Through Indigenous Eyes

By Shiyé Bidzííl
Dean Dedman Jr.

The story of the Standing Rock movement as told by a local drone pilot and visionary

Compiled by Dyan Diamond

True North House
publishing
worldwide

True North House Publishing
Worldwide

First Edition

ISBN: 978-1-387-44852-4

True North House Publishing

Worldwide

Please contact TrueNorthHouse@live.com before using any material from this book. Thank you.

Find Shiyé Bidzííl/ Dean Dedman on Facebook

Cover art: David Carter
Cheyenne River
www.DavidLouisCarter.com

Graphic design for cover: Michael Pierre Price
Ojibwe
www.MichealPierrePrice.com

Dyan Diamond
Aniyunwiya
www.DyanDiamond.net

ISBN 978-1-387-44852-4

9 781387 448524

90000

Thank you

First of all I want to thank the Creator for allowing me to open my eyes to see the truth for what it is with no disguise. I want to thank every single person I have ever met and acknowledged throughout my history. I want to thank the people of the movement. I want to thank all the people who work with IEN. I want to thank Tom Goldtooth, Dallas Goldtooth. I want to thank the people of KLND. I want to thank the people of Standing Rock. I want to thank all the people, the council and Dave Archambault II. I want to thank every single water protector. You all know your names. I want to thank every single camp that is in resistance to a lot of things. I want to thank all of the elders of the Navajo Nation. I want to thank all the elders of the Lakota Nation. Both of my great Nations. I want to thank my children, Kymani Drake and Kaiden Sky, and my precious baby girl, Kinyaa'aanii Laylah Rose.

Table of Contents

Chapter One..................................2015 – April 2016....................Page 9

Chapter Two................................May, June, July 2016..............Page 21

Chapter Three.............................August 2016...........................Page 39

Chapter Four...............................September 2016.....................Page 55

Chapter Five...............................October 2016.......................Page 69

Chapter Six................................November 2016....................Page 89

Chapter Seven.............................December 2016..................Page 133

Chapter Eight.............................January 2017......................Page 197

Chapter Nine..............................February 2017.....................Page 249

Chapter Ten...............................March 2017.........................Page 303

Chapter One

"Find a purpose in life so big it will challenge every capacity to be at your best."
~ David O. McKay

Dean Dedman Jr., aka Shiyé Bidzííl, was born June 9, 1985 in Bismarck, North Dakota. He is Hunkpapa, Lakota and Diné, Navajo. He was born for the Bitterwater clan. He lived in Chinle, Arizona until he was 12 years old. His family moved to the South Dakota side of the Standing Rock reservation. He graduated from high school there and spent two years at the Institute of American Indian Arts in Santa Fe, New Mexico. He studied communications, production and film.

He carries two cultures within him. Navajo and Lakota. Long before the Standing Rock movement began, what most Americans think of as camping was a way of life for his family early on. He loved his paternal grandparents and missed them very much after they passed. He still believes in life beyond this world. He believes in science and in other-worldly things like aliens and UFOs. Outer space always fascinated him. He grew up loving dinosaurs and superheroes. He is a huge SeaHawks fan and he was greatly inspired by Linkin Park's music and music in general.

He always loved art. He never remembers not drawing or painting. It wasn't something he was inspired to do, it was just something that he naturally did.

After college he returned to Standing Rock and worked in the casino for a while. He met a woman there. They married and had twin boys (Kymani Drake and Kaiden Sky) and a little girl (Kinyaa'aanii Laylah Rose) together. They moved to Tacoma, Washington. It was a tumultuous relationship.

He struggled like most young, Indigenous people who live on reservations do. He loved being a father though and found a lot of love in his children. He was always making the best out of any situation and looking for the humor in things. He was also always looking for wisdom to connect to.

Early in 2015 he writes on Facebook:

Sacrifices + responsibility = a great and prosperous life.

He begins to share videos and photos on Facebook. Mostly of his children and nature. He loves the outdoors. He truly loves every part of nature and Mother Earth, his Unci Maka.

His creativity is always working. Not only is he an artist, in many, many mediums, but he is a poet as well. In 2015 he writes:

I see myself in another realm of reality.

I lay and ponder on this cold prairie grass.

Remembering all the good moments coming to pass.

Sad at times I may feel.

But nothing matters but the thought of you.

Vivid emotions like quantum physics.

Never yet understand.

But idea of life and love.

An eternal bond of emotions blush.

My heart is cold.

My heart is lost.

I may have lost my way.

But still have my cross.

Quantum salvation in linear time.

Feelings frozen.

Waiting for your touch of elegance.

Your beauty.

Your mind.

As his marriage falters, he writes:

We are all victims here, but ones we hurt the most are our children. Children are sacred. They hold power we adults don't understand. They are our hopes and dreams. They are stars ready to shine. They shine their light on the lost and hopeless. Even in the darkest places, they will guide you. So never underestimate our children. Never neglect them. Stop for two seconds out of your day and smell the roses with them, for they will show you a power far greater than the human soul. It's called LOVE.

He thinks of himself as free spirited and open minded. Someone who thinks outside of the box. He's always looking for more information on space and science. He begins to share some of the struggles of Indigenous Americans on Facebook. He shares information on the Apache Nation and how they are occupying sacred land that is marked to be destroyed by mining. He is aware and watching. He shares stories about the first Indigenous American to go into space. He is always proud of his Indigenous people.

He returns to South Dakota in 2015 and gets a job at a grocery store. They try to be a family and do things we all think of as usual. They take walks, eat pizza, watch their favorite tv shows. They explore the area and go on little adventures. Little things make him happy. Homemade birthday cards and dinners at home. He takes his kids trick or treating. He bakes cookies for them. But he is restless. He feels like there is more for him.

In 2015 he turns 30 years old. His relationship with his wife goes back and forth. He dreams about his paternal grandmother.

Last night I had a dream of my grandma. I was running through a thick forest and came upon an old cabin. Inside this cabin I saw my uncles. I was sad and worried, but my uncle went into another room and came back with my grandma. She was in good spirits and healthy. I awoke in tears. After all these years she came to me. She hugged me and told me in Navajo that everything is going to be alright. I miss her so much. She was in a happy mood. I believe she was happy to see me. God bless Nalii. Love you and miss you very much. I hope you come back to see me in my dreams. WAKING LIFE.

In March of 2016 a package in the mail changes everything for him.

Finally my new Phantom 3 Executive Kit has arrived this morning. Assembling and downloading the DJI GO app now. Ready to touch the Dakota Skies!!

A couple of days later, he writes:

Well I'm new to this. I had recently ordered a Phantom 3 Drone Advance EXECUTIVE KIT. Unfortunately I do not have an up-to-date iPhone or iPad! My iPhone 4 is an old dinosaur. So I'm patiently waiting to take it out for a spin!!! Going to be very cautious at first. These things don't come cheap. Anyone out there willing to lend me an iPhone or iPad iOS 9 or higher? Let's go test this bird.

He works it out and posts on March 6, 2016:

My Phantom 3 first flight!! The tiny town of Mobridge.

He shares his first drone footage. And he is up in the air, chasing his kids around close up. His first drone footage looks like a professional is flying the drone. He takes to it fast and has amazing flights right away. His mind starts spinning ways he can capture footage in new and unusual ways. He checks out apps that can help him reach the fullest potential of the drone. A flame has been sparked.

I feel tired, but can't sleep. Okay, maybe I'm just anxious for tomorrow morning's P3 Flight. Gonna test out my polarized filters to try and get a perfect morning sunrise.

March 8, 2016

He takes the drone out and gets aerial shots of Lake Oahe. He tags LaDonna Tamakawastewin Allard in his Facebook photos. It is as if he was meant to fly that drone. He flies beautifully. People start to notice right away. They comment that he is an artist with the drone. He flies every opportunity he has. On March 11, 2016, he announces his new business. Drone2bwild. He offers photography to videography.

He spends time getting to know the applications that work with the drone. He spends lots of time editing and honing his skills. He continues to fly often. He flies over the house, the river, the town. He is truly a natural with the drone. He is fearless in flying. He pushes the drone to go as far as possible and get the best possible shots.

"The most destructive thing I've ever done was believe someone else's opinion of me."
~ Teal Blue Jay

On March 20, 2016 he shares a Facebook post about the Dakota Access pipeline. It is from someone in Iowa. He continues to fly the drone often. He shares his drone footage on his Drone2bwild page on Facebook. He gets a backpack for the drone so he can carry it easily on hikes. He films his town, Mobridge, South Dakota, and edits the film with details and music. He has an incredible feel for using the right music and finding the best ways to display his drone footage. People start paying even more attention. His Facebook posts begin to get more reactions and comments.

I love my life
I love my talent
I love my skills

Talents + Passions = a lot of editing!!!!!!!

March 25, 2016

The view from the other side.

It was a perfect morning. No wind. Not too cold. A little misty sprinkles, but that didn't stop this beautiful flight to the other side of the Missouri River to capture these breathtaking views.

On March 26, 2016 he announces:

DRoNE2BWILD will be covering the RUN 4 WATER gathering that will be taking place. Starting in Wakpala, South Dakota at 11am and ending at the waterfront on Main in Mobridge, South Dakota. So come, be a part of something bigger.

March 28, 2016

He releases the video: Dakota Access Protest. The Run For Water. He gets lots of compliments and comments. It is an amazing, beautiful and informative video.

This is what took place this past Friday. Thanks for letting me be a part of something bigger. Thanks for all the comments and shares. I love my work. I love my culture. Feels good to know I'm putting my mind toward accomplishing my dreams.

That same day he shares a post about the beginning of the original camp for the Standing Rock movement. Community members ask for help to set up a camp in Cannonball, North Dakota. They need help hauling wood, mowing, building tipis; everything. The camp will be in resistance to the Dakota Access pipeline. They believe that the Dakota Access pipeline would cause harm to the Standing Rock Nation. They are setting out to stop it.

March 31, 2016

Who's all coming to participate in the gathering tomorrow? Starting in Fort Yates all the way to the Cannonball Camp. Encouraging everyone to come and be a part of history and change!!!! We seriously don't need a pipeline running through our lands let alone the Dakota Access pipeline!!!!

April 2, 2016

Things are really picking up fast in his life. But there are always those steps back, and he had those too.

Had the worst Friday ever!!!! Lost my Drone!!!! Got the car stuck looking for my drone, lost the keys looking for the drone. And after all this I find out my Uncle O passed on!!! I'm sad. I'm worn out. I'm tired. RIP Big O. I'm gonna miss you and will always think about you. Didn't get the shots I wanted because of the dang wind!!!!! Things didn't go the way I had imagined!!!! 6 hours later I find my drone!!! (Thank God for GPS/Google Maps!!!!!!)

On April 6ᵗʰ he shares a Chase Iron Eyes for Congress post. And on April 7ᵗʰ he shares that his drone photos are in the local newspaper, The McLaughlin Messenger.

April 8, 2016

When the decision is made always remember this is our HOMELAND!

#Drone2bwild #NoDakotaAccess #NoDAPL

He shares a video he put together. He is photographer, camera man, director, editor - everything. And he pulls it off beautifully. This video shows lots of wildlife affected by oil spills. Lots of oil spills. Then footage of the horse riders. And then there are Indigenous people gathered. There is drone footage of the 4 directions gathering. Cars are lined up on the road for miles. And the first tipis being set up. He gets many kudos in the comments. The video gets thousands of views. He responds: My videos will be shared with this generation and the next.

The truth be told

The love of our lands

And the humbleness of our hearts

Thanks to all of you. Help support our waters and lands.

Stay tuned for the next video coming to a Facebook near you.

There are many issues to the Dakota Access pipeline. The land the pipe is to be put into is a major concern for many reasons. He shares an informational graphic showing how much land the Lakota Nation has lost over time due to treaty breaches by the United States government. The loss of land in the past 100 years is staggering.

We Matter!!!!!!!!! Digging up the blood of Mother Earth and burying PIPELINES beneath the ground will always have consequences!!!!!!

"It's the same old story with the government and the agencies and big oil. We don't matter. They're coming again. When will it stop? I'm not expendable. My grandchildren are not expendable. We have to fight to live."
~ LaDonna Tamakawastewin Allard

His home life is still up and down. He is madly in love with his children, but his relationship with his wife is often on the rocks. He continues to work menial labor jobs. Food commodities help the family survive.

April 13, 2016

He continues to fly his drone. He announces that he can now live stream videos on Facebook. Facebook's new live feed feature enables any camera to stream to Facebook live. Even his DJI drone camera. He begins to get more serious about his drone business.

We specialize in aerial photos, videos, or live streaming of events. We do weddings, funerals, get-togethers, outdoor hunting & fishing, camping, business, before & after photos, sports events, pow wows, horse races, and search and rescue, etc. etc.

He posts drone footage of his uncle's memorial service. He posts drone footage of Mobridge at night. On April 18th he announces that he will be providing drone footage of the release of a bald eagle. The eagle had been shot in the wing, but was now healed and ready to be released back into nature. This was to take place April 21st. On the 16th and 17th of April, he attends the 2016 Mobridge Annual Art Show and flies his drone. He captures the art show from a drone's perspective.

April 19, 2016

It's not if the pipeline will leak, but when.

He shares an informational graphic about the Dakota Access pipeline. The Dakota Access pipeline threatens the drinking water of millions of people – far beyond the Standing Rock Nation. An estimated 18 million. The next day he shares a photo of people sitting in a circle at Sacred Stone Camp and invites people to come and be a part of history.

"My goal is not to be better than anyone else, but to be better than I used to be." ~ Unknown

He announces his support for the Standing Rock Sioux Nation. He shares a photo of men on horses, riding in support of No Dakota Access pipeline. He is increasingly involved in the movement. He gets business cards for Drone2bwild.

On April 22nd he posts about Iyan Wakanya Gagnapi Oti. Camp of the Sacred Stones. And the water protectors who are staying there. It is in Cannonball, North Dakota. They are standing against the Dakota Access pipeline. The Army Corps of Engineers will have public meetings soon on the Standing Rock reservation. Community members are encouraged to go to the meetings to speak up. There are many concerns around the proposed pipeline beyond the fact that it would eventually break and pollute the water. There are treaty rights violations. There are concerns over sacred burial and cultural sites being disturbed. There has not been a full environmental impact study done yet.

April 24, 2016

If you care about water rights then please read this bulletin!!!! ASAP!!!! ASKING FOR ANYONE in Navajo country INTERESTED IN BRINGING UP A DINÉ FLAG TO THE SACRED STONE CAMP LOCATED ON THE STANDING ROCK Sioux Tribe Reservation @ Cannonball, North Dakota. Help join our stand for all our tribal waters. Come, be a part of history. Sincerely, Dean Dedman Jr., Hunkpapa/Diné

The question is: What is it going to take for the pipeline company to understand that what they are doing is going to cause something more drastic and dangerous?

It comes down to COMMON SENSE!!!

On April 24th youth runners from Cheyenne River set out from Cannonball, North Dakota for a 500 mile relay run to turn over a petition against the Dakota Access pipeline to the Army Corps of Engineers. They are running to Omaha, Nebraska to deliver a message: The Dakota Access pipeline should not be built.

April 26, 2016

Well my drone can legally fly anywhere in the U.S.A. Yay.

He shares a photo of his drone license.

I am encouraging everyone to come forward and tell the Army Corps of Engineers who and what you fight for. And that's this whole area of our place called our homeland. This place is all worth fighting for. This place between the real world and the spiritual world. A place called Standing Rock. Tell them all our chiefs' stories of struggle and how we fought to stand up for what we believe in. We are people just like everyone else who came from across the great oceans. The only thing that separates us and everyone else is that we live our way of life in a well humbled, respectful matter of everything around us. The earth. The sky. The planets. The stars. Everything beyond the great unknown. We are connected people. Part of a system that is connected throughout time and creation. We have the stories, we just need to tell them.

April 27, 2016

As Europeans arrived in North America and met all the different Nations of Indigenous peoples, they often named the Nations incorrectly. Sometimes they went off of a neighboring Nation's description. Sometimes they were just plain mean. The proper name for the Nation that is called Sioux is Oceti Sakowin. It means: Seven Council Fires. Sioux is from a Chippewa word and means "little serpents."

He releases a new video that he's worked very diligently on. It is a gorgeous video. He proves himself as a stunning visual artist. He titles it: Protect Our Homeland!!

4 Directions Walk Run Ride of your life: April 29: 10 am Grand River Casino

U.S. Army Corps of Engineers, Colonel Henderson, wants YOUR input on the permit for the Missouri River crossing of the Dakota Access pipeline. This permit (and the Oceti Sakowin) is Big Oil's final obstacle to construction which has already illegally begun. April 29th is also the 148th anniversary of the Fort Laramie Treaty of 1868. Join in this historical event. He wants to hear from the Youth of the Nation, and the people affected by this proposed pipeline. Which is all of us.

A pipeline leak will destroy Standing Rock and Mobridge's water supply and pollute the Missouri River for generations to come. Fact: it is inevitable that DAPL will leak. Stand with us against Big Oil. Walkers are invited to converge on Grand River Casino this Friday. Bring your picket signs opposing DAPL. Motorcycle ride: 59 miles from Prairie Knights Casino to Grand River Casino. Spirit Ride on horseback 3 miles from junction 12 & 20 to Grand River Casino. Spirit Walk: 4 miles from the Sitting Bull Monument to Grand River Casino.

Protect Our Homeland, Dean Dedman Jr., Lakota/Diné

My closing thoughts for the night. Something to really think about, whether you're a concerned community member or in the circle of the council.

PUBLIC AWARENESS FOR OUR PEOPLE. Words of enlightenment.

Everything should always be public! Why hide or keep certain information behind closed doors? We should all be informed. If we can handle 500 years of suppression, battles, war and getting de-culturized, I'm pretty sure we can handle the truth. Why keep it from the people who probably voted you in office? Please be a leader and talk in front of me, not behind my back. Please be a leader and do what's right for our homeland, not for what you can benefit from the white culture! A tribe that survives is a tribe that is connected to all of its people, rich or poor. That's the problem. We shouldn't compare each other, but rather accompany each other. We are all here for the same reason. To prosper, respect, acknowledge our values and to help each other. Protect our homeland. Don't join them to profit yourself. Please make the right choices and stand up for what's right in life. Follow the path of our warriors, buffalo and chiefs. And go down in history for making change. Don't get suckered into bad politics!!

When I awake in the morning my spirit will rise to Creator to seek wisdom for this coming fight against this pipeline.

April 29, 2016

STAND

TOGETHER WE

SHALL PROTECT OUR

HOMELAND AND OUR COMMUNITIES.

Encouraging everyone to also bring HUGE SIGNS WITH BIG BOLD ANTI-PIPELINE MESSAGES SO THAT THE DRONE WILL BE ABLE TO SEE THE SIGNS CLEARLY.

WELL THIS IS IT EVERYONE!!!

OUR LAST CHANCE TO STAND UP AND RUN, WALK, RIDE ON HORSEBACK AND MOTORCYCLE TO GRAND RIVER CASINO...WHERE THE ARMY CORPS OF ENGINEERS LEADER WILL BE AWAITING OUR VOICES AND THE THUNDER OF OUR MARCH. WE STAND NOW.

I now call on the bike riders from the NORTH. I now call on the horse riders from the WEST. I now call on the spirit walkers from the SOUTH. And I now call on the spirit runners from the EAST, the direction which our SUN rises to GIVE OUR MOTHER EARTH its NATURAL ENERGY upon OUR HOMELAND. To shine its LIGHT on all of our creations, which our ANCESTORS brought forth from the creator. So I now speak my MESSAGE to Colonel Henderson and I say let OUR WATER transcend itself upon OUR LANDS so it can be absorbed and brought forth to the sky of our EAGLES. CARRY it far so OUR STAR PEOPLE can BLESS it with the POWER of THUNDER and WISDOM. To let it fall with GRACE from the SKY and let our cycle continue. As it should always remain for all of time and CREATION for my Lakota people and also for my Diné people of the SOUTH. Give thanks to water for it will always remain a LIFE SOURCE for all of the LAND and CREATION. Wasté.

People call the day emotional. They share pictures and videos of the meeting with Colonel Henderson. Many allies show up to support Standing Rock. Many people attend and voice their concerns about the Dakota Access pipeline.

May 3, 2016

If the Army Corps of Engineers really share our Indigenous concerns, then there should be no problem NOT SIGNING that pipeline into action!

"Water is life. Without water there could be no life." ~ Justin Rowland

On May 8, 2016 he shares Unicorn Riot's link on his Facebook page. It is about Sacred Stone Camp and the resistance. Unicorn Riot is an independent news source. Alternative media is starting to get involved, but coverage is still little and sporadic. There is no national media coverage at all.

On May 9th he shares a post about a meeting with the State Department in Tioga, North Dakota the next day. TransCanada's Midland Pipeline Project could potentially tie into DAPL (Dakota Access pipeline). There is another call for people to show up and voice their concerns. And there is a confirmation that California aquifers are contaminated with billions of gallons of fracking wastewater. The problem is growing rapidly and action is getting more urgent. The people of Standing Rock grow more determined.

Dakota Access pipeline threatened to cross sacred treaty lands. Dakota Access threatened to dig up precious earth through sacred sites. They threatened to violate the human and spiritual rights of Standing Rock. All for money, jobs and oil. The jobs are not lasting jobs. They are temporary jobs. And there are not nearly as many jobs available as reported. Also, the oil was going to be exported. It would be sold to other countries. It would not even benefit the people of the United States. The only people who would profit would be Energy Transfer Partners, who own Dakota Access. President Obama blocked the construction of the KXL pipeline. Would he stop the Dakota Access pipeline?

I relax my mind this very night and start to ponder.

Taking in this nocturnal beauty I call sleep, my mind starts to wonder.

I close my eyes and find my mind drifting over a thousand cries.

My homeland I hold dear is in danger, destruction is near.

My heart is pounding like a thousand drums, gaining strength, it makes me stronger, ready for battle we can't hold on any longer.

My turtle shell of life gives me humility, pass it around. Prayers of wisdom, values of truth.

Protect Our Homeland.

Slay the mighty Snake, banish him far, beyond our lands.

To a place where no one will understand.

Soon again my eyes let me see the stars shine bright this very night. Through all the dark skies that shadowed our lands throughout this night.

Pray every day and every night.

Soon we will win this very FIGHT!!!

Dean Dedman Jr. 2016

Chapter Two

May 2016

I'm finally finished with my video titled: 4 Directions.

So pop some popcorn and be ready to enjoy my talented progression I call video ART! The video is 34 minutes long. I want to thank everyone who came out to support this cause about our lands and waters. Now with every eye on my awareness videos I would like to start producing other videos on issues we still have here on our Nation and on other Nations. Hope you enjoy my visions.

The video features drone footage of motorcycles, walkers, runners and people on horseback coming together from the four directions. It is a beautiful and emotionally moving video. Many people participate. It ends with the community meeting with Colonel Henderson.

They gather to voice their concerns about the proposed Dakota Access pipeline. First, that it is in direct violation of treaty rights under the 1851 and 1868 Fort Laramie Treaties. There are concerns over protecting sensitive cultural and burial sites. Concerns that no one has consulted with the Nation who would be affected. Concerns over the danger of the pipeline breaking and leaking into the river, into well systems and ground water. Concerns that there has not been a full environmental impact study. Concerns for the water. Concerns for the survival of future generations.

"We are not going to stand idly by and let this happen." ~ Joye Braun

"If this pipeline is to go through, you would be desecrating sacred lands." ~ Candy Mossett

It is noted that just last month a leak of TransCanada's Keystone pipeline dumped nearly 17,000 gallons of oil in South Dakota. It was the largest spill in state history. The company building this pipeline would be the same TransCanada that would have built the Keystone XL pipeline if President Obama had not vetoed it after a long grassroots battle against it by Indigenous activists, environmentalists and many others.

In the video, Colonel Henderson says it is an honor to be there. He thanks the elders. He thanks everyone for being a part of the democratic system. He says that his grandmother lived in Mobridge, South Dakota and used to fish out of the river. He says that the Army Corps of Engineers has no position on this. He states that their only goal is to abide by the law. He says that he shares the concerns about the impacts of this pipeline.

"Mother Earth has been abused, the powers have been abused, this cannot go on forever. No theory can alter the simple fact. Mother Earth will retaliate, the whole environment will retaliate, and the abusers will be eliminated. Things come full circle, back to where they started. That's revolution." ~ Russell Means

He shares the 4 Directions video with groups and on pages. He uses social media in masterful ways to network and to get the information out to the people. Everything seems to be coming to life on Facebook pages. People are reaching out and being educated and connecting.

He also shares that Bernie Sanders is planning a Fargo, North Dakota rally. The presidential election in November is already on everyone's minds. He supports Bernie.

May 12, 2016

Inspirational Warrior

My Spirit rises from Standing Rock, but I never forgot my desert lands of Navajo Nation. Chinle REPRESENT!!! IT'S BEEN 10 YEARS SINCE I'VE FELT THE ARIZONA AIR.

On this post he shares Nataanii Means' music – Warrior. He often shares music videos and is especially connected to Indigenous artists.

Spiritual quote of my day. My prayer before every project.

"Confusion is a gift from God. Those times when you feel most desperate for a solution, sit, wait. The information will become clear. The confusion is there to guide you. Seek detachment and become the producer of your life."
~ Unknown

May 14, 2016

He shares a post: Diné Navajo Nation against Trump

Let my people go. He disrespects Nation to Nation. He dishonors and neglects. Vote no for Trump.

"You can build all the buildings you want but America will always be Indigenous land!"
~ Supaman

He continues to fly the drone and to share photos. His videos continue to get more and more views.

May 18, 2016

A run to always remember. To keep in our hearts and minds. To hold within us the power of movement and unity among our culture and community of young and old. Stay focused. Stay strong. For the fight is never over. It's only just begun! Wasté.

More petitions are started and shared to stop the Dakota Access pipeline. He shares information on other Indigenous issues also. And there are a lot of Indigenous issues.

There is a push for Obama to pardon Leonard Peltier that year. Leonard Peltier is a member of the American Indian Movement who was framed for killing FBI agents. Peltier became a symbol of the mistreatment of Indigenous Americans in the criminal justice system. He has been in prison for 40 years.

There was the news of the Carlisle Indian Industrial School releasing the remains of Navajo children who had been buried on the campus there. The Indian school murdered the Navajo children and after 100 years, they would finally return home for proper burial. There were stories of horror and death in many schools for Indigenous children and it was a sad victory to reclaim these precious Indigenous children.

May 20, 2016

The news is hard to take. Digging has begun on the Dakota Access pipeline. Even though the federal permit has not been approved or issued. Bakken Pipeline resistance fighters are arrested at a refinery in Indiana. North Dakota's Standing Rock, Oceti Sakowin, long time victims of displacement and persecution, are now fighting an oil pipeline that is scheduled to be built through sacred lands. He shares the Sacred Stone Camp GoFundMe page to help build camp and provide resources for the water protectors.

"We must have the guts to stand up to the fossil fuel industry and tell them their short-term profits are not more important than the planet." ~ Sen. Bernie Sanders (I - Vermont)

May 21, 2016

He shares a post by Dave Archambault II, Chairman of the Standing Rock Sioux Tribe. The chairman announces that digging has begun in Emmons County, North Dakota. However, Dakota Access does not have permission to cross Lake Oahe and cannot complete the pipeline without this permission. The Chairman notes that the council met with several federal agencies, including the Environmental Protection Agency, the Department of the Interior and the Advisory Council on Historic Preservation. And that they are all putting their concerns in also.

"The tribe is dedicated to the protection of our treaty rights, our reservation lands, and our people – and we will ensure that the federal government upholds its trust responsibility when it makes its decision regarding the Dakota Access pipeline." ~ Dave Archambault II

May 22, 2016

No Dakota Access pipeline Announcement!!!!

Save Our Waters. Save Our Human Spirits.

My work is passion. My art is soul. My awareness is alive.

He releases a new video with music and still photos. His videos and posts are starting to get even more attention now. People are viewing and sharing them often.

3/4 of Mother Earth is full of water. On this tiny little planet in our solar system and in our infinite universe. Don't be blinded by selfish profit. I'm afraid in the next 100 years we won't have a planet anymore. Everything we've known to coexist with will be GONE FOREVER, AND NO AMOUNT OF MONEY CAN BRING IT BACK!!!!!

"1.3 million gallons of oil are spilled into U.S. waters every year." ~ ReZpect Our Water

Indigenous rights and water protector groups start to spring up on Facebook and in the media in general. Groups that have been around for a while start to get more views and interactions. These groups educate people about all of the issues that affect Indigenous people.

#SacredWater is the most worthy cause to fight for! Respecting and protecting water is a way of life for Native Americans. Shiyé Bidzííl makes this clear in his video about Standing Rock's fight against Dakota Access pipeline. I've been so fortunate to witness and learn first-hand this deep respect for the most vital of elements required for life. When we speak and fight for water, our intentions must be for the greater good of humankind.

#WaterIsLife #ProtectWater #WeNeedCleanDrinkingWater #NoWaterNoLife

May 23, 2016

This evening's thunderstorm brought life and renewal to the lands. Sitting out by the lake, I felt free. I love the senses Mother Nature throws at you. The naturalistic force of water coexisting with our human spirit is a very powerful feeling. The power of every ripple expanding outward. The sound of water flowing through my mind fills me with good knowledge and wisdom beyond anyone's understanding...you would have to be there to experience it. The sound of thunder awakens all of earth's children.

You can have all the money in the world, but when you leave this earth you can't take it with you, so why care about your wealth? Higher spiritual beings know that when we go we will carry the earth and all its beauty within our souls. When we pass to the next realm of spirituality. This process we have here on earth is only the beginning. Something big oil and government will never grasp!!!! Only us true Indigenous people know and experience true power like that.

A very polite Caucasian woman comments on this post that although she is white, she has this same spiritual experience with the earth and animals. He apologizes and says sometimes he needs to remember there are others who have the same awareness. He is never too proud to apologize and always fast to include all of humanity in his extended family.

On May 24ᵗʰ he shares a quote on Facebook that will come to mean much more than he can imagine on this day.

"Here is the world. Beautiful and terrible things will happen. Don't be afraid."
~ Frederick Buechner

My chairman. Supporting his grassroots. A message for him.

MAKE THE RIGHT DECISIONS

MAKE THE RIGHT CHOICES

SHARE A PIECE OF YOUR HUMAN SPIRIT

SHOW OUR CHILDREN

WHAT WE AS A SIOUX NATION

CAN ACCOMPLISH

BRING US OUT OF THE PAST
INTO A GREATER AND MORE
PROSPEROUS FUTURE
WITHOUT DESTROYING OUR WAY OF LIFE
Wasté. Dean Dedman Jr.

May 25, 2016

There is a call out for prayer. Members of the Oceti Sakowin and allies prepare to stand up against the Dakota Access pipeline. Dakota Access has begun construction on the pipeline illegally. The call is for prayer for the water protectors and for all of the Standing Rock Nation. Dean leaves his job at the grocery store on this day. He does not post on Facebook for several days then on May 31ˢᵗ he lets everyone know that he is still alive and kicking.

June 1, 2016

Meeting Native public media at KLND 89.5 FM Community Radio. Expanding my opportunities. Wish me the best.

Big oil companies have already been using Eminent Domain to claim the land they need for their pipelines to go through. It is another concern for the Standing Rock Nation. Environmentalists are fighting against the abuse of Eminent Domain in Iowa. He posts about it and continues to support all efforts to keep oil in the ground.

He shares a post about the historical significance of the day for Navajos. On this day in 1868 Navajo leaders signed an agreement with the United States government. This agreement closed concentration camps in New Mexico that had been imprisoning Navajo people since 1863. Many Navajo people did not make it back to Navajo land; the sick and the injured who could not keep up. There were many, many long walks and trails of tears for Indigenous people all over North America.

"Growing up in Chinle we know stories about women jumping off cliffs with their children or wrestling soldiers off to save their family. They would have rather died than go on the long walk. On this day in 1868 my ancestors were allowed to return to the four sacred mountains. Many, MANY were lost to and from that concentration camp. But today I thank every single one of them, because their blood, strength and power flow thru my veins. Today, like any other day, is a good one to reflect and thank the Great Mystery for our way of life. Hozhó." ~ Nataanii Means

The divestment movement has begun. Organizations commit to pull out their investments from banks and financial institutions that are funding the pipeline projects. Banks are beginning to be spotlighted for their bad investments in oil. People are beginning to pull their money out of these banks and to look to local credit unions instead.

Some news comes that is hopeful. It is reported that construction on the Dakota Access pipeline has been halted. Indigenous archaeological finds have shut it down. But in Ontario, the Grassy Narrows First Nation is demanding cleanup of mercury contamination. Indigenous Nations have long been ignored and forgotten. The Standing Rock Nation know that it is a battle for Mother Earth.

"Are our lives worth less?" ~ Grassy Narrows First Nations Chief, Simon Fobister

Indigenous people from all over are becoming educated and educating each other. The rise in awareness is slow at first, and then it begins to catch fire from the intellectual sparks of others. Dean understands that he is a part of the forward movement. He shares Dallas Goldtooth's post from REDx Talks. Indigenous leaders and allies are networking. They know that the future is at stake for all Indigenous people.

"What if America loved Native American people like they loved Native American culture?"
~ Unknown

Most Americans seem to have no real understanding at all of Indigenous issues. They are quick to wear an "Indian" costume, decorate their homes with "Indian" trinkets, or use an image of what they think of as an "Indian" as a sports mascot, but the reality is that these are Indigenous people. The original Americans. And they are being treated horrendously by the United States – throughout history and today.

Treaties are broken every day. It has been happening throughout the history of the United States government. The government takes away land and resources and holds Indigenous Americans in containment camps, also known as reservations. The government has attempted to take away the culture, language and spiritual practices of Indigenous Nations since it first began.

Indigenous Americans are oppressed. Each Nation is sovereign. Each Nation is a Nation within a Nation. Every enrolled Indigenous American holds dual citizenship. To their own Nation and to the United States. But the United States government has controlled the Indigenous population in brutal and outrageous ways by controlling the Indigenous Nations. They have little say in the fate of their own Nations.

As a result of being kept in containment camps, many Indigenous reservations suffer from the same issues. Drug and alcohol addictions. Suicide is rampant. Domestic violence and violent crime in general plague the Indigenous people. There is not much opportunity for career or personal growth on most of the reservations and the people suffer without the ability to dream of a better future.

Just to illustrate the ridiculousness of the relations between the Indigenous Nations and the United States: Indigenous Americans were not allowed United States citizenship until 1924 even though they served in the United States military and are the original Americans. It wasn't until the late 1970s when Indigenous Americans were allowed to practice their own religions, even though everyone in America is supposed to be free to practice the religion of their choice. The United States government has been trying to kill off Indigenous culture and people since the beginning.

Yet all Americans today are in the debt of the Diné, Navajo. They helped to win World War II with their code talkers. He shares an article about a Diné code talker who takes his journey to the spirit world.

One thing no white man, Nazi or Japanese ever broke was our Diné Language. I am proud to be Diné.

Protests over the treatment of Indigenous Americans are never in the forefront of the news, but over time many celebrity activists have spoken up and protested alongside Indigenous people. Muhammad Ali, Marlon Brando, Dick Gregory, Richie Havens and Buffy Sainte-Marie were among the celebrities who tried to bring the struggles of the Indigenous people to light in the past.

His creativity is spilling over and he paints and researches new things he can do with his drone. He enjoys learning new technologies and takes to them easily. He plans on getting drone footage of buffalo. He is always in touch with his Indigenous culture and his roots.

"Eventually you'll end up where you need to be, with who you're meant to be with, and doing what you should be doing." ~ Unknown

June 5, 2016

Call outs for people to come to Sacred Stone Camp begin. The first call outs are to the youth, by the youth.

Water is Life.

Without Water all of existence

Will no longer be.

Water is EVERYTHING!!

Share cause you CARE!!

June 6, 2016

Having a good morning, need coffee. Writing proposal, policies and disclaimer for a new drone media direction for KLND airways.

Things appear to be going in a new direction for him. He is working with KLND local radio. On Facebook, he shares music from Supaman, A Tribe Called Red, Frank Waln and other Indigenous artists. He shares Indigenous music about the resistance against big oil and other Indigenous issues.

The music is often meant to heal generational trauma. Indigenous people have been terrorized for so long that not only is there current trauma, caused by the current events – but there is also historical trauma that goes back generations from past trauma to ancestors. He honors his past and recognizes the future for the next seven generations.

June 9, 2016

He turns 31 years old.

Feelin life.

Feelin good.

Feelin soul.

Givin thanks.

4 another day.

Coming.

My life.

In my control.

Hey ya hey ya.

June 10th

4 all my aboriginal people of the planet and beyond the spirit world!! OUR SPIRITS WILL NEVER BE BROKEN

June 14, 2016

He encourages everyone to get to the polls and vote for Chase Iron Eyes for congress. He believes it is important to get Indigenous people into governmental offices so they can represent all of the people. Indigenous Americans are vastly underrepresented in the government of the United States.

"Love is love is love is love is love is love is love is love, cannot be killed or swept aside."
~ Lin Manuel Miranda

June 15, 2016

Good morning my circle of Indigenous radicals...@ the lodge of good voices. McLaughlin, SD KLND 89.5 FM Community Radio.

"You are the hero of your own story." ~ Joseph Campbell

In reaction to the Orlando, Florida shooting at a night club, he shares a photo with the caption: Orlando shooting is the deadliest mass shooting in U.S. History.

Wrong. Wounded Knee is. Where the United States Government massacred 250 Sioux men, women and children! Calling the Orlando mass shooting the deadliest in U.S. history whitewashes this country's violent past.

Another example of how we are forgotten. We are alive and standing strong in the face of the U.S. Government!!!!

At this moment in history, Indigenous people are in Washington, D.C. for the Reject and Protect gathering. Indigenous hip hop artist, Frank Waln, performs in front of thousands on the last day of action. Standing Rock Indigenous youth activist, Bobbie Jean Three Legs and LaDonna Tamakawastewin Allard appear on live feeds at Times Square in New York City where they dance.

June 16, 2016

Yet another oil spill near Native American land is failing to grab national attention.

When will the rest of America start listening to Indigenous people?

June 21, 2016

Ever wondered what happens when an oil pipeline bursts underwater? This footage of an oil spill in Moscow that caught on fire last week will give you an unforgettable picture. Share the video today if you want to say no to new pipelines being built in your backyard.

June 22, 2016

Good morning everyone!!! Everyone who loves radio, tune in, stream in on our website and radio 89.5 FM The lodge of good voices!!!

Shiyé continues to look into FAA rules and online training so he can legally fly the drone. He learns all the ins and outs of what it means to fly a drone in the United States. He reads a huge manual of official drone rules and policies. He takes it very seriously.

"Nature is my religion and the earth is my church." ~ Unknown

June 27, 2016

It's official. 4 directions printing solutions coming real soon here. Stay posted. Bringing new opportunities to Standing Rock & beyond.

He begins a new business. A printing company. He begins to make graphic images. He enjoys graphic arts and he is very good at it. He also starts making comedy skits for the radio station with coworkers. He stays busy.

July 1, 2016

Today I accomplished 3 goals.

1. I touched the heart of a true friend.

2. I opened new doors for myself.

3. I got on the radio for the first time and played DJ. It was an awesome experience.

Stay focused and opportunities will present themselves.

On July 2nd the buzz around camp is that there are actors coming to promote awareness of the movement. Shailene Woodley and Ezra Miller show up at camp. Water protectors get photos with the actors and post them on Facebook.

We are all going through some changes. Delete. Add. Flippin through dem pages. Leaving this past gone. Today's problems, nothing wrong. Hilarious problematic views. A touch of drama. Nothing new. Same old switch. Different day. Facebook decay. To the future our eyes see, never hold back. Be all you can be. We all going through some changes. Be awesome. Be free.

#DedmanPoetry©2016

"Give a man some corn, he eats for a day.

Teach a man to grow corn, he kills you and steals your land." ~ Unknown

July 5, 2016

The Hulk is being watched!!!!

Actor, Mark Ruffalo, is on the government's terrorist watch list. He was added to the list after he promoted a documentary about the effects of natural gas drilling.

More attention is being brought to the movement every day.

Good afternoon @ The Lodge of Good Voices. Gonna be on air playing Shiyé Jamz.

July 7, 2016

Shiyé Bidzííl (Navajo) translated (English) Meaning: My SON IS POWERFUL

July 10, 2016

LOVE ME HATE ME
GREATNESS PREVAILS
Accomplish GOALS.
Soaking up Satisfaction!!!

My WORLD is beautifully Chaotic!

SUM 1
HIT THE
RESET
BUTTON.

It is always a love/hate relationship with Facebook for everyone. Sometimes Facebook works with you and sometimes it is an enemy. But it is always important for the Standing Rock movement. He has his own challenges with Facebook and social media.

CHANGING THE WORLD
ONE POST AT A TIME

FACEBOOK
HALF LIES
NO TRUTHS
WHO DARES?

RADIO AND GHOSTS
BROADCASTING
THEIR SPIRITS!!
PERSEVERANCE
I WILL BE HEARD!

July 11, 2016

MY MORNING PRAYER.
I'm looking to You
My Creator
You're my Rock
You're my Savior
You're my God

I'm looking to you

My God is an awesome God

He reigns from the Heavens above

Whenever I feel troubled and lost

He saves me with the message of love

I'm alive and I'm blessed enough

People doubt, and they question us

I've been left and shunned, in the depths of scum

gotta get me up to repent and flush

my sins out, so when I think about

back then, I'm happy that this is how I live now

switched routes, staying in the right lane

find light in the Lord, gotta bright faith

life saved, eternally grateful

I am weak, and I know that I've shamed You

but You want my heart, and I really wanna try

I give it all to You, give You all my life

I'm looking to you.

"It's never too late to be whoever you want to be. I hope you live a life you're proud of, and if you find you're not, I hope you have the strength to start over again." ~ Unknown

Will the grass roots PREVAIL??!!!!

He shares Joye Braun's photos of semi-trucks carrying huge oil pipes. Things are starting to look very serious. DAPL is still working with no permit.

July 13, 2016

The Dakota Access pipeline is being built as we swipe Facebook.

Separation will

Only weaken

Our strength.

July 14, 2016

He shares a post by Linda Black Elk. Another issue of the Dakota Access pipeline is the desecration of land that grows plants and houses animals that are vitally important to the Indigenous people for healing, ceremony and sustenance.

"As we were driving north on Highway 83 through Herreid, South Dakota, I saw the construction of the Dakota Access pipeline as it rapes its way through beautiful prairies, wetlands, and ancient wild rice beds. My family sat in stunned silence as we drove past the indescribable destruction...a literal bloody gash, a gaping wound on the body of our Mother Earth. It was so violent...so sickening." ~ Linda Black Elk

This land is a gift.

It's everything we want it to be.

July 17, 2016

Shiyé Bidzííl's

Journey Begins!!

Water the SKY

And make RAINBOWS!

July 18, 2016

It's my time zone.

It's my hour.

Gathering my thoughts.

Building power.

The question is...

Can u handle?

He continues to work at the radio station even when he has to hitchhike to get there. He continues to promote his printing company. He shares his art on Facebook. He shares art from other Indigenous artists and helps promote them.

July 21, 2016

I love goals

And inspiring others!

I love my direction!!

July 25, 2016

He shares his latest video. RUNNING TO DC

THIS IS DEDICATED TO ALL THE RUNNERS WHO ARE RUNNING 4 THEIR LIVES HEADED TO WASHINGTON DC 4 THE SAKE OF OUR WATER AND OUR LAND. PRAY 4 EM, AND HELP SUPPORT EM THRU EVERY INCH AND MILE THEY ENDURE AND SACRIFICE FOR THE GRACE OF OUR MOTHER EARTH. PROTECT MOTHER EARTH AT ALL COSTS!! RECONNECTING OUR ROOTS ONE STEP AT A TIME.

#EarthWater #SacredWater #WaterProtectors

Directed & Edited By: Dean Dedman Jr.

Photography By: DRoNE2BWILD, Dustin Thompson and Bobbi Jean Three Legs and google pics!!!

July 26, 2016

Getting my very first tattoo!!

ON MY NECK!!!!!!!!

By Tattoo Artist, Chaske D. Nebow

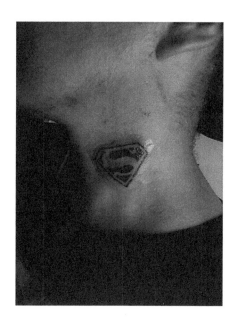

On this day he shares a post that says the Army Corps of Engineers has approved the permit for the Dakota Access pipeline to cross the Missouri River.

It's gonna take more than a simple signature to stop our uprising of Nations!!!! We will fight, we will stand, and we will prevail!!!!!!!!!

He shares a video of an oil spill.

ARMY CORP OF ENGINEERS OPEN YOUR EYES!!!!

THIS IS WHAT'S GONNA HAPPEN!! IT'S A MATTER OF WHEN.

"As Natives of North America, we don't own the land we walked on for thousands of years. We belong to it."
~ Unknown

A meeting is called for July 28th in McLaughlin, South Dakota. All pipe carriers, sundancers and Oceti Sakowin warriors are called to gather for prayer. And to organize a plan to defeat the black snake.

There is a Lakota prophecy that says there will be a great black snake that will run through the land and bring destruction to the people and to the earth. This prophecy has been told from generation to generation since Crazy Horse first envisioned it.

July 28, 2016

He shares a map.

The location of Sacred Stone Camp. By the Cannonball River in Cannonball, North Dakota.

Also known as the FRONT LINE!

"I am running for Oceti Sakowin, all Indigenous people, and for many future generations ahead. We are running for our lives against the Dakota Access pipeline. It's right in our backyard. Now is the time for the people to hear our voices. We are here and we will stand strong." ~ Bobbi Jean Three Legs

The news of the permit being granted is devastating, but the water protectors regroup and fight even harder. People are urged to call the Army Corps of Engineers' Regulatory office to demand that they reverse the permit. Other Indigenous Nations are asked to support the efforts to stop the Dakota Access pipeline. The Standing Rock Nation sues the Army Corps of Engineers over the permit approval. The youth runners make it to Dayton, Ohio on July 30th for a dinner with actress Shailene Woodley.

July 30, 2016

Now is the time to protect Mother Earth!

Chapter Three

August 1, 2016

DRONE PILOT

The month my story of the drone began. The rest is history.

    Actions now happen daily at camp. Larger actions are organized. Three days of prayer and discussion on the State Capitol grounds in Bismarck, North Dakota are slated. Water protectors ask for the North Dakota legislature to stop construction of the pipeline until tribal lawsuits are addressed.

August 3, 2016

We are all the family of earth, they have taken us away. In their new clear war.

Taught us to compete and abuse.

And blame each other. While we're all being used.

"PLEASURE MAY COME FROM ILLUSION

BUT HAPPINESS CAN COME ONLY OF REALITY." ~ John Trudell

    I had a dream last night. In my dream I saw all the diggers and DAPL personnel packing up and leaving. I watched as they disappeared over the horizon from where they came. It felt so real. When all of a sudden I awoke and realized it was a dream. Was this a vision of what is to come? The crazy thing about this dream is this was the first dream I've had in a while. I never had a dream like that, especially feeling so real. Well I pray that perhaps this is power telling me the future. I wouldn't really know, but hope for the best.

This morning Dakota Access sent a 48 hour construction notice to the Standing Rock Nation. Now is the time to stand with us.

We need your heart and soul. Not a polluted mind. Not that I'm pointing out your mind is polluted, but a strong human being who will sacrifice anything to protect our Mother Earth's final resources. You don't have to be an angel or a devil to understand that!! You have to give up anything and everything if it comes to it, to protect Mother Earth. Harness the power of Mother Earth. The storms. A tornado. The wind. An earth quake. That's true power. It will help you. And guide you to a better understanding of the aura of the known universe!!! And to every living thing associated with life....AND THAT'S WATER!!!! #NODAKOTAACCESS

On August 4th an announcement is made that the Standing Rock Nation is filing a temporary injunction on the Dakota Access pipeline in federal court. This injunction is being filed while they are waiting for a court date for the original injunction. Dakota Access is stopped from drilling under Lake Oahe for the moment.

Major call outs for people to join Sacred Stone Camp are put out. Donations are asked for, but they ask mostly for bodies to come and stand on the front lines of the actions. And for help with cooking, firewood and community endeavors. Prayers are also asked for.

On August 5th, 2016 the youth runners make it to Washington, D.C. Actors, Shailene Woodley, Rosario Dawson and Riley Keough are there to stand with them. They arrive at the Army Corps of Engineers' headquarters. These young people ran relay from Cannonball, North Dakota to Washington, D.C. They rally and speak about the devastating effects of the Dakota Access pipeline in the area for several days.

Dakota Access continues to work illegally on the pipeline. They clearly violate North Dakota laws and treaty laws. Water protectors get video evidence of the violations every day. Dakota Access has its own security personnel and they work to intimidate water protectors. One of the first ways they try to intimidate is by taking photos of water protectors' cars and license plates.

August 10th

Going to the construction site where they are building the pipeline. Gonna get footage and audio!!!! #NoDakotaAccess

Everyone please come and show DAPL we all care about our water and we are here to protect all of our lands and water here at the construction site!!!!!!!!!!

#ProtestInPrayer #WaterIsLife

He puts out a call to action for all Oceti Sakowin warriors. He shares videos from inside camp showing what is happening. He asks for prayers. This is a big day for the movement and called day one of the occupation. The water protectors, both Standing Rock Nation members and allies, block the entrances to the pipeline construction sites.

"There was a call to action from our relatives in Sitting Bull's territory. They are at a camp called Sacred Stone Camp. Let's go help them out. Can you imagine our warriors not responding to Crazy Horse or Sitting Bull's call!!!! Sundancers, this is what you prayed for this summer, the water, the children, everything. Time to be about your prayers. We are on our way because it's our responsibility to protect sacred water." ~ TJ Running Bear

August 11, 2016

He shares a beautiful photo from Waniya Locke, a language teacher, who has been reporting eloquently on Facebook since before the first day of Sacred Stone Camp. The photo is of men standing around tipi poles at dawn. She writes, "Calm, Prayerful, Strong this morning."

My BLOOD!

I am a descendent of Hunkpapa, LAKOTA

But born for Todichinii

"BITTER WATER CLAN"

Everyone stay tuned in on KLND radio and webpage and Facebook page for live coverage and feeds from the front lines of the resistance!!!

In the comments he says that people are being arrested.

He shares actress, Shailene Woodley's video. It's viewed almost 300,000 times. She stands in solidarity with the Standing Rock Nation against the Dakota Access pipeline. Law Enforcement and DAPL security are staged for confrontation. Water protectors chant: Mni Wiconi – Water is life! Fists of resistance are high in the air. They stand in front of the law enforcement.

This is it. 500 years in the making leads us to this day. We are Lakota/Dakota Nations. And we are here to stay!! We are the last natives standing in a country that was stolen from us in the first place. We don't claim and/or invade!! We live and share a connection to Mother Earth because that is the way to live. In unity. We were the ones who stood up and won the battle of Little Bighorn. We never surrendered to the government! We stayed strong with our roots in the long war of oppression and resistance!! 500 years!!!!!!!

Time to show the world we are still here to fight 4 our waters and lands!!!

Get off of our treaty lands!!!

As the day goes on, reports come in that eleven people have been arrested. Water protectors try to block the gate to the work site and get arrested.

They brought in a small army to arrest peaceful water protectors who were seated in prayer on public land, using their first amendment rights.

August 12th

I'm trying my best to get drone footage for everyone, but they've been scrambling all our signals. But I got pics!! Will post as soon as I can.

They may have scrambled my drone signal, but I still managed to get some awesome footage. It is still on my raw files!!! So I will be posting them soon here.

There is talk about finding remains of Oceti Sakowin ancestors in the ground at the digging site. Ancestors are buried all over the land that is being desecrated. But no human remains are reported to be found and the digging continues. Two council members were arrested the previous day at the action.

Dave Archambault and Dana Wasinzi !!!!!!!!

No gate, fence or boundaries can hold you guys back!! Very proud of what you did and that shows the world and DAPL that you guys stand strong 4 all of our peoples here on Standing Rock!!! Warriors in my book!! Stay strong brothers.

Modern day warriors, they stand for what we all believe in. They lead the front line.

KFYR-TV, a local Bismarck television station, picks up the Shailene Woodley story at Standing Rock and gets an interview. Other Indigenous Nations are asked to come and bring their Nation's colors to display at camp.

Drone2bwild brings you to the front lines of the DAPL protest.

Gathering of Nations has started!!!!

Lots of water, Gatorade, sandwiches, snacks for all of our water protectors who are standing strong on the Dakota Access FRONTLINES!!!!! Courtesy of Gary John Montana!! Heading to the frontlines now!! #NoDapl #StandUp #Thanks

August 13th

Drone2bwild brings more aerial pictures of what's been going on. Highway 1806 on the Cannonball Ranch near the Standing Rock reservation. Originally on treaty lands!!

Photos by: Dean Dedman Jr. #Drone2bwild

Feeling spiritual.

It's all about the power of the human spirit! Not the illusion of money!!

August 14, 2016

As we gather, we unite. Many Nations coming together for a day we will hold in history as the day natives stood against BIG OIL! Grassroots Strong. We sing the songs. In our hearts we pray to protect us this day. Stand strong. Stand proud.

He puts a call out for drone pilots to come to Standing Rock to support.

Drone2bwild will be at the front lines on Monday when DAPL workers return!!

"What we are doing is speaking for those who can't. We are speaking for those who came before us, those that will come after us, but we are also speaking for those who fly above our heads, those that slither at our feet, those that run in the fields, those that swim in the river. We have an awesome responsibility that was laid at our feet. We must answer the call and face the storm, with no fear." ~ Courtney Yellowfat

Sacred Stone Camp puts out a call for all boats. Water warriors are asked to bring canoes, kayaks and paddle boats on August 20th for actions. He comments that he will be there with the drone. Water protectors are participating in daily actions. They live feed the events as they happen.

He shares Drone2bwild's video of the river.

This river is gonna look a whole lot different when oil is leaked into it!!!!

His sister is supportive and helps him locate a tent. He gets a ride back to camp. He continues to work with the radio station, KLND. They ask for people to call in with updates about DAPL actions so they can report them. There are reports of North Dakota possibly deploying National Guard to help the highway patrol and sheriffs. Water protectors are strongly told to bring no weapons to camp or to any actions. They are directed to stay in prayer.

If anyone at Sacred Stone Camp has any SD cards, would be cool to use them so I can store more footage of tomorrow's gathering with the drone @ Cannonball Ranch on Highway 1806.

August 15th

Update: DAPL workers have begun digging!!

He shares a Drone2bwild video. It is drone footage of the digging as it begins. He flies right over the construction equipment. Then he flies up to the road where all the protectors are. A long row of cars line up the road. He flies over people who are walking. He sends the drone way down the road, then back. He flies over big trucks with empty beds as they pull out of construction zones.

It has begun!!!!! Update: they are digging into our Mother Earth!!!! Terrorists of land and water!! United we stand!!

He also shares drone footage of the first arrests from the 11th. The drone flies over while law enforcement officers calmly walk up and arrest two men. He shares more drone footage of the construction areas and the law enforcement officers blocking and protecting the entrance to the DAPL construction sites.

"What you are looking at is an armed human barricade of police officers protecting a corporation's plan to pollute the water of a so-called 'sacrifice zone' against a group of unarmed, peaceful Native and non-Native citizens standing in prayer to protect the water supply for this and future generations." ~ Angela Bibens

The Bismarck Tribune reports that Dakota Access has filed a suit against the water protectors. They are asking a federal judge to order water protectors to stop interfering with the building of the pipeline.

Drone2bwild brings awareness to Dakota Access pipeline!! It's gonna affect everyone along the Missouri River, including the Standing Rock reservation border. Hoka

There is still not much media coverage of events, but it does get some attention nearby. KXMB local news interviews him for a segment about the drone and the water protectors. In the news clip he says:

Everyone on the rez calls me the drone guy. I've got over 1000 shares on some videos. A lot of people are hurt and sad and crying. This needs to be documented so it can go down in history.

The hearing for the injunction filed by the Standing Rock Nation is announced for August 24th. It is to be held at the Federal Court building in Washington D.C. There is a call out for people to be there.

August 16th

He shares several Drone2bwild videos. They are drone footage of above the camps. Sacred Stone Camp now has an overflow camp. They are calling it Oceti Sakowin Camp. The camps are still small, but they are growing daily. He shares more drone footage of many cars coming into camp and people arriving. He captures wonderful footage of above the water they are protecting. His videos are getting tens of thousands of views now. He shows the first aerial shots of camp with just a few tipis and some small tents around them.

Cheyenne River Tribe brings me more people every day. They are cruising by and honking!!!! Oglala and Cheyenne join Standing Rock Nation.....there are hundreds more coming.

DAPL people to let you know: WE ARE GATHERING ONE MILLION STRONG!! EVERYDAY OUR NUMBERS GAIN. #GATHERINGOFNATIONS #RESISTANCE #NATIVERIGHTS #WATERRIGHTS

Day 4 of the uprising resistance. We gather and sing for the water. Our strength is in our numbers. When destruction is coming to water and the earth, we, as native peoples, have come together to protect and honor Mother Earth. That's what the government will never understand.

No highway patrols and DAPL workers today. Water protectors take over the work site. Originally on treaty lands. While the head of the DAPL workers filed a restraining order on Dave Archambault and protectors!! Seriously, let's see if they can restrain 2,000+ natives and all races of all colors!!

His drone footage is sent around the world. Japan, Germany, Ireland, England and all over the United States. People around the world are getting to know the movement through his beautiful drone footage. People thank him often for his work.

Wow. I'm doing an awesome job. Feels good to be a part of history and I'm documenting everything. I want to thank everyone for your help and for being tuned in to what #Drone2bwild has been doing for the Standing Rock reservation. Thanks for all the info and advice and heads up on things. Much appreciated. I have been filming this since the start and I will continue to film it whether there are military helicopters or not. This drone is not intimidated by military force. I will document every single action of this movement. If you want to help in any way you can send micro SD cards. Need a lot of them so I can gather as much video as possible. Wasté

August 17th

Standing Rock Tribal Council puts out a call to all Indigenous Nations of the world. They ask for support in the way of proclamations, resolutions and letters of support. This call out is signed by Dave Archambault II, Tribal Chairman.

Dean continues to work with and to promote KLND 89.5 FM, local radio station. He shares drone footage of the radio station.

We've out reached to over a million people out there, this little radio station here on the Standing Rock reservation. So keep sharing and letting the world know what's been happening here with the Dakota Access pipeline. Thank you. Keep up all the awareness.

The Drone2bwild page views have picked up by 100% in one week.

I have captured the world's attention. Using just my drone has been very beneficial to my Native people across NDN country and beyond. It really does feel good to be a part of something that will forever capture the eyes of the world. Big media has yet to shed light on what's been going on here at the front lines of the Standing Rock reservation. But here I am with this little Phantom 3 Advance, flying around, filming as it happens. The resistance of my people and destruction of my earth. It really does hurt me to see DAPL digging into her and mining her spirit. But what brings me up is the power of prayer through all my peoples who have been gathering in hundreds and soon to be thousands. Big Oil corporations, like Dakota Access, may have all the power through money, but true power is the power of the human spirit. And I'm capturing it all with new drone technology. Many people may be taking beautiful pictures of Hawaii or filming a beautiful beach somewhere around the world with their drones. As for me, I'm capturing my people as they stand for the water and land. My name is Dean Dedman Jr. I am Hunkpapa, Lakota and Diné, Navajo.

I was born for the Bitterwater Clan. And I will fight for my water and document every part of it. Thank you to all the people worldwide who have been keeping up on the footage. I will continue to film it as it progresses. Mini wiconi. Water is life. I am capturing history in the making.

He shares drone footage.

I came to camp this evening. The protectors are still gathering. The numbers are growing. There is an official camp called Red Warrior Camp. This is the drone perspective on the new camp. The long tipi you see is called the council lodge.

Day 5 of the protest and people seem to be at peace here at the camps. DAPL people have yet to come to the site. No highway patrol either, but they were stopping and blocking traffic coming from Bismarck, ND. Helicopters have been spotted flying around, but without 50 calibers...I repeat there are no armed helicopters in the area. Remember this is a peaceful protest. We pray and sing. That's the power of prayer. They are working on the other side of the river. They start at 8am and end work at 5pm. So Drone2bwild is planning on crossing the river in order to share with the world what has been taking place on the other side. I will plan on flying sometime in the morning. Stay tuned. This is another update from Drone2bwild and KLND radio.

August 18th

No arrests!! But someone has blocked off the road by taking a back rear tire off a vehicle!! But we are calling out to tell people there have been no arrests and everything here is at peace. This is what's been taking place since no DAPL or highway patrol are on the scene.

He shares a video of the vehicle and also a video of many flags hanging on a fence. He says, "The flags still hang!" This was the original flag row. He also shows signs and concrete barriers that have been spray painted with messages of support for the water.

People on social media talk about the original proposed location for this pipeline. It was first proposed to cross the Missouri River north of Bismarck. But the people of Bismarck, who are mostly Caucasian, rejected that route because they believed it would threaten their water supply. So Dakota Access moved their plans onto the treaty land of the Lakota.

Many Indigenous people believe it is just a continuation of the genocide that has been occurring since Europeans first landed in North America. Just a continuation of the efforts to wipe out the Indigenous people and culture.

The leading issues with the Army Corps of Engineers and the Dakota Access pipeline (owned by Energy Transfer Partners) are the blatant violations of the law. The National Historic Preservation Act was being ignored. Cultural, burial and ancestral village sites would absolutely be affected by the digging and drilling into the land. Criminal acts of trespass under the 1851 and 1868 Fort Laramie Treaties are being outright ignored. Tribal consultation is being completely bypassed. There is still no full environmental impact study.

August 19th

DRoNE2BWILD catches up with Quese IMC. Here to spread the love and stand with his people. Quese IMC brings his people's flag to stand with Standing Rock Nation!!

Drone2bwild is ready for the canoe gathering!

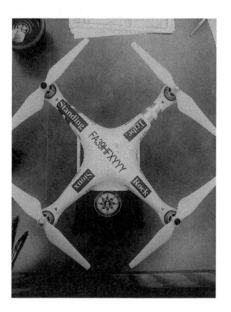

We will be broadcasting live as it takes place.

Join us! Aug 20th at 9am as we take to the water to say #NoDAPL

We will resist the Dakota Access pipeline.

We float in unity and paddle for solidarity against the Dakota Access pipeline!!!

August 20, 2016

Dean provides drone footage of the canoe gathering. He gets amazing video of the canoes on the water. The camps are growing fast. As are the views his videos are getting. Numbers are rising daily. He also posts beautiful drone footage of the crowd. Many water protectors hold signs. One amazing sign says: We Are Water. The water protectors hold signs off the side of the bridge and he gets a wonderful view of it with the drone. This video gets almost 300,000 views. 10,000 people share it. The water protectors love the drone. They wave and yell at it. They put up their fists in solidarity with it.

Today, we give recognition and love to the sacred water of Mother Earth! Water protectors took to the waters of the Cannonball, ND at the Sacred Stone Camp.

#NoDakotaAccess #NoPipelines #KeepItInTheGround

Drone Footage by: Drone2bwild Photography & Video   Music by: A Tribe Called Red

It's really so awesome to see my brothers and sisters bring the Navajo Nation flag to stand in solidarity with Standing Rock nation. Proud to see the flag!!!

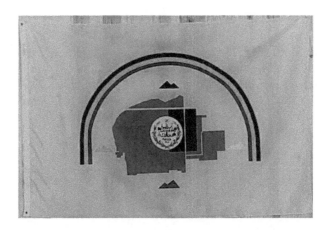

August 21ˢᵗ

Calling out to the protectors of the earth all over the world. The Red Warrior Camp is growing every day!! Many nations beyond the 7 councils are coming together. And there are still many more on their way!! Support Sacred Stone Camp and Oceti Sakowin Camp!

The Apache Nation announces their support for Standing Rock. The Apache Nation has lost much land, little by little. It was taken away for its timber, copper, silver and water. Treaties are not upheld. They are currently standing to preserve one of their sacred sites, Oak Flat, from being destroyed by copper mining. They are also protecting the water that would be used to mine the copper.

August 23rd

He flies the drone over the water to the other side. His footage shows the drill pad, which will be used to drill under the water, in the early stages. He takes the drone down and gets a look at the construction equipment they are using. He flies the drone over the pathway of the pipeline.

Today we united our prayers with songs. In solidarity we marched onto the Memorial Bridge here in Bismarck, North Dakota to show the world watching and the residents of Mandan and Bismarck that we are a peaceful people of the lands and the waters.

ALL NATIONS

ALL RELATIONS

ALL WATERS

Other Indigenous media use his drone footage in educational videos. Sacred Stone Camp uses his videos often. Many people encourage him and continue to share and react to his work.

August 24th

We are a peaceful people. We are unity. Today was the day of the hearing. The camps came together to pray and give thanks to Mother Earth. And also to tell the world that they ain't backing out. We are here standing strong against Dakota Access!!! We have all of our resources. We have all our allies and Nations behind us. We all come to this spot to tell the world that water is life. Water is the source that sprouts all life in the known universe. Protect all water.

August 25th

He realizes he will need financial support to continue his work with the drones. He sets up a GoFundMe page. He does not share it all the time, but he does share it and others help him. Other drone pilots have been arriving and documenting history with him. One is Myron Dewey with Digital Smoke Signals.

Way before Oceti Sakowin heard the name Myron Dewey! Lol it was Shiyé Bidzííl and all his struggling truths.

Just wanna shout to everyone that we are all doing an awesome job.

August 26th

KLND 89.5 Radio DRONE UPDATE:

This is what progress is happening from the other side. With the last drone flight two days ago, things have moved and changed to signify that there is construction happening over there.

He gets a good shot of the drill pad. There is hardly anything there. Some pipes. It is fenced in. The drone footage shows a very large, wide strip of land that has been bulldozed. He flies over DAPL workers who are getting out of trucks. He flies over the water.

We are a peaceful people...but yet the media portrays us wrong. We are here. We are strong. Because we are a people who have deep ancestral roots of Mother Earth. We only have one planet. Let's protect it with our lives!!!!!!

You can't drink oil, keep it in the soil!

August 28th

It's time to put all our differences aside and remember why we shall remain.

We gather here from all parts of the world to pray and protect our waters. To give thanks to all waters of this planet, and to remember we were always connected to the roots of our ancestors. FROM THE LANDS, THROUGH OUR WATERS, TO THE SKY!!

He shares an amazing drone video of horses as they come into camp. They are followed by a long line of vehicles. Camp is growing fast.

August 29th

HEY so tomorrow if you're at camp and you brought a banner, bring it to the North Camp at 6pm. We're going to be taking pictures by Drone2bwild Photography & Video's drone of ALL banners. Come out and rep #NoDAPL, your nation, whatever! We're going to arrange them to show everyone's messages.

August 30th

BREAKING: Army Corps of Engineers has granted the final easement needed for DAPL's 3.8 billion dollar project. DAPL had a permit at the time of the hearing, which allowed them to pre-construct and drill on the east side. They were granted the Mineral Lease Act Easement for the Army Corps Land on the west side. Although there are no documents to show that they have the permit to drill, they are already working on the west side, on private land. Today construction materials were delivered to a site on Highway 6 for the drill pad.

August 31st

There is an action and he is there to live feed it on Facebook. Live feeds from Standing Rock are often choppy and interruptions in service are common. There is a young, Indigenous man who is attached to a large construction vehicle. Two law enforcement officers try to cut through his thick arm cast with a hand saw to remove him. It is not easy to cut and they are there for a while.

A large crowd of water protectors is gathered around, chanting and trying to persuade the law enforcement officers that what is happening is wrong and they should not be protecting an oil company against citizens of the United States. The law enforcement officer stops for a few minutes and a water bottle is handed up to the Indigenous man. The law enforcement officer gives him a drink of water and starts working again. The crowd shouts: Water is life!

At times the water protectors seem menacing in their efforts to stop the law enforcement from protecting the pipeline. There is desperation in their voices. They understand the seriousness of the situation and try anything to wake the law enforcement officers up to it. They call a black law enforcement officer a slave to the white man's oil. They tell him he should be standing with his own people rather than protecting an oil company. To other law enforcement officers, the water protectors say they have no souls. A law enforcement officer says that they have trained for this. That enrages the crowd. Water protectors start chanting: The whole world is watching!

An hour in, law enforcement blocks access to the action site. People have to park and walk farther. More law enforcement shows up. Fire fighters are there too. Dean tries to talk to them, but no one will talk on live feed. He asks them if they are trying to give their families clean water today. Water protectors carry signs. One says: Injustice anywhere threatens justice everywhere. The crowd chants for the Indigenous man who is still locked down to the construction equipment: This is what a warrior looks like! They get loud. The law enforcement officer stops trying to cut him off and everyone sends up a big cheer.

They start cutting again soon. People make pleas for the Indigenous man. "He's our brother, please do not hurt him. He would do anything to protect his water. You don't understand." They encourage him to be strong. They tell him that they love him. The officer starts cutting in a different direction and the Indigenous man moves uncomfortably. People get upset and women start crying, "Lilililili!" The officer stops and takes a breath before he starts cutting again.

The video feed cuts off unexpectedly a couple of times. It is common for live feeds to suddenly go down. When the last feed from Dean comes on, the crowd has been pushed back, far away from the construction equipment and the lockdown. There is a line of law enforcement officers standing between the water protectors and the Indigenous man who is still being cut off of the equipment. Water protectors stand facing the officers. They say that this is a violation of their rights. That it is suppressing the right to assemble, suppressing the right to report events as media. That it is against the constitution of the United States.

Water protectors say that they are there to protect the water for their children. One Indigenous man tells other water protectors to not disrespect the officers. He reminds them that they are not there to be mean or to be violent, but to stand up for the water. He reminds everyone that they are there to pray for the water. People start drumming and singing Indigenous songs. The law enforcement officers look uncomfortable while they sing.

Eventually the Indigenous man is cut off of the equipment and taken to jail. He is released later that evening.

Morton County Sheriff, Kyle Kirchmeier, tries to counteract the water protectors on social media and announces that he is very proud of the job the deputies did that day. Law enforcement attempts to use social media to show their side of the story, often telling stories that make the water protectors seem like they are not peaceful and prayerful.

Chapter Four

September 1, 2016

Things are happening at camp beyond #NoDAPL actions. It has become a strong community of people who take care of one another and celebrate each new day together. Horsemanship Day is announced at Oceti Sakowin Camp for September 3rd. Everyone is welcome to take part in the activities.

We bring this forward as an offer of time and space to celebrate each other in this resistance and enjoy a day of building solidarity with the many, many Nations standing with Standing Rock who have come from across the continent!

September 4th

He shares Democracy Now's video:

Dakota Access pipeline security guards attack Native American #NoDAPL protesters with dogs and pepper spray.

The videos that come out from other live feeders on Facebook are crazy to watch. Water protectors sprayed right in the face with pepper spray. A young woman who works for DAPL encouraging her dog to go after water protectors. Dogs biting water protectors. People kneeling to have a milk of magnesia concoction poured into their burning eyes. And these are not law enforcement officers who are inflicting this abuse. It is the security guards who work for DAPL who are hurting unarmed, peaceful, prayerful water protectors. The world stops in horror.

Here at the FRONTLINES!!

Ready to protect our treaty lands!!!

No matter what it takes, we will stand our ground!!

I am no longer affiliated with the KLND radio station and for that the drone has been taken from me. Reasons I don't even want to get into. So help Drone2bwild get back in the air. For now I'm on the front lines documenting everything from my phone. Stay safe and peace, love to everyone who has been following #Drone2bwild and its aerial media.

Once again, thank you to every single one of you out there. For all your support and messages of prayer and protection.

His followers are growing in numbers and strength. They try to help him however they can. Calls are put out for donations, solar powered chargers and other equipment to document and broadcast. A drone is donated to him so he can continue his work, documenting the events of the #NoDAPL movement.

September 5th

He notes that he is feeling motivated with Pete Nichols at the Cannonball River on his Facebook status. Pete is working to get a drone and support for him.

Thanks for everything you've done for me bro. I really appreciate it. Hope to collaborate more with you guys!!! I will be back up in the air in a couple of days.

He shares a YouTube video:

Robert Kennedy Jr. talks renewable

Dean's drone footage is in the video. It is really beautiful footage from high above, covering a march.

Robert Kennedy Jr. says he couldn't be there today, but he wishes everyone luck and expresses gratitude. He extensively talks about renewable energy. He thanks the water protectors for fighting.

As I scroll the Facebook page of Morton County Sheriff's Department, I notice how many lies they tend to post. SMH

I'm angry for the moment, but emotions can't get the best of me, especially in times like this!!!! But we are turning heads and changing the world's environmental views on Indian land. We stand strong. We stand for all of the world's waters!!!!

My kids. So happy to see them all together.

He shares a photo of his children. He is no longer with their mother.

"You will not be forgotten as long as I'm in this White House. Indians will have a seat at the table when important decisions are being made about your lives. Washington can't - and shouldn't - dictate a policy agenda for Indian country. Tribal nations do better when they make their own decisions." ~ President Barack Obama, Nov. 5, 2009

Anonymous puts out a video. It is a warning to the DAPL security guards and law enforcement to stop harming the water protectors. It is shared widely on Facebook. Jill Stein is there and she is on the frontlines with the water protectors.

"We are not human beings having a spiritual experience. We are spiritual beings having a human experience."
~ Pierre Teilhard de Chardin

September 6th

All are welcome to come and spread the love!

He shares a short video of drone shots of the main entrance into Oceti Sakowin Camp. The road is lined with flags from all different Nations. Flag row, it is called, and it is stunning.

He live feeds on Facebook from a construction site where water protectors are gathered. He stops at a trooper's car and the trooper engages in conversation with him. The trooper is polite and respectful. Dean asks questions. Would there be any workers coming to the site today? The trooper says he doubts it, but he says he is not in communication with any of the workers. Or the security guards. He asks if the trooper thinks the security guards will do something when he leaves. The trooper seems concerned and asks if he is worried that they will. Another water protector says yes. The trooper says he will talk to them. He says it is unfortunate that anyone got hurt the other day with the dog attacks.

This law enforcement officer is compassionate. There are many along the way who are, but those stories are harder to find than the majority of the horrible, violent stories. A few law enforcement officers are reported to walk off and quit their jobs. There are even rumors of some who join the water protectors in the fight for clean water.

The largest Native American protest in HISTORY is happening right now.

Right now one of the largest Native American protests in history is ongoing, without so much as a single mention from the mainstream media.

He shares a live feed of a law enforcement officer ordering a young drone pilot to bring his drone down out of the sky. The officer tells him that there is a law against flying the drone. The officer is menacing and tries to coax the drone pilot into giving up his drone. He tells the pilot that he has to present certification to fly a drone. People gather around the drone pilot as the officer tries to get his drone. Dean and the group of people walk the drone pilot down the road and away from the officer to protect him. Nearly 70,000 people watch this video.

It wasn't Drone2bwild's drone, but the North Dakota Highway Patrol is harassing our drone pilots who have been covering this movement. Yet they have helicopters hovering/flying at close proximity to the crowds. Way below 500 feet. They were almost about to take his phantom 4 away but the crowd intervened. #DronesRule

We are utilizing drone technology in this matter because we are fighting a pipeline and we will use every resource we can get our hands on. And also for our Protection. The eye in the sky sees everything. I don't get how the government breaks all their laws throughout history, yet when a drone pilot steps out of FAA regulations it's a big deal!!!!

New Drone Tactics in mind!!!

September 8th

Chinle Stands With Standing Rock

He shares Navajo Nation's post. They are collecting supplies to take to Standing Rock in his hometown of Chinle, Arizona. After the dog attacks, many people send resources and support to Standing Rock. He is particularly proud of his hometown in these efforts. His followers send him information and heads up notifications. He asks his followers for information at times.

Can someone confirm this?

He shares CNN's post: North Dakota guard members possibly headed to pipeline protest.

Sources tell Valley News Live that the North Dakota National Guard is being called in to help with security at the Dakota Access pipeline protest going on near Cannonball, North Dakota.

This is a pic that Drone2bwild took of the canoes and kayaks that came in from Bismarck today. They left from Bismarck yesterday. After a fierce rain storm, they have arrived. They had a water ceremony and offered fish from the northwest coast. Drone Footage coming soon!!

He shares drone footage of Rosebud camp. It is where his campsite is. In this amazing video, the drone runs along the river. It flies over campers, tents, tipis. Over a horseback rider. Camp is growing into a small town.

September 9th

Creative people, including musicians and artists of all types are drawn to camp and show up to support. He posts a video of Immortal Technique, rapper, performing at Red Warrior Camp at night.

September 11th

There is a call out to impeach North Dakota Governor Jack Dalrymple and to fire Morton County Sheriff, Kyle Kirchmeier. Dean encourages everyone to sign the petition.

September 12th

He shares a post from Democracy Now! an independent news source. Last Thursday, Morton County, North Dakota, issued an arrest warrant for Amy Goodman, a reporter from Democracy Now! The charge: Criminal trespass, a misdemeanor offense.

North Dakota authorities have issued an arrest warrant for Democracy Now's Amy Goodman because she exposed the fascist police dog tactics of private security companies during the #NoDAPL protests. What is the world coming to? We are all gonna be getting arrested for telling and exposing the truth. That's the American government for you.

It's crazy how us journalists are getting profiled for telling and showing the truth, but yet the DAPL security have not yet been charged for their actions last week!!! What is America coming to? The whole world is watching!!!

We will always remember the year 2016. The year we natives came together to stand up for all of earth's water supply. History in the making. This video is how this all transpired from a few water protectors to now a worldwide phenomenon of earth and water protectors verses the fossil fuel industry. My work will forever be in cyber space. This is non-violent direction action. We come with prayer and good intentions. We are here. We are water protectors.

Video By: Dean Dedman Jr.   Song: Electric Pow Wow   Artist: A Tribe Called Red

The video is of the North Dakota frontlines. The drone flies down a long line of law enforcement officers. There are many water protectors standing in front of the line of law enforcement on the road. The video shows law enforcement officers walk up to a line of water protectors and arrest them. Next, the drone footage shows the ground being dug into by heavy equipment. Then he flies above the water.

September 13th

He shares the latest breaking news:

Allies have locked themselves down to excavators and halted construction on the Dakota Access pipeline an hour and a half west of camp.

Friday's federal intervention stopped construction near the Missouri River, but work on the pipeline continues in many other places. We won't stop until they stop and being an ally means taking action.

Around twenty people have just been arrested, including journalists. Police have SHUT DOWN all road access to the site and are carrying assault rifles and less-than lethal weapons.

WE NEED YOUR HELP. PLEASE SHARE. MAINSTREAM MEDIA IS NOT REPORTING IT.

"Dissent is the highest form of patriotism." - Howard Zinn

"BE BRAVE TODAY, SPREAD THE MESSAGE." ~ Prolific The Rapper

September 14th

He is interviewed by the Overpass Light Brigade. He is recognized for being a local guy who has inspired many people to come stand as water protectors through his drone footage. People are now coming from all over the United States and beyond. In the interview he says,

I was living in Mobridge, South Dakota, where Lake Oahe is located. Since the fight has come to the lands of my people and ancestors, I took it upon myself to come here to the Cannonball River to stand and fight for the waters and lands that we all share on this planet. I have been camping here going on five weeks now. I have sacrificed everything in order to be here and do what I am doing. I'm planning on staying here until the very end and until we water protectors put an end to Dakota Access and its atrocities towards our sacred sites.

September 15th

The movement extends far beyond camp. Thirteen water protectors are arrested at the Department of the Interior. There are growing pains inside the camps.

"Things tend to get torn apart around camp because you forgot we been in prayer since April 1. Handle yourself and treat each other how you want to be treated!!" ~ Wiyaka Eagleman

"People don't understand the whole deal with the pipeline still? Remember that movie Avatar? Basically us natives are the blue guys. And the greedy oil assholes are the military coming to cut our big tree down."
~ meme from Sacred Stone Camp

September 17th

Drone action is an everyday mission at the camp.

Good Morning to all who keep up with our Indigenous media. Today is gonna be a beautiful day so get out there and enjoy the camp. Participate in the horse races we got going on at 2ish. I just wanna say that we are all doing an awesome job helping each other in a time like this. Our ancestors would be so proud of us. We are change and that's a good thing. So always remember to pray and sing for the waters. Soon we will all look back on this year and remember all those water warriors, protectors and youth who made a stand for the water and Mother Earth! So I will end this post in a positive way. Stay safe out there and remember why we are here.

Today's rain storm; the camp was soaked and muddy everywhere! Days like this our hearts can rest because there's no work going on. So we continue to pray and sing as we continue to gather hour by hour. Welcome to Red Warrior Camp.

He shares new drone footage of Red Warrior Camp. It has really grown this month. People are asked not to film inside of the camps on the ground to protect one another. Every night there are community bonfires, singing, dancing and lots of laughing. One of those nights he is able to get drone footage of fancy dancers who came to honor the people with their dance.

"You don't always get what you wish for, you get what you work for." ~ Unknown

September 18th

Just a statement about my drone and where and how I use it.

I have been flying the drone in every air space here but the navy air space. And YES even RED WARRIOR's lil bitty air space. I will say this now, before all the groups and camps came around, before all the media extravaganza, even though we all had cell phones, I was the only one with the power to film great quality footage. But not just film great awesome footage, but to allow me and the viewers to go where we couldn't go and see things that we couldn't see from the ground level. So basically I've been here since day one and I fly the drone every day. It has been the one and only best non-violent direct action in history. I have also been capturing a lot of vital, important imagery that will play a huge role against Dakota Access. And of course the drone covers everything that goes on within the camps; like the horse races, kids playing in the river, canoe actions, people coming and leaving from camp, the gathering of the many Nations that come into camp. You name it, this drone has either been there, flew by, or was skipping across the waters.

I've flown this drone to the limits to get all those unique shots that everyone loves to see. There are around four other drones at the camp as well, but mine is the most active and the most involved with a lot of different aspects of the camps, even the RED WARRIOR CAMP. I believe I have earned that level of respect. And if anyone has any concerns about the drone or where I've been flying then please come up to me and talk to me. You can't miss me. And what would be most helpful is for everyone who has been here for as long as me, to please feel free to educate the new campers on what flies here at camp so they are aware of the drones and also just to be safe. I want to assure you and everyone else that it's not the FBI, CIA, BIA, or DAPL's drone. It is my drone that flies by. The drone that I operate is all white. Now most other drones within the camp fly high over. As for me, I love to fly in low. So please don't be scared. This drone is on our side and has been on our side since the beginning.

Now with that out of the way, I just want to make my position clear on where I stand within all of this media. And also to let all security of the camps know that I AM LOCAL MEDIA!!! I don't need to go through procedures. You should be aware of me by now, and some of you security are also locals yourself. We know each other. So please, easy on your actions when it comes to me. Other than that, all of you are doing a fantastic job. Keep up the good work.

I fly my drone with speed and agility. I am aware of all the subjects which not to film. I do respect the certain areas of the camps. But please, I am Drone2bwild Photography & Video. I know my own rules and I know my place and that's reporting on behalf of all my Standing Rock Sioux Tribe peoples. This is where I'm from. And this is who I represent as an enrolled member. So a message to all of the camps that come from many different trails. REMEMBER YOUR ACTIONS, YOUR DECISIONS, AND YOUR PLACE HERE. IT IS GREATLY APPRECIATED. I would like to say this, MAKE GOOD CHOICES AND PLEASE THINK BEFORE YOU ACT. AND REMEMBER, WE STANDING ROCK LOCALS STILL HAVE TO LIVE HERE.

NOW I WANT TO REASSURE THAT EVERYTHING THAT I HAVE STATED WAS ALL OF MY OWN WORDS. I DIDN'T MEAN TO OFFEND ANYONE, AND IF I DID I WANT TO APOLOGIZE. MY WORDS ARE MY OWN AND NOT THAT OF THE CAMPS. MY MESSAGE WAS TO JUST ADDRESS THE USE OF THIS PARTICULAR DRONE THAT I FLY EVERYDAY. WE ARE ALL HERE BATTLING THE SAME SNAKE. SO LET'S PUT OUR MINDS TOGETHER AND SLICE THIS SNAKE'S HEAD OFF!!! THANK YOU. ANY QUESTIONS OR CONCERNS FEEL FREE TO MESSAGE ME.

We march in solidarity to offer prayers to our desecrated sacred burial sites that DAKOTA ACCESS PIPELINE DESTROYED A FEW WEEKS BACK WHEN THEY PULLED THE DOGS OUT!!

WE OFFER OUR PRAYERS TO THE LAND SO THAT OUR ANCESTORS WILL REMAIN WITH MOTHER EARTH AND ALL OF HER CREATIONS. We march and pray to keep our water protectors' spirits lifted high and to keep us strong and to empower all of us with the knowledge of the earth. WHEN WE DO THIS WE ARE COMMUNICATING WITH MOTHER EARTH. As Indigenous peoples of the land we hold that knowledge close to our minds and hearts, but really we keep it in the pipe of the Chanupa. The sacred pipe. So every day we continue to do this with prayer and tobacco.

I, the drone pilot, can capture all the visuals of this destruction as it is laid out before us. Documenting everything has been a focal point for the Indigenous media. We will soon provide footage to help assist and bring justice to the Dakota Access pipeline workers, their security and the corporation itself. And one more note. They will try and build on this land as quickly as they can. And when you start working faster and quicker it only ups the risk of something happening while in full operations which could eventually lead to cracks; or worse, a leak. We know that they are working on this project now and they are working to build it fast. Personally, I believe I can speak on behalf of all Indigenous people here on OUR LANDS that we will have this DAKOTA ACCESS PIPELINE 100% TOTAL SHUT DOWN, BECAUSE THIS IS MORE THAN JUST A PIPELINE. IT'S ABOUT THE ENTIRE WORLD'S WATER SUPPLY!!! NOW IF YOU WATCH ALL OF THE FACEBOOK POSTS OF ACTIONS ....THE WORLD IS ANGRY AND ACTIONS ARE HAPPENING WORLDWIDE!!!!! WE WILL STAND UNTIL THE LAST PIPE AND DRILL IS OUT OF THE EARTH AND TO ALSO HONOR OUR TREATIES. TO DEMAND THE RETURN OF LAND THAT WAS TAKEN FROM US FOR EXPLOITATIONS OF GREED BY THE SO CALLED AMERICAN GOVERNMENT. UNPOLLUTE THEIR MINDS AND POCKETS. START UTILIZING RENEWABLE ENERGY TO THE BENEFIT OF THIS PLANET. WE WILL PREVAIL AND WE WILL TEND TO MOTHER EARTH AND HER CRIES. BECAUSE WE ARE ALL NATIONS. WE ARE ALL RELATIONS. AND WE ARE ALL WATER.

WE ARE THE WATER PROTECTORS!!!! AND WE WILL PROTECT ALL OF EARTH'S WATERS IN THE GREATEST STAND KNOWN IN AMERICAN HISTORY AND THAT OF THE WORLD.

Written by Shiyé Bidzíil

September 19th is the day that Prolific The Rapper posts his music video. He shares it, saying, "I think the world deserves to see the truth about #NoDAPL"

Title: Black Snakes / A Tribe Called Red x Prolific The Rapper

Original Song: Pow Wow Stadium by A Tribe Called Red

I have tried my best to portray what I felt at camp, I felt LOVE. Love for all people, all living things, Mother Earth herself, and concern for future generations. I felt what this world needs at this time, Unity beyond race, concern for one another and togetherness. I felt peace and calm. Then when the police came I felt the opposite. I felt lies, setups and oppression, but I'm trying not to dwell on the negative. My only wish with this video is that it helps in some way. I wasn't sure how to help so I just started filming.

Much love to everyone on the front lines!! Much love Standing Rock, Oceti Sakowin, Turtle Island, all Indigenous Nations overseas, all spiritual leaders, and all beautiful Human Beings of all colors (Black, Red, White, Yellow, Pink, and Orange haha! jk). You're all important and I love you all equally!

When I was at camp I got the feeling that this is the beginning of something new, something that excited me and woke me up. Something bigger than what I thought it was and it's beautiful. The energy, courage and unity I felt at camp was inspirational.

To EVERYONE at home, let's keep spreading truth for those on the front lines!

If anyone seeing this goes to Standing Rock, I would encourage you to be humble, sit by the microphone where they talk and listen to the leadership teach good things. It's a beautiful happening. Don't go to lead, go to help. Peace, love and prayers to all, including the police, sheriff, government and Energy Transfer Partners; maybe they will have a change of heart. And if not, I'll see you on the front lines!

September 20th

David Archambault II, Chairman of the Standing Rock Nation, speaks in front of the United Nations Human Rights Council in Geneva, Switzerland. He asks for support in the fight against the Dakota Access pipeline project. Standing Rock is very serious about stopping the pipeline and going about it in every way conceivable.

Dean shares a photo of rapper, Iam Drezus, at Sitting Bull's memorial.

Took a break today to go see and pay respects to a true legend, Sitting Bull. #TatankaIyotake

I've been flying every day and today I just upped my skills with drones!!

The art of the Bow!!!

He flies the drone up fast to look like it was shot into the air like an arrow that Iam Drezus pretended to shoot.

This camp has brought a lot of my Indigenous hip hop natives here. It's pretty cool that I'm collaborating with one of them. Iam Drezus has been real from the start. I've been shooting a lot of drone material with him around camp. His song and video will be out real soon. It's been a blessing in many ways to work with all my favorite people here. Stay Real. Stay True.

He also shares drone footage from the day before. It is of horse riders on a hill. It is gorgeous footage of the land, the horses and the people. He is getting a lot of compliments from other Indigenous media people. Dallas Goldtooth, from Indigenous Rising Media, shares his footage with compliments.

September 21ˢᵗ

He shares a link to support a statue that was built at Standing Rock. It is called: Not Afraid To Look. Art has been a beautiful way to increase awareness for the movement. At the same time an announcement is shared around social media: Emergency Commission approves a 6 million dollar loan to cover the cost of law enforcement. Law enforcement presence has grown as camp gets bigger and the actions grow. He only leaves camp to wash his clothes, shower and charge his drone occasionally.

September 22ⁿᵈ

Today at camp: Overcast with the first day of fall. Goodbye sun, welcome cold weather. Are we all ready for this coming winter? As you see we are all still here. We are all still strong. We are native people and winter is our home. Stay strong! Stay united!!

He shares drone footage of flag row. It is a touching tribute to all of the Nations who have shown up to help in the fight for the water.

September 23ʳᵈ

He shares a Drone2bwild video of canoes coming into camp. There were large and small canoes with lots of people. He asks people to tag the video for the northwest coastal tribes.

The Northwest Coastal Tribes come to join our stand against DAKOTA ACCESS PIPELINE!!! Here you can see them coming in from the Missouri river up the Cannonball River.

"Follow your dreams even if it means standing alone.

Be different but stay yourself." ~ Unknown

Ok who's all at camp?

Who wants to be at camp?

And who all was at the camp

But want to come back?

September 24th

I feel uneasy! But I'm ready and prepared for anything that is coming my way!!

Our voices are being heard!!! Listen!

On September 25th he appears in Steven Jeffrey Chrisjohn's live feed.

I was the first person here to get it all with the drone. The cool thing about it was I had the drone, everybody else had phones. The drone gave a better perspective of how the movement was evolving. I get a lot of compliments from everybody when they see the footage. That's why they came. They wanted to be a part of what they were seeing visually. These drones brought a lot of attention. The drones stepped it up a notch.

The drone comes in toward him and he reaches up and plucks it from the air. He says: There you go.

This is what I fight for everyday along the Cannonball River! She has done nothing to us but provide us with beautiful nature and the cleanest waters! And yet the Fossil Fuel Energy Corporations have made it their destructive mission to extract and take all of her precious resources. All in the name of GREED and their addiction to dominant power over the earth and its creations. As Indigenous people we will pray for her and spiritually educate the world watching that there is a way to live with the earth. And there's a way not to live with the earth. We choose the way of the earth!!! Mni Wiconi #NoDAPL #WaterIsLife

Through the power of prayer we will prevail.

He shares drone footage of bison running. They are majestic animals. They are sacred to the Lakota people and to many Indigenous Nations. In an effort to educate people about the bison, he shares information.

Bison almost went extinct around 1900. But they were saved. Once they were 50 million in number, now they are only about 500,000, but they are coming back. It was the European settlers who almost got rid of all of the bison. Indigenous people used every part of the bison. Their lives depended on the bison and revolved around where the bison roamed. But the Europeans were greedy. They saw bison as limitless in numbers and as a way of making a lot of money. They hunted them for a few parts that they could easily sell, then left the rest just to rot. By 1890, extinction of the bison was very close.

There was a darker factor in the near extinction of the bison as well. The American government could control and kill the Plains Indians much easier if there was no food for them. So bison hunting was encouraged. Plains Nations starved to death until the remaining Indigenous people were pushed onto small bits of land. That opened up the west to the European settlers.

September 26th

The use of brand new technology with the wisdom of the elders as they tell their stories brings a new life to my culture.

He shares Indigenous Environmental Network's video. He contributed to the project. It is an exciting time with technology meeting ancient wisdom. But there are prayers and sacred ceremonies and fires that no one is allowed to film. Campers are informed about all the media rules for camp right after they arrive.

Media Hill sits on the side of Oceti Sakowin Camp. It is also called Facebook Hill. Campers can usually get a signal there. Signals are hard to come by most of the time. And there is charging power there. Solar and bike powered. People can charge up their devices and get a live feed up from above camp there.

"We're still here. We came from the star nation.

It was told by our ancestors that the first creation was the sacred stone and the second creation was the water.

When those came together they created a sacred sound - that sound is the life energy.

When we say Mitakuye Oyasin, we're praying for the two and four legged, the winged ones and the ones that swim and crawl.

So we pray for all life. We pray for our children and your children.

We recognize that Mother Earth is a source of life. Not a resource."

~ Chief Avrol Looking Horse, spoken in Lakota.

September 28th

Things begin to ramp up. Tensions are high at the actions. Actions are being held at multiple sites where construction is happening. Private security, hired by DAPL, still have dogs and pepper spray. They bully the water protectors. Every action becomes more dangerous for the water protectors. More water protectors are being arrested and the charges are reaching and unclear.

September 29th

To everyone of North Dakota!!!! Stand up for what you believe in, not for what you hold in your pocket!!!

We have brave children who also stand up for our earth's waters!!!! And they still have pointed guns!!!!!! SMH

Protecting and promoting public safety?

Children in the midst of an armed Riot Squad. Were they ready to shoot? Seriously? Why carry if there's no intent. Intimidation? That's not any better. ?? #NoDAPL

He shares a photo of children in a crowd with armed police. There are children of all ages at the camps. A baby was born at camp. High school students from Standing Rock go to camp. A school has been started. Children are greatly important to the movement and highly protected.

Chapter Five

October 1, 2016

My relationship with Mother Earth!

The mountains are my bones,

the rivers, my veins.

The forests are my thoughts

and the stars are my dreams.

The ocean is my heart,

its pounding is my pulse.

Racism against Indigenous Americans is rampant in the Standing Rock area. Especially in Bismarck. A clerk of the court was reportedly reprimanded for stereotyping an Indigenous American. Police often racially profile Indigenous Americans. Most of the Caucasian/European communities are very separate from the Indigenous communities.

"The only people who are mad at you for speaking the truth are those people who are living a lie. Keep speaking the truth." ~ Unknown

Camp has taken on a life of its own. There are banners being made, dancing, singing, drumming, storytelling, horseback riding, traditional games and current ball games. Elders and youth alike are engaged in prayer and ceremony. Shelters are being constructed. Security and medical groups are formed. Everyone contributes something to camp. Some people cook, some chop wood. There is always something to do. Everything is donated.

October 3rd

BACK TO CAMP!!!! AND IT FEELS GOOD!!!

October 4th

He adds photos of the helicopter pilot taking photos of camp as he flew overhead.

They wanted a close up of the camp, why couldn't they just come to camp!!!!! Lol

These guys got caught WHITE HANDED!!! Flying over camp with false helicopter numbers on the side of their aircraft.

Ok, I just realized that through this whole battle, I have not yet worn a NoDAPL shirt of any kind!!!! Hmmm. I wear XL. I believe it's time to slap on a shirt!!

There are rumors that camp has been or is going to be raided during this time. Camp leaders and live feeders reach out and calm everyone. They tell the campers to ignore the bad information. People at camp start to think that infiltrators are putting out these rumors on social media.

DIRECT ACTIONS 24/7 365!!!! WHO'S WITH ME??

Human beings MUST PROTECT OUR WATER AT ALL COSTS!!!!!!!!!!!!!!!!!!!!!!!!!!!!!!!

He makes a video with music about water to help educate people about what is actually being fought for. Water covers 71% of the earth's surface. It is essential for all life forms. One billion people over the world do not have access to safe drinking water. It is estimated that by 2025 more than half of the people of the world will be facing problems with safe drinking water.

Water protectors go to court that morning. Court often is postponed. Caucasian water protectors get off with fewer chargers. Justice is all over the place. Civil rights are being violated. Morton County reports that since the beginning of August 96 people have been arrested. They point out that only 14 are residents of North Dakota.

When I look at him I see inspiration IN MYSELF and a BRAVE STEP FORWARD TO A WORLD WIDE PHENOMENON ON THE FIGHT AGAINST BIG OIL. HE OFFERS US STRENGTH IN ALL OUR HEARTS, AND SHOWS US THAT NO MATTER WHERE WE CAME FROM, OR HOW WE GREW UP, OR WHAT COLOR WE ARE, OR WHAT STANDS IN OUR WAY, SHOW NO FEAR AND STAND UP FOR WHAT WE ALL BELIEVE IN. THAT WE, AS HUMAN BEINGS, CAN BREAK THE CHAINS FREE FROM THIS STOLEN COUNTRY AND PREVAIL AS NEVER FORGOTTEN WARRIORS TO THE END. FOR ALL OF WATER AND OUR HISTORY. I WILL ALWAYS GIVE MY RESPECT TO THIS MAN. BRAVERY. STRENGTH. A TRUE SUPERMAN IN MY BOOK. MUCH RESPECT Happy American Horse!!!

October 5th

This morning is big!! Keep me in your prayers!!!

He shares video from his Drone2bwild page. People are gathered near an intersection. Law enforcement is there also. People are in a circle on the road and the law enforcement is spread out. There are huge military vehicles right down the road from the action.

They are blocking the road into St. Anthony's. This is on highway 6.

We keep doing this every day and we will stop them from working. We stop the process, we stop the oil, we stop all fossil fuel industries. They have riot police and military convoys. We have unity and prayers!!!

"You don't need someone's permission to save your language." ~ Lyla June

PBS Rocks!!

WE NEED YOUR HELP. PLEASE SHARE IT. MAINSTREAM MEDIA IS NOT REPORTING.

He shares a PBS News Hour video: Indigenous People of America. More than 100 Native American tribes have joined a protest in North Dakota against a major oil pipeline.

The major media coverage is so minor. People send and tag him in posts of support often. Los Angeles city council votes unanimously in support of Standing Rock. Support pours in from around the globe. The International Indigenous Youth Council asks everyone to join in International Days of Prayer and Action from October 8th through the 11th.

October 7th

Yeah! A Tribe Called Red stands with us!! Standing Rock!!!

He shares an article: Thousands joined A Tribe Called Red in solidarity with Standing Rock water protectors against the North Dakota pipeline.

ENERGY TRANSFER!!!!! THE WORLD IS ENRAGED!!!!!! ENERGY TRANSFER!!!!! THE WORLD IS WATCHING!!!! ENERGY TRANSFER!!!!!! THE WHOLE ENTIRE WORLD IS STANDING WITH STANDING ROCK!!!!!!

THEY BETTER STAY AWAY FROM MY GRAND CANYON. THEY ARE TRYING TO TAKE EVERYTHING!!!

MISSISSIPPI STANDS NEEDS YOU ALL AS WELL!!!! LOCKDOWN ON DRILL SITE EVERYDAY!!

In Mississippi, a group calling themselves, Mississippi Stands, stands strong against the pipeline. They block a road to a construction site and nine people are arrested.

October 8th

Law enforcement is out for the drone pilots this day. Myron Dewey of Digital Smoke Signals is detained, his drone is confiscated illegally and then he is let go. Myron live fed the entire situation on Facebook. And in another area, Tom Goldtooth and Dean are also detained. Law enforcement wants to charge the drone pilots with drone harassment and intimidation of DAPL workers and security.

Just to let everyone know, Drone2bwild's drone did not get seized.

In a very choppy live feed from outside of the Morton County law enforcement building, he gives an update. He says that he showed the police the drone footage in question. That he was questioned for thirty minutes. The drone footage was from the Little Heart River.

They are doing everything in the book to get the drone out of the air. They break their own laws.

October 9th

HOLY CRAP THEY'RE DELETING MY LIVE FEEDS!!

BREAKING NEWS: U.S. Court of appeals REJECTS Standing Rock's injunction request to halt construction on #DAPL during the appeal process.

People are still coming to camp in large numbers. Especially on the weekends. A young, Indigenous man from Arizona sets off to run 1,400 miles to protest the pipeline.

October 10th is now known as Indigenous People's Day. Actions have been planned for the significance of this day.

He puts out a choppy live feed. Signals are very weak and it is very difficult to get a good live feed out from the actions. A helicopter and a small airplane circle over them constantly. Everyone wonders if the aircraft are cutting off their ability to go live.

Our movie star got arrested!!! Way to go girl. We love you!!!!!

News that actress, Shailene Woodley, was arrested spread around Facebook like wildfire. Dozens of water protectors were arrested with her.

What are you protecting? Today is OCTOBER 10th, 2016. NO MORE COLUMBUS DAY!!! This is a good day to release this video. We're going strong here at camp. Stopping DAPL construction with NON-VIOLENT DIRECT DRONE ACTIONS!! With Myron Dewey and me on the brink of the LAW for flying our drones to expose the truth. Drone harassment!!??? Get out of here! As drone pilots, this is our job. To protect our lands and waters from above. The injunction has been lifted, now DAKOTA ACCESS has the right to finish the job at all locations. When they come WE WATER PROTECTORS WILL BE READY!! WATER IS LIFE!! MNI WICONI!!

Credited Photos & videos by: Drone2bwild, Desiree Kane, Johnny Dangers, Myron Dewey & google pics!! Music By: A Tribe Called Red

Why do Energy Transfer Partners, a billion dollar company, have such a close relationship with law enforcement?

Morton County Sheriff, Kyle Kirchmeier, said that our non-violent actions are, "More like a riot than a protest."

Is this even necessary? Morton County and North Dakota have all the weapons.

This video shows peaceful water protectors with no weapons – then a sheriff's deputy with a pointed gun.

We are water protectors.

We are unarmed.

We dance.

We pray.

Mni Wiconi.

The pipeline encroaches on Indigenous lands.

The pipeline is disrupting areas of cultural significance.

Morton County what are you protecting?

The $3.8 billion Dakota Access pipeline is set to span some 1,200 miles, from the Bakken oil fields in North Dakota to Patoka, Ill.

This is the movement.

This is what we're protecting!!

For Mother Earth and environmental injustices worldwide.

#NoDAPL

What are you protecting?

He is becoming more and more well known in the movement. People come to camp and ask to take selfies and photos with him.

To all my friends and relatives, if anyone wants to help Drone2bwild and his DRONE ACTIVISM ENDEAVORS PLEASE FEEL FREE TO SEND ANY SUPPORT OF ANY KIND. IF YOU HAVE ANY DRONES AROUND. JUST SAYING BECAUSE AFTER WHAT HAPPENED TO TOM AND I WHEN WE HAD THE DRONES OUT THAT DAY AND AFTER WHAT HAPPENED TO MYRON WHEN THEY TOOK IEN'S DRONE AWAY!!! THESE ARE TACTICS OF WAR. IF THEY ARE GOING BEYOND THE LAWS AND SEIZING DRONES WITHOUT A WARRANT, IT'S BOUND TO HAPPEN TO ME.

EVEN THOUGH I STAY ONE STEP AHEAD OF LAW ENFORCEMENT, IT'S ALWAYS GOOD TO ALWAYS BE PREPARED. SO THAT'S WHY I'M POSTING A CALL OUT TO ALL WHO HAVE BEEN FOLLOWING MY WORK HERE AT THE OCETI SAKOWIN CAMP. IF THEY'RE GONNA START JUST SEIZING DRONES AWAY FROM DRONE WARRIORS, THEN WE ARE GONNA NEED TO START ASSEMBLING AN ARMY OF DRONES TO BACK US UP FOR THIS LONG MARATHON OF A BATTLE FOR OUR TREATY LANDS. BECAUSE WE'RE COVERING THE WATER PROTECTORS AND ALSO USING THEM FOR SURVEILLANCE. DRONES HAVE BEEN A BENEFICIAL KEY TO THIS VERY MOVEMENT, AND WE NEED THEM TO KEEP US IN THIS FIGHT.

WASTÉ ALL MY PEOPLES!! HAPPY INDIGENOUS DAY!!! MAY YOU WITNESS HISTORY WITH ME! AHO.

In Reno, Nevada on an Indigenous People's Day march, a man in a white truck drives into the crowd. He injures at least five people. The next morning, Headline News from CNN finally reports on Standing Rock.

October 11th

Dave is here at Prairie Knights Casino. He will be at camp tomorrow. Dave stands with Standing Rock!!! Dave Matthews and others played at PKC, brought to you by Chase Iron Eyes and the Standing Rock Schools!!

The crowd loved him. So much that the educational schools of Standing Rock gave him a star quilt.

October 14th

More people and groups are coming into camp all the time. He shares drone footage of a bus coming into camp and announces: The Bemidji Charter bus is at camp!!!

October 15th

GONNA BE A SHORT WEEKEND WATER WARRIORS. BE READY.

"How can you incite a riot in the middle of the prairie on gravel roads? Who are you going to incite? The prairie dogs? The cows?" ~ Joye Braun

OK so this is my 3rd time posting this!!!! For some reason it was deleted and deleted again. I see they're working hard to break our First Amendment rights.

I got the privilege to meet an inspirational journalist and reporter, Amy Goodman, from Democracy Now! She was the main reporter covering the stories as they unfolded that day with the pepper spray and vicious dog attacks handled by mercenaries who were hired by Dakota Access. A day we will never forget!!

She came back to face the music and her charges for just doing her job as a reporter. She was covering the attacks on Natives and non-Native PEOPLE of the LAND.

And Morton County has not yet even brought these spiritless mercenaries to justice. That's the way North Dakota is. And as long as their OIL is being pumped from the BAKKEN, this state of North Dakota will continue to show military force. You see the BAKKEN is North Dakota's baby, it's their GOLD and they're gonna do whatever it takes to protect it. For profit only for them to prosper, with no regards for the future or any citizens.

History seems to be repeating itself. Just like over a hundred years ago when they said that the sacred Black Hills were ours, then broke the treaties all because they discovered GOLD!!!!! A country built off slavery to feed its GREED. Now America is so addicted to this way of progress. This country is NO LONGER the land of the FREE or home of the BRAVE. They talk about laws and how to follow them. Before the settlers and government were even established, the INDIGENOUS PEOPLE already RESPECTED and followed Law. And that was the pristine law of Mother Earth.

Morton County and the rest of the government need to re-learn their own history and get it right. If anyone should be caught for trespassing, it should be MORTON COUNTY and all those IMMIGRANTS who sailed across the GREAT OCEANS. YEAH WE MAY NOT HAVE HAD THE SUPERIOR TECHNOLOGY BACK THEN, BUT WE HAD A SPIRITUAL CONNECTION WITH THE EARTH and that was POWER we all shared equally and also gave back to Mother Earth.

TO THIS DAY the GOVERNMENT will NEVER understand it, spirituality and physically. Personally this country sickens me to the bones. This system of a so-called government is BROKEN. And when a system is broken, it no longer works. It's time to bring a new system: THE INDIGENOUS SYSTEM.

DEAN DEDMAN JR. 2016

He still finds moments to connect with Mother Earth. He shares a beautiful, short video of sunset from camp.

Yesterday's beautiful evening. Despite all this Dakota Access fiasco, you gotta step back and enjoy the views Mother Earth and Father Sky provide us here at the Oceti Sakowin Camp.

I guess you can say we watched the North Dakota sunset.

October 16th

He shares a prayer on Facebook.

My mother shared this with me. For me. To protect me because that's what mothers do. Protect their children. She gave life to me and in return I will do my best to protect her. Love you Mom, your son.

October 19th

Time to re-write history my people, and it starts at Standing Rock!!
ADAM BEACH IS AT CAMP!!!!!!

#DRoNE2BWILD FOLLOW THE MOVEMENT

BISMARCK/MANDAN REPORTERS, IF YOU CAN'T TELL THE STORY RIGHT THEN JUST DON'T COME AROUND THE SITES ANYMORE. INDIGENOUS MEDIA CAN TAKE IT FROM HERE.

INDIGENOUS MEDIA HAS BEEN AROUND FOR THOUSANDS OF YEARS. WE ARE THE TRUE STORYTELLERS. IT'S IN OUR BLOOD. IN OUR HISTORY. IN OUR CHILDREN. PASSED DOWN FROM EVERY GENERATION TO THE NEXT. WE WERE HERE. WE ARE HERE. AND WE WILL CONTINUE TO EXIST IN THIS WORLD AND ONTO THE NEXT.

I PRAY ALLEGIANCE TO OUR FLAG OF THE STANDING ROCK SIOUX TRIBE, AND TO THE WATER FOR WHICH IT STANDS. MANY NATIONS, UNDER CREATOR, UNDIVIDABLE, WITH VALUES AND PROSPERITY FOR ALL.

WE ARE DIGITAL WARRIORS. HACKING AWAY AT GOVERNMENT GREED IN A WORLD OF NUMBERS AND CODES. UPLOADED SPIRITS FROM THE CREATOR'S MAINFRAME. EVOLUTIONARY MIND PROCESSORS OF CHAOS AND CONTROL. BROADBAND OF NATIONS RISING BEYOND THE LIMITS OF CYBERSPACE AND INTO THE GREAT UNKNOWN. ARE YOU REAL? OR AN ILLUSION OF PROCESS?

October 20th

GOOD MORNING TO ALL MY PROTECTORS OUT THERE IN THIS CRAZY WORLD OF OURS!

People are encouraged to get involved in many different ways. There is a call list beginning at the White House and going all the way down to Morton County government. There are petitions to sign. There is a list of banks that have money invested in fossil fuels to divest from. People are asked to send money and other donations for everything from legal aid to winterizing camp. People are asked to be a part of the social media educational campaign and to share information about Standing Rock as it comes out.

October 23rd

I'm here and ready to capture it all! We are ready and standing our ground. Our sacred ground. Peace be with us all.

He shares a report that around fifty law enforcement vehicles are on the way to the front lines. He notes that law enforcement is not just local any more. Law enforcement of all different types is showing up from all over the country.

BREAKING NEWS: DRoNE2BWILD TOOK FIRE THIS MORNING. THEY SHOT THE DRONE BUT DIDN'T TAKE IT OUT. I HAVE FOOTAGE OF THREE LAW ENFORCEMENT OFFICIALS SHOOTING AT IT LIKE IT WAS DUCK HUNTING SEASON. AND WITH NO REGARDS OF WHO IS IN THE AREA.

They shot at it a total of ten times, but they never shot it out of the sky, that's for sure. Like I said, it's gonna take hell and brimstone to get me out of the sky. I'm loading up my footage now.

It is a federal crime to shoot down any aircraft or drone. He has video evidence that law enforcement discharged their firearms at the drone. He shares the drone footage.

"Regardless of the situation, shooting at any aircraft — including unmanned aircraft — poses a significant safety hazard. An unmanned aircraft hit by gunfire could crash, causing damage to persons or property on the ground, or it could collide with other objects in the air." ~ Federal Aviation Administration

Up close and personal with militia police. This law enforcement officer runs towards the drone and this is the guy that shoots at it. As you can clearly see, it swings to the left due to the impact of the bullet. Afterwards I get two other law officials trying to shoot it down. Crazy. Filing a complaint is already in the works.

In one of the biggest moves yet, water protectors take back unceded territory of the Fort Larmie Treaty. In the early morning of October 23rd water protectors set up a new frontline camp. This Treaty Camp is directly on the proposed path of the Dakota Access pipeline. Water protectors block the road to keep this camp safe. They vow to stay peaceful and prayerful.

October 24th

TODAY THE BATTLE CONTINUES. BLESS MY DRONE FOR TODAY MIGHT BE ITS LAST FLIGHT.

FACEBOOK LIVE IS PROTECTING US ALL!!!

OBAMA IS A BROKEN DREAM, CAUGHT IN A WEB OF CORPORATE GREED, JUST ANOTHER ILLUSION OF FAKE FREEDOM. SMH

DRoNE2BWILD BASICALLY EMBARRASSED MORTON COUNTY'S FINEST. SEE FOR YOURSELF.

He releases more footage of the drone being shot at. He puts it to music. First, an officer drops a bullet before he shoots.

A total of eleven shots, but only ten accountable on the drone video. This video clearly shows North Dakota Law Enforcement and DAPL security professionals at their best, but personally I think they need to go back to the shooting range. Although Drone2bwild was shot during the making of this video, it still flies the skies. Watching over all of the water protectors. PLEASE SHARE AND SPREAD THE TRUTH ABOUT WHAT IS REALLY GOING ON HERE IN NORTH DAKOTA!!! #DRoNE2BWILD #WATERISLIFE #MNIWICONI

I'm legally taking action against Morton County Sheriff's Department. These outlaws will be prosecuted to the fullest extent of the laws. NO matter how much this North Dakota state is backed by oil money, I will prevail in court.

More buses full of suited up soldiers are spotted heading out of Bismarck. They are believed to be National Guard. His mom warns him with photos she took of the buses.

October 25th

He notes that he is feeling motivated. He has already done a few interviews with media. Mostly independent news media. There are still complaints about the major networks ignoring the events at Standing Rock. He does an interview with AirVuz about the drone being shot at. He explains that the sheriff said the drone was flying at a helicopter and the passengers feared for their lives. There is absolutely no evidence of that happening anywhere in any of the videos. In a later interview with Drone 360, he says,

Law enforcement is saying that because they're breaking laws and they're using that excuse to justify shooting the drones. My drone was shot, but it was still flying. It's like the drone is protected by something. Without this drone technology we wouldn't be where we're at with this battle against the Dakota Access pipeline. Drones are very beneficial — they're our eagle eyes in the sky.

DRoNE2BWILD WILL BE ON NATIVE AMERICA CALLING ON FRIDAY THE 28TH OF OCT. @12:00PM CT. TUNE IN AS HE TALKS ABOUT DRONES AND HOW THEY CHANGED THE MOVEMENT FOR GOOD. AND ALSO TALKS ABOUT HIS DRONE TAKING GUN SHOTS FROM MORTON COUNTY LAW ENFORCEMENT. AND TO ALSO ANSWER QUESTIONS TO ALL WHO TUNE IN. PEACE AND RESPECT TO ALL OUT THERE. SHARE SHARE SHARE.

THEY HAVE MADE THE CALL!!! RIGHT NOW AS YOU READ THIS POST, DAPL & THEIR MILITARY MORTON COUNTY POLICE HAVE STARTED TO MOVE IN. THEY ARE JUST NORTH OF THE TREATY CAMP IN A SMALL TOWN KNOWN AS FORT RICE. THEY HAVE ALL THE WEAPONS. THEY HAVE THE BATONS, THEY HAVE THE PEPPER SPRAY. THEY HAVE THE MILITARY. WE HAVE OURSELVES AND OUR PRAYERS. AND THAT'S THE ONLY THING WE WATER PROTECTORS NEED, AND THAT'S TRUE POWER. THE POWER OF THE HUMAN SPIRIT. PEACE FOR ALL WATERS OF MOTHER EARTH. STAND UP AND STOP THIS DESTRUCTION BEFORE US. PRAY FOR THE STRENGTH TO ENDURE 500 YEARS OF COLONIAL CHAOS. THIS IS IT. WARRIOR UP AND STAY TRUE TO OUR INDIGENOUS ROOTS. GET THIS MESSAGE OUT AND GET AS MANY BODIES WE CAN GATHER AND GET TO THE FRONT LINES RIGHT NOW. WE NEED YOU. WE NEED YOU ALL.

Drone Warrior meets Mark Ruffalo. Pretty cool dude. He looks at me and says OMG I know you!! I know you!! I think it's supposed to be the other way around.

Several songs are written for the Standing Rock movement. Trevor Hall's music video, Standing Rock, on YouTube is a wonderful song with a video that shows a lot of camp life and actions.

THIS SONG JUST MOVES ME. TOUCHES MY HEART. SOOTHES MY SOUL. PEACE FOR ALL WATERS OF MOTHER EARTH. STAND UP AND STOP THIS DESTRUCTION BEFORE US.

"Sometimes people try to destroy you, precisely because they recognize your power - not because they don't see it, but because they see it and they don't want it to exist." ~ Unknown

October 26th

DAPL SECURITY TERRORISTS IN THE MIST.

Here they are parked on top of DESECRATED SACRED BURIAL SITES. If their own American LAWS don't find them guilty, our ancestors' spirits will.

He shares drone footage. He flies the drone over law enforcement. It's foggy out. The drone lingers around some DAPL trucks. One guy throws his glove at the drone in exasperation.

A-List celebrities in camp so instead of guns they threw their gloves. I guess you can say they tried to give us a helping hand in prayer!!!! Hahaha

Someone reports that the FAA has issued a no fly zone in the Cannonball area. It is said to be a temporary restriction. It gives law enforcement a monopoly on the airspace.

Very late night, he starts a live feed from Prairie Knights Casino and Resort. Many popular live feeders are there. Prolific, Nataanii Means, Dallas Goldtooth. They are laughing, telling jokes and having a moment of fun. Layha Spoonhunter and Erin Wise who both work with Indigenous youth are there also.

October 27th

They are coming.

They say, "YOU CAN'T JUST COME IN AND TAKE OVER SOMEONE'S PRIVATE LAND." SMH. Well here's some huge history for you ProDapl invaders. We were here first. And you picked the wrong place for this battle. We are Lakota/Dakota, the last warriors who stood up to the U.S. Government. Time for some education on this country's history, this so called America built this country by taking over and stealing our lands through broken treaties. We are here to take it back. Now you know the feeling when someone takes over your land. Karma. It's the 21st Century and we INDIGENOUS people are using The Latest Technology and Social Media to take our land, our water, and our country back to the laws of Mother Earth. The only law we respect and abide by. I call it the 21st Century battle of our treaty lands and INDIGENOUS rights. Each and every one of us here has power more powerful than your fire arms, your LRAD weapons, your Riot gear, your Laws. That power is our individual spirits. Our roots. Our connections. It doesn't matter where we come from. To us, we are all one. This you will never understand because you ProDapl invaders have lost your connection to your soul and human spirit. But we pray for you. Perhaps one day you will reconnect yourself back to Mother Earth. But until that day comes WE'RE TAKING BACK WHAT WAS OURS AND THAT'S THIS COUNTRY. THIS IS BIGGER THAN A PIPELINE. BECAUSE AFTER WE'RE DONE CUTTING THIS BLACK SNAKE'S HEAD OFF, WE ARE COMING FOR YOU AND YOUR ILLUSION OF A SYSTEM.

My heart. My nations. My soul. My relations!

MORTON COUNTY SHERIFFS ARE ALL RUNNING OUT OF OPTIONS. THEY ARE ALL GETTING Desperate!!

Need people on 134 at the dirt road. Where the little bridge is. Law enforcement is headed there. Get the word out. There are snipers on ridges. Helicopters and planes overhead. Bring horses and all cars. You are committing terrorist acts on U.S. citizens and you are being watched. Law enforcement is fully dressed in riot gear. They also have LRAD weapons.

In a live video, water protectors burn things in the road to keep the officers back. Black smoke billows into the sky. The officers continue toward Treaty Camp in a long row.

Pray

In one of the most iconic moments of Standing Rock, Myron Dewey is live feeding the brutal camp raid. He asks Dean how he feels about law enforcement being on treaty land.

Dean: I feel disrespected. I feel hurt. I feel hurt that these guys won't ever understand. I try to tell them, but... The only reason why we're moving back is because they're armed. They have guns, tear gas, riot gear, weapons and rubber bullets. That's what it takes for them to push us back. They carry weapons because they're scared.

Myron asks him what the land means to him.

Dean: This land means everything... LOOK AT OVER THERE, LOOK AT ALL THE BUFFALO! LOOK AT ALL THE BUFFALO! LOOK AT ALL THOSE BUFFALO!

In the live video you can see a herd of buffalo coming over a hill. Water protectors start screaming and celebrating. The law enforcement officers look behind themselves.

Dean: THEY'RE COMING FOR YOU GUYS! BE CAREFUL! HERE THEY COME!

Shiyé Bidzííl AT THE FRONT SPEAKING THE TRUTH. AND FOR THAT I WAS PEPPER SRAYED, BUT I WAS QUICK TO COVER MY FACE.

The feeling of this happening to my Standing Rock breaks my heart. But it boosted my soul when I saw our Tatankas coming from the MNI WICONI herself, stampeding toward these corrupted lawless military police. YOU SEE WE ARE CONNECTED TO THE EARTH AND ITS CREATIONS. FOR ME, I KNOW THE TATANKAS HEARD OUR CRIES AND OUR PRAYERS. THEY WERE COMING TO HELP US. PROTECT US. OUR

PEOPLES WAR WHOOPED AND CHEERED. WE HAVE ALWAYS HAD THIS CONNECTION TO OUR SACRED ANIMALS OF THE LAND.

One of the greatest feelings I will never forget, the look on their faces. Even with all those weapons & military vehicles, they all looked back & for those few minutes they had this look of fright in their eyes. That scared feeling, like when Custer knew he was at his last stand, scared to death, as he hid behind his own men & dead horse.

For those few minutes of seeing them coming I FELT like I was safe. My heart burst with peace and harmony. So I told those police officers that they would never understand our connection to the earth. I told them that they hear us. And they are coming for you. Never underestimate the Tatankas of this great Lakota Nation. They were all getting scared. I saw the fear in their eyes. One of my many moments of this historical event from this great movement. We are truth. Living and breathing our spirits every day. They may have taken it tonight, but we will take it back tomorrow. Trust me. They don't know what's coming. We are gonna go down in history. For my Standing Rock Nation. For my earth and waters. For my family and all my peoples of the great Oceti Sakowin Camp!!!!!

"There's people being really hurt there... It's very scary and these people are just like us. We can't forget our humanity in the face of these kinds of things." ~ Mark Ruffalo in a CNN interview that night

Mark Ruffalo is right, LISTEN TO HIM. We also need more people here on Standing Rock. This place is turning into another Wounded Knee as you can clearly see from the atrocities of today!!!! This country is truly going to hell. And I can't believe no one sees this as a national threat!!!!! WAKE UP WHITE HOUSE.

During the violent raid of Treaty Camp, a security guard who was hired by DAPL got in his truck and started speeding toward Oceti Sakowin Camp. Water protectors tried to stop him and even used their vehicles to stop his truck from hitting other water protectors. The DAPL hired security guard got out of the truck with a weapon. He was surrounded by water protectors as he walked into water. The water protectors diffused the situation and kept everyone safe. Even the DAPL security guard. Eventually BIA came and arrested the man.

By the end of the day law enforcement had used all of their weapons. Rubber bullets, pepper spray, batons, LRADs. Many, many water protectors were arrested. All ages, races, genders. Prayer warriors were ripped out of ceremony and arrested. Their arms were marked with numbers, like the Nazis did to the Jewish people. They were loaded onto buses. At the jail, some were strip searched, humiliated and forced into dog cages. They were not read their Miranda Rights. Due process of the law was not followed in any way.

This is very sad to see; hurtful, painful. Time to step up our prayers and actions. These lawless officials seriously don't know what's coming. Everything else the spirits will handle.

The lengths DAPL is taking to put this snake into the ground. Fear is what brings weapons. Only through strength brings us tactics!!!!

"Upon suffering beyond suffering; the Red Nation shall rise again and it shall be a blessing for a sick world. A world filled with broken promises, selfishness and separations. A world longing for light again. I see a time of seven generations when all the colors of mankind will gather under the sacred Tree of Life and the whole Earth will become one circle again." ~ Crazy Horse 1877

Very early morning October 28th Dallas Goldtooth reports that there are three vehicles burning on the bridge. Military style vehicles. It is reported that law enforcement drove them to the bridge and parked them face to face and a fire started. A barricade is set up on the bridge and no one is allowed to cross.

The illusion of FREEDOM AND THE CORRUPTED!! SMH

"America's freedom won't be held back by a bunch of dirty natives with their phony spirituality and dumb ecological concerns." ~ Kelcy L. Warren, CEO Energy Transfer Partners

PIPELINES ARE DESTROYING THIS PLANET AND CORRUPTING THE SO-CALLED LAWS AND PEOPLE OF THIS COUNTRY. ALL IN THE NAME OF GREED AND ADDICTION. AMERICA'S NEW BREED OF TERRORIST INCITES VIOLENCE ON THEIR OWN CITIZENS AND ABORIGINAL PEOPLE WHOSE LANDS THEY TOOK. THE ORIGINAL LAND KEEPERS FROM GENERATION TO GENERATION.

NBC SLOWLY OPENING AMERICA'S EYES ON STANDING ROCK.

He shares NBC Nightly News as they finally cover the Dakota Access pipeline protectors. NBC: Dakota Pipeline: Police in Riot Gear Arrest Protesters

WHAT HAPPENED TODAY I BELIEVE WILL ONLY GET WORSE. NORTH DAKOTA WILL GO TO ANY MEASURES AND BEYOND ITS LAWS JUST TO PROTECT THAT BAKKEN OIL. EVEN IF THAT MEANS SWITCHING UP RUBBER ROUNDS TO REAL ROUNDS. THIS WHOLE STATE IS GETTING CRAZY. IT'S SIMPLE....ALL WE WANT IS CLEAN WATER. THAT'S ALL.

THIS IS WHAT US PROTECTORS WILL BE FACING EVERY DAY NOW. THE ONLY REASON THEY PUSHED US OUT IS BECAUSE THEY HAD WEAPONS. SHOOTING AND HARMING PEOPLE IN PRAYER. USING HELICOPTERS AND FLYING THEM VERY, VERY LOW. SHOOTING AT HORSE RIDERS, RESULTING IN KILLING A HORSE AND SHOOTING LIVE BULLETS AT RIDERS. I KNOW WE HAVE TO STAY IN PRAYER, BUT HOW CAN WE WHEN WE ARE PRESENTED WITH THIS KIND OF BRUTALITY AND VIOLENCE? TBH WE STAY TRUE TO OUR SPIRITS, BUT IT'S TIME TO STEP UP AND TAKE SPIRITUAL-TACTICAL ACTIONS AGAINST THESE MONSTERS.

WE DON'T NEED GUNS. WHAT WE WILL USE IS OUR PRAYERS AND TECHNOLOGY AND WE WILL HIT EM WHERE IT HURTS. THEIR POCKETS. AND BY THE TIME THEY GO BROKE, THE WORLD WILL SAY WE HAD ENOUGH. AND NO ONE WILL FUND, ASSIST AND PROVIDE FOR THESE MONSTERS.

A MESSAGE TO ALL SURROUNDING STATES: DO NOT IN ANY WAY ASSIST THIS CORPORATION. FREE YOUR SELF FROM THAT ILLUSION. ALL THAT BAKKEN OIL AIN'T EVEN GONNA BENEFIT THIS BROKEN COUNTRY BECAUSE IT'S BEING SHIPPED OUT TO OTHER COUNTRIES. MAINLY CHINA. THE CORPORATIONS, BANKS, AND THE MAJORITY OF THIS COUNTRY'S POLITICAL LEADERS, CITY OFFICIALS AND LAW ENFORCEMENT; THESE ENTITIES ARE THE ENEMIES OF THIS COUNTRY. SO PLEASE SHARE THIS EVERYWHERE FAR AND WIDE. PEOPLE OF THIS COUNTRY OPEN YOUR EYES AND WAKE UP FROM THAT ILLUSION AND GET BACK TO YOUR ROOTS. STAND UP FOR WHAT IS RIGHT. NO MORE BEING OPPRESSED BY OUR GOVERNMENT. AFTER THIS POST IS LIKED AND SHARED. TAKE A DEEP BREATH AND ACCEPT YOUR NEW FREEDOM. THE INDIGENOUS FREEDOM AND THE LAWS OF MOTHER EARTH. RESPECT AND SHE WILL ALLOW YOU TO LIVE FOREVER. AND THAT'S WHAT WE CALL BALANCE AND TRUE PROSPERITY. THE ORIGINAL DREAM KEEPER OF THIS LAND. PEACE BE WITH ALL OF YOU. WE ARE CHANGING THE WORLD FOR OUR FUTURE, OUR PRESENT AND OUR PAST!! ONE OF THE GREATEST MOVEMENTS IN HISTORY OF THIS WORLD. THE OCETI SAKOWIN.

Perhaps we can take a moment to step back and have a day of peace and prayer. We need to rest our hearts and souls. To allow our minds to take in the power of knowledge. We need to all come together as one whole Oceti Sakowin Nation. Let's sing, let's pray, let's celebrate and give thanks to the Creator for he has given us another beautiful day. We know they are close and watching us. Let's give 'em our full attention with prayer and songs. We know they fear us already, that's why we see the weapons they hold so tight. So let's sing and dance to rejuvenate our spirits. And also respect and bring in all the spirits of these great ancestral grounds that are all around us. We will celebrate so loud that the whole valley and out to the river of life known as MNI WICONI will echo as far as the ripples can see. So loud that it sends them back because they can't handle the beats and the war whoops. So loud that they will drop their weapons and abandon their armored vehicles and run back to where they all came from. When we all come together and focus all our energy on one single continuous song and prayer, we can actually feel the presence and soon the physical force of our ancestors, land, animals, and most of all THE POWER OF MNI WICONI.

As you can see and also feel the power of my work through the beautiful flights over Oceti Sakowin Camp to flying through the hail of gun fire when battling lawless corrupted North Dakota law officials. This is one of many stories I share through Drone2bwild Photography & Video. Known around camp as "DRONE WARRIOR" I stand and fly for justice and the Indigenous way of life. A drone environmental activist who exposes from the sky. I am changing the way we experience movements such as this historical gathering of so many Nations that come here to help us protect our homeland and waters from corporate greed.

DRoNE2BWILD IS ATTENDING A HUGE FUNDRAISER AND WATER PROTECTOR AWARENESS GATHERING LOCATED IN SANTA CRUZ, CA ON JAN, 14ᵀᴴ, 2017. MUCH APPRECIATED FUNDS FOR THE TRIP AND FOR MORE DRONE FUNDING FOR THE DRoNE2BWILD PIPELINE TOUR 2017. NEXT STOP TEXAS!!!! PLEASE SHARE. THANK YOU, DEAN.

"18 million people get drinking water from the Missouri River where the disastrous pipeline will be completed! Call out to ALL Water Protectors to join us! Let the world know we come in prayer! Share! Speak out! Join Us!"
~ Johnny Dangers

October 29ᵗʰ

It's pretty obvious our 1st Amendment Rights don't EXIST.

There is news that the United Nations are sending representatives to Standing Rock.

"Let's see... No fly zone... LRADs... massive canisters of pepper spray... rubber bullets at point blank range... constant helicopter surveillance... infiltrating provocateurs paid by the corporation... police and national guard intermixed with DAPL security, all dressed in riot gear... attack dogs... military guns and vehicles... hmmm, what could be next?" ~ Overpass Light Brigade

Why I'm fighting to save this planet. For my children. I miss them very much. They give me the strength to continue this fight. I love you guys so much.

FAA RULES GROUND ALL AIRCRAFT INCLUDING DRONES...THE NEXT DAY THERE'S HELICOPTERS, PLANES, AND MORE DRONES!!!! BEAUTIFUL TIME TO TAKE FOR THE SKIES.

October 30ᵗʰ

We are having our Indigenous Civil Rights violated in every way from our own government. The Chaotic States of Messed up!!!

He shares someone's photo of many law officers taking one protector down on the day of Treaty Camp raid. There are many images like this one floating around Facebook. Photos of violence by the law enforcement toward the peaceful, prayerful water protectors.

A fire is set not very far from camp. For the first time in over a month there is no airplane or helicopter flying over camp. Water protectors believe it has been set by DAPL security. There is no rush to put it out by the fire department and it burns for hours. Fortunately, the wind was blowing away from camp.

Anonymous puts a message out for North Dakota Governor, Jack Dalrymple. They warn the governor to back off of the water protectors. They threaten to release documents showing a conflict of interest for the governor.

Support is still coming in from all over the world. Colleges, groups, families all send photos and words of support to the water protectors on Facebook. They gather and march and protest in their own areas.

October 31ˢᵗ

If you're looking for me, I'll be on MEDIA HILL AT OCETI SAKOWIN.

Chapter Six

November 2016

Flying a drone over the pipeline, I deliver the news in a very unique way that draws attention to what we are doing here. Right now I'm going to check on our buffalo because they have them caged up. But I don't stay in one spot for too long because they might shoot at the drone.

We're gathering people. We utilize Facebook to get our stuff out. We can't get in there, but the drones allow us to go in and we can go anywhere we want. As drone pilots, they give us a sense of freedom. That's how I feel when I fly a drone because this drone is untouchable. Ain't no one gonna stop this drone unless you're a real good sniper. So that's how we've been attacking it. And of course there are laws, FAA, all these laws in effect, but do you see them following laws? They manipulate laws. But they expect us to abide by the rule of law. We don't wanna abide by the rule of law though because it's not the right rule of law. The rules of Mother Earth are the natural laws. And we're gonna bring back the laws of Mother Earth. We appreciate, we respect and we don't take.

Many shocking stories of horror come out in the days after Treaty Camp raid. One of the most heartbreaking stories during Treaty Camp raid on October 27th is from an Indigenous woman named Red Fawn who was arrested. Red Fawn was there that day helping the injured water protectors get to medical treatment. As a large group of law enforcement officers took her down to the ground and forcefully held her there, a gun went off. She was charged with shooting at the officers and is facing many, many years in prison. Everyone believes that the gun was not fired by Red Fawn, but by law enforcement officers in an attempt to frame her. #FreeRedFawn

November 2nd

In the news, President Obama says they are examining options to reroute the Dakota Access pipeline and he is going to let the situation play out for a few more weeks in North Dakota. It is horrible news and makes a lot of people very angry. Especially in light of the Treaty Camp raid and all of the violence that was used on the water protectors. It is reported that the Dakota Access pipeline is nearly completed. Letting the situation "play out" literally puts water protector lives in danger.

Tara Houska, from Honor the Earth, tweets: @POTUS you've asked #DAPL to cease construction, but your administration is working w/police hurting Native Americans. #NoDAPL #Hypocrisy

WHO WOULD LOVE TO SEE THE DRONE GO UP ON LIVE FEED OVER THE BARRIER ACROSS THE BRIDGE??

Going up with the drone in 10 minutes. To show sacred sites and to show how close they are to the water. Go to Drone2bwild and check it out.

STANDING ROCK'S VERY OWN LOCAL DRoNE2BWILD EXPOSES THE PIPELINE YET ONCE AGAIN. ARE THEY BUILDING A FORT TO KEEP US OUT? ARE THEY BUILDING HIGHER SO WE CAN'T TAKE OVER? PEOPLE OF THE WORLD, I KNOW YOU STAND IN SOLIDARITY WITH MY STANDING ROCK, BUT THE REALITY IS WE NEED YOUR ACTUAL PHYSICAL PRESENCE HERE. I, DEAN DEDMAN JR., AM CALLING ONE MILLION PEOPLE TO STANDING ROCK FOR DIRECT ACTION. IT'S UP TO THE WORLD TO PUT A STOP TO THIS PIPELINE AND ALL OTHER PIPELINES IN THE WORLD. IT'S UP TO YOU AND US AND ME. LET'S MAKE THIS CALL AND STAND.

He live feeds from camp. He is surprised that he can. It is a bright, sunny day. The skies are blue. He shows the airplane flying over. He says, "This plane is jamming signals." He goes to the top of Media Hill and finds

Myron Dewey there, flying a drone. Myron shows him what the drone sees. It is Turtle Island, a sacred site near camp. It is a very large hill. DAPL hired security guards are standing right there with law enforcement officers.

Dean asks for people to give him hearts. In Facebook live feeds there are emojis people can use. The heart is one of them. Lots of hearts cross the screen.

Security is sitting on sacred sites, burial sites. Right on top of the hill. There are stones marking the burial sites where vehicles are parked. They are on grave sites. There's military. Our people are strong, singing, in prayers.

He comments that the Department of Justice has a representative there, but she can only watch. Several times the live video cuts off, shuts down. He has to move away from Myron to get it to come back on. They laugh about it.

The camp is on the edge. Everyone is on the edge. It's not going to stop until we get a million, million warriors and a thousand horses. I advise you to sacrifice everything and come out here. We need actual physical presence. If anyone is sending any supplies we need firewood, we need stoves and we need you. Alaska, if you are watching, organize a bunch of wood and come to camp. They cannot hurt our resolve.

Myron says that there is some type of jammer that is being used to shut the drone signal down. He says that there are water protectors in the water, although it is very cold out and they could get hypothermia.

Dean walks around and interviews people for a while. He talks to a news person who says that he is the only local news person who will cover the actions. He complains of being ridiculed by his coworkers. Dean tells the newsman that he is glad he is there. He interviews a woman who tells him that an Amazonian tribe did a prayer at the base of the water. She tells him that 500 clergy members are coming tomorrow to do actions.

Wiyaka Eagleman stops by his live feed and reports that water protectors built a bridge and crossed over the water to Turtle Island. Law enforcement took the bridge apart and met the water protectors with big canisters of pepper spray. There were law enforcement officers in boats. He says that water protectors were shot with rubber bullets. He says, "One of the youth got shot in the back with a rubber bullet and started spitting up blood."

He walks around again. A lot of people are standing around on Media Hill, most of them on their phones. He interviews a young man who tells him that after the bridge was built and the officers tore it down and started gassing people, water protectors jumped in the water and swam to the other side. A reporter got shot with a rubber bullet. He says, "They're not even supposed to be on that land. They're protecting a multi-billion dollar corporation."

Dean mentions that on Facebook, where you can check in to show where you are, a million people have checked in to Oceti Sakowin Camp. Facebook users from all over the world did this as a show of support after individual water protectors were targeted after checking in to camp on Facebook. Law enforcement is definitely watching Facebook, along with the supporters of the Standing Rock movement. Eventually those supporters are called, "digital warriors." Digital warriors make an impact on the movement with support of all kinds.

You need to come. I'm from here and I've been here for months. You just got to be out here. It's heartbreaking, it's emotional; it's real stories. That corporation over there cost us, it's a lawless corporation, they are going to do everything they can to put that pipeline in. Way back in the day, they wanted the Black Hills because they had gold in them. This is the same thing, except the oil is the gold. They are going to do everything they can because they are addicted to that oil, to that money. Obama waiting two weeks, I don't understand. He lost my respect. I would ask for all those medallions back.

He uses his camera to zoom in on the action.

There it is guys. DAPL security is aiding the Morton County police. They have DAPL security completely covered up in black. There goes another plane. There are literally planes flying over reservation space.

Treaty land, reservation land and the air space belong to the Nation. The United States government broke treaty laws and trumped themselves right into the air space. They invaded another Nation's land with their weapons and intimidation in order to put a pipeline in that would eventually have problems, leak oil and taint the water source for the Nation and 18 million others who depend on that water source.

A lot of people say they want to come but they can't get through. But the only road that's blocked is 1806. You can come in anywhere south from the rez. Turn back around and come back. A lot of people are questioning if this place is on lockdown. This is the only place you can experience real freedom.

He says he will post a map of routes. He reads a couple of comments posted on the live feed.

What is this all about? Apparently you are just tuning into Facebook if you're asking that question. You guys just have to come here.

He continues to walk around and interview people. Most of them have just come back from the frontline. The live feed continues to get cut off and come back.

A young man says, "A bunch of young people not posing any threats get shot at with less than lethal rubber bullets at point blank range. It's disgusting. I'm from Iowa. I was here before, just got back. I think it's going to take numbers to stop this."

He asks if the young man was scared and the young man says, "Anyone would be." *He encourages everyone to call Obama and tell him that two weeks will not work.*

A woman named Paulette Moore shows up and gives a full report on the action. She says that by 8 am water protectors had built a bridge across the water to Turtle Island. The police started showing up early with non-lethal weapons and mace. Water protectors brought a drum. People swam over to the other side after the bridge was taken out. They stood and got maced and hit with rubber bullets. She reported that it went on for quite a while. The water was cold and the water protectors risked hypothermia. She says that Lorenzo Serna, from Unicorn Riot, an independent news source, was in the water for more than an hour.

Another person walks up and shows them a rubber bullet. It is mostly made of very hard plastic with a hard blue cover. It is large and they laugh about thinking it was a microphone. He encourages all of the digital warriors to get screenshots of it for evidence later.

Paulette continues to describe the events at Turtle Island. Water protectors used boats to go back and forth for the wounded. She says that she did not see any arrests. She tells that one of the law enforcement officers almost fainted and needed water. She wonders what the law enforcement officers' dreams are like.

"It's about native resilience and Indigenous people really defining the issues of our day. Having this language of Mother Earth and the spirit of Mother Earth that people feel so drawn to. All we're required to do as Mohawk people is to be grateful. That's it." ~ Paulette Moore

He talks to a woman from the Department of Justice. She has not been to the frontline yet. She says she cannot say much or really do anything. She says they are a group of mediators who facilitate dialogue.

Another young man talks to him and says, "Honor the treaties. We got maced for no reason at all. One guy going around macing with no warning at all. I just pulled up my mask and threw up my hands. They're the ones who have fear, those with the weapons. All those ancestors on the hill, they are going to get them. Their souls are so lost."

In another report he is told, "We went up there, I was going back and forth delivering blankets for the water protectors who were in the water. People were getting hypothermia. I was pulling people out of the water when they couldn't see because they'd been sprayed in the eyes so they wouldn't drown. Today I put down my camera and forgot about documenting this and just gave it my all."

"I was at the frontline just updating the world on what's going on. They are desecrating sacred sites. They told us yesterday as soon as we moved off, they would move off. But they are still standing there." ~ E'sha Hoferer

The feed stops and starts up. He interviews a member of the clergy who is there for the next day's action. The minister says, "We're here to follow the leadership. So often the church has tried to lead, but we want to be clear that we are standing alongside our brothers and sisters at Standing Rock. I think it will take prayer to stop *this. This is equivalent to a civil rights movement. If the human community follows what's happening here this could be a watershed moment."*

"Today what I witnessed was a little bit of struggle. A little bit of oppression. On that side were all the officers lined up. On this side were all the protectors lined up. A couple of protectors had prayers in the water and were shot at. I witnessed prayers for the other side. I was able to be at peace. I got to feel the other side. They felt our compassion at the end of the day. We were together in prayer." ~ Steven Jeffrey Chrisjohn

This Facebook live feed gets nearly 150,000 views. People are tuned in. The digital warriors are ready to help.

Protecting my homeland is my number one priority!!! I know the world is standing in SOLIDARITY, but we really need you to actually be here. FR sacrifice is what's gonna change the world. CALLING ALL DRONES TO STANDING ROCK TO DOCUMENT HISTORY.

That day new information about the Treaty Camp raid comes out. A youth riding a horse was shot at with live, lethal bullets as he was riding away from law enforcement. A horse had to be put down after a law enforcement officer shot it.

"Human rights abuses galore. People being held in dog kennels. Police Brutality, Reckless Endangerment, Lines blurred between DAPL security/police, Zero Police Accountability, Police taking orders from unidentified masked men, Illegal Search and Seizures, Unjust charges pressed on Journalists, Egregious Felonies placed on protectors, Excessive bond sought by states attorney, NO CHARGES ON POLICE OR SECURITY TO DATE (none for the dog attacks, or illegal shooting of drones, or the DAPL infiltrator who broke through a barricade chasing protectors with an AR-15). And for what? For wanting a FULL ENVIRONMENTAL IMPACT ASSESSMENT. For wanting fair inclusion of the tribe's concerns on projects that affect their water, graves & sacred sites. For wanting human rights abuses to stop. For wanting clean water." ~ Prolific The Rapper

It is reported that every day that the pipeline is delayed costs DAPL six million dollars. People feel that is why there has been such an escalation of police violence against the water protectors. North Dakota's governor declares a State of Emergency and this enables him to ramp up law enforcement and to bend the laws as he sees fit.

Water protectors are encouraged to stay peaceful and in prayer. No one understands how one angry, violent move could wipe them out better than the Indigenous people.

Tonight as I stand here on Media Hill, I look across and see huge lights shining towards the camp, while a thousand spirits gather to give us strength. The lights shine down to the water and twinkle off the ripples. It only takes one person to make a statement. Walk up that hill with courage and bravery. Hold your heart with the water and the people. Raise your arms and accept true power of water and earth!!

That evening he appears on Steven Jeffrey Chrsjohn's live feed.

I'm Dean. I'm a local media here. I've been doing this since before it hit big. And flying over the action today was a pretty amazing sight. We tried to live stream it today, but the helicopter started coming in close and started jamming the drone signals. But we still got it on raw footage.

It was a beautiful thing to see, a river, the water, separated the protectors from the DAPL security and all the lawless officials. It was pretty intense. I believe they were shooting at the drone again too. For me, as a drone pilot, capturing these things that are going down as history, it really does mean a lot to me. Because capturing these actions with this technology that people are somewhat still trying to understand, drone technology, has been very beneficial. I stress that ten times because it has allowed us to go see; like a couple of days ago, we took it over to the drill pad and what I did over there was a great accomplishment because I gave the world what I saw through the drone. And as soon as I posted it, it hurt a lot of people's hearts. It inspired a lot of people, it encouraged a lot of people and it gave people a sense of hope, even though it seems disastrous, the pipeline going through and all.

But right now at this point, when we are fighting this pipeline, when we look over there and we see all those lights, some people feel hopeless. Some people, in their hearts, feel like they don't know what to do. And some of them are wondering how can we defeat, how can we destroy, how can we stop this big of a corporation that has worldwide investments. And a lot of people say prayers. You gotta keep praying. And even though they pull all their weapons and all their guns and shoot us with all the tear gas and rubber bullets, soon enough they're gonna run out of ammo. They're gonna run out of rubber bullets and tear gas.

There may be a lot of warriors taken out, but there are going to be a few that are still standing there. That's all it takes is bravery and courage. And not to have fear, because fear leads you to other places. In a way those cops, they have fear. They fear us. We're just Indigenous people. We're peaceful. We're connected to a lot of things they don't understand. And when you don't understand something, you fear it. That's why they have all these weapons.

As of today - right on top of burial grounds there, they put up huge spotlights that are overlooking the camp. Basically, they are trying to be the camp's porch light. You can see the whole camp wherever you go at night. All it takes is one person, one person to walk up this hill and walk into that light. One person to swim across that water and to walk up on that hill with no fear. It takes one person to make a statement. And when you get up on that hill, just raise your arms and accept the water and the earth. You might be shot, you might be arrested, but in a way that shows DAPL security and Morton County law enforcement that they're not dealing with any ordinary warriors. They're dealing with brave warriors. Warriors that are willing to sacrifice everything they have. To sacrifice their freedom and walk up that hill. That just goes to show that one individual is that strong and has that much power.

When we combine as one Nation that makes us powerful. That's the kind of thinking of every medicine man, every child, every woman, every warrior and everybody that's here. Every media here. That's the kind of courage and bravery we should have in our hearts and in our minds. And that will get us through another day. And in the end, we are going to be successful because we have heart. Let's see all those hearts guys, let's see all those hearts. That's the kind of strength you have to have in this kind of fight, when you are fighting a pipeline like that. You gotta be brave.

November 3rd

"After a week of violence inflicted by law enforcement on unarmed peaceful water protectors, over 480 clergy and people of all faiths arrived in solidarity with Standing Rock. In solidarity, they repudiated the Doctrine of Discovery, denounced the Dakota Access pipeline, and affirmed the position of the water protectors on the ground." ~ Indigenous Rising Media

Clergy hold a prayer march up to the blockaded bridge. Then they burn a copy of the Doctrine of Discovery at camp in a ceremony with the water protectors. Then some protest in the North Dakota State Capitol building. 14 are arrested.

He live feeds and shows his drone footage from the previous day.

This is what I can do with the drone. This is my calling. All this land has history. That's what they don't understand. There's one tipi standing in solidarity right by the water. Those people are brave. DAPL comes up and raids in the night.

He flies the drone very close to the action. The drone looks right at the police. The drone goes over the water protectors. The people are praying for the water. They are praying for the spirits on the hill. When the drone goes around, the fists in solidarity go up.

COME ON GUYS WE INDIGENOUS MEDIA DRONE PILOTS CAN DO BETTER SURVEILLANCE THAN THAT!! AND CORRECTION, THEY'RE NOT PROTESTORS THEY'RE WATER PROTECTORS. GET IT RIGHT KFYR-TV. YOU GOT TO BE ACTUALLY HERE TO HEAR, SEE AND FEEL THE REAL STORIES AND THAT'S THE TRUTH. PLAIN & SIMPLE.

He shares KFYR-TV's video: The Morton County Sheriff's Department has released video footage of bison being herded by protesters near a #DakotaAccessPipeline site on October 27th.

We were conquered by their technology long ago. NOW IT'S TIME TO USE TECHNOLOGY AGAINST THEM AND DESTROY THIS CORPORATE TERRORISM!!

Water Protectors only praying for Turtle Island. They were met with pepper spray and rubber bullets. But still we stand. And that is powerful. #NoDAPL #Drone2bwild

Spirits are everywhere. They are wandering energies of disturbed sites. Today I heard the story of a policeman who started convulsing and all of a sudden fainted. A story of two officers who were previously involved with the pipeline as hired security, who got shot and murdered. Was this coincidence? Like I told them last Thursday, this will come back on you. We must pray because these officers are in danger of spiritual retaliation, let's pray we can save a few.

I want to show the people that drones can be used for good, because right now when people hear the word drone, they automatically think FBI, Homeland Security, CIA, and DAPL! So using this technology has really educated the people at camp about drones and now they welcome the use of the drone. The drone is here to cover these events as history is being made each day. This camp is expanding and getting bigger by the day. Everyone is still on edge and waiting for the next move that DAPL will be making. Will they still be working secretly? Will they bring in more security forces? Questions like these run through my head and amongst the camps, but for now we are all here bringing the awareness and solidarity of all these Nations that have shown up to stand with us to put an end to this Black Snake. Drone2bwild Shiyé Bidzííl

SORRY GUYS, DUE TO THE RECENT NO-FLY ZONE IT IS NOW A FAA RULE NOT TO FLY OVER DAPL AND THE WHOLE AREA. ENCOURAGING EVERYONE TO GIVE NORTH DAKOTA FAA A CALL AND DEMAND THEY DROP THE NO FLY ZONE. TODAY I CLEARLY SAW DAPL HELICOPTERS AND PLANES FLY DANGEROUSLY LOW AND AT CLOSE PROXIMITY TO EACH OTHER, VIOLATING FAA RULES

THEMSELVES. AND YET THEY ARE SCARED OF A LITTLE DRONE! SMH. SO YES, HIT THE PHONES AND FLOOD THE ND FAA HEADQUARTERS. THANK YOU. FLY HIGH.

November 4th

It is reported that the FAA has lifted the flight ban in North Dakota. Barricades put up by law enforcement have prevented the water protectors from seeing the progress of the construction of the pipeline without the drones. DAPL seems to be working around the clock. With no access to the construction sites, the water protectors cannot physically stop the building of the pipeline.

November 5th

Representatives of the Seven Council Fires of the Oceti Sakowin gathered to reignite the sacred fire of the resistance camp and establish the "horn" of the nation, a camp layout where seven lodges are placed in a circle formation. The last time such an event occurred was in the late 1800s! That's The Power of this movement. That's The Power of our Prayer.

He shares AJ+'s video: Meet the drone operators of the #NoDAPL standoff. He is interviewed in the video.

The role I play is eyes of the sky. I'm an enrolled member of the Standing Rock Sioux Tribe and I am protecting my homeland as a drone pilot. People want updates on the pipeline and to see how it's progressing. What I see with my drone eyes is that they are building. Two days ago the pipes were all just pretty much laying there. Now they are all connected.

The drones provide a sense of safety to the protectors. Many have been tear gassed, pepper sprayed and shot at with rubber bullets. As the actions were going on by the water there, a lot of people told me they felt safe because there was a drone just above them watching what was going on.

CALLING ALL DRONE NATIONS 2 STANDING ROCK TO PROTECT OUR TREATY LANDS & TRIBAL AIRSPACE.

November 6th

YOU DON'T NEED A HELICOPTER OR A PLANE! ALL YOU NEED IS A DJI PHANTOM 3 DRONE AND WALLA INSTANT EXPOSURE OF A PIPELINE SO GUARDED THAT GETTING THROUGH ON FOOT WOULD BE DANGEROUS. THANK YOU TO DJI DRONE MAKERS FOR GIVING WATER PROTECTORS THE UPPER HAND IN THE SKIES. They may have conquered us in history because of their superior technology, but at this time in the 21st Century we Indigenous water protectors are using technology to fight and answer back.

He is interviewed by more media outlets including Yes Magazine. "Everybody's mad. Everybody feels hurt and broken," said Dedman. "But we can't let them break us. We just got to stand here and do what we can."

November 7th

He is on Steven Jeffrey Chrisjohn's live video on Facebook. They are in a stairwell at Prairie Knights. All of the live feeders get very creative putting out information on the live feeds. But even at Prairie Knights, Wi-Fi signal can be hard to come by. Sometimes it is very slow.

A lot of people who are keeping up with the movement are asking what's going on - we haven't seen many live feeds. That's because they have a scrambler. They are doing wrong and they don't want anybody to see it. They are censoring our media. Even if we have four bars, we still can't get online. The best way to deal with it is with the drones. The drones can reach far distances and they can't mess with them. That's why you haven't seen any live feeds coming out of camp. Especially on the front lines, they can't live feed. Because of censoring. We are just watching them. We are exposing them and they don't like it. Drones have come a long way since the first drones.

Call outs - I'm calling all drone pilots to Standing Rock. Whoever has a drone, bring it here. This is history right here. This is the only chance you will get in your lifetime to capture this. They are violating every human right and we want to capture that. This is the time now. I encourage more drones to come to Standing Rock. I want you to come and be a part of history.

I have two videos ready to come out, but we can't upload easily. That's been a problem. I finished one video tonight. Watch every minute of it. They are welcoming us at Sitting Bull College so we can upload it.

This movement changed my life in ways I never thought. I've disconnected myself from all the worldly things. Thanks supporters. Thanks for all of the encouraging messages. I take them with me every day out there. It's for the people, it's for our ancestors.

"Our story has been told by other people, not Indigenous. This story is going to be told by the people who are here. The people who stay at camp." ~ Steven Jeffrey Chrisjohn

On November 7th Graham Biyáál, a youth runner from Arizona, along with many other runners, arrive at Standing Rock. Indigenous Rising Media puts out a lovely video and uses Shiyé's drone footage.

"We are not here as conquerors, but as stewards." ~ Graham Biyáál

Indigenous Rising Media also puts out a video of over 400 people who marched in silence for a prayer action with the International Youth Council.

"We're praying for our people. We're praying for the land. We're praying for the water. We're also praying for all of you...in uniform. All of you who have to be here." -Terrell IronShell

November 8th

He takes time to thank people on Facebook for their donations. A video he made comes out on Indigenous Rising Media. It gets more than a million and a half views. It is a beautiful video. The lyrics by legendary John Trudell are added to the background of the video. He is now working with Indigenous Rising Media.

"Crazy Horse

We hear what you say

One Earth, one Mother

One does not sell the Earth

The people walk upon

We are the land

How do we sell our Mother?

How do we sell the stars?

How do we sell the air?"

~ John Trudell

November 9th

Today should be a day of celebration & prayer. Songs & unity. Yes. The Trump is president, but we, and all of the nation, should not feed into that fear. Don't be scared. Because that fear gives him that tyrant aggression and that is not power. It is more a weakness to a system that is broken.

Instead we will all do our part to show the world that we are the land of the free and home of the brave, and that starts from within our hearts. We are strong. We are alive. We are living, breathing testimonies of 500 years of oppression & spiritual genocide to our Indigenous brothers & sisters. Elders & children. I walk without fear on this dark path to our future. I do not dwell on the present or our past. But strive to a future I know exists for all of human kind. Humans, such beautiful beings, but yet so destructive to each other and the environment. Compassion, generosity and wisdom. Share my strengths & courage to all people of this world who stand for our mother and against the injustice that has infected this beautiful planet's heart. We return to our roots, for what we are about to face is a force that hides in the shadows. No matter how difficult this task may be, we hold strong with prayer. We harness our individual energy. Mother feels it. She will awaken. ~ Dean Dedman Jr.

Trump's election to the United States presidency is bad news for the water protectors. They believe he will try to re-open the KXL pipeline. They believe he will pressure the Army Corps of Engineers to grant any easements DAPL needs. They believe he will push forward the Enbridge pipeline expansion projects. It is known that Trump has financial investments in fossil fuels.

Our hearts and souls are and will always be unbreakable.

A day of prayer and celebration. This is the moment we all feel around the world. Calling the rest of this country and the people of the world. Hear us. We are alive. We are living breathing proof that life is beautiful in every way.

He live feeds:

Good morning. We're taking this day to celebrate. A lot of people are hurt, crying, upset that Donald Trump is president. I tell them, don't cry, don't be upset. You're only feeding into the fear and the fear gives him the power. You don't want that. So we take this day to celebrate. We appreciate the land, the water, the earth, the sky. All the animals, the four-legged, the two-leggeds, us. Don't worry. Don't doubt. Donald Trump can only make this movement bigger. The whole country is uprising. They are doing actions. They don't like Trump. I personally don't. But we move forward. So everyone who sees this post, come to Standing Rock. Come to Oceti Sakowin Camp and feel that power that you see in the live feeds. Come to this camp and you will fully understand what we are doing here as water protectors.

"We're taking Thanksgiving back. We're no longer honoring what it stands for. We're honoring the earth. We would like for you to come and celebrate Thanksgiving. Celebrate the earth and all the times she's loved us and nurtured us. This is the moment everybody's been waiting for." ~ Ernesto Burbank

I want to take a moment and I want you guys to take a moment, wherever you are at, in your office, on your phone, outside, by a river. Close your eyes and channel all of your energy and give it back to the earth. Because the earth is power. She's a living, breathing planet. She's hurting, she's crying. And for us Indigenous, we are sent here to protect her. But we need you to physically come and stand here with us. And support and accept the laws, the true laws, the one and only true laws of Mother Earth. We don't need to enforce them; we know and we accept and we respect. That is the meaning of true law. We don't need to police, we don't need to militarize. That is true power, Mother Earth's law. That's what we're here for, every day we are fighting. We want to call you out. Come out here and experience this all. And you will see why and you will feel it. And it's so powerful that a tear will come out of your eye.

But we need to disconnect from the system. Materialistic stuff, money. When we do that, we are reconnected to the earth.

I respect and appreciate every one of you who follow and respect my work. I carry all of those messages you send me right here in my heart. And it empowers me to do more and motivates me. As a visionary artist and as a human being it makes my soul strong and from the bottom of my heart, I love all of you out there. I'm doing it for you, I'm doing it for your kids, I'm doing it for the people of the world - and most of all, I'm doing it for my kids. My twins and my baby girl. That's all I have in the world left. And I want them to have a future that's bright and beautiful. Not destruction and chaos. That's what I'm fighting for. *(He gets teary and Ernesto puts his arm around him.)* Thank you guys.

November 10ᵗʰ

He is in a live video feed with Didi Banerji and Ernesto Burbank. They are on Facebook Hill at camp. He encourages people to put up the hearts on the live feed. He is wearing a NoDAPL sweatshirt. You can hear Ernesto's laugh. They are all cutting up and laughing. He and Ernesto ask for people to bring sheep, a staple of the Diné.

Come join the love. All the hearts is what keeps us going every day. One tribe, one people, one nation, one world. Laughter is medicine. Call the White House. Bring drones. Disrupt the system with the power of love and prayer. *(The signal is disrupted then comes back.)*

That drone is like our eagle flying over. They are our warriors, technological warriors. They don't want the drones to fly.

Council fires are lit. Sacred fires are lit. Bernie's bringing caravans of things. We are the revolution he calls for. If you believe it, you can do it.

"The ancestors, the spirits are here. That's why we know we can do this. You come down, you put tobacco in that fire, I can't even tell you." ~ Didi Banerji

Just because Trump is president doesn't mean it's over. It's going to boost this movement to the next level. The power of prayer is more powerful than anything. Money don't mean nothing. It's just a piece of paper.

The mood is very light despite the circumstances and the cold. They sing and invite rapper, Drake, out to camp. Chad Charlie shows up and shouts himself out. Chad tells some jokes. The laughter is good to hear. Then Chad does the robot and gets more laughs.

Erin Wise, who works with Indigenous youth, stops by and they shout out the youth of the movement.

"There's so much happiness, so much love out here." ~ Ernesto Burbank

A young man stops to talk to them. He tells them he just arrived from Arizona and his group brought firewood and other help. He gets lots of hugs and love. Everyone is invited to come and be a part of the love.

I am now in a position of great vision. I know my presence and expanding directions. I am high in the realm beyond the clouds of mother. Aerial knowledge of wind and power. I am everywhere, but you will not find me. I am true freedom of land & water. The star beings hear me. I call on sky protectors to guide me. Lead me through this spiritual journey of digital revolution. I am now in a position of great vision. Technology evolution. Transmitting swiftness on eagles matter. Thunderbird's strength, I climb the ladder. In a world of chaos this is my home, my sky, my power. Soaring universe. Transcending hours. Calculating altitudes. My vision empowers. I am HIGH HAWK watcher of Mother. Dean Dedman Jr. 2016

Yes Anonymous, bring down the entire system. Make the money disappear. Shut down every bank that supports DAPL. And we know you have been watching. We know you are out there. Time to put down the mask and prove to the system that you also are everywhere. Crunch time. #BreakingDatabasesWorldwide.

DAPL has built a militarized construction site with tall walls around it, razor wire and spotlights. Heavily armed military, police and mercenaries hired by DAPL patrol the site around the clock. It is officially a war zone, but the law enforcement will not admit it.

Actions continue. Water protectors gather for ceremonies to honor the desecrated land. They pray. More water protectors arrive and buses are being set up to transport even more. An estimated 15 to 20 thousand people are staying at camp.

On November 11ᵗʰ Dean is seen in Steven Jeffrey Chrisjohn's live feed. They are at the casino in a stairwell to get a signal and some quiet. Steven talks about Ernesto Burbank, a Diné tattoo artist who is standing with Standing Rock. Steven says that there has been a lot of singing, praying and sweat lodges at camp. Steven introduces Dean.

They are caging up our tatankas. The buffalo nation is locked up. They are feeling the same oppression as we are in this valley, within the valley of the Oceti Sakowin Camp. We can relate to them because they have been caging us up for 500 years. It's a fort up there. That's how scared they are. Maybe an 8 foot wall, before that is about 5 or 6 piles of razor sharp wire with an 8 foot trench.

I'm always on media hill. Most of the time, I'm in the sky, I see it on a screen. Camp is so big, it keeps growing. We're calling out everybody. We're putting them on the spot. Because right now with the change of presidency, we have a greater enemy within our country. We're going to stand. We're going to fight it. We're not moving to Canada. We're going to stand right there in the valley of Oceti Sakowin. After we're done with this pipeline, is the next pipeline. We'll do the same thing. We're going to fight for our mother. We're going to fight for environmental rights. What we want to do is to bring together worldwide awareness, bring together all the scientists who study earth because when you have knowledge and study it with science, it's a good thing. Science and spirituality that us Indigenous people have, it's the same thing. Just from different perspectives. But we can learn from science and that's a good thing for us.

He puts out another live feed later that day. He has to do it in a couple of parts because the feed is disrupted.

We shouldn't worry about what others say. Stay true to your path. And always keep a look out for coyote. We have to stay focused, all of us. Everyone. Even the elders need guidance. A lot of issues come because they feel like they get disrespected because a youth stands up and says something, not out of disrespect, but out of concern, because we are the seventh generation and within that seventh generation there are a lot of respectable minds. But we should always respect each other, elders, warriors, people, children.

The children are who we really need to listen to. I know they are quiet. They are too busy playing, being children. Not a care in the world. They don't really understand what's going on in this world. That's the way to live, as children. You look at them; go into camp and watch them play. They are carefree, they are living, breathing, happy, joyful.

Yes, we are going to help the buffalo. We're going to say prayers for them. But you can't let these things misguide you. Someone said once you start getting on Facebook live and showing all these things at camp and there's too much, but somebody's got to do it, you know. So I just took that leadership. I wouldn't say leadership, I just took that role. The drone gave me that role.

What I've been doing with the drone has been phenomenal. It's given everyone that view from above. Everybody loves it. In a way sometimes I do get heat. I got heat about the Crazy Horse video. Oh man, it touched everyone's heart and it blew up. I would like to tell everybody, I read all your emails and I read all your comments and I really respect what you guys have all been saying. I take those words and I use them. I use everything you guys give me and I turn it all into positive. That's the way to live it.

I always try to carry myself very humble and I don't let things bother me. Even in the face of a line of riot police, you can't show them your fear. You can't let them see you're scared. It gives you more strength. That's the way you got to be at camp. That's the way I fly the drone. I go in deep, I'm not scared. I don't know why I do it, it's fun, it's crazy.

I got one negative review on the Crazy Horse video. The council fire, the way I presented it. I do get permission before I fly in anywhere. The benefit with me is that this is my home. I live here. I know how it is. I present these movies in a very beautiful and creative way. I work with everybody in media at the camp. I work with security, I work with everybody. I have love for all you guys out there.

So I got one negative remark, he emailed me and he was saying that I was very disrespectful to the elders, to my people, to the whole nation. But I always have respect. I know the limits. I was allowed to film it. I had two minutes to film it. The sacred fire wasn't lit yet. Unfortunately there were other drone pilots who didn't get the message and they disrupted the prayer circle. But they were caught and their footage was deleted. Everyone thought it was me, but I was already out.

I have respect for people I don't agree with. I have respect for my enemies because when you show respect like that, no matter who they are, it's just good to give respect. It's better than being disrespectful. Always hold your values high. Don't let all the money misguide you. There's a lot of money coming into the camps. We all hear the stories. Money is the root of all evil. You gotta be strong. Money leads into other temptations and we can't allow that. We can't be misguided. We're all here for one thing. We're here to destroy this pipeline. It's getting harder, but nothing is impossible. Everything is possible. That's the way life is. You got to live it. Breathe it, eat it, sleep it.

For all my people out there, that's how you have to carry yourself all the time. No matter what. Whether you are going onto the front lines or filming it with a camera. There's some people who come here and want to be a part of the spiritual essence, but they want to do the media thing too. Personally it's really hard to do more than one thing. If you want to do media, then be here to do media. If you want to do spiritual, then just do that. For me, I'm here for the drone. But in a way I still pray every day. I pray every time I fly the drone. I close my mind and just think positive every day like that.

But it's hard. I get criticized every day for things. I get criticized from a few people within my own community, but I'm not going to name any names. That just escalates it more. But I have a message for those who criticize me. You might not think that I'm doing very much. One person even asked me what have I done for this community. Come on guys, press all those hearts out there to let me know how much I've done for this whole camp, for this whole world to see. There you go. (He smiles at all the hearts.) I've been doing a lot. I've been busting my butt. A lot of people say, Dean, you got to get your rest, but I'm addicted to this sometimes. I love creating the videos, I love flying. A few people don't think I'm contributing, but sad to say, they need to involve themselves a little more in camp.

As far as me, I'm on Facebook 24/7. Facebook can be a good tool and it can be a bad tool. Like drama. People spreading drama on Facebook. We don't want that. If you have drama, you guys need to learn how to take care of that. Man up or woman up. We are here for one thing and that's to protect the water. We all have our parts. We're all going to do whatever we can for the water.

The elders, the kids, the media, the drone pilots, we're all working together. And that's the way it should be. Not bickering. We are strong. All that negative force, it's a part of the spirits. You all have to be careful out there. And yes, coyotes always do have their place. You guys gotta stay true to your path, your life and your mission and what you want to accomplish will eventually prevail and succeed. And that pipeline will just disappear. Poof, like that. And Donald Trump, poof, just like that, he'll be gone.

This is what tears us apart as native people on all the reservations, we need to stop. Stop all the lies, stop all the drama. Stop all the stealing. There's a lot of donations for camp, come on you locals. You want something, you gotta work hard from the heart. When I was growing up in Navajo Nation, we worked hard. There's a lot of trees down there. We have our own resources. I know we have call outs for all the help we need, and that's appreciated, that's awesome, but at the same time we need to go to all of those trees and just start cutting them down. That's our own resources right there. Start building our own camp.

Back on Navajo Nation, we used to go to camp and cut our own wood for winter. A big ole mountain pile of wood. And we herded our own sheep. We pumped our own water. We didn't have light. We had kerosene lamps. It was basically a hard earned living from the heart. And it still is that way. And that's the way it should be. Even though it's all given to us here. We have a house, we can turn on the faucet for water. We flip the switch; we got lights. Of course it comes with bills. And that's the thing I totally separated myself from. I haven't paid a bill in probably about a year now. I disconnected myself so much. Sometimes I need a prayer for myself. I do need a break sometimes. When you guys don't see me for a couple of days, that's just me disappearing. I don't even tell you because I need that time to calm down. We all do need breaks guys.

I pour my heart out, I give my vision. I don't know what else I can offer. I offer my love every day. I offer my skills, I offer my strengths.

You can receive all this great knowledge if you just listen. Just listen. Even though the guy might be wrong or the prayer might be wrong, just listen. It's your number one tool. Yes, I am human. *(He sighs deeply.)* That's what you guys gotta do when things get stressful. Take a deep breather. Please guys, we're all here for one thing. We just need to settle down. We can't be bringing in this negativity within camp. We have got to keep camp spiritual. Keep the camp in a positive way. Trust me, the rewards are going to be so powerful. It's going to bring in more people. The more we have a positive camp, the more people we can bring. Look at all of the positive actions all over the world. One million, two million people. Bring them here. That's what we need. We need a lot of people here. So this is another call out. But bring the positivity here. We're all grownups, we should all have common sense. We should all be good then.

"Don't be too hard on yourself.

There are plenty of people willing to do that for you.

Love yourself and be proud of everything that you do.

Even mistakes mean you're trying." ~ *Unknown*

November 12th

"America 2016 - the year corporations brought the wars of the Middle East home and sent military sound cannons, national guard, mace, rubber bullets, and now trenches and 8ft of razor wire against its own people. They have turned sacred land in Standing Rock into battlefields. When we look back on this event in the history books, what will you tell your children you did to stop them?" ~ *Kevin Belcher*

"Each and every policeman I've seen at those direct actions has been more heavily armed than I was when I was an infantryman in Vietnam." ~ *Sam Adam of Veterans For Peace*

This is the buffalo update: We know that DAPL & Morton County's lawless officials have been rounding them up for the past two days and slowly shipping them out. Where? We don't know. Now their fate is unknown. These trucks are our best shot. This was taken two hours ago. So they can either be in Bismarck / Mandan area or within a hundred mile radius. So any info on these 18 wheelers with loaded sacred buffalo, please call PETA right away.

He shares aerial drone photos of the buffalo pen and the transport trucks they are being loaded up onto. He also shares disturbing live feeds from actions that day. Water protectors are nearly run over by DAPL security and DAPL workers. A DAPL worker in a truck fires off live rounds from his handgun, waving the gun around the crowd like a crazy person.

In a live video he interviews a former police officer from Chicago, Illinois. Jeff Ginter was at Oceti Sakowin to support the water protectors. Jeff came in reaction to seeing law enforcement officers abuse their power; using rubber bullets, gas and batons. Jeff says that the law enforcement is going overboard with their tactics. He is surprised that law enforcement would work to protect an oil company over individuals.

"As a former police officer, there are a lot of good cops out there, but it just takes a couple bad ones to make us all look bad. We have a conscience and we can't just leave that behind. Embrace that desire to serve people and to help people. It's okay to step away from a job you don't like. It's okay to leave. There are other jobs. You don't need to do this to your own self-esteem. You have to look at yourself in the mirror. This isn't a Christian act. Shot in the face, whether intentional or not, it's just too much." ~ Jeff Ginter

The Crazy Horse video from Indigenous Rising Media is getting a lot of attention. Many people are sharing it and watching it. It was edited by Josué Rivas Fotographer.

Wow! My vision is shared with the entire world. And with the voice of Trudell, our ancestors will hear us. The world will feel us. And Donald Trump will fear us. The earth will awake.

Donations are pouring in from around the world. Green Latino's group present Standing Rock Chairman Dave Archambault a check for $2,500. Everyone is encouraged to donate, to call the White House and other government offices and pray.

November 13th

We sing it, but we can't give it all out. We sing it, we sing all night long!

He live feeds a couple of short videos from Prairie Knights. Someone is playing a guitar and you can hear tattoo equipment in the background.

November 14th

There are gatherings, marches and rallies all over the United States in protest of the Dakota Access pipeline. People stand in solidarity with the water protectors. November 15th is being called a #NoDAPL National Day of Action. Actions are planned from one coast of the United States to the other.

November 15th

From the heart we tell our stories. We are living, breathing, alive and the truth from the wolf to the eagle. Plus updates for camp.

He live feeds with Ernesto Burbank. They are in the hallway at Prairie Knights.

Robert F. Kennedy Jr. will be at camp. I've talked to him already. At 2pm. He will be at Media Hill. Most of us call it Facebook Hill. For a press conference. I will try to stream it live. I get to hang out for the rest of the day with him. I will show the whole world how DAPL is operating up there. The world will get a glimpse of what we are dealing with. Military operations, it's more than just DAPL workers protecting this drill, this pipeline. What I've seen up there with the drones is that it's more. We'll see what we're dealing with. It's the government for you.

The live feed is interrupted. This is now known as getting "DAPLed." Live feeders joke about being DAPLed all the time.

We are still investigating the buffalo. I can provide eyes in the sky, but we can't get info from the ground. I did see a post that they were getting auctioned off. January 7th. That is the fate of those buffalo right now. They are our relatives. What they did to them is pretty much what they are doing to us. They build a wall, a castle, a fort, to show how scared they are.

High Hawk with the power, it gives me that sense of freedom. When I fly that bird, it gives me freedom. I can be anywhere I want to be and see anything I want to see. Come out for Forgiveness Day. It's no longer Thanksgiving Day. We're taking it back. Thank you but we're taking it all back. We probably won't be eating turkeys any more, we'll be eating buffalo and sheep. They sacrifice their lives to let us live. We say a prayer for their lives before we butcher. We say a prayer to accept their energy, their bodies, their meat to feed us. That's sacrifice between us and the buffalo, the four legged. Respect all four leggeds.

About protecting the mother, the children and the future for seven generations. We encourage you guys to all come out. Experience the true feelings. I do my best with my skills and talents to bring this all to you in Facebook world. I give respect to all of you guys who stay tuned. We love you all out there. If it wasn't for you guys, the world wouldn't know the message. Share it. You guys are brothers and sisters and family. Some people don't have money, some don't have a ride, but nothing is impossible. Live your dreams to the fullest. Do good in your life. Stay positive and life will be happy.

We fight every day for what we believe in, that's Mother Earth. We fight spiritually, mentally, physically. For our planet. To help her and guide her and keep her safe for future generations, for all the four leggeds. We are the stories. Mainstream media can never capture that. We are walking, living, breathing stories. To the very first Indigenous people who left their marks on those rocks, that is in our DNA and that's what they can't take from us.

Even when everything feels lost, we are still here. Our spirits still stand. This world is in chaos right now. Trump. But we'll use that. All those Trump supporters, he supports that pipeline over there. Calling out all those million masked men, Anonymous. I know you're listening because you are listening everywhere, right? You leave us so many Facebook feeds about how you are going to protect and stand and bring justice to the government. Now it's time. It's time to put your mask down and reveal your true power. A true warrior doesn't need to hide his face, because he wants to be recognized and show that enemy who took him down. You don't need to hide your face. True warriors come from inside. Calling out all of Anonymous. Calling out those who hate Trump, the ones who are marching in every city in the world and uprising. Come here. We got the whole plains you can invade and embrace the power of camp. There's a better way.

Shout out to Angelo. He sits every morning at the fire. He is the fire. To Francis Fisher. Wonderful woman, beautiful soul. She is one of the great actresses from the movie, Titanic. I got the privilege to hang out with her all day. It was fun. A shout to Leo DiCaprio. You gotta look at the drone footage. It's true, factual information. It's straight up the truth. You can't get any closer to these DAPL terrorists. If you want to see the actual truth, Leo, I encourage you to watch. I know you're watching bro. Can't wait 'til you get here bro. You're a big inspiration to me. Big shout out to Heather from Sundance films.

He introduces Lindsey Nash. She is organizing the We Are Diné group. He says that she is the biggest help.

The women of this world are so powerful. So powerful because they give birth to real men and that's why we respect mother, because she gives us our children. All men should give respect to all of the women of the world, because they are so powerful. They have the energy, determination and strength to bring a new life into this world. I give my respect to all of the women of this world. You are all strong and powerful. Just keep doing what you do. If you are a single mother you are doing it good. You take care of your kids, you provide for them. You're getting them ready for the world.

And we need all support for Red Fawn. Prayers. She needs us more than ever.

He asks for hearts for Red Fawn and more hearts float across the screen.

November 15th

How is #NoDAPL #MINIWICONI #StandingRock not trending? My feed is full of water protectors spreading the knowledge in every nook and cranny. Oh yeah, that's right, mainstream media is controlled by the powers that be, therefore the truth isn't being told. History repeating itself. While all you guys are protesting Trump, calling him racist, the cops in riot gear are using weapons, pepper spray, clubs, guns, rubber bullets, live rounds, agitators...arresting mostly Natives for loving and praying, selecting by skin color. This corrupt establishment must be stopped.

Robert F. Kennedy, Jr. of the Waterkeeper Alliance is at Oceti Sakowin Camp. He is there as a show of solidarity with the water protectors.

"What this company [Energy Transfer Partners] is doing is criminal. They are using a loophole to wrap around a 1,200 mile pipeline." ~ Robert F. Kennedy, Jr.

Bernie Sanders speaks from the White House that day to nearly a thousand water protectors led by the International Indigenous Youth Council. They call for President Obama to stop construction on the Dakota Access pipeline. They ask everyone to go to Standing Rock and stand with them.

November 16th

He provides drone footage for Indigenous Rising Media. The video is of a human medicine wheel. It is a beautiful video of people on the ground wearing the four colors of the medicine wheel. This video gets over 700,000 views.

He is interviewed by Jordan Chariton from The Young Turks, an independent news source.

I took the drone beyond the limits. It shows the truth. They tried to shoot the first drone ten times, but missed. At all times we fly with safety; safety is first. What people really need to see is the destruction of this land and the only way to see it is by the drone. People came because they saw the drone footage. Drone technology has done a lot. Long ago, they had better technology when they first came here, but now we are turning it around. And we're going to win. Without the drones they could build this without anyone even knowing.

One of the protectors told me that he felt protected while he prayed at the hill. That's the power of these drones. They are here to protect and expose. It's a water protector. It protects the water and the skies. They have a lot of respect for the drones. Water and land and the whole Mother Earth is at stake here. We're protecting our Indigenous rights.

He live feeds from an airplane. He is flying over camp. The look on his face is pure joy.

Later that day he does a live feed from Prairie Knights. From a hotel room with Didi Banerji and Ernesto Burbank. They are in good spirits and ready to give updates.

I got the privilege of flying in a plane. I got to see the camp from a plane perspective. When we landed DAPL said we were illegal, but we were legal. The guy flying the plane knew all about the FAA. A lot of people are saying they brought the drill in. But the drill itself is not here. I've seen it. They are preparing all the accessory equipment. The drill is not there at this moment.

Some Diné sisters said they brought the mutton. Sheep, buffalo, all that. We love that. Still waiting for the Navajo president to show up. *(They make jokes.)*

Didi talks about the camp cough - she has it. She is on some medications and that is why she is at Prairie Knights. People gave her a room so she could get better. She expresses her gratitude.

There are questions about Red Warrior Camp. There have been rumors that people from Red Warrior Camp have been getting a little too aggressive on the frontlines. There are rumors that they have been asked to leave camp.

We are here in unity and that's not unity. We may not always agree, but we need to stay in unity. We are all here for one thing and it is going to get to the extreme. They are using live rounds. I want safety for myself too. So if anyone can get your hands on some bullet proof vests, I wouldn't mind that. All seriousness, pretty soon there is going to be serious bodily harm or death. This is serious. It's going to get more serious. They are trying to push it.

Someone shares a breaking news link to his page. Planes are spraying Indigenous people with chemicals. It was not confirmed. People said they would not be surprised.

November 17th

"This is a very important moment in time. I see these struggles happening all over America and all over the world where folks are finally saying no to the fossil fuel paradigm. We are finally raising our voices and what better

place to start than our First Nation's people who have been suffering from this system since the very beginning of our nation." -Mark Ruffalo

While we were out yesterday at the Mandan airport I noticed the infamous yellow and white helicopter gassing up and getting stored in aircraft housing. After we landed the airplane, we were met by two officials who stated there is a no fly zone and they weren't nice about it either. But we abided by all the FAA laws and rules. The restriction altitude was 3500, we were flying at 3700 feet.

November 18th

The Bismarck Tribune newspaper reports that a judge has thrown out felony charges against several water protectors who were arrested during Treaty Camp raid on October 27th.

November 19th

More good news comes. This time it is out of Norway. The largest bank there sold its assets in DAPL after being urged by a petition from Greenpeace Norway.

In other news, Kelcy Warren, CEO of the company that owns DAPL, says that the Standing Rock Nation did not voice their concerns about the pipeline during the planning process. This was clearly a lie and was proved as such when the Standing Rock Nation released audio from a 2014 meeting when the Standing Rock Nation voiced concerns to DAPL representatives. It is also revealed that DAPL could be in financial jeopardy because it signed contracts promising oil deliveries by January 1st, 2017.

In crazier news, A Washington state senator introduced legislation that would make it a felony to protest. A new legal term called "Economic Terrorism" was created. In the courts, water protectors are not treated equally at all. Reports come out of Caucasians being given misdemeanors for the same charges that Indigenous people were given felonies.

And Morton County Sheriff, Kyle Kirchmeier, announces that unlawful structures are being built at camp in an effort to fortify for the winter. He says their efforts are insufficient to protect themselves from the weather. Water protectors call for Sheriff Kirchmeier to be prosecuted for violence against water protectors. Some North Dakota law enforcement officers are doxed. Anonymous releases all of their personal information online.

A United Nations human rights expert accuses United States security forces of using excessive force against the water protectors. United Nations officials denounce the inhumane treatment of the Indigenous water protectors. An official of the United Nations calls law enforcement out for detaining water protectors in overcrowded cages on concrete floors without giving medical care when needed.

"Some of the 400 people held during the demonstrations suffered inhuman and degrading conditions in detention."
~ Maina Kiai, United Nations Special Rapporteur

Actions against DAPL are occurring all over the country. A Citibank in Chicago is blockaded by water protectors. Actress, Susan Sarandon, announces she has divested from Chase Bank. She shares information for people who want to do the same.

November 20th

"Water is Life!!!! Indiscriminate use of tear gas, mace cannons, flash bangs and concussion grenades on the peaceful crowd. I was gassed pretty hard multiple times on the left flank." ~ Johnny Dangers

The breaking news is that law enforcement sprayed water protectors with water cannons in below freezing temperatures throughout that night. Later, law enforcement says they were trying to put out fires that water protectors set. In live video feeds it is apparent that this was a lie. Water cannons clearly target lone water protectors who are nowhere near any fire.

167 water protectors are injured. 3 of those are elders. 26 are taken to local hospitals. Including a young water protector who had her arm nearly blown off and an Indigenous water protector who was shot in her eye. 7 people are hospitalized for severe head injuries.

Judging from the injuries, the police obviously targeted the heads and legs of the water protectors. The whole situation began when water protectors attempted to clear two damaged military vehicles from Highway 1806 so the bridge could be opened again. Water protectors are urged to call to report the hate crimes to the FBI.

November 21st

I am here, you will not find me, but I am here. Things have gotten worst for my people. But I am here, I am safe.

November 22nd

He shares Sheriff Kyle Kirchmeier's statement in response to the incident at the Backwater Bridge on November 20th. The sheriff stutters through the press statement.

I counted 103 uh uh umms! And he couldn't even finish the statement. They know they are in a world of trouble.

"Earth is my church.

Nature is my spirituality" ~ Unknown

This is a live update of North Dakota's Infamous Law Officials protecting their DAPL Security and their black snake and drill site.

He shares a live feed from the Indigenous Rising Media Facebook page.

The drone is flying over land, but you can see the water. He flies the drone around Turtle Island.

There's the helicopter guys. We don't want to get too high because they'll start crying. This drone is not trying to take them down. The helicopter is violating FAA rules, flying way too low. Reports are these guys have been sitting on this hill all day.

On top of Turtle Island, he flies over big antennas on military looking vehicles. He flies over the land where the pipeline is going into. He flies over the drill pad next. There is a lot of activity. There are many trucks and lots of equipment.

They are currently drilling. Thanks to that guy, DAPL worker, who just exposed himself. Going low over the drill site.

He takes the drone way down over a trailer. He flies in close to the DAPL workers. Then he goes back over the path of the pipeline.

When it consumes your spirit, this is what it does. Destruction. Desecration. No regard for life or earth or water or stars. Look at this. Security probably knows the drone is flying over them. Let's go scope out.

This is their communication tower here. Right by the pipeline. This is the site where all the flags of unity used to stand, but no more. They disconnected the drone. It should come back shortly. When you fly next to that tower, they shut down the drone. But we got GPS and we aren't going to fly blind. I don't even need this screen. DAPL doesn't understand how skilled us drone pilots are. We're going in close to the frontlines.

The picture comes back. He flies behind the law enforcement. He flies the drone to where the water cannons were shot off at the bridge. The drone gets a good look.

There's a big crane. What are they doing? They've reinforced their barrier walls. That's how scared they are of us. There's lots of vehicles behind the barrier. Look at all those busy bees, up to no good. Let's get out of there before they try to shoot us down. This is the place where they had the water cannons in freezing temperatures.

The video is cut off. He comes back online with another live feed.

My beautiful water. Creator protect her. This is a live update of North Dakota's infamous law officials protecting their DAPL security and their black snake and drill site. Part two.

The drone flies over the water. The skies are bright blue. It is another brilliant flight.

We are live with the drone here. We are going over to the east side to see if they are drilling. We'll find out here in a minute if they are drilling.

The drone travels a good distance before it reaches the drill pad. The drill pad is protected with barriers. He turns the drone around and flies back over the river. He talks about technology and how the drone might get shot down. The battery goes to low and the feed cuts off.

He shares another short video with drone footage of law enforcement putting up barricades at the bridge.

He also appears in Steven Jeffrey Chrisjohn's live feed that day. Just as he lands the drone, Steven tells him that the people on the feed want to know who he is.

Come on people, you know who we are. We are water protectors. Drone warriors, water protectors, this is us right here blessing the drone. We only have Facebook live right now because there are no actions.

Morton County page – the stuff they put on there is ridiculous. Kirchmeier needs to take a speech class. The cop behind him took over and said he was happy with the way the cannons worked out. They have tactics they won't tell us about. They say they did it all because someone threw a rock at a guy fully geared up in riot gear. In retaliation they threw concussion grenades, tear gas. They said they were only using water cannons to put out fires that we started. But you can see on the feeds that they were not putting out fires. They say they are using tactics for riots and for crowds. One water cannon targeted one single person out in the open. Now is that a crowd? So basically these guys are lying.

This guy needs to get out of this office. All the politicians need to get out of office all the way up to Obama and Trump. They all need to reevaluate themselves. They all need to go back to their mommies and their daddies. They need to learn lessons from their own elders. Of course their own elders probably don't know any better either. They just gotta go back and find themselves. We don't hold nothing against them. We hate their actions, but we can't hate. If we hate, we're no better than what they're doing. They're doing all this stuff because of hate.

If you see the live feeds, DAPL workers saying we are the scum of the earth. Do I look like a scum of the earth? I'm Indigenous. I'm right here to the heart. Now how is that scum of the earth? I'm a protector of the earth. They need to relearn their vocabulary. What I seen up there with the drone, going across all that desecration of sacred sites and lands, that's scum of the earth. And when I go flying up close and personal to them, I know they're probably watching. That's me, spraying pepper spray in their face and shooting them with rubber bullets. And I fly away. Freedom of the drone. And that's the freedom I have and they can never take that away from me.

They might shoot the drone down, but five more get resurrected. Because the people love and support what we do. And they can never take that away from us. They cannot take that away from any people of color here who stand in solidarity with us. They can never break our souls. They'll never break our pride. They'll never break our human spirit. Physically and spiritually.

For all those DAPL workers and all the government officials, you guys need to go back home. You need to go back to church. Go learn your Christian ways. Let's see where those Christian ways take you. You guys need to go back to spirituality ways. Become one with the earth. Disconnect yourself from all that greed and addiction to money. Our God is everything around us, living and breathing. Smell it. *(He takes a deep breath.)* It's a beautiful thing. Isn't it? I'd like to thank all of you guys who tune in every day. I love you guys with all of my heart. And I'm protecting you, your family and your next seven generations to next seven, to next seven generations down the line. On a personal note, everyone that keeps up with the Indigenous Rising Media page and IEN, we need some red bulls. Thank you very much.

Veterans are self-deploying to Standing Rock. They are organizing themselves. They are scheduled to arrive December 4th. They believe there will be hundreds coming to stand with Standing Rock. Chris Turley, a young, Indigenous veteran, is walking to Standing Rock. He is raising money and will donate it to various veteran crisis charities.

Dean is seen on Angelo Wolf's live feed that evening.

When we combine everything we all have, we are powerful. We're beyond them now. We can use this technology above them, behind them, around them. That's what spirituality does when you have it in your heart. They can't stop us. That's true power. There's no kind of police tactics they can use that can stop us.

This is beyond Obama now. It's beyond Trump. It's in our hands. All the people at camp. We are going to change it. The world is with us. Money does talk, but prayer and spirituality walks. Beyond and into another realm. I'm happy to accept what's beyond that.

November 23rd

Good Morning people! You've been Facebooked!

He shares an early morning live feed from a hotel.

Let's just say I'm blessed to have another beautiful day here in North Dakota!! Eating breakfast with all these potential DAPL workers! Grand slamming them this morning!

Dean: Wow. It's been a long, wonderful morning and here's what I'm eating today.

He shows a table of men next to where he is sitting. And then his plate.

Dean: Complete with some syrup. Sitting here, eating here with all the people here.

He looks around the room. There are all kinds of what looks like DAPL workers. Some of the DAPL workers have been seen on live feeds during actions. He starts singing.

It's a wonderful morning. Sitting here with Angelo, but I cannot reveal his face. I still gotta wake up here.

Drone2bwild got a new drone. It's called a Phantom 4. I sent it on its first flight and it got shot down right away by DAPL. I decided to fly the IEN drone, so we smudged that one and me before it went on its flight.

November 24th

His followers help him raise money for new drones.

"Thank you! You keep the ancestors' bird's eye view of these atrocities alive, by droning them to us. So we know the truth. I wish we had millions to give so we could replace every drone shot down by these domestic terrorists. Happy thanks giving." ~ Rosalie Dobson

He live feeds from Prairie Knights. It's very foggy and wet outside. Snow is falling.

Good morning everybody. As you can see it's snowing out there. I'm thankful for living another awesome day. For a recap of yesterday, a drone went down. We just got it and it got taken away. It was a Phantom 4. As I live streamed over the drill pad, lower than anyone has ever gone before. You can see it on Indigenous Rising Media page. It's snowing today, but that's not going to stop the drone. I believe there's some actions going on. And in Bismarck too.

We don't call it Thanksgiving, we call it Taking Back Day. Later this evening, I'm going to shut off my phone and spend some time with my kids. Stay safe, warm and positive. And be prayerful.

In another live feed later from camp, he shows drone footage of the action at Turtle Island. It is a gray, cloudy day and ice has begun to form in the water.

We are no longer calling it that day. We are at Turtle Island. Going to zoom up to these guys' faces now. Let's fly by them again. We'll send them prayers. We're gonna circle these guys. They want to be at home, eating turkey. The snow is falling. Soon all of this water will be frozen. Then we won't have to make a bridge. Now we're gonna go check on the Backwater Bridge. Let's see how many cop cars are here now. Everybody's at home stuffing their faces with turkey or watching the parade. You can see a big difference now. Look at this, there's only a handful of cops, compared to yesterday. All the protectors come out because there's not many law enforcement here. We're gonna cut the black snake's head off today.

There continue to be rumors of camp being raided. Water protectors on the ground give out reports that it is not true. There is a video circulating of two female water protectors who are harassed by law enforcement in a local restaurant. Tensions between the Caucasian/European community and the Indigenous community escalate in the area.

There is an action in Bismarck. Water protectors take over a street and set up a table. They cover it in red paint to signify all the Indigenous blood that has been spilled.

All of those stories about Thanksgiving that you probably read and were taught as a child, they are all false. The Thanksgiving stories they teach today are wrong. They were invented to cover up the horrendous genocide of the Indigenous people. Europeans have been trying to kill off Indigenous people since they arrived in North America. They celebrated with huge feasts when they massacred whole villages of Indigenous people. That is how Thanksgiving started.

Things progress quickly that day and he puts out another live feed soon. He live feeds several videos. They are drone footage of the action happening at Turtle Island. He shows the water protectors walking over a bridge they built from one shore to the other at the base of Turtle Island. There are lots of signs supporting the movement. Many people gather. They yell and wave at the drone as it flies by. He flies up to the law enforcement on top of Turtle Island. He gets close. It looks like law enforcement has a hose on the side of the hill. His feed freezes off and on. He does not panic when the screen goes blank.

DAPL security and Morton County are outnumbered on this day. We are taking our lands back North Dakota.

You're tuned into Indigenous Rising Media. They are scrambling the drone signal because they don't want us to see how limited they are with their resources and tactics. They don't want to be embarrassed and show how, on Thanksgiving Day, they forgot to protect their oil money. But there's only a few, maybe 100 to 200 cops and we've got thousands. So this day is our day.

They've got military Humvees, LRADs. We got canoes, boats. (*He flies over the protectors crossing the bridge.*) This is what we'll be doing all day, live feeding. Police and military are outnumbered. North Dakota, all your tax money has been spent on hurting others, so think twice about paying your taxes. Here's the scum of the earth. That's what a DAPL security worker said about us, but it's really true about them. They have no respect for sacred sites, they have no respect for themselves, no respect for their families.

"America is really gonna front and celebrate 'Thanksgiving' like they aren't terrorizing Native Americans right now?!" ~ Unknown

In another live feed:

It's a beautiful day and we're taking everything back. We're taking Turtle Island back. If you've seen the drone footage, we've built bridges to walk across the water and we're hitting them from all different directions. There are other actions taking place around the taken land that the police don't even know anything about. Morton County is pretty much outnumbered. They don't have the manpower or even the capacity to try to protect their pipeline. They've called in more from other counties to come help. Let's see if they come help on this holiday when they are probably at home just eating turkey. I don't know if they want to come out and it's cold out too. Another update is that they do have a water cannon out on Turtle Island that they are aiming toward the protectors. I'm going to take the drone up again and get a closer look at what's going on. You guys pray for us because prayer is powerful and it's beautiful and we're taking back our lands, our sacred sites, our treaty lands. We're taking back everything that our peoples already had for thousands and thousands of years for seven generations beyond seven generations beyond seven generations. Stay tuned. Share. And know the truth.

The live feeds continue:

This is the drone guy. We just got confirmation that law enforcement said they have permission to shoot down the drones. It's illegal to shoot down drones, especially if they are around the water protectors, but I fly everywhere. Listen in on this.

He turns on a radio. There is static. Then a voice says, "It's very apparent from their social media that they are listening to us on the radio."

They are aware that we are listening to them. We are changing history! I'm going to go fly again.

I want to give a live update. Been flying the drone all day and exposing all their little tactics they try to do. We had a radio, listening in on what they are doing and they are finding out what we are doing from all of our social media pages. They were stating on the radio that they need reinforcements. Telling us that they are outnumbered. So in the meantime, as we are doing this live video, they are having Thanksgiving dinner on top of Turtle Island. Which is crazy.

I flew over there with the drone, went down the road, right over their heads. It's like they are allowing the drone to fly around. They don't have a gun in their hands to shoot it down. They have turkey and pumpkin pie. It's crazy. They were stuffing their faces and looking up, oh there's the drone. I got drone footage of them having dinner, just taking a break.

We heard over the radio that they said all the drones flying overhead are pretty hardcore. They did also say, which is not confirmed with the FAA, that they intend to shoot down any drone, but if it's around the protectors, they will not shoot. But they will shoot the drones. So anyone from the FAA, or call them and let them know at FAA, that Morton County has taken it upon themselves to shoot the drones. And like I stated before, it's illegal to shoot down any drone because it's considered just like an aircraft. And it is stated that is illegal, no matter what the situation is. No one is allowed to shoot down a drone, recreational or military.

We did get confirmation over their radio channel that they did seize a drone, but it was not Drone2bwild's drone. So that's a quick update, get it all from the drone pilot himself, exclusive footage is coming out of the Indigenous Rising Media page.

Today was a good day. We took back all the land. But out of respect, we don't want to take over the sacred sites because there are powerful spirits there. Today is about giving respect and giving thanks to Mother Earth. Because without her we wouldn't have this beautiful home we have here.

He turns the camera around and shows a very, very full camp. He is on Facebook Hill and there are lots of people there. He points out clouds parting in the sky.

It's a beautiful day out here guys. Look at all the flags flying in solidarity. There's hundreds of flags put up here throughout the whole camp. There's the sun trying to look out from behind the clouds.

One thing that I want to point out is that every day we have rumors that this camp is being raided. Advising all women and children to go. That's based on paranoia and fear. We as protectors shouldn't allow that to overcome our spirits because it makes us go crazy. But it's 110% untrue. It's just what they want us to think. So once again, we are not getting invaded. For the past couple of days we took the drones up and there's not that many security out. And right now they had to call in reinforcements and I doubt they even came because they're at home eating turkey.

While everyone is cutting the heads off turkeys, here at Oceti Sakowin Camp we're cutting the head off the black snake. It's been a good day of actions. All of the water protectors, the veterans, everybody came in. I want to do a quick shout out to IEN (Indigenous Environmental Network), the wonderful crew I work with. I'm blessed to be a part of their vision and journey. And I'm blessed to share my vision and journey with them and to share with everybody around the whole world that's been tuning in.

He looks at the live feed comments.

Yeah, there was a woman up here earlier stating that they were raiding the camp. But when something like that happens guys, don't believe it. The true source of real information is IEN, we keep tabs on all that stuff. We monitor every rumor, every page, every post. For me, being digital means that I stay in tune with social media. I stay in tune 24/7. But as of today, when the sun goes down, I'm shutting off my phone so I can spend time with my kids and my family. Enjoy a nice dinner. We're going to pray and to give thanks to Mother Earth. So I'll be gone for a couple of days. But I'll be back. I want to thank each and every one of you guys out there for showing all the love. All the love. All the hearts. And yes, I will always stay on my game.

So tune into the Indigenous Rising Media page and you will see about ten live feeds. I did live feeds all day. Just hitting them with the live feeds, hitting them with the live feeds.

Oh, right now I'm looking over there and they are bringing in five more police vehicles, going to Turtle Island. They're either going for backup or they are just late for their Thanksgiving dinner.

So today was our day. We took back what was rightfully ours. We did it out of unity. We did it out of solidarity. But most of all we did it out of positive prayer. And that's how we succeed. This is the beautiful thing about life. We live it every day. We live things in a positive way. It's about good and evil. It's about not letting the evil take over the world. But we do need evil to inspire the good in us to inspire others. It's the yin and yang.

I'm going to end it here. You guys have a wonderful Thanksgiving, but we're changing that. Before you sit down and have dinner with your family, close your eyes and be thankful that we are living, we are breathing, and today we lived a good day. And give thanks to Mother Earth because she is everything right now. It's our time to start standing up and to start representing and to start respecting Mother Earth because she is precious. And we will stop all fossil fuel corporations from digging any more resources out of her. And we are going to show the world that Mother Earth is a living entity. A living source of life. One little planet, a little speck, a dot in a whole ocean of ocean of ocean of space is earth. And we come here and have life, we have water, sky, air and that is the meaning of life. We are here to experience it, not to destroy it.

You guys take care. Peace out.

He is often interviewed by independent news media. TYT (The Young Turks), Jordan Chariton, puts out a video of an interview with him. They talk about the drone that was shot down. He had tried to fly very low over DAPL's vehicles.

Dean: The reason I went so low is because I didn't see anyone around. Obviously it's cold so I thought they were hiding out in their RVs or trucks. But as soon as they knew the drone was really low, where they could get out and shoot it, that's what happened. There's an image of a guy in all black gear and ski mask and all I saw was the guy shooting right at it and *(he snaps)* it went off.

Even though I hit the return home button, it still said the aircraft was disconnected. And at the same time I had to gain altitude. We waited two minutes but nothing. But this time when I go back, I'll circle around high enough where they can't shoot it. We'll see what kind of footage we can get.

Rhianna Lakin, a drone pilot, works with him closely. He calls her his sidekick and she provides amazing support. Other drone pilots come to support Standing Rock as well.

He is photographed by water protectors like they are paparazzi. He has become famous from the drone footage he has been providing. More people show up because of him. His followers encourage and support him and the movement.

He often lends his drone footage to other media outlets. He is generous in his sharing. He is also generous with sharing the help he is given with other water protectors. If someone needs a meal or anything, he is quick to help.

He shares an announcement that Taboo from the group, Black Eyed Peas, will be heading to Standing Rock after Thanksgiving.

November 25th

Protect our mother

Reports are flying out of Bismarck that water protectors were arrested in the Kirkwood Mall for forming a circle and praying. Law enforcement put up razor wire around Turtle Island. And in devastating news, the Army Corps of Engineers announces that they will clear Oceti Sakowin Camp on December 5th. The governor of North Dakota asks for federal help with the eviction.

November 26th

He live feeds drone footage from the Indigenous Rising Media page. His feeds get fifty thousand views and more. They are widely shared.

Update on DAPL construction and Turtle Island.

As you can see, they've put up razor wire all around this whole island. It's like a little fort. With the little swimming pool at the top. And they've damaged the canoes. They were outnumbered and they were scared and they feared for their lives. But we stood in solidarity to show them that we can take over whenever we want to."

Law enforcement officers stand on top of the very tall hill and watch the drone pass by. It is a crisp, cold, sunny day.

They underestimate the power of the drone. It seems like they are trying to mess with the drone. The drone's flying a little funny. I've been flying it for a while though. Let's see if they point their guns and try to shoot this drone.

There it is guys, did you see that? They tried to shoot it. They don't care if they are breaking the law. Now if they were good shots, they would have taken it down. Get a screenshot of them pointing the gun at the drone. Thank you guys.

He flies around and around the officers. Then he flies over the water protectors on the other side.

We got a circle here, a gathering. It's protectors on the other side standing in a circle. This drone is above the protectors, it's above a lot of people, so if they try to shoot at it, that's illegal. Let all the new protectors know who are just getting here that this drone is on our side. It's protecting them.

A large group of water protectors march toward Turtle Island. He flies the drone over them.

Here's an all unity and solidarity march. The power of social media, there's so many comments coming that I can't even read them. But after this I will read them and get back to you. There they are. Desecrators. Protecting a pipeline. I'm going to be a little cautious because they are shooting at the drone. This drone is keeping them on their toes. One drone and it has all of their attention. The power of the drone. It can fly all over the land, our land. And there's nothing they can do except watch it. Smile Morton County.

And here's the spot they were all meeting at on Thursday. I hope they gave thanks to Mother Earth before they broke bread. Right around this tree is where a family was buried. They are right over a family; their bones, our ancestors. Our people. How would they feel if we were parking our cars and walking all over Gettysburg or their cemetery grounds? They would be offended.

They made a statement that they are doing nothing wrong. And they were using water cannons as a crowd dispersal tactic. The drones capture their wrong doings. That guy right there, he waved. They want to shoot this drone down. I gotta do it guys.

He flies over them again. He gets even closer. Then he flies back.

We keep them on their toes. Let's get out of there while we're doing good. We're going to go ahead and fly above this beautiful water.

There is a lot of comedy going on. Indigenous people have learned to laugh despite the circumstances they are put under. Several Indigenous comedians are at camp and live feed hilarious videos in the down times between actions. The humor rolls over onto Facebook and Morton County Sheriff's page is hacked with ridiculously funny changes. Morton County takes the page down and does not see the humor.

There is a press conference to address the December 5th deadline by Chairman Dave Archambault and a panel.

He shares drone footage of above camp in an Indigenous Rising Media live feed. Camp has grown unbelievably. There are so many people there. The tipis, tents, campers and other structures are spread out all over camp. It is fifteen minutes of beautiful drone footage. He goes over Turtle Island, the drill pad, the pipe.

As our Father Sun sets we pray for our mother.

The Army Corps say they will take 15,000 people off this camp. We'll see. The countdown begins to December 5th. Making the call out, all veterans, all water protectors. We're gonna need all of you guys to protect this camp and to protect mni wiconi. And to cut the head off that black snake over there. When this ends I want you to say a prayer for all of us here. 15,000 protectors. Stay tuned. The best stuff you'll see with drones.

Later that evening he shares a live feed from a concert held at Prairie Knights Casino. Actress, Francis Fisher, is there, along with several musicians.

November 27th

He puts out a live feed.

Giving a quick update. North Dakota has not gotten any snow yet, but I hear there's a big snow storm coming. The show last night was freaking awesome. I pretty much live streamed for a couple of hours for the whole world to be there, to see all of the artists and experience it all. They were killing it. It was freaking cool. It's the best show I've been to in my entire life and it was free. This show was free and it was benefiting the whole movement and every one of those individuals who were on stage were so empowering because they all had such strong voices. The youth were amazing as well. But last night they put on the show until like one and the Pavilion was telling us that the show was over. But we got to see everybody we wanted to see. It was an amazing show. We caught the Myron on there, he's so hard to find. Prolific was on there - give him props, he's going home for about four days and he'll be back. For me I just woke up tired and I'm about to get something to eat so from there I can properly feel a lot better. Thank you guys out there for everything that you do. All you guys are amazing. Stay in touch. Have a nice day.

He posts from the Indigenous Rising Media page

Indigenous Rising Media drone shot by police.

They are shooting weapons at the drone. Little pellets. Shot the lens and propellers. So FAA does it matter what they are shooting? Everybody take screenshots and review it. *(He shows little holes in the propellers.)* They are shooting at the drone with pellets. It's illegal to shoot down a drone.

Bismarck I am here! What's up peoples! FR! Who's around?

In the comments, his followers tell him to not announce where he is. They encourage him to be safe.

November 28th

He shares photos of law enforcement officers lying on the ground.

These are pics of the Morton County snipers pointed at the protectors down below. Drone2bwild sees everything in the sky!! So I drone in and catch 'em shooting the P4 multiple times with a shotgun. Video was live but Facebook took it down. Raw footage coming soon.

He does a live feed from the Indigenous Rising Media page. It is very snowy out. He flies the drone over camp. The wind is howling.

Winter is here!

Alright guys, this is the camp and winter is here. This is Shiyé, also known as Dean. I'm here on Indigenous Rising Media because they shut my feed down. This is what we're doing with the drone. We're taking it to the extreme in wild weather conditions. Share this out guys. The drone is still working. Here is the water of life. It's freezing. We are at freezing temperatures and there's snow here at camp and we are still droning. This is a North Dakota winter for you guys. My hands are freezing. People from Hawaii, send us your sunshine. Here's how it is driving around in the snow. *(He shows a car sliding around on the road.)* The drone is starting to freeze up guys. I'm going to go ahead and bring it down. This is live footage of the camp right now. I'm going to take the drone home and warm it up before it freezes. First I'll go down flag row.

"I am a ten year, two times war veteran. I am not a protestor, I am an Ogitchida. I am here to protect these people from you. I am a defender of the constitution. I came to see this for myself. I saw the rubber bullets, I saw the gas, I saw the attack dogs, I saw the water at freezing temperature. I saw the riot gear and the violence inflicted on so many U.S. citizens. I saw how you've been mistreating my people. I am the first of many warriors to come."
~ Zhooniya Ogitchida

"The world will not be destroyed by those who do evil, but by those who watch them without doing anything."
~ Albert Einstein

He is often seen in other people's live feeds. He appears briefly in Lindsay Nance's that day. It is snowing and he says that he needs to go to the casino.

Facebook has stopped all my Facebook live feeds! Even though I have full connections. Time to start up another account just for live feeds!!!!

Later he starts a live feed. He is at the casino with Didi Banerji.

Finally I can go live !!!!!

Hey Facebook, for some surprising reason Facebook let me go live again. Thank you Mark, you are an awesome person. Mark Zuckerberg, you don't understand the power that you have with your technology to connect the whole world. Don't let your mind get corrupt by those oil companies. You don't need the oil corporations, you don't need any negative thing like that. You have the power to connect the world. It's up to you bro, Mark Zuckerberg. I do have faith in Mark, he has a good heart, he has a brilliant mind. Bro, do good for the world. Go green, do not help the oil corporations. When you make that kind of money you have a responsibility to be more humble than the next guy. Always remember Mark, all that money you make, it's not about control bro, it's an illusion.

Our family is getting bigger at the camp. 15,000 strong and thousands of veterans coming. It's hardcore. We have all kinds of military here. Majors, lieutenants. They are coming here to remind all the military why they do what they do. The thing is to protect innocent civilians, so they're going to check everybody.

They're there to protect us, they know we're innocent, that's why they're coming. They're going to be between us and the military because we need protection.

He shouts out several friends who are in the military.

I got a message to all the National Guard out there. I respect what you do from the bottom of my heart, but if you are doing it to make money for your education, I would suggest that you come to camp and learn the Indigenous knowledge. It's free because knowledge is free. We should never have to pay for knowledge. You just got to listen to learn. It's the power of the spirit. Everything in this world should be free, there should be no money. The only laws that I abide by are laws of Mother Nature.

For the people of Bismarck and Mandan, I love you. As much hate as you say and type, we've all taken it all in and it empowers us. It empowers me, it empowers my mind and my physical being. I know there's a lot of people in Bismarck who support NoDAPL.

Yesterday we had drone action by the Phantom 4. There were snipers on Turtle Island, pointed down at the protectors. So it was my duty as a drone pilot to protect, to fly in and capture everything that was happening and I did.

He puts out a couple of live feeds that evening.

Good evening everybody out there. I have a statement. I just want to do an update on the North Dakota governor's statement about coming in early and evicting all the water protectors. Personally, I believe it's just a media frenzy. What they want to do is called a media tactic. They want to call this early to get everybody scared. To get everybody riled up, to start spreading confusion within the camps and all the leaders, but it's not going to work. This is a message to all my water protectors out there. They just want us to be scared. They want to incite fear and make us confused, make us start getting scared early, but it's not going to work.

They're scared, that's why they're putting it upon themselves to make that statement tonight in this blizzard that's going on right now. How are you going to go out in the middle of a blizzard and stand there? It's all a media tactic and you hateful faces that are on here, I know that you're part of DAPL. I'm going to take that negativity and turn it into love. That's how much power I have. Look at all the hearts! I love you guys! I love you guys!

I want to state again that the statement the governor made, I believe it's just a tactic to scare us. Don't believe it. Don't believe anything that North Dakota says. They just want to incite fear in us. Fear, fear, fear, that's what they want. But we don't fear them. Don't you fear them.

I will take it upon myself to say a prayer for the North Dakota governor and everybody out there. Be safe coming up to Bismarck. We passed by about six cars that went off the road, even an RV. Remember that the hardest thing for the human people to do and understand is to have patience. Even if it takes two hours, three hours to get to your destination, where you got to go - understand that patience is a virtue. Be safe about it people out there in North Dakota. Drive safe.

I'm happy that Facebook let me go live again. Another message out to Mark Zuckerberg, remember bro, you have the power to connect the whole world and unify with the technology that you call Facebook. We're going to rename it Earthbook.

I'll do live feeds this evening, stay tuned and share this feed with everybody, with all your friends, all your groups. See you guys later.

The next couple of live feeds come up soon. It is very snowy outside and the road looks very dangerous.

Alright guys we're live feeding again. I just want to let everybody out there know this is on Highway 6 right now. This is what's happening. There's BIA, that's a tow truck and that's a truck. Weird. BIA all the way up on Highway 6. But that's cool though.

Like I said earlier, what they came out with, that's just to get media attention, but we've got more media attention than they ever will and whatever happens on December 5th, we're ready on Dec 1st. We've got military, we've got army, we have Navy Seals, we have special ops. We have veterans that served for the good of protecting this country from domestic terrorism and that's what this is right now. This is domestic terrorism against water protectors, so all you vets out there who are coming, I love all of you guys from the bottom of my heart. You're not doing it for the country, you're doing it for your family, you're doing it to protect your children. That's the true meaning of protecting and that's what we're doing right now. We're protecting our mother, we're protecting our water, we're protecting our children, we're protecting our families.

Alright guys another live book feed, no wait guys, I take that back. This is an Earthbook post. Everybody's been commenting about Kevin Gilbert. He's a human being. He does a live Facebook video and gets a million views automatically. And of course when you have a million followers what happens? It's going to get cut off because it's all about censoring. Just like me, I got cut off trying to talk truth. There are a lot of water protectors who have a lot of truth and there are a lot of people sharing our truth and that's what happened to his page. So we can keep sharing everything he has to say. I'm going to go back to camp tomorrow and I will locate this guy and get more truth out of him. So I'm logging off Earthbook now.

November 29th

Oceti Sakowin Camp is now the tenth largest city in North Dakota. Despite the snow and harsh conditions, veterans and civilians alike are still showing up to help protect the water.

Indigenous United States veteran, Chris Turley arrives at camp that day. He has walked from Oklahoma in support of the Standing Rock Nation and movement. It is estimated that the veterans will show up in the thousands.

Mississippi Stands group is still active. Two water protectors locked down to an excavator that was removing boring sludge from the drilling of the pipeline. One water protector was two weeks into a fast to bring awareness to help stop the pipeline.

It is reported that the FAA is once again banning water protector drones from flying at Standing Rock. The only exceptions will be made for journalists who get special approval beforehand.

Drone2bwild will be going live and addressing this statement and his continued role as pipeline exposer and drone water protector.

Soon he live feeds from a hotel room. Angelo Wolf is with him.

The drone guy addresses the FAA statement about the banning of drones at Oceti Sakowin Camp. These are his thoughts and his words to the FAA and Morton County and the world!

I want to start addressing issues. It says that the FAA has banned drones from the pipeline project at Standing Rock protests. Drone footage of clashes with police at the campsite have gone viral. Of course they have gone viral because the drones capture everything. They are the eyes in the sky. They captured everything last Sunday. You can clearly see that they are pointing their water cannons right directly at one single person. Now is that a crowd? You guys review the footage.

Now these helicopters are supposed to be in support of law enforcement. Now law enforcement, what do you consider support? Does this include the helicopters going dangerously low? Does that include the helicopters coming down and trying to crush the horse riders as they are trying to run freely on the Plains? Now these are big, heavy aircraft which can cause a lot more damage than a single drone. Now think about that guys. FAA, whose side are you on? Are you biased? Unbiased? Are you on the side of the protectors? Of the drone pilots? Are you on the side of Morton County?

Now let's look at this, let's wind it back. Out of all of this stuff, it's about safety. Now every time I go out, I go out with 110% safety. I'm always aware where there are aircraft flying around. I go really low. Normally I'm flying around five feet above the ground. Now that's not way up in the sky where the aircraft is. So I cannot damage the aircraft. But note this, once the law enforcement see it, the drone is coming, they radio the helicopter and airplanes to change their flight patterns and they start going into the area of the drone so they can use that as an excuse. I have stressed that many times. I watch this. I'm really observant.

Now here's my statement about this, Drone2bwild is still going to be flying, still going to be documenting this, still going to be capturing all this evidence and still going to be doing what I'm doing. And that's capturing evidence as they try to shoot at the drone. I'm going to capture everything as it happens because it's my right, it's the drone's right. It's the first amendment right.

Now FAA, you think about that. The first amendment right, before you start banning drones, think about it. What's more dangerous? A huge helicopter with a lot of gas in it as it crashes and burns, or a simple drone when the most damage it can cause is the propeller hitting somebody and causing cuts. But it won't go to that because this Drone2bwild pilot here is pretty skilled with what he does. I have been flying every day just to hone my skills. I will continue to fly. I will continue to cover this because it's my first amendment right. That's what's going to cover me. And you will see that. You can see it on the live feeds. Watch me fly. Watch what I do. You'll see if there's any danger about it. The only thing that is dangerous is the people who have weapons. Now, that's my live statement to the FAA.

You can actually ask for permission to fly your drone even though it's a restricted area - what do you think the possibilities of that being granted to you? Most likely everyone says zero, but you know what, three months ago I got a call from the North Dakota FAA guy. Before he stated the rules to me, he said that he loved what I was doing with the drones and that's coming from the FAA guy. So maybe I should. If I have to, I could have my followers whip up a statement, a petition for me and inbox it to me and have it ready for me and we'll get this petition going. If we have to have a thousand signatures, we'll make it viral and trust me, the whole world's behind my back and will sign it.

And all you haters that are on this page, you can go ahead and snoop in on our stuff, all I gotta say is can you fly a drone? No. Sit back and watch the world change right in front of your eyes.

I know a lot of people have respect for what I'm doing. I know I have to jump through hoops and fly low by FAA rules and regulations, but somebody's got to do it. Somebody's got to push these FAA regulations to the limit. Somebody's got to push this drone technology to the limit. And I'm going to be that person, because that's my life mission to do. This technology that we have, we gotta push it. You know the rules and regulations, we gotta push it. If there's a really skilled pilot out there, don't let the rules and regulations hold you back from creating something really beautiful and magnificent.

The other day, they took it down, but I'm going to put it back up, my Phantom 4, recently bought for 1200 dollars. I took it up to Turtle Island, the second flight for it. The Phantom 4 that I have is like the hawks and eagles that fly in and swoop and get their prey. Now when I say prey, I mean documentation. For those proDAPL people. But they got shot up. They're learning though, Morton County is learning.

The first time they tried to shoot it, it even got really close to them and they couldn't shoot it. You guys remember that, right? If you do remember that footage do some screenshots and put it in the comments so everyone can see. They really embarrassed themselves. Morton County's finest, they all need to go back to the shooting range.

But like I said, I gotta give it to them, they are using their brains finally. Now they are using shotguns that have pellets that spread out. So the Phantom 4 ended up getting shot. I'm sure you guys saw the video. Repost that on this feed guys so everybody can see what I'm talking about. They shot the propellers, they shot the props up. If I shake the Phantom 4 there's still pellets inside of it. But it still flies. I'm going to open it up and put those little pellets in a baggie. And that can be evidence right there. They shot the camera screen, but they didn't shoot the camera. My drone got shot at, but it is still flyable. I just need some props, if anyone is kind enough to throw a pilot some props. I have a feeling we're going to go through a lot of props.

But yeah, they're shooting at the drones. I had a top secret radio and we were listening in on the radio to Morton County trying to be secret. And I'm going to tell it all. We listened to everything they said. The drones are the eye in the sky. We need to start taking down these drones, they said. Those drones are giving up our locations. They said, these drones are just getting too hardcore, we need to start shooting them down. So did the FAA let them, did they know about that? No, basically they are just making their own rules and breaking their own rules. They don't care. But they love, they love, they love to enforce their rules on us. So is this country free? No it's not. We're literally fighting for our freedom.

But when you enter the camp it's the best feeling in the whole world. You can go there and disconnect yourself from everything. You disconnect yourself from money. You disconnect yourself from bills. You disconnect from all these illusions that are in this system that is created to oppress and squeeze and stress your soul out. That's why we cannot live as true human beings, because we are being oppressed and pressed and pushed and controlled and forced. We're being limited by this government.

The true freedom is Indigenous freedom. When this universe was created there were the natural rules and laws and those are the rules and laws of Mother Nature. And the government needs to look into that. Because you don't need, when you have Mother Nature and her laws, you don't need to forcibly force those on people or animals or the plant life or the water. It's a well-balanced system.

That being said, I'd like to thank everyone who's tuning in. Get that petition out there for me. Share it around.

I want to give a shout out to my sponsor, DroneGear. Alex Kavanagh, he's a wonderful human being. Thanks for everything bro. Not to mention all of you people who tune in every day. I love you from the bottom of my heart. I appreciate you 110% and I personally try to get back to every single one of you guys. You guys feed me a lot of good information. Everybody asks me if I went to the meeting, but I don't need to go to the meetings because I get such good sources of information.

I want to give a shout out to everyone at camp staying warm. When you look outside it's pretty breezy.

Some of his live feeds just show the weather. He live feeds just a couple of minutes of him walking with huge snow goggles and a mask on his face. It is white and snowy outside.

Later he live feeds with Ernesto Burbank.

Alright guys we walk in the face of winter, because buffalo nation is within us all!! Oh it's cold. This is my bro, Ernesto. I want you to support him.

They are walking through very deep snow.

Walk in the face of the storm because the Buffalo Nation is within us all the time. We walk through the storm. Alright guys, normally I have a mask on, but I can taste the snow. Snow is life. Water is life. Snow is water. It's pretty cold but we're Standing Rock, we're Lakotas. I'm Lakota, I can endure this. They tried to get us out of here, but it won't happen. It's not going to happen. We're not going to go anywhere. See us walking through the snow right here? I'm going to get a water tattoo right there *(he points to his neck)* and later on I'm going to get a drone tattoo right on my wrist. You guys come out here. I will go live with my tattoo. Love you guys all.

Finally Drone2bwild is getting his water mark tattoo...ON HIS NECK!

He plays music by Drezus, Long Live The People, while Ernesto gives him a tattoo on his neck. He tells everyone that he did drone footage for Drezus' new video, Black Snake Killas.

Check it out people. It's a watermark tattoo. A water protector tattoo. It didn't really hurt.

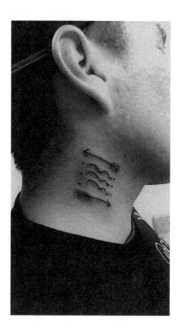

So I wear this in honor of all of the women who have been arrested and charged falsely like Red Fawn!! This tattoo goes beyond RED WARRIOR, BEYOND OCETI SAKOWIN, BEYOND SACRED STONE.........ALL THE WAY UP TO THE LEVEL OF THE SEVEN COUNCIL FIRES. And with that said: The flesh that this watermark rests upon will forever always be protected for generations to come.

Tonight "DRONE" got his watermark! Ernesto Burbank is the guy behind the tattoo machine.

"History is a lie.

Religion is a control system.

Money is a hoax.

Debt is a fiction.

Media is manipulation.

Government is a corporation.

The system is an illusion." ~ Unknown

DRONEGEAR sponsors Drone2bwild!!

Alex Kavanagh thanks bro I'll see you in L.A.!

In a short live feed, Alex says that DroneGear is supporting Dean now. He says that they are sponsoring Dean now. He calls Dean, "family," and Dean says, "I'll see you in LA." They hug and Alex leaves.

"I supported the drone pilots when I could whilst shooting many interviews for @tidesoftravel. I decided to sponsor Dean with our Inspire 1 X5, 5 batteries and a @dronecrates case for it. We will continue to support Dean with equipment as he needs it. They're illegally shooting down drones." ~ Alex Kavanagh

"there is peaceful

there is wild

i am both at the same time" ~ sum

November 30th

The Bismarck Tribune reports that 124 felony charges against the water protectors have been dismissed by a state judge. 15 have already been dismissed. The judge said that Morton County did not show probable cause that any of these water protectors conspired to endanger people or property by fire or explosion during the raid of Treaty Camp on October 27th.

It is also announced that people coming into camp can no longer bring supplies with them. They cannot bring, "anything that goes to sustain living there, including wood, food, and blankets."

"They need to evacuate. The executive order is clear that it's public safety. If they ignore it they have to live with the consequences of potentially freezing to death." ~ Maxine Herr, a spokeswoman for the Morton County Sheriff's Department

They are in the middle of a snowstorm that already dumped over eight inches of snow. Winds are blowing strong. Many roads are closed and driving is near impossible. Most of the water protectors could not leave even if they wanted to. Camps are filled with people of all ages; families, children, elders and animals. Everyone was safe inside camp, so the eviction notice during a snow storm seemed very cruel.

Navajo veterans are scheduled to leave December 2nd for Standing Rock. They would return home on the 6th. News of the eviction was not stopping any of the veterans groups.

There are already veterans at Standing Rock and they have already started to stand. Live feeds of law enforcement talking over a loud speaker system to the vets are watched by the world. First the law enforcement tries to sweet talk the veterans. They thank them for their service. They tell them there are veterans on their side too. They tell them that water protectors have been throwing dangerous things at them and that they set cars on fire. But when the law enforcement cannot sway the water protector veterans, they become more defiant. They tell them they can use any force necessary to arrest them. Law enforcement says the vets are forcing a confrontation.

The veterans are shown standing between Indigenous water protectors as they pray and armed law enforcement officers. During many actions law enforcement used a loud speaker system. Often they just repeated themselves. It was just one of the many, many psychological tactics they used in their warfare against the water protectors.

He live feeds on Facebook from his own page from Bismarck.

A'ho people that tune in every day. This is the wonderful Dean. I'd like to let everyone know that it's been a beautiful day so far. The snow has stopped snowing. It's still cold. Can't feel my hands. But it's a wonderful day in Bismarck.

What I'm going to do today is I'm going to go around and show all the love of Bismarck. If I have to infiltrate the mall and do actual live feeds, I will. I'm just offering my heart and my love. If they don't want it, that's their problem. I'm going to see if I can get a cop on the life feed saying water is life. This is my mission today.

I'm not at camp right now. And no for all of those pro DAPL people, I did not give up my tipi. I did not give up my Hogan.

As a media person, we go far and beyond that, we expose things. We infiltrate things. So right now I am on the north side of Bismarck. So just be prepared, I will be on and off live feeds. Maybe live feeding some people who just don't know what's going on. Crazy. That's my mission today as a drone pilot. Personal live feeds and what they think about December 5th. Catching everyone's personal thoughts.

Let's go into this store. We'll see what they think. Hit me up if you are in Bismarck, if you want to eat with the drone pilot and I'll take you out to eat later.

He walks into a convenience store and asks, "Do you got anything good to drink here? What's the best thing to drink?"

Clerk: I got a fountain over there and all those drinks over there.

Dean: Do you have water?

Clerk: Uh, yeah.

Dean: Water is life, right?

Clerk: Yeah.

Dean: 110% water is life.

Clerk: I'm busy sir.

Dean: He's busy.

Dean walks out of the store.

Dean: So basically you see, I went in right there and they say they are connected to the movement, but he was too busy. Too connected with the illusion of job and making money. Working with people who are trying to buy all the stuff. Maybe I should go back in and try to get him to buy me something. No, let's go over here. Where people are getting gas. Gas is oil. Let's see.

He walks over to the gas pumps.

Dean: Hey sir, how are you doing today?

Man: I'm good.

Dean: What are you doing today?

Man: Trying to get my snow blower working today. I haven't ran it in three years.

Dean: What's your position on what's going on down south?

Man: You mean with the pipeline?

Dean: Yeah.

Man: Well, I'm anti pipeline.

Dean smiles at him. That's great, as you pour gas, but we all do it. We're working on it though.

Man: Yeah. They could put it someplace else.

Dean: What did you think when they were trying to put the pipeline near Bismarck and the people said not here and they moved it down south?

Man: I wasn't aware of that.

Dean: You didn't know about the meetings about the pipeline?

Man: No, but I'm not trying to pay attention to that.

Dean: That's the thing though. You weren't in tune. So what do you think about the December 5th evictions?

Man: They said they are going to evict the people?

Dean: Do you know how many people, how many water protectors are down there?

Man: Five to ten thousand people?

Dean: Aww, you're way off. 15,000 people plus with 6 thousand vets coming.

> *A car passes and Dean says they are water protectors.*

Dean: Oh I'm just going live. You are on live feed.

Man: It's kind of messed up. If people don't want it there, I don't know why it has to be.

Dean: Have you heard about all the negative things Kirchmeier is doing down there?

Man: Yeah and I don't agree with that. Or all the racism around Bismarck. I don't agree with that either.

Dean: How do you feel about Trump?

Man: I don't like him. But I think that's another reason people think they can get away with all of the racism because he's going to be the president now.

Dean: Do you think we have hope for this world?

Man: Oh yeah, there's good people out there.

Dean: Thanks for this interview. You have a good heart. Thanks for sharing. I love you bro.

You guys heard the words from a Bismarck resident, he's against the pipeline. Now like I was saying guys, Bismarck isn't all evil. There's no evil anywhere. He's not evil. That guy, that was cool.

I should have had him buy me something. No, I take that back, I shouldn't because all those pro DAPL people out there, every time we ask for something they say all we are doing is our GoFundMe accounts.

You know what I think about those GoFundMe accounts, I want to withdraw all that money and burn it. Prove that it doesn't matter. Let me look into some of these comments.

You are awesome. I'm not awesome, you guys are awesome. I'm just a voice. This is how I feel. You guys are all awesome! Out there in this Facebook world. I wouldn't be the voice if you guys didn't tune in all the time and spread the message and share it. This is what I do now. Personally, I didn't want to be the face of Facebook or a Facebook live person, I miss my personal life. But someone's got to do it, right?

Here's a few words from the fire starter himself. *(It is Angelo Wolf in a car.)* See, he does this to me all the time, puts me on live feeds. But this is the love of water protectors. This is what we do. This is what we're going to do all day. We're going to walk around Bismarck and Mandan today and meet random people and see if they love the water.

> *He goes back into the store.*

That's the guy that was too busy. Are you still busy? Can I talk to you? He looks like he's kind of irritated toward us. He told me to get out of the store. I only had simple words for him, but he got irritated.

So there you go. He's looking at me all messed up, man. He was like, get out of my store, I can't stand you. And there was one guy who was pumping gas that doesn't support the pipeline.

> *He gets in a vehicle.*

I gotta call this guy about breaking news. Oh, one more thing before I cut off this live feed, KYFR, K-Fire, personally contacted me wanting to do an interview because of the live feeds I'm doing, but I told them you're going to have to pay me some money that's going to be contributed to camp, and we're going to be live. If you are going to do an interview with me, Shiyé, we're going to have to do it live, because I cannot trust them. If they are recording it then they will manipulate it and they said we'll talk later. So I told them next time you really want to do an interview with me, we're going to go live, live. That's the only way. Now when I do get on that K-Fire, if I do, boy, Bismarck, Mandan, I got something coming for everybody.

In another live feed, he watches Angelo Wolf doing a television interview.

"We're not going to back down. If you want to do media, tell it straight. Sometimes they make us sound violent and rioting, but we are not. Sometimes you don't believe the things we post, but we are living it." ~ Angelo Wolf

There are reports that Bismarck Ace Hardware store will not sell propane to campers. It is reported that law enforcement told the store not to sell any materials that could be used as an incendiary device.

They want us to go to Ace Hardware and see if they will sell to us. We'll go with a whole crap of money and see if they will sell to us. I think we will infiltrate Ace's before they close down. We'll check out that store.

He does a live feed from the hotel.

I'm now on Angry Patriot Radio discussing updates on the December 5th evictions of Oceti Sakowin Camp! Here's just a few of my thoughts!!

Good afternoon all my wonderful, lovely, beautiful souls out there. Today, right now, currently I'm on a four minute break, but I'm on Angry Patriot Radio talking about the actions that can possibly take place on December 5th. And also the concerns of today that this morning's announcements have been all over the news about the governor of North Dakota stating that anyone who's coming in with supplies is going to be facing a thousand dollar fine and might even be jailed. What they are doing is that they are stopping all means of supplies and that means shelter, food and anything to keep warm. They are stating that they are cutting off everything from the world so that we can freeze and starve.

But the one thing that the governor of North Dakota forgot is that they're dealing with Indigenous people. We have survived for centuries and we never needed that technology that you guys love so much. Yeah, right now we may be in a hotel, we might be driving a car, we might be using a cell phone for Facebook, but we are really connected deep down to earth. We are survivors and we always, always will prevail. Never, ever underestimate the power of the Indigenous people of this world, because you got another think coming.

With that said, I believe it's pretty much an act of terrorism against their own people. People of the United States. This ain't no land of the free. This ain't no home of the brave. This country here has gone to crap. Pure and simple.

My mind and my heart are strong, but my outside emotions are angry. But I control that anger. Never ever let that anger get the best of you. Or the fear inside of you. No matter what the situation is, no matter how chaotic this is going to get.

I want to give a message to all my peoples at the camps, all my best friends, all the people I love and all the children of the camp: We remain calm and all things will work out. Always keep that positivity and always take a deep breath.

I also wanted to state that that's six days. In six days we will be cleared out. The Great Tunkasila created the world in seven days, let's change it in six days.

The interview with the Angry Patriot Radio show was odd and unsettling. The host of the program did not seem to know much about Standing Rock or the movement. Or maybe he did and was trying to infiltrate. The host was abrasive, to say the least. It was hard to tell what the guy was up to.

Chapter Seven

December 1, 2016

CNN covers Standing Rock live on their morning show. Things have ramped up even more with the eviction notice looming. Standing Rock is finally getting major media attention.

He notes that he is feeling thankful.

As a drone pilot, I once had a dream to unite my culture with technology to improve our connection with the world, and now that dream has become a reality.

So they arrested a drone today. SMH #FreeHighHawk The drone went up to cover the veterans' prayer and they managed to hack it and took it. #NoDAPL

These guys are true freedom warriors who are once again being portrayed as criminals. The Morton county tactics are so ridiculously stupid.

He shares Morton County Sheriff's poster. Three water protectors are wanted. It says that they have committed crimes near the Backwater Bridge. These three men helped disarm the DAPL hired security worker who drove into camp and pulled out a gun during the raid of Treaty Camp.

December 2nd

The veterans are coming in from all around the country. Kash Jackson is there from Illinois. He is a straight talker. He has a common sense view of the situation and the world. He is a pleasure to listen to and is seen on many live feeds during the actions with the veterans.

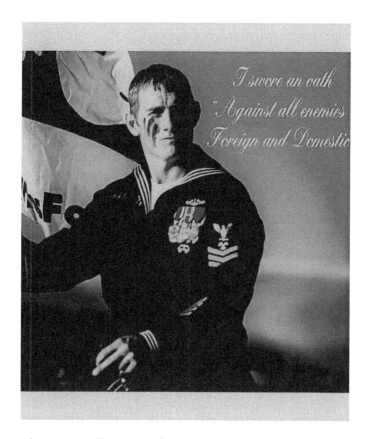

"I swore an oath against all enemies foreign and domestic.'" ~ Kash Jackson

I'm here at camp now. Some vets are going to be making a solidarity walk. CNN is here and I'm going to try to talk to them and see why they are here.

He live feeds from camp on the Indigenous Rising Media page.

He interviews a young man who is a veteran. He tells Dean that he came so he could actually see the situation. And it is bigger than what he thought.

Dean: Now who do we have here? This guy! Are you still walking?

Chris Turley: No, I'm not walking anymore. But I made it.

Dean: You made it! Tell me about your journey.

Chris: It was a good one. It was long. It was an awesome experience. I met a lot of good people along the way.

Dean: As you were walking, did you meet any resistance? Any negative people that zoomed by you, or was it just all positivity while you were walking up?

Chris: It was all positivity. I ran into some law enforcement and they showed me protection. They watched my camp at night while I was sleeping. They knew my mission, my goals, my intent and they watched over me, they protected me.

Dean: Awesome. Seen this guy on the feeds and pictures, and you actually meet this guy in person and he's pretty tall. *(They laugh.)* Coming from me, you got mad respect. You proved that you don't need a vehicle to get out here to camp. You don't need to have money to get here to camp. All you need is determination, spirit and heart. And if you have that, you can walk anywhere in this world.

Chris: That's right. You convince your mind and your body will follow. Remember that.

Later he live feeds on Facebook from a hotel.

Today's been good. I've been doing a lot of research. I also took a little break from flying every day. But as I was taking a break, you never actually take a break. The Angry Patriot Radio guy wanted to know what was going on at camp. I told him he needed to go to camp. A lot of people were saying, don't trust him. I don't. But I listen. You can actually learn stuff from listening to ignorance.

He shows the wanted poster for the three water protectors.

They stated that someone had a knife. If you look at the videos, it was the DAPL guy who had a gun. Clearly these guys are heroes. They are not criminals. They are wanted for protecting the water. For protecting the camp from the guy who ran his truck into camp. These guys are heroes. Show all those hearts. The more you push the hearts, the more they can't delete it.

This is how far they go. Where's the evidence? We have evidence of everything that happened that day. But he went to Morton County and got everything dropped. Why? Because he felt threatened. What if that would have been one of us? A water protector? We would have been charged. We would have gotten shot, straight up.

You can see what's been going on for over 500 years. I want to show you another interesting thing about censoring media. Ernesto got his feed shut down. We are working on putting another page up for him. This is how far Facebook censors things. You can use Facebook for good or bad. Mark, remember you need to use this Facebook technology for the good of mankind.

Anyone who's wanting to purchase Phantom 3's, hit up the DroneGear page. Support DroneGear. They are supporting the revolution at Standing Rock. Indigenous Rising Media 110% support this. Show all the hearts. Get all those mad, angry faces off this page. Look into them.

I've been getting messages, we see you, we know where you're at. This is 110% truth. We confirm everything. This is where I put out the most awesome drone footage.

We got three days left until the revolution blows up. It's not an eviction. It's three days until the world finally sees. It's going to blow up. The people of the world are going to witness something so grand. There are caravans coming to Standing Rock. They aren't scared of the thousand dollar fine and getting things taken away. Go straight through Bismarck. Honk your horn. Don't let the fear tactics keep you away. There are ways to get here. Come straight through Bismarck.

Drone2bwild is going to go back in the sky. I'm going to fly over and see what's going on at the platform at the drill sites. The eastern site is where the drill is going down. That's my goal of the day. Thank you for all your support and messages. Thank you for everything from the bottom of my heart. When I came into this game, I just wanted to fly the drone. The vision I had was to bring in and unify a lot of drone pilots to use the good of these drones to promote and to help save and to fight and to connect our hearts back to the earth.

It feels good because it came through. There's so many drones, when one goes down, we give thanks for those drones. That's how much I believe in what I do. Where would we be without drones? I like to promote that right there. *(He points to the water protector tattoo on his neck.)* You have to gain this tat. There's a few people who like to ask, why did the drone guy get one? I was here from day one. I have been down front on the frontlines, not all the time, but I have been down there. People say all I do is sit and look at a screen. I watch all of you guys. I protect all of you guys on the frontlines. I protect the tipis, the buffalo. The vision I have with the drone is higher than anyone can realize. I'm just a connection, a channel. But the drones are bigger than that. And all the drone pilots.

This is a revolution. Laws and constitutions and limitations, no one has control of the sky. We shouldn't be told what to do. As long as we're doing it from the goodness of our hearts, we can do anything here. Don't let this government, this constitution, boss you around, control you, bully you. That's just them trying to follow the system they think keeps them safe. That's just them protecting their million dollar houses and all that money that's gonna make them feel happy.

The system is only made for a person to be safe in one lifetime. They forget that life goes on. Seven generations. You have to think about your children and their children and their children after that. I'm fighting this for my children. And your children and their children. I'm doing it for the heart of Mother. We are connected. Realize it, understand it, accept it. Don't be afraid of it. When you feel that, it feels good. It feels better than anything you've ever felt in your life. That's the message I want to get out in the world. I'm going to go to camp. Going to be doing some live feeds. Can't use music, there's a copyright issue. That's why I was banned for a day. I have to be careful using the music. Support the movement. I love all you guys.

Share it up water protectors and support this man. I got an exclusive with a Bismarck taxi driver.

Dean: I heard you can't take anybody down there (to camp) anymore.

Driver: No we're not taking anyone down. They are dropping out of airplanes and getting enterprise rental cars. Also I picked up some guys, I don't know who they were, but they were military police. Some got into vans with Chicago license plates. Illinois license plates.

Dean: Do you think they were up to something?

Driver: They were military. I think they were going down to the protest.

Dean: When did they tell you to stop doing that?

Driver: Almost immediately after it started.

Dean: Do you know how much money can be made, just taking those people down there? You go down highway 6, right?

Driver: Yeah, we go down highway 6. But if we do it, for political reasons, it looks like we're supporting the protest. Half the people in this town just want this to go away. They're not even looking at this crap, toxic oil that they want to go under that river. I don't trust these oil guys, you know?

Dean: I know.

Driver: I've never seen such an abuse of power in my life. Every cop in the nation coming down here and shooting people. A girl got shot in the head. People got shot with rubber bullets. Were you down there for that crap?

Dean: Yeah.

Driver: Really?!

Dean: Pretty intense, pretty crazy.

Driver: It's just awful. That's just sad. It's terrible.

Dean: You're a resident of Bismarck?

Driver: My whole life.

Dean: Do you feel like the tension is up around town?

Driver: Oh yeah. They just want this protest to go away. They're like, just put the pipe in. They're running everybody out. They've turned it into red man against white man. A bunch of crazy liberals, good for nothings, causing trouble, that's what they think. My friends don't like my stance on it. My stance is that I don't want a pipeline. It's all crap. These people, in my opinion, who are doing this, we should kiss your ass to keep this pipe out. Canada won't even refine this crap that they want to pump under our river. They say it's never gonna leak. It's already leaked. You can't even drink the water.

Dean: Do you think they would still be mad about it if it was going through Bismarck?

Driver: Oh yeah. Yeah. Give me a break. We all know why, they don't have the money to sue. We got all these people up here, we'll sue! Somebody gets sick or something like that, it's in Chicago. It's in the black areas, it's in the red areas.

Dean: Of course, it's the lower levels of society.

Driver: Absolutely. They can't sue. They don't have the money to sue.

Dean: Have you been down there to camp?

Driver: I went through. I took Amy from Democracy Now. I took her guy to the casino so he could bail Amy out of jail.

Dean stops the video and says: Alright guys. This is a way, way early morning exclusive. Before we continue on with this wonderful man's opinions and where he stands with this fight, from now on we're going to share this video a million times and we're all going to push hearts because this man came out of the shadows. He stands against the pipeline. He supports what we are doing. His son does, his family does and a few of his community members. We all need to protect this guy, support him and show him all the love and solidarity, because what he has to say next is extremely truthful. Let's share this feed. *He starts the video again.*

Driver: Were you down there when Amy got arrested?

Dean: I've been down there since day one. So you stand with Standing Rock?

Driver: Yes Sir. Absolutely. Absolutely. I hope nobody gets hurt. You guys are doing the right thing. You can't flash a gun, you can't flash a knife, they will shoot you. You give them a reason to open up, these cops will shoot you.

Dean: Yeah, did you read about how the DAPL security almost got to camp, had a gun and was pointing it around? The protectors that took care of that are now wanted for that.

Driver: You get one hairball, I can understand somebody saying, aw, you pig and throwing snowballs and rocks or whatever, but one knucklehead comes down and he flashes a gun or pulls a gun out. Ohhhh. *(He puts his hands on his head.)*

Dean: Crazy the way the system works these days, huh?

Driver: All they have to do is to get a picture of somebody. And if somebody gets shot, they'll plant a gun on somebody. This is corrupt crap. These cops are corrupt. They'll kill you and blame it on you in a heartbeat. They're all cops and they didn't mean to kill you, but that's what they're paid to do.

Dean: Did you know on Thanksgiving Day, we were praying for the sacred sites around Turtle Island...they were literally on top of the hill having Thanksgiving dinner - Six feet below that, our ancestors are buried there.

Driver: I don't know nothing. All I'm picking up is bits and pieces.

Dean: It's crazy bro. Follow the pages.

Driver: Stay standing out there.

The video shuts off.

Dean: He came out of the shadows and contacted us. His son did. I'm looking forward to connecting with him tomorrow and apologizing in all respect. A true and honest man who knows how to tell the truth the way it is.

Energy Transfer Partners snaked its way to the inhabitants of this community. They manipulated citizens and law enforcement with a dark insidious shadow over the good values of this town. But one night he said it all.

Don't hate him, respect him. Show him all the love. As I watch the comments go up, I can still see a little hate. To all the people putting out that hate, you're wasting your time. You could be doing better things with your time. They cannot type all day. They obviously don't have anything to do.

He's a hard worker. He's a true American citizen. Everybody that sees him around town, shake his hand. He's going to need all of our love, support and protection. Let's make sure this guy is going to be okay.

Anger is a waste of time. Anger is a waste of energy. All the troll's hate is powerless. Love is unity. Strength is power. It's time for Bismarck and Mandan people to step out of the shadows. Don't be scared. There are good people in this world that love and care about you. It's time to stop the racism and the hate. Come down to Standing Rock. We will pray for you.

Just like we come to Bismarck to support the businesses there. We shouldn't boycott ACE Hardware, they just don't understand. Let's all make them understand. Make the people of your own community understand. It's time this whole region could learn a lot from one another. I say we don't boycott because it only goes down to their level. We support instead. The tribe brings millions and millions for that community there. If we work together, we can prosper together.

It's time to set good examples for our children. Corporate greed must stop. Money is only an illusion. If you laugh at it, you don't understand. You cannot take money to the spiritual world. You cannot take materialistic things to the next world. This is deeper than anything. This pipeline, it's beyond the pipeline. It's about saving the earth. Because our children's children's children will not have a place to live. The planet will go black. There will be no more light. *(He makes the screen go quiet and black.)*

What part of the story you don't know yet? The connection to Mother Earth? Or the violation of your rights as a human being? If you do not know the full story of what's going on and you are just waking up in Bismarck or Mandan, look up pages. Indigenous Media Rising, Drone2bwild. Put up links for good media sources.

People of Bismarck and Mandan, it's time to write a letter to law enforcement. We've all had enough of them. They're only making this area look disgraceful. Take out the hate. When all those law enforcements go to your church, tell them. When you see them in your town, tell them. It's finally done. Put down your badges. And your batons. Throw down your egos. The last statement they said is that they come to the camp in those uniforms, it's war. It is not war, it's just fear.

We've been holding onto this fight for so long. It's time to change. The screen is black because there's still negativity in these comments. When it starts showing a lot, a lot of hearts, then the light will come back on again. See! Light is on again.

I thought I'd just give you an entertaining live feed. A post Facebook tried to sneak off and hide. The power of social media. Yesterday was a victory for all people who stand up for water. Obama, in his last remaining days as President of the United States, he steps up. He finally steps up. So he denies the easement. But it's time for all of us to come together. Even Bismarck and Mandan.

Tell Morton County it's time to put down that barricade. I know you miss the casino and all those fishing routes. It's time for Bismarck and Mandan to stand up for what's right. Go up to the barricade and tell all those officers what's right. We probably can't live without money, but we can use it in a good way. Stop hating each other. That Highway 1806 is a pathway between two cultures. Continue to pray. But Bismarck and Mandan, it's time to stop DAPL from embarrassing and making you look bad. It's time to tell your fellow officers to put the guns down, take off the riot gear. Tell them to come home. It's almost Christmas time.

It's time for both sides to stop hating. Remember love and unity. BisMan, it's time to make a page for all the people who support the water. You could have messages for your community. Time to tell Morton County to take down their hateful Facebook pages. Yes, we are all family. We all want to say the truth, but when it's time to say the truth, we are scared to say the truth. How do we do that? We need to stop manipulating the truth too.

You can clearly see that we have drone footage of your officers being violent with water protectors. Tell Morton County to stop lying. It really is time to stop all of this. I know everyone's sick and tired of it. It is not hard for the leopard to change its spots. It's time to open everyone's eyes. Plain and simple. Continue to have that hate in your heart, we're not going to change the world. We're going to be stuck to that illusion of a system. Aren't you guys tired of the system? In my opinion, it stresses out the soul. Next we're going to talk about how they are illegally using drone weapons.

December 4ᵗʰ

Free gloves for all the kids who love to sled down Media Hill. Stay warm out there water protector children. Our hand print is the symbol of our media, let's keep 'em warm.

He is on Ernesto Burbank's live feed on Media Hill.

There's news today about construction being stopped, but I don't buy it. Look at the rows and rows of cars. People are coming in. That's amazing. That's the power of the people.

He live feeds from Media Hill. There are people everywhere. It is very crowded.

We are live here on top of Media Hill. We'll take the drone up in a little bit, but this camp is filled. This is the camp coming in from the south. Over twenty thousand strong. We even got the winter camp on top of the hill. Not to mention there's still a line of cars. There's more caravans coming. This has been going on for the last couple of days.

We are prepared to stay here and protect our mother, our land. And we've got all of our brothers and sisters of all colors here to stand with us for the land and for human rights. We got media over here. Now all the major media people are here. It took what the police have been doing to all of us, but we are glad they are here. Remember media, Indigenous people have been telling this story the way it should be told, so have respect for that.

For the drone updates, I did a video and called out the drone guns. I told them to bring it and it got cut off. I don't know why. It was just a statement. They're probably crying around again. But we're gonna take the drone up for safety reasons. I'm not going to live feed it. But you'll see it eventually. Just stay tuned and share the Facebook pages.

I'm going to be taking the Phantom 4 up that the police shot up. It still flies. It takes a lot to shoot these things down. But let me say this, they started with rubber bullets. Everybody saw those videos, right? They couldn't shoot the drones. So they stepped up to shotgun rounds. They shot the drone, but they did not take it down. Now they stepped up to using anti-drone weaponry. Apparently they are not supposed to be using it, but that technology does exist. So of course they are going to use it.

These guys are scums of the earth, way up there on the top of that hill. They're using law and rules to overrule us, to do what they can. And the FAA, I believe there's still a ban, a no fly zone. But there is a helicopter flying around here. And guess what guys, we're going to play a game here. Guess the color of that helicopter. Yes, of course the skies are only open for the military and DAPL security. Yes, yellow, yellow. No blue. Just yellow. The one that's been flying here every day. Apparently the sky belongs to them. Drone2bwild is still going to fly. The FAA is going to let us, if we do the paperwork, but we don't got time for paperwork. This is Indigenous airspace and we shouldn't have to sign a paper to fly this sky that's meant for free. This is our land, this is our earth and this is our sky. And we have that total freedom of flying wherever we want to.

But remember we always do it with safety. We don't fly over and try to attack those guys. We attack them with visuals. That's why they're attacking the drone pilots. If everyone saw that video by AJ+, I'm going to say it again, that was a very awesome and beautiful video about what we do here, about us drone pilots and how the drones couldn't be stopped. They flew where they wanted, when they wanted, even at night. Documenting everything as it all occurs. Now they are trying to put a stop to the drones by using drone weaponry. Oh there's a drone right there.

The sky is so blue. There is a drone flying overhead. There are so many people everywhere.

Drones still roam and fly free. Let me show you something. *(He shows the screen of a tablet.)* Anti drone gun looks like something Batman would use. They could be hiding out in the ravines and we wouldn't even see them. So how can we fly and document with this kind of equipment out there? We're just going to have to step up, new tactics. What we've done and what you guys saw on the AJ+ video, we're going to have to step it up more than that.

And that's what we're going to do today. We're going to push drone technology way past anything we've ever done before in this whole world. Because that's what drone pilots do. Stay supportive. Everyone pray for us. There's a drone. A digital bird. You cannot stop the power of the drone. Beautiful. Here's the drone I'm going to fly. Let's get a close examination of what they did.

They couldn't shoot it with one rubber bullet, so they used shotgun pellets. *(He shows where the pellets hit the drone.)* But they couldn't knock it out of the sky. These propellers are moving so fast. I put new ones on, but the old ones were shot up. This is what you call a Phantom 4. $1200. But we sacrifice. $1200 can be shot down just like that. But with the support of the world in what we do, ten more drones get resurrected guys.

Here's another thing that happened. I'm flying this with no lens on it. There's no cover. They shot through there. The power of this drone, look, it's still flying. I will take it up later. I'm still tempted to do a live feed on my Drone2bwild page.

Any other drone pilots out there, come and fly the sky with us. We need all the help we can get. I know those drones cost a lot of money. I have sponsors and I know you guys haven't seen it yet, but I have a DJI Inspire pro 1. That's like the thunderbird of drones. Today I got a zoom lens in. So I can fly way up high and look close at the ground without getting close. So that's a good thing. I believe what they have doesn't scare me. I'm not trying to sound like I'm unstoppable, but I gotta believe it like that and keep that determination in my heart and in what I do. I'm going to keep flying high. I'll still be flying close. I'll just have to change up tactics. *(The live feed shuts down for a minute.)* Of course the signal is jamming again. They are going to jam it.

He reads the comments. Then he talks to William Hawk for a few minutes. William says he is there to meet every single veteran who comes to Standing Rock. He comments on how cold it is.

This one here is my last one, besides the Inspire. The last birds. There are people bringing more drones and I'll be here, raising my drone in the sky. I'm spending some time with it because when I take it up, I hope it comes back. We've sacrificed a lot of drones. I believe Myron has sacrificed a lot of drones as well. Doing what we do. And that's why we respect each other. We should respect each other in all ways. Always remember that. Who wants me to go out into the crowd and get a couple of people's perspectives?

He talks to a man who has helped to make and bring around 500 mirror shields to Standing Rock. He talks to Dean about filming drone footage of the mirrors turned up to the sky – so they look like a river. "It is not a direct action," the man explains. "It's just inside of camp. Just to unify camp and have some fun today."

From a drone perspective, I can't help it. I'm going to go live with that. I think it's gonna be beautiful. I can already see it in my mind. Starting up high, swooping down low, doing some side things. I got this.

He interacts with several people on the hill. A young woman tells him she just flew in and security at the airport swabbed her hands for explosives. And she was not allowed to rent a car.

I'm going to walk around the hill here and get a couple of interviews. We got a snowman standing in solidarity too.

He shows a sign that says: Standing Rock Awakens the World.

He sees a man he calls Ben. He tells him to sing the drone song. Ben sings, "Drone to be wild...."

Dean: What do you have to say about all the trolls that are on this live feed now?

Ben: I love you trolls. Please continue to troll because you make our jobs easier.

Dean: You're just wasting your time, sitting there on the computer. It's a waste of time. You could be out there doing something productive instead of spreading hate on social media. For all the water protectors, ignore the bad comments. It's a waste of time. Forgive them and don't care about what they say.

He walks around and meets more people. There's a woman from Cannonball. Someone gives him an orange. He shows children sledding down the hill. They are laughing and having fun.

We have all the kids. With all this tension going on, in the midst of all of this, we have children, beautiful children. Having fun and enjoying life. This is what we are fighting for. Children here are playing, having fun and enjoying themselves.

I better just get the drone up. I can't help it. I'm going to get the drone up and go live on Drone2bwild. We even have a dog over here. See all that? All these protectors, twenty thousand plus. Note to all media people trying to get a pass, the line is long here.

He walks over to a guy who has a huge, professional looking camera.

Dean: Who are you shooting for?

Camera man: Channel 4, England.

Dean: Tell the story with heart bro.

Camera man: It's not up to me to tell the story. Another guy is doing that. I'm just getting pictures.

Dean: Tell him you insist on telling it with heart.

Camera man: I will tell him. I will insist.

He finds Tonia Jo Hall and asks her to tell a joke. She says, "Are you a vet? Then why are you wearing all that cammo?"

Dean: She got me *(he laughs)* on my own feed. Everybody stay tuned to the drone page. I'll be going up.

He live feeds from camp again. He is in a tent. He is with Rhianna Lakin, a drone pilot.

"This is Rhianna," he says, pulling her up off her chair. "She's been very helpful and we've known each other about a month now. She came up to me, I had no drone left, and she came and she saved me from being grounded. She offered her Phantom 4. And I used it. She's a really great assistant. Wonderful from the heart. Tragically, the drone that was feeding from right inside the pad. That was her drone. Sorry."

He asks her how she felt about losing her drone. She says,

"How do I feel about it? I feel that was a good ending to that story for the drone."

He gives her a drone to replace her lost one.

Drone Nation protects Oceti Sakowin Camp

He live feeds from the Drone2bwild page.

The Phantom 4 can't fly, so we've got a secret weapon. The Inspire Pro 1. Alex, if you're watching, Rhianna brought in the zoom lens too. The original Phantom 4 can't fly. Stay tuned. I'm going to fly.

He is soon flying live on Facebook. He flies the drone over camp. There is a lot of snow and a lot of people. He shows the drone screen on his life feed.

DJI Inspire Pro 1 flying above the lit up Oceti Sakowin Camp! Literally traffic backup. The power of the spirit and prayers have been answered tonight! The world will sleep in good dreams and inspirations, for tomorrow we will be ready to finish off the head of the snake and evil in the world.

Look at that. It's literally a city. This is Oceti Sakowin Camp at night. A city. A breathing, living city.

There is a long, long, long line of cars coming in to camp. It is nighttime and the car lights twist and turn way down the road. It is a remarkable sight. Chris Turley is with him. Rhianna is also with him and starts talking.

Rhianna: We're walking. While he's looking at drone settings, I'll give you a look at camp at night. There's the dome. Lots of people coming in. This camp is the tenth biggest city in North Dakota. I hijacked Dean's phone. I'm not as good as he is at spitting out the poetry and emotion. I'm going to walk around and pretend like I'm him for a minute. It's like a city here! People are piling in here. We'll give you an eye in the sky of what the road looks like.

Before I turn the camera around, let me say that I've been in the drone industry for four or five years and I've never met another drone pilot that's as courageous as he is. Send him some hearts right now.

The drone comes up close.

Rhianna: Here he goes with the hand catch. I'm telling you, he's the most fearless drone pilot I've ever met. That was a beautiful hand catch right there.

Dean: I'm not going to send this drone up again because it's too cold.

Rhianna shows the long, long line of cars coming into camp.

Dean: Who knows what's to come, but for now, everyone's celebrating. It is what it is. The drones need some rest. It's been cold out here. Nobody's leaving, those are people coming. They'll find someplace to stay. Coming in for victory. I can hear the music starting. I can hear the drums, the singing. Tomorrow there's more activities.

Over 20,000+ water protectors, veterans and people from all walks of life are pouring in from every direction. What a sight to see and feel. Also every veteran from all branches has come to stand for the country they have fought for. This is not a movement, but a revolution of change against oil corporations who filter our communities and leaders with greed and corruption!!!

If you went to the Drone2bwild page, that's the second time I've flown the Inspire. I've been flying a lot of Phantoms. I fly with ease and I'm really confident in my flight. But when I took that up, it's different. It's a new kind of drone. A top of the line drone. I felt like I was back at my first flight with the Phantom. That was contributed by my sponsor, DroneGear, Alex. I get 110% support from them and not only them, I get support from other sponsors too. I get support from every one of you that follows the drone page.

Drone2bwild is on live radio to spread the truth from the good to the bad.

He is on Keeper's Mind Pool Radio Network that day. One of the hosts says that he has been having problems with phones and technology all day. He is on the way to Standing Rock.

A female host comments that there was some good news that day, the last easement was denied by President Obama. Dean calls in.

Dean: I am filled with love, solidarity, happiness, fortitude. For today's events. It was a crucial day, a day of everything. A day of hope, a day of remembering, a day of veterans. I thought there was an action going on, but there wasn't an action going on. Our voices got out there to the world and what I saw was people coming here. They are coming in. We took the drone up to the sky and saw a city of people. It's a small victory to an enduring battle. This is only the beginning. They denied the easement. They cannot drill under the river. Now they have to go in with a full environmental statement. People who are at one with the earth and the sky and science will study this. Study the wildlife. It's basically devastating if it goes under the river. This is what we'll have to push to win the war. Between Fargo and Bismarck there's a lot of traffic and cops are stopping people. They are trying to stop traffic from coming in.

Full environmental statement. We need to push this and really follow them and find everyone who is involved and make them do their jobs right. They had people come in and look at the ground and they said, oh there's nothing here. But they are stepping on sacred sites. Camp is celebrating. There are people everywhere. I had to tell people to create a circle to let the drone take off.

On a live feed, he shares AJ+ video about the drone operators of Standing Rock and how the drones were being shot at.

That is one of the most powerful drone feeds today. Over 2.2 million views. We're breaking the rules to protect the land. These people right here have no regard for any human life. *(He shows a photo of a cop who is shooting at a drone.)* They misuse power. Because they have weapons on their side they think they have power. They think they are God. But they're not. They're human souls. They're simple human beings that have been blinded by illusions and consumed by all the greed. And this is the system playing out for them. That's why they're pointing weapons at the drones like this guy here. That's why they have a military vehicle right here.

If you saw the footage from this video, you saw how they use the water cannons. And Morton County gets on to make a statement and back themselves up that they use it for a crowd operation tactic. You guys saw that. There was no crowd there. There were basically just protectors there all by themselves out in the open. And they were clearly just spraying them.

He shows a photo that shows that there was no crowd. Water is being sprayed on a single water protector who is standing all alone.

Now FAA what is your take on this? You guys have been hiding in the dark. You should step forward and make a statement about the drones here at Standing Rock, limiting them in the sky. You really want to talk about flight regulations and all of that? You need to look at the Morton County helicopters. The airplanes, flying at night, no lights on. You should get them for stalking. And the helicopters too. Using them for a weapon. Flying dangerously low over the horse nation. All they were doing was riding and galloping free on the land like their ancestors. And you gonna fly at them and disturb the peace like that? We know the truth because we experienced it that day. That Thursday.

You guys can lie all you want, Morton County. You're lying straight through your teeth and it's all going to catch up to you. Because all of these people tuned into this live feed, they are going to spread it out and spread it out, and spread it out. And this is the truth that is coming out. It's a replay of the truth. We didn't need the major news networks to put this out there. We put this out there ourselves. Thanks to AJ+, Drone2bwild, Myron Dewey, he's dedicated to this cause. This was one good video here. Powerful video. Powerful drones.

He goes back over photos from AJ+ video.

Each and every one of these officers here. The spirits will eventually catch up to them. And they will either be cursed, or we don't know what's going to happen. These officers, we're all worried about them.

And there's the first drone footage of the first week of actions. Our own tribal chairman, Dave Archambault, was arrested for going beyond the lines to protect from the desecration of burial grounds. And for trying to protect his ancestors in the ground, they arrested him. Along with Dana Yellowfat, council. You can see clearly that they come to this land just to control us. To bully us because we are Indigenous people. That's why they put this here.

Like the taxi guy of Bismarck said, they come down this way because they have more money than this tribe will ever have. I'm going out of my way to document things in a different way because sometimes it's hard to document the truth. You got to do things you don't want to do and go beyond the privacy. You gotta bend the rules a little to actually capture the truth. The truth is, we are Indigenous media capturing the desecration of our sacred sites. And also using the drone to capture the visuals of our people, of our water protectors, in a way so unique that it's changing drone footage to this day.

We've got a couple more days before the big day. Remember, this isn't an eviction, it's the start of a revolution. Morton County, DAPL and that helicopter and plane that flies all over the place, they'll know what we are talking about. They're trying to stop all water protectors from coming. I got a call from some friends in California that today they tried to buy tickets to get here to Standing Rock. Once they mentioned Bismarck,

North Dakota, the airport officials said, No. There's no tickets available. So you can say clearly that they are trying to shut us down, trying to shut us out. But people are coming in caravans.

December 5th

Indigenous Rising Media reports that around three thousand veterans prayed at the barricade on Highway 1806. They are asking Dakota Access to stop the pipeline. They are also serving as human shields to protect the unarmed water protectors from law enforcement.

Later that evening, in a Forgiveness Ceremony, veterans kneel in front of Indigenous elders and ask for their forgiveness for how they have been treated by the United States military. Throughout time and now.

There are reports all over Facebook that the Army Corps of Engineers have denied the final permit to drill under the water. Videos and live feeds of water protectors celebrating come out. Some are cautious and do not really believe it.

Dean is on his way to Bismarck.

Awesome I got a room. Double queen with rewards. Check in time at 4.

All these hotels have been really nice. I'm on a mission to interview someone else. We got something in the works. Digital Smoke Signals and Drone2bwild are teaming up again. We have to. They are using anti drone weapons. We're going to have to send drones to record the drones that they are shooting down. Of course, you never trust the feds. We all knew that.

It's probably going to be like this all day. Are they drilling in this weather? Nobody wants to be outside today. Are they invading camp? No, it would be all over the live feeds. Here comes North Dakota winter. This winter gets a lot worse than this guys. Twenty thousand plus at camp and they are still coming in. Cars all night. Snow turns into water and water is life.

When you want to report the truth about some things, how can we get the truth out? Will they really tell the whole truth? When they aren't aware of a larger audience, they will tell the truth. I'm going to find the taxi guy and apologize to him. And maybe we'll have another good conversation.

He looks outside at the snow.

This snow is crazy. I think this is actually a blizzard warning. Mother Nature is on our side. You think DAPL security is still out there protecting? Maybe just a few. Polish TV spoke very good about us. That's cool. All over the world. I literally have the world following. I try to get back to every message. This is a blessing. The ice is going to freeze and it's going to be hard for them to drill. You guys have to learn how to relax.

Dutch TV said we all had a grand victory, but the battle isn't over yet. CNN is a joke. They were trying to find me for a couple of days. They gave me their phone number. Maybe I should call them. But I want to interview them. It's not as much fun over the phone.

Tis the season to be droning. No, we can't drone in this weather. What happened yesterday was a victory. There were fireworks, drones, children playing. I want to get the Mavick, it's not out yet. Now they have the drone guns, so it's not necessarily stealing, they just take them out of the sky. Of course DAPL is going to pay their fine. They have the money to do it. They are going to do whatever it takes to get that oil.

The Bakken oil field is like the Black Hills. And what happened, settlers found some gold and the Black Hills were no longer ours. They got the gold out. Who likes gold anyway? Diamonds too. Just remember, diamonds, children get killed digging up diamonds. Think twice about where it comes from.

Iam Drezus comes in and gives love to Dean. His new video has footage from Drone2bwild in it. They talk about a veteran who was kicked out of the Ramada Inn. Dean says that he looked into it, but the guy did not want help.

Bismarck, North Dakota

I'm being targeted people, by a black van!!!

Proof guys that the trolls are out there patrolling!! Just give 'em an hour!!!

Trolls are real. You stay on live feed in a place where you know where they are for an hour and BOOM, they are in your face. That's proof right there.

We're gonna have a little live feed press conference here. Two minutes. What are you guys' thoughts? When the trolls just come out of nowhere. *(He's in front of ACE hardware store.)* Alright ready, let's do this. I just want to get something for the camp though. You afraid of the power of the media? I'm just going to do this professionally. I'm going to go in there and buy some propane.

He goes in and first looks at snow shovels. He asks a guy about propane tanks and he says they have them up front. $34 he thinks. He shows Dean where they are. $24.99.

Dean: When it's filled up, is it safe to travel with it? Do you have bungie cords?

The guy says they have bungie cords for sale. He tells Dean that the tank can't be clanging around in the vehicle. He asks if Dean wants him to grab one and fill it.

Dean: Yes. Thank you Sir.

The guy gets a tank and goes to fill it up. Dean puts his camera in his pocket. Someone checks him out. He is told that it will be ready outside. He walks outside.

Dean: Why do I feel like everybody's watching me? We've all got to be warm. It's cold out here. Just trying to stay warm.

He talks to the guy as he fills the tank. He thanks him and puts the tank in the car with a seat belt.

Dean: You feel the tension. All we want to do is keep warm. That propane there, it's coming to camp tomorrow. I'll give it to somebody at camp because it's all about giving. You really feel the tension. The mall is the worst place. That hardware store. The guy was okay, but the women were looking. This is all a lesson learned guys. Study it, read it and time it and watch the comments. There it is guys. Trolling 101. This is the last Facebook live that's going to come out for a while. Cause they're all over the place.

But in a little while another live feed comes out. A man approaches him in the mall. The guy confronts him in a nasty and angry way. He tries to put his camera up in Dean's face as he live feeds.

"Tell us what's going on at camp. Why aren't you staying there at camp? Why are you at a hotel? I thought you were a protector. But you're staying at a hotel while everybody else is at camp in tipis. People can't even go to a restaurant and eat without you asking them questions, I'm just doing the same to you," says the man, obviously irritated.

Dean calmly tries to walk away - but the angry man follows him. Dean just keeps walking and the man finally goes his own way. Dean walks out of the mall.

He says, "They are coming out of everywhere!"

And soon another live feed comes from the Ramada Inn in Bismarck. Dean is with a friend who is driving. He shows a man in a mask walk up to the car.

Masked man: Get your protesting asses back home!

Driver: Dude, I got nothing to do with this.

Masked man: Get your protesting asses back home!

Dean: Let's just go. Just go.

Masked man: That's right, go! *(He looks into the window of the car.)* Turn your phone on, go ahead!

Dean: Just go! Go!

Masked man: All you protesters GO HOME! Us North Dakota people are going to f* you up!

Dean: Go! Go!

Masked man: Every f*ing one of you!

Dean: Just go!

Masked man: Every f*ing one of you!

Driver: I can't go, they've got us blocked in here.

Another guy walks up on Dean's side of the car and puts his hands in his pockets. He has a mask on too.

Dean: We're going to go!

Masked man: We know who you are! We follow you too! We f* your wives at home! We hope you like it!

Dean: Damn guys.

Masked man: Keep it up! We're going to f* you up too! You threaten our people!

The guy on Dean's side of the car pulls a camera out of his pocket. It looks like he's going for a gun. Dean ducks down.

Dean: Call the police! Everybody call the police at Ramada Inn!

Masked man: I'll f* you up!

Dean: How are we gonna go home with you guys blocking us?

Masked man: You leavin?

Dean: Yeah!

Masked man: Don't come back! I don't want to warn you again.

The masked man just keeps screaming. The guy on Dean's side of the car is holding up a phone - looks like he's taking a video or live streaming.

Dean: We're going. We're going!

A man walks out of the hotel and begins to take a video of what is happening.

Dean: Just go!

Driver: I can't. They've blocked us in.

Dean: Hey guys, this is serious! This is no joke. They blocked us in!

The masked man starts to walk over to his own vehicle. It is parked right in front of them so they cannot get out. There is also a truck behind them. The truck belongs to the other masked man.

Dean: You guys take good pics of all of this!

The camera man who walked out of the hotel is still taking video. The masked man throws snow at the camera man. The masked man runs around the vehicle chasing the camera man. The masked man finally gets in his vehicle and finally moves out of the way. The man who was standing on Dean's side of the car goes back to his truck and gets in. Dean ducks down again as the truck door shuts.

The masked man speeds off. Dean's driver moves the vehicle forward. The camera man walks up to them. He's still holding up his phone.

Camera man: I got both their license plates.

Dean: Cool, cool, cool, cool. There it is guys. He was following us for about five to ten turns. Not safe here.

The camera man shows him the video. It is a view of outside of the car as he walked out of the hotel. The masked man is yelling at the camera man and pointing his finger. The masked man tries to grab his phone.

Camera man: Why would you do that?

Masked man: Let me see that phone!

The masked man starts chasing the camera man around the car.

Camera man: What are you going to do?

Masked man: Come on MF*er!

Camera man: I'm a guest at this hotel, dude.

Masked man: All of you! Every f*ing one of you! Let's roll!

The masked man starts to walk away. The camera man follows him and then the masked man charges at him.

Masked man: Wanna get f*ed up?

Camera man: I've already called the police, dude.

The masked man gets in his vehicle and speeds away.

Camera man: Are you going to follow them? Hey, we know you! What's up?

Another man comes out of the hotel and asks what's happening.

Camera man: A crime against these guys. And this guy, he's actually a part of it.

He points at the truck that is still blocking them from behind. The man goes over to the truck and tries to stop it. When the truck starts to move, the man puts his hands on the front of it, like he's trying to stop it. But the truck keeps moving and leaves.

Camera man: He just threatened them.

Dean: Okay guys. You can clearly see from what just took place ... it's the way you are, it's the way you dress. We're targeted. Obviously, they don't want us here. But we got it all on live feed. Oh crap it's cold.

A woman walks up to them. The camera man shows Dean his video again and they get a picture of the license plate. Dean zooms in on a good shot of the plate and the woman reads off the numbers.

Camera man: I got the other one too.

The woman reads off the other license plate number.

Camera man: Both from North Dakota

Woman: There happens to be a sheriff's ball going on inside of this Ramada right now. So there's a lot of sheriffs inside there right now. We can try to talk to somebody and tell them those license plate numbers.

Dean: This is what we got to deal with when we're trying to protect the earth, the sky and what we believe in. Insane, for real. But, you hold your spirit strong, you have a strong heart. Don't let it break you guys.

He shakes hands with the woman and says, thank you. He thanks the camera man too. The feed goes out then comes back.

Camera man: You need to file a police report.

Dean: I'm going to file a police report. We are no longer safe here in Bismarck. Pretty crazy guys, pretty crazy.

Immediately, digital warriors start posting about this and researching who the men who terrorized Dean. Their license plates numbers and screenshots go viral quickly.

Mission complete Shiyé Bidzííl

It is Ernesto Burbank's live feed.

Ernesto: DAPL Santa Hohohoho *(He has on a Santa beard and hat. He laughs that laugh.)* Mission complete, mission complete.

Dean looks out from around the car seat - he's in the back with Chris Turley.

Dean: It was mission save Drone2bwild guy. There's a lot of people who are out there crying and worried. Even my mom and my dad. But Drone2bwild is safe. The events that took place, there's things you gotta do in the media and I took it to the extreme, but they had to be exposed. You saw what they were. It's a terrible thing that they work like this. When they can't stop your media, this is what they do. It does incite fear. For one second there. But at the end of it all, this is what we needed to see. You saw it all. The whole truth. It's all online. Look around at what's going on. Look in the comments and you'll see who the trolls are. The official trolls. The lawless trolls.

Everybody that follows my page, I want you to start policing in unity. Look into the trolls that are on my page. Study them. Because the Drone2bwild guy is too busy flying the sky. He's going to go back to flying the sky. He's going to go back home and he needs to stay at home. There's good people in Bismarck, but there's bad people too. In the shadows they lurk. I found that out today. They're real, they're out there. They'll twist things up and as much as we want to take this to justice, it'll never happen. It'll never be solved. Because they're covert in the ways they do. Ain't nothing I can do about it, nothing but pray.

You talk about that one guy, and I'm not going to say his name, because they might come after me again. They want to put fear in you. But my heart was strong.

I'm here and I'm safe and my heart's still beating. Covert ops, walking around in Bismarck, solo. Don't ever do that alone! But that's how much bravery I had. I knew they were lurking all over. I know, I know, I know. I will never do that again.

Chris Turley: You dudes who messed with him, you all lucky you didn't find me. You all lucky you found him instead. You come at me like that and it's going to be a whole different story. Right now, I'm a guy who believes that violence does solve problems.

Dean: I just fly drones man. *(He leans over Chris and hugs him.)*

Chris: We got him, he's safe. He's staying with us tonight.

Ernesto: *(Still NoDAPL Santa - now with big black snow goggles on.)* Don't let them put fear in you. That's what we got each other for. To help.

Dean: This is true. This is the way the world operates. I know you guys told me last night, be careful, but I had to do it.

Ernesto: We gotta raise our boy's spirits a little bit. He got shook a little bit. NoDAPL Santa doesn't encourage any violence. No violence.

Dean: Besides all the fun and jokes, serious guys, I'm okay. My phone is blowing up. I want to say this though. As much corrupt, illegal and terrorizing things they did against me, I just want to say, thank you corporate mercenaries, undercover people, running around in secret.

Between all the laws in this government, in this country, I'm going to take what you guys did and you guys just blew up the drone. People love the drone, it's gone worldwide and I'm gonna use that for the good. Thank you guys, thank you. I'm sorry it was risky and I'm sorry I got a lot of people scared out there. But look at my followers, by the time I got out, the truth was already out there. You gotta watch the live feeds and look at the comments. Thank you followers from Drone2bwild.

December 6th

He's riding in a car. It is snowing very hard.

We are in the midst of probably the biggest blizzard in history. I want to announce Iam Drezus' new music. Black Snake Killa. Going to have this on BandCamp and all the proceeds are going to camp.

Next is a live video of Myron and Dean.

Dean: So there are fear tactics going on. There's a lot of bullying going on after the decision by the Army Corps. Creating fake accounts.

Myron: Agitators that are going online. Creating fear.

Dean: They're trying to control the media and Myron's always getting cut off.

Myron: We were able to find them making fake accounts. Don't argue with them. These people have lost their spirit. Don't get caught up with the fear tactics. Block 'em. Move on. Do not engage. Do not try to educate them. Snow is about three to four feet. Someplaces about twelve feet.

Dean: We are all going to have to start stopping those proDAPL accounts. There's still those negative faces that come across here. Start blocking them. Back the blue, those are fake accounts put up by Morton County law enforcement. They are only set up to spy. There's also fake water protector accounts. They are trying to make us look bad. Those guys are law enforcement, they are everywhere.

Dave Archambault saying go home, he's just concerned in a way. We have to start sustaining ourselves. The casino is being consumed by all the water protectors. We all made the call, but we all gotta realize that when there's this many people it eats up the resources. We have to come out here and depend on ourselves. Come here prepared. Back to Dave Archambault. He wants to let everyone know winter is coming. We do need a break. We've been doing this all year. There's going to be a lot of storms. Take care of your children who are here. If you need to go home and rest, then go. No one is holding you here. You are free to go or you are welcome to stay. It's just a concern because winter is tough here. Winters are strong and extremely cold here.

Here's the next tactic. Block all negative comments, block all negative comments. We almost solved that terrorizing at the motel. But will law enforcement go all the way and prosecute this? I don't know. We need to fight the angry faces with hearts. They are using media tactics.

What I've seen in Bismarck and Mandan, it's a dark shadow. I fear for all my Native friends and family who live there. I grew up going there. We're all the same place, we're all the same region. That DAPL just divided a lot of good people. I saw that for myself.

We all have that hate in our heart, but don't attack with negativity. It's pointless. You are just sharing that same hatred and attitude that they have. Leave them be. Feel free to block them. Look into their pages. We are all our own media here. Even the negative ones. We are filtering out the negative ones. Soon they won't be able to even look into this. That's the power of social media guys.

Yes, I did get help. No one is going to take control of that account. Feel free to investigate all on your own. We're learning about all the negative people. Get all those trolls out of here. Look through this feed. Get them out. There are fake water protector sites as well. Don't buy into any information like that. If there are posts about doing harmful acts or going against council, screenshot that and send it to us. As far as Indigenous media, I'm only recruiting Indigenous. I respect all of you out there.

He is with Angelo Wolf later at Prairie Knights Casino.

Angelo: Me and Dean have some stuff to talk about this evening. Dean just got back in, roads are nuts. Please drive safely. We're here at the Prairie Knights Casino and right now the Casino is being drained of all of the resources. A lot of people are still coming here - I have said this before, when you come here you have to be self-sufficient. You have to be able to take care of your own. This is the point where you cannot rely on camp to provide you with the necessities to live here.

Dean: Always be aware of trolls. Try to take care of them. Look for the trolls. See the negative faces. We're going to block all of you guys. It has to do with government, law enforcement and all the people about the constitution. But remember, the constitution, we have the right, the right to protest and fight for clean water. So when you really want to uphold that constitution to a higher level.

Angelo: Think about being a human being. Think about having clean water. We are trying to take care of everyone.

Dean: First amendment right - freedom of speech. We're going to be reading all of your comments and questions. We are not trapped here. We are gathered here because of the snow and cold. But as soon as this blizzard clears up, we'll be back. Anonymous, you used what happened to me to promote Anonymous. It's time to take off those masks and reveal who you are. If you really do stand with us, take off your masks and do a live feed. I ask you to do that. If not, step away.

(He reads some comments.) There's hateful videos of me? If you could give a link to those, do that. I encourage all of my followers to do all of your own investigative reporting. Look into those fake accounts. They are infiltrating the camps even. This movement is so big that we can't keep up with everybody. I cannot keep up with every comment.

You guys are all my investigative team. All 640 of you right here. Remember, even if it's on your own page, it's coming for mine - you still need to let us know and block them. Block all trolls. And no more negativity. No matter what it's about. That just puts more fuel on the fire and it's not going to win. All we can do is pray. Pray, pray, pray. Cause what I seen up there in Bismarck, a dark shadow just covered the whole city of Mandan and Bismarck. People are scared. Today I tried to get a room and they denied me. I said, why, is it because I have this, because I look like this? *(He points out his bullet proof vest and cammo wear.)* She said no, but basically they denied us because of an image of us. What happened when those two guys attacked and terrorized me, I could relate because that's how they see us. But it's okay, after I got my things out of the room I said, thank you from the bottom of my heart. That's all I said. I just walked away.

I like that #NoTrolls. Start putting that out. We're going to pull ourselves together with all the information you've been providing me... look at that, there's still trolls. No trolls. Hey trolls, you know what you guys did, I called you out, I proved to the world that a troll can find you in an hour if you hang around Bismarck. And he did. You know why he did? Because he was looking for me. That's the power of the followers that I have. And they don't want that. They want to put their messages through too.

I'm back at home, Standing Rock Sioux Tribe. I feel safe. Although the casino is packed with water protectors and other people. And people from Mandan and Bismarck who come here to play and that's all they do. We don't hold nothing against that, we support that, because down here we support nothing but entertainment and fun. We're all human beings.

Angelo: And human beings need water.

Dean: Remember guys, don't antagonize the trolls. Even though I called them out. Keep it to a minimum. Watch what you say because it can be taken out of context. *(People point out trolls on the feed.)*

We're building an arsenal of drones again. They have technology and took them out. We believe there's border patrol here.

Angelo: We have confirmation on that. Border patrol is out here. I think Florida is sending some folks here.

Dean: See that comment, Trolls need water too, dummy. Screenshot that one and everyone block him or her. Every time you see a troll, snapshot and block them. Report them.

Angelo: I don't block trolls. They keep my day going.

They laugh.

Dean: People are taking care of each other. Hunkering down. I want to express that you guys are doing a wonderful job. I really want to thank all of you. You guys do all the hard work. You make my work a lot easier. Because my work is just getting what I see out there. And what I saw out there the last couple of days ago was dumb. I know it was a stupid move, but I had to literally put myself out there as bait. And bring them out and show the world that they're around, they're everywhere. And they come at us because they don't like what we say, they don't like what we're about.

Angelo: We can't let hate win.

Dean: There's so much hate in the world. Stand tall guys. Soon all that hate will go around you. I was this close to breaking it, but I didn't. I used it. What really empowered me the most is all you guys encouraging me with your words, you letters, your messages. *(He points to the screen.)* Look at Thomas R. Trump. We shouldn't point, but look into that Trump guy. *(They laugh.)* Alright guys, basically we did infiltrate a lot of trolls on this page right here. It looks like there's more trolls on this page than on the drone page.

Troll patrol! Troll patrol! Who are trolls? Let's get a definition. Trolls are people who track. Trolls could be anybody. They disguise themselves as water protectors, they are pretty much out there. They label back the blue. They're cops, they're ...

Angelo: We don't have anything against law enforcement.

Dean: We don't.

Angelo: But these are taking it to a whole different level.

Dean: But I assure you there is corruption in the system of North Dakota and cops are a part of it.

Angelo: But there are good people in Morton County.

Dean: There are good people within Morton County and the highway patrol. During those actions, those non direct actions with Jill Stein, when she came, and I had that conversation with the cop - you felt that goodness in his heart - like he kinda knew what was going on was wrong - there are good cops here.

Prolific The Rapper walks over to them. I'm really proud of this guy and I'm glad he's safe. He's always doing important work and keeping people safe.

Angelo: On top of that, one of the police officers on Turtle Island, he sat down and then he walked away from the line. He knew what was happening was wrong. There are good people on the force. We don't hold any hate against anyone. We gotta rise above the hate.

Someone was asking about Sophia. She didn't get her arm amputated, which is good news. Also, Sioux Z, she lost sight in her eye. And this is her fighting for clean water. Somebody wants to jump in. She's actually here. She came down.

Didi Banerji gets in the live feed. She's coughing. Everyone loves that she came down.

Dean: Everybody on the drone page is actually very well connected. You asked how you could help, actually what helps the most is investigative reporting from you guys at home. You guys know more than we do. This is the time when everybody is doing their part right now. You are the minority here trolls. *(He points out more trolls on the live feed.)* Hearts, hearts, hearts, show the love. Indigenous people are about surviving. I'm going to close it out here. Remember, do the research and investigation.

Drone2bwild page shares a message from the Standing Rock Medical Healer team:

Medics, security and veterans have been checking on people at camp and sending vulnerable people to Prairie Knights Casino.

Please share with Oceti Sakowin Camp: There is a large coordinated caravan going to Oceti Sakowin camp with a plow. They will clear the path from the north gate to the dome and straight out to the south gate. They are looking for and asking that all vulnerable people be transported to the Prairie Knights Casino. There will be a second caravan of empty four wheel drive trucks that will transport.

Information has already been gathered and shared about the man who harassed him in the mall and the two men who terrorized him at the hotel. The information came out quickly. His followers researched and found the men in no time.

Sometimes when you're in the face of ignorance and evil, it's best to just walk away.

He puts out another short live feed.

What happened to the drone? What happened to all of the drones? When you can't take down top notch pilots, you have to use drone weapons. We are working on that though. I'm not going to say any more. You'll find out. I want to apologize to Mark Zuckerberg because without all of this I wouldn't be able to talk to all of you. I'm hitting them hard, those pro DAPL guys.

Update on recent PRO DAPL propaganda link!

This is a live feed. He is on the phone with a woman.

Woman: According to North Dakota - they've had law enforcement from nine states here helping. They say that it meant many families went without a loved one for a while. They say that many protesters used scare tactics. They say that it's nasty there, violent nasty. There are peaceful people, but not all. Some protestors would publish the addresses of law enforcement officers.

Dean: It's Bull.

Woman: This is them publishing bad information.

Dean: What happened yesterday, scare tactics? That's what they did. We haven't put up videos. We can use them later on. Law enforcement, there are good and bad. They can't hide it. People know. They want to keep people under control. When people start talking, they want to hold them down. That's what happened to me.

I got on a radio show and they screwed me over. I did it without looking into it. I thought radio, it would get the message out there. It was Angry Patriot Radio. They, I believe, support Trump. When I went off and spoke my heart about what I believe is the right thing to do, that is when they targeted me. That's the power of what we're standing up to. And it's a scary power. But we're brave, we stand.

Look at what happened to me. It was intense. But you gotta stand your ground and do what's right. They were stalking me. I know they were on that page. They were trying to come in with the phone, but what did I do guys? Walked away.

I shouldn't have to explain myself. Because if I do try to explain myself, if I try to tell them the goodness, it's just going to go in one ear and out the other. It's pointless to try to explain to them and to prove you're right because they know you're right. That's why they are stalking you. Anything with the trolls, just publicly post them everywhere. *(He reads comments.)* That's right, don't trust CNN. We don't need major news networks. Because look at this, we only have one phone here and with the power of social media we are all the media right here. Just one person exposing what I did yesterday, I had to show the world that there is a dark entity that's taking over Bismarck. You guys all saw it yesterday. You guys all saw it with your own eyes on that live feed. It's pretty intense and they want to put statements out there that they were threatening our families. What did they say? Things that shouldn't be said. And all the trolls that are lurking on this feed, you remember that. Trolls, you have a heart. Find it.

December 7th

Updates: ND law enforcement?? Or Pro DAPL protestors?? Shiyé Bidzíil believes it's a whole network of systems that force the rule of law and promote fear in the lives of many.

He shows the video of the incident at Ramada Inn.

These guys blocked us from the front and the back. I'm going to play the video and get the comments. They just came out with a link that says we're threatening law enforcement officers' families, but here they are threatening ours. This guy didn't say anything.

He is talking about the man who was standing on his side of the car. He thinks it could be the guy who harassed him in the mall earlier.

I think he followed me from the mall. If you watch their body movements, they are obviously law enforcement, or they are working for law enforcement. During that whole ordeal there was a gathering of law enforcement officers. It took them about fifteen minutes to come after that. As I was sitting in the lobby, there were law enforcement officers that I've seen at Standing Rock. We did see each other, but we didn't say anything.

I believe it's a network of people who are intertwined with rich families from Bismarck. This guy here is pro DAPL.

He shows a picture of the guy from the mall.

He kept following me everywhere. Take a good look. Remember he states that he's here to protest for the constitution. But remember the constitution protects our right to protest. There is a link to that guy's video on YouTube. As he was asking his questions, he was wanting to get something out of me. He wanted to antagonize me. But I gave him his freedom of speech. I let him speak whatever he wanted to speak. I just walked away. That's really all you can do.

He's a social guy, he's always live streaming. If you're a social person all over Facebook, you would easily be looked up by law enforcement officers. Why haven't they found him yet? Because it's all a set up. They are all working together. It's psychological warfare. They like to stalk like that.

They like to pose as water protectors. That's the extremes they are going to so they can infiltrate our camp, our messages. They are a part of that system that wants control and for things to go as easy for themselves to keep all that wealth. They run their everyday lives with the same routine, they like to keep people under control. This guy likes to keep people under control. Just keep looking at him guys. I'm pretty sure the mall has video evidence, but the law enforcement didn't even give any kind of statement. This is all going on report later, but we are going to write it in Indigenous law.

This is Shiyé Bidzííl and you all know how I feel about Anonymous...but I have a real good feeling about this one.

He shares Anonymous' message to Morton County Sheriff's Department. Anonymous tells them they need to arrest the people who harassed Dean or there would be consequences.

He shares Bismarck Police Department's post:

Shiyé Bidzííl will ADDRESS THIS LIVE!!

Let's prepare all the EVIDENCE GUYS. Who's with me as I journey back to write up all the necessary "EYE WITNESS REPORTS" to file charges against these MASKED VIGILANTS who stalked, chased, blocked and terrorized. ((WE ALL SAW THE LIVE FEED)) So we can properly prosecute these criminals to the full extent of their LAWS!

Bismarck Police said they responded to a report of a possible vehicle/pedestrian crash. But when they arrived they found it was an altercation between several people. They were investigating it as a case of reckless endangerment and disorderly conduct. The suspects have been identified and are being investigated.

All I want is my freedom!!!

He starts a live feed. He shows Kash Jackson's photo with an upside down flag. The upside down flag is very misunderstood. In the military it is an official signal of distress. It is not disrespectful. People often flew the flag upside down at camp and it was very appropriate.

Alright guys, this is where my heart's gonna get poured out. And I'm going to tell you why. In this world, before all the rules and the countries and governments and laws, before all the forces of corruption and money and greed, a long time ago when we all used to be free. When we used to experience true freedom, and I still do, there's certain people in this world that want to take us out. They look for us every day. I bet right now they are all around. They don't like when anyone expresses what I was talking about. They don't like those kind of words.

Right now, within this live talk, they are there, watching me. The followers, they take care of me, they make me aware. The guy that was stalking me at the mall. Now what they're trying to do is to put fear in me. You guys know what, I got this. We got to step beyond that system guys. But then again, you don't want to be that stupid.

It's crazy that all of us gotta have fear like that just to live in this day and age and world. But we could make it all go away. Just step away. Go back to doing what we used to do before this movement. Go back to watching tv and working 9 to 5 jobs and continue that every day cycle of living, that stuff that makes us feel comfortable. And then they'll leave us alone.

But that's not me. I'm not about that. I'm about doing something greater in this world. Even if I have to jump through hoops to show these corporations that there are a lot of good people with good hearts and humble hearts and good minds.

Right now I'm in the sky. I'm in the sky. I'm all around. They're always trying to find you. But right now I bet they're right within this feed right here. They pop in and out. Of course we're not quitting now. Yes, share that video. You guys all know what the guy at the mall looks like. Apparently he's after me now. You know why he's after me? Because I have a voice. And I could stand up by him and not say anything and walk away.

Cause he has nothing but ignorance. It's not about being distracted by fear. It's about overcoming fear. I'm high in the sky. Be careful of the guys with the shadowed out pics, like Lonnie. Right there he is. Snap shot him, send him and block him. You guys know what to do. I love you all. Just remember, you got to have a camera behind your back.

I strongly feel the need to print and place at every public location & hotel of Bismarck/Mandan due to the terrorizing of unarmed water protectors this past week. The holidays are coming and we feel the need to feel safe as we begin this new year. With blessings for our earth and water.

He shares a poster.

Wanted: person of interest

For the intentional use of force against unarmed water protectors (It is the sheriff's picture.)

December 8th

Wake up everybody. It's 3am.

He live feeds from the hotel. He is in a stairwell at the casino.

Minds are rested, our times are tested. Falling leaders, up rise all of our spirits, no matter how much we endure, we stand. No matter how much hate and fear goes through our minds. Trolls will never stand. Cause we got you. We got you all locked up. Throw away the key because these trolls are never getting free!!!!

We got a very special day. It's going to be a lock up all trolls. I am going to Bismarck tomorrow. I was told not to go, but why am I trying to hide? I need to press charges and get restraining orders. I was suffering from some fear. It's hard not to let it get ahold of you.

Going to Bismarck tomorrow to Ramada Inn. Going to play it out there. We'll stay safe. We'll have TYT Jordan there. I'm going to tell the story about what I was doing up there all by myself. I wanted to document what was going on. I went to Walmart, ACE hardware, the mall - that's where it all started. I was stalked there.

He did what he did because he wanted to get something out of me, but I didn't let it bother me. I just walked away.

Jordan will be with me. With his camera guy. Probably a couple of good warriors too. We're going to walk through the streets. Maybe the mall too. I want to tell what I was doing with my camera.

All these stories saying we are reckless, we are a threat. I'm going to dress casual. We had on fatigues and stood out.

I was trying to get a room. Lady said no. Asked if she was sure. Another lady said there's a room, but she said no. She looked scared. I thought, that's how I looked at the guys who approached the vehicle. She doesn't have to think like that. So much fear is running around Bismarck.

We need to get control. We don't need to capture what they say. No comments. Just delete them. I'm accumulating all of the trolls.

I don't know how I did it. I don't know how mine stands out more than everyone else's. Everyone is amazed at what I can accomplish with you guys.

I need to start flying again. We did have drones coming, but Morton County put a stop to it. Someone has been arrested for trying to bring drones. All these water protectors - there's too many water protectors, we're faced with a major blizzard. I think I'm getting separation anxiety from flying my drones.

I think those guys are trying to call me out. There's a guy in Bismarck who wants to give me a drone, but he's acting very shady. Someone kept trying to lure me up to Bismarck.

I think the government is utilizing all the weapons they can to stop us. Anti-drone weapons? Anybody heard about them? Some guy passed along info. Going to start looking into that.

This whole week I've been lost. In Bismarck, I was lost. I started feeling that dark shadow. I was there trying to capture how we Indigenous get treated up there. He was just trying to be himself, but he was threatening. Water protectors wanted to punch them, but didn't and I'm glad.

Sometimes there's ghosts in this casino, it's weird.

I feel a lot better now. I'm not going to travel alone.

He is clearly still shaken up after being terrorized.

I was with IEN, but it seems like they have dissipated. Doing their own thing.

Everyone's disappointed in our chairman, Dave Archambault. I couldn't believe it myself. They say there's a reason he told all the water protectors to go home. I have been telling people to go home, they're sick, they're arguing. Just go home, we'll still be proud of you.

I'm the person who holds the whole thing that goes on here. I felt like I had to apologize for all of that crap that went on. I didn't really think it would affect me, but it messes with your head. I won't be too hard on myself.

Be ready for tomorrow. I can get through it, but when it's happening right there in the moment, it's scary. Maybe I let the guy at the mall get the best of me. I have read all the threats. The guy from the mall kind of changed up his tactics and is trying to be nice.

The world has my back. Ready to round all you pro DAPL and trolls!! So beware when you lurk on my page because you will be caged!!!!!

He posts photos of the masked man and the man from the mall. He tells everyone to be aware and to watch for them.

Somehow they got one of these guys before I even came up to file charges!!! TBH I don't trust this whole area of crime and law.

He shares information: The Bismarck Police Department put out a statement. An arrest has been made. The first masked man who terrorized Dean at the Ramada Inn: A 33 year old Bismarck man. They noted that although an arrest had been made, the investigation was still ongoing. He was released within hours.

Everyone shared this post – it was even shared in French.

He is bonding out in a few.

I haven't yet gone to the police station to file charges. This guy, Jesse, is going to be bonding out any minute now. Within the next ten to fifteen minutes. He is not supposed to be around me. The guy that they are accusing of ... I want to know how they know this is even the guy. I don't understand why they didn't interrogate him to find out who the other guy is. His bond is $2,000. I'm meeting with lawyers and important people right now. I want to see if any of my followers want to review my live feeds and see if they can catch the trolls talking.

I know they were following me the whole day, the whole week. It's about putting these pieces together. I need all of your help. To be honest, I don't like the way this is playing out. Anonymous pushed them to find somebody real fast and throw them up there. Probably just a pawn in this whole system that is corrupt. We'll all catch on. This is just a small piece of how North Dakota is corrupt. People know it too. It's all connected.

The higher people in Bismarck didn't want this pipeline because it was going to poison their water, so they pushed it down there toward the tribe. Now they want to invest money in it. They didn't want it up north, so they pushed it down south. That's a good time to make some money off of this pipeline. We're building a huge web of all of this. It's branches of the military, the government, people in Bismarck, the underground, law enforcement, criminals they control like little pawns like the masked guy. I really don't believe he did it.

December 9th

Snowmobile attackers.

It is late night/very early morning. Dean and Myron and Prolific are on the road. They are talking about the snowmobiles that just ran up on them and tried to make them wreck. They come to some lights in the road and Myron stops. The snowmobilers are putting the snowmobiles away. Myron asks if they are okay. They say, "Yeah, awesome."

As they pull away, a truck behind them starts chasing them. They start going really fast. Dean holds the camera out of the window and it's noisy in the wind.

Dean: I hope my followers screenshot all of them. Do you want to call 911? The vehicle is currently in pursuit of us.

They get the license plate number and call it out on the live feed.

Myron: So he's actually turning around and pulling into a house right behind us. I'd like to GPS us. They are still on the road back there. Call 911 real quick and document a little about what's going on here.

Dean: Come on followers, throw those hearts up.

Myron calls 911. A dispatch tells him that the officers are following them and know where they are.

Myron: They are coming out on the road now. They just dropped the snow mobile off. He's coming out after us. He's coming out after us. He's right behind us!

Now the chase gets really crazy. They are going really fast. The truck acts like it wants to rear end them. They pull away from the truck. Dean puts the phone outside the window again and the wind is loud. They pull way ahead. There is snow and ice on the road. Then the truck catches up. It is so close that you can hear the guys in the truck yelling and whooping.

Dean: Followers I hope you were taking screenshots. My hand is cold! It's cold. I'm good guys, but my hands are cold! Here he comes, he's coming faster, he's speeding up! Speed up! Speed up! That officer needs to get back on Highway 6 and go fast. Keep the hearts going. Just be safe. Screenshot all these trolls. The cops are behind us, way back there.

Myron: I'm going to continue to go south and slow down. He's going to try to go around us. I think my car is smoking.

Dean: They are slowing down. They are probably going to turn around.

The truck is still behind them.

Myron: We're coming back from Bismarck. It started about 11:20 and that's when we turned on the phones to document. They are still right behind us. They haven't slowed down. Going about 60 miles per hour. They almost rammed us, they slammed on their brakes and they almost hit us.

Dean: They dropped the snowmobile off at a farmhouse. We know where it is.

Myron: Here he goes again. Now he's right behind us. They want to hit us. They are going about 90 miles per hour. They want to hit us, but no police officers whatsoever. Seat belts guys. We're at almost 100 miles per hour now.

Dean: Ohhh nooo. The truck is closer. They are not going to slow. Ohh they're just going to hit us! They are right behind us. They are backing up a little. He's trying to get on the side of us.

Myron has been on the phone with the law enforcement dispatch. You can hear her say, "I need you to pull over. The police can't catch up."

Myron: I'm going down to 40, but they are trying to ram us.

Dispatch: You need to stop driving.

Myron: Let me get to a good spot. Going down to 30.

Dean: Keep watching guys, keep watching.

Dispatch: Have you found a good place to pull over?

Myron: There's snow on the side, I am slowed down to 30.

Dean: We're going to verify the license plates and I want you to get the names of the owners.

Myron: They're coming right on us again.

Dean: They're watching us on the live feed. They're probably following us. Snooping around on the pages. They're turning around. Now they're coming toward the officers. They are driving north and east, back to Bismarck.

   They finally are able to pull over. The screen goes black.

Dispatch: The officers are going in their direction and they will find them.

Myron: I see a cop coming down the road, but he's not doing anything. I turned the lights on. We see a vehicle coming. It looks like the officers. The officer looks like he stopped. He's about four miles away from the vehicle.

Dean: There it is guys. If this was Indigenous snowmobilers, they would have already been arrested.

Myron: You can't say things like that. You have to give them the benefit of a doubt.

Prolific is telling the story on his own live feed. They tried to ram us. We had to go about 100 miles an hour.

Dean: There were four or five guys though.

Myron: There's something wrong with the front of the car. I don't think they hit us.

Prolific: They slammed the brakes on and slid toward us.

Myron: We're in a good spot. We're safe. There's cops up there. We're going to give them the benefit of a doubt that they are chasing this vehicle.

   Dean's followers start to give him information about the truck that was chasing them. The police call them. They say they are right behind them. They tell them to not be alarmed. The police pull up.

Dean: As you can see, they flashed the lights on us.

Police: What the heck is going on?

Myron: We just got chased.... by snowmobiles.

Police: On the highway?

Myron: Yes. They were harassing the cars. They pulled into a farmhouse and put their snowmobiles up. We thought you had them pulled over, but I don't know.

Police: What do you want to do about it?

Myron: Press charges.

Police: Do you have a video of it that you can show me right now?

Myron: We're live.

Police: What's more important?

Myron: That's not it. We'd like to know who they are.

Police: We won't tell you. You can file statements. Let me get some statement forms.

Dean: He's not happy. Followers, screenshot the photos, VIN number, color of truck put it in there and on the timelines, get it out there. For the officers.

Police: I talked to them. He told me why he was doing it.

Myron: Our lives were threatened and you're acting like nothing is happening. It's not okay. It's not okay for women and children who were around.

Police: Bring me some video.

Myron: If you talked to him, why wasn't he detained?

Police: I know where he is. Do you guys have ID's?

Myron: We'll bring down all of this information tomorrow.

Police: Okay

Dean: Holy crap. That's just pure friggin crap.

Myron: I know we can't win. I wasn't going to lecture him, but we do know that the officer knew who it was. I wanted to see if getting emotional did anything to the officer, but it did not. We have to follow the colonial law. We have to document everything. We're going to follow the protocol of the law.

Dean: (Sighs heavily several times.) Bless, bless, bless. Did you guys notice that, on this feed? After they disappeared, the trolls are not on the live feed anymore.

Prolific: Thank you guys at home for helping.

Dean: It's so...there's this power that we can't get beyond. Spiritually we can, but these laws...

     Myron's feed disconnects.

Dean: Screenshot all those trolls, we'll look into them. Before you block them, look into them.

Prolific: It was a pretty dangerous night, but we're okay.

Dean: Go back through all these comments here. Get all the important information then block them. Because I noticed they were watching. Then when they disappeared, the trolls disappeared. The tire is alright, I believe. Those cops won't listen. It's going to be like this until someone with the right kind of values, integrity... I will go Facebook live and point out when and where it started and how far the chase went. The world we live in. Racism will never die.

     He live feeds from a hotel room later that morning.

     We are getting targeted because we are reporting the truth to the world.

     Good morning everybody. Time to play some music. I got some sleep, feel pretty good. So let's get inspired again. We are getting targeted because we are the media. We have the ability to expose the truth.

     He stands up and puts his gear on.

     We got some more drones in. Rhianna is testing them out. We're going to try to get them across to the other side. And as for me, I got more evidence against all those people out there.

     He is playing music loudly. He shows pictures. He puts on more gear - his hat, his boots.

     You know what I got. Big blown up pictures of actions. A good friend of mine, he does this stuff. That's the kind of music that gets you pumped and prepared. Because you never know what you're going to go through as an Indigenous reporter.

     We have crucial evidence, but I'm not going to give it out yet. From the other terrorizer from the hotel. I hope I didn't scare anybody last night. They're just a bunch of young.... Song is A Tribe Called Red. Everybody should know that.

     Do I know if they are drilling? Most likely they are. This pipeline is going to go through. But right now the real battle.... it's not a physical battle, we can't go over there with non-direct nonviolent action because they have insurance. Everything they've lost since we've been stopping them, they are going to get it back.

     Look at that. The trolls aren't here. They must have been up late last night because they're not here this morning. Thanks for giving me all the information. Morton County had some police trolls. I bet those police were sitting there on the side of the road pushing those angry faces.

I know people say I can't go out there and antagonize. But that's why they are after me. Because of all my followers. I love all of you guys. No angry faces because they are sleeping in. Thank you for all you do. It was pretty awful what the cops said, it punched my heart. All this started out since Trump is gonna be president. All this hate came out. Who is Bismarck? They didn't want the pipeline. These big families. I know them because they used to come to Prairie Knights Casino. They didn't want the pipeline, so they went below them.

Now they say, let's invest in that pipeline and make some money. Some of those big family members in Bismarck, they are tied into all of this. Law enforcement, Morton County, government. A big shadow of corrupt. A special kind of corruptness. It involves a lot of people. Rich families in Bismarck, law enforcement, but not all of them.

There's a little group of law enforcement who still stand for the good. They believe in protecting the people. My heart goes out to them. They see there are good people, such as me. Thank you to all those law enforcement who never dipped into corporate greed and corruption.

It ties into people they arrested. They used them to get what they want. They threaten them with putting something on them. DAPL workers, there are some that are just pure evil. They don't like Natives. They're into motorcycles and patriotic stuff and guns and weapons and Trump. All conquered people should know who to bow down to, but what makes them say that? This is a free country. They start misusing their freedom. They think they have the freedom to conquer whoever they want to.

You shouldn't have to enforce your freedom. You understand it. All those hearts. I've been studying them. It's hard to do investigative work on social media. They make fake profiles. But some of them left all their personal pictures and information. We know who you are, just like you know who we are. You should get better videos. More original.

Message to all those people who want to threaten us. Open your eyes and listen. This ain't gonna get any better. Make it better. Quit passing that hate. Promote that love. I've seen people spreading hate and then in their family videos they are spreading love. You guys do have love too. All you trolls out there. Don't let DAPL turn you into an evil person. We're all people, just like you. I do remember seeing some of you guys at the casino, gambling away, being entertained. We are all family, we are one.

They feed off the evilness. If you're going to feed off of anything, feed off the love, feed off the good values. They all have children. North Dakota corrupt organization. It starts all over North Dakota and they invest in the pipeline.

It's like the Black Hills. Money is survival to these people. I can understand and accept that, but we gotta do it in a good way. Not take and hurt and kill. We can do it with love and blessings. You probably just laugh at my videos. I'm glad I'm entertaining you guys. Trolls. they are terrorizing and patrolling. I'm going to do another live feed later. Pray for everybody. Peace out.

Op, there's a troll. Tag their link to their Facebook page. Spread it out first before you block. Look into them. We got people who own businesses in Bismarck, their family members that hate us and then young people and then below that the older generations and above that the law enforcement. Between those two are the criminals they control. Then above all of that are all the top secret people. There are trolls that are good too. There's a branch of all Army, Marines, National Guard, Navy trolls. All the military trolls. Military is born to use fear and force. Then branches of the government. Then people of the city, rich people who have invested in the pipeline. Then their families. They are all tied in.

Here's the sad one. They come from the reservation or camp. A small section of that is true honest corruption that is within Standing Rock tribe. Sadly it's within all tribes. They are not physically trying to target us, they just are against what we say. It's a small rez and we all know. There is corruption within Standing Rock. It's sad to say.

To stand up to this corruption, you have to have a strong heart. You have to stand in front of a million dollars and say no, I can't do this to my people. Stay focused. Trolls messages don't mean nothing. To stand against corruption you gotta have a lot of strength. It will push down on you, but it's okay. Put the world in your hand, not on your shoulders. Put it in your heart. Corruption is hard to resist. Money is hard to resist. We live below poverty levels. So when money comes, we take it and we spend it right away. I've learned that money don't mean nothing. For all my Indigenous brothers and sisters, this is money. This is the guy who put his name all over this corruption first. When people say they need money, I give it to them. Help each other. It's just money. This is what we need to burn. All of it. It's paper. I don't let it control me. I control it.

Don't let money consume your hearts guys. All you guys out there, all the people of the council, use it for the protection of your people. All those million dollar GoFundMe's. Don't go out there and buy a new truck. It may say that I have that much money, but I'm low again. 110% the second terrorizer that was at the hotel, he's going to be going to court next.

He does a late live feed from a hotel.

Update. We are powerful more than that.

Spiritual warriors all the way guys. It is calculated. We are gonna put one hell of a lawsuit on every single officer, criminal, and we have good officers that will speak up for us. *(He reads comments on the live feed.)* What gathers all these people is my heart. Since this movement began it opened my eyes to another perspective about how to live. I understand that no matter how much evil you have in one person's heart, you can change for the better. No matter what you've done or who you are, there's always a way to find good in your heart. You just gotta find it. Heart can never go away. It takes one little heart floating across the screen there. It's the power of spirit.

I've seen the trolls. Let them do it. If it makes them feel better. I don't feel harassed, I feel empowered. No matter how much wrong people are saying to you, it takes one person, one spoken word to change a lot of things. It starts with forgiveness and you can forgive yourself.

The Army Corps is raising the water. Think about it like this. They feel our prayers. That's why they are literally raising the water because they feel we need more water. They are slowly getting the meaning of water is life.

That's why I love every single one of you guys. You don't see me for how I look or what I've done wrong. You see me for what I have here under my shirt, my heart. I don't see any trolls in my heart. It's getting to them. They're feeling the power. Words can only go so far. Where my focus goes, all of our energy flows. I feel so safe. This is the safest I've ever felt in my life. I feel so safe because of all of you people out there and everyone who believes in me. It started with the drones.

Drones can open minds and ways. As much hate and evil as there is in Bismarck, that's not going to stop me from walking around and being free. Don't ever let that fear go into your heart. I was close, but I turned it all around. The reason why I'm here is because we're all human. Even all those trolls out there. You are all human too. You all have families, children, people who you love dearly in your heart. You work hard every day. You've earned that house, those cars. But always remember, don't ever judge anyone. Whether they are higher above you or lower than you. We're all equal. That's the way creator set it out to be.

If you took my insights and words seriously that means I must have some kind of power, I don't know. At the end of the day, you have to smile. And when you smile at the face of evil, eventually it will smile back at you. I'm always good. It's the strength in your heart. That's what leads you to a greater way of wisdom and life. A lot of people are going to hate me from a lot of different directions, but we're Indigenous, we're from the four directions.

All those trolls out there, I'm going to turn those angry faces into hearts. It empowers me. It truly does. I love all of you guys out there. It's changed me for the better.

A woman walks up and he hugs her. She's from the water protectors' legal protectors. He reads comments again.

You were right Gary. It played out the way you knew it was going to play out. But don't judge them. Leave them be. All we gotta do now is learn from our mistakes, learn from our pasts and make a better future for ourselves and our kids.

If this pipeline goes through, so what, it goes through. We just have to keep living our lives. When you make great change in the world, you make happiness with a better future. Turn negative into positive. Don't look at those evil comments, let them be. That's just them making themselves feel better. But I assure you one thing, what you guys see, let it go. Because there's something more grander that's going to happen. So big that I can't type it in a post right now. Trust me. Ride the eagle when you dream. Spread those wings. Feel the air above you.

The drone allowed me to feel freedom more than anything. It never gave me that feeling of oppression. It allowed me to fly anywhere. Wisdom, integrity, bravery, courage, love, generosity, everything. I'm from the Bitterwater clan. And I think I'm going to go to sleep and I'm not going to wake up for...I might just disappear and never come back.

I feel better than ever guys. I do. Wow. I'm going to go to sleep though. It's up to you guys from this point on to continue forward to look at me, to entrust in me, to allow me to go forward with you guys. And if you don't, I don't judge you, I don't hold anything against you. Know this, whatever you said to me and gave to me, I will always carry it on to the future. It's knowledge. Whether it's good or bad, you learn from it.

December 10th

He shares Angelo Wolf's post:

We need drones. If you're able to help us out, please hit me up. They've taken our drones and we're working with a limited supply at the moment. We're documenting everything that DAPL does.

He does a live feed from a hotel.

I had to make a couple of changes. My page maybe was hacked.

The live video goes in and out. He reads comments when it is up.

I'm doing pretty good. I'm feeling a lot better. I caught up with sleep. I'm trying to promote the funding page because me and a couple of warrior friends are going to go around and do some stuff.

They are going to let some water out and it will flood camp if it goes too high. They are drilling. No drone needed. They are drilling. The structures of camp will flood. It will slowly rise depending on how much they let go at the dam. Army Corps of Engineers are doing it to stop DAPL or just to get people out of camp.

If you feel like you still want to come help, you are going to have to be self-sufficient. Make sure you can tolerate the North Dakota winter. There is another snow storm coming.

Angelo is feeding at same time. He says to watch his feed instead of Dean's. They laugh.

They put the sacred fire out today at Oceti. They burned it out. That means the elders have moved out of camp. Main sacred fire is out. Others are still burning. A lot of Red Warrior camp have packed up and left. Crow Creek boys and horses are still there.

As far as droning, we are down a lot of drones. I do have an Inspire that DroneGear gave me, but it's on lock down. Until I get it back, I am on hold.

I don't think it's safe to mail a drone. Quite a few people tried and I didn't get them. Send money instead. 2017 is going to be a new year and I want to go around to other pipelines.

Angelo is still live feeding. He is thanking people who helped get rooms. Food arrives. Dean is back. He is eating.

Thank you for all the good letters, messages, everything. Tina sent an iPhone 5, I didn't get it. I haven't received anything. When you mail anything, LaDonna posted that mail is getting stolen or stopped. I'm going to start changing it up and using people who aren't connected now. You can't trust anybody.

Does it help to buy a Standing Rock t shirt? I don't know - lots of people are promoting that they are supporting camp, but they aren't accountable.

The memorial ride is on for the Dakota 38. There was a march in D.C. for Standing Rock and Leonard Peltier today.

The latest about Red Fawn. They dropped local charges, made them federal charges.

Who is stopping the mail? You don't even know where it starts and where it ends anymore. Could be a lot of things. So much mail that it's just overwhelming to get it here. It is a federal offense to mess with mail.

Updates on the snowmobiles - we are writing our statements and that's all I can say right now. It's more going to be legal battles now. There's going to be lots of lawsuits coming out of this.

Are feds infiltrating? No idea. No proof.

Don't be frustrated, just be happy. I had a pretty rough week, but I got over it. Don't let those people bring you down. The only thing we know is that we don't know nothing.

I accept all of you guys for who you are too. We're all human beings. Everything you do leads you to this point and then leads to you something better in the future.

I saw the fly by video - if we go any closer, drones will scramble and get shot down or lost. Something is scrambling them. Even on a full battery. We know there's something going on, so I don't want to lose any more drones. I'm watching other drones go down. I can drone over camp though. Stingrays – I am studying up on them. They are supposed to be illegal.

I am so proud of our people. We are so strong. Our ancestors are with us. I am here because of all of your prayers and our ancestors and I believe this. Bless you all too.

Twenty-four minutes ago Chase gave a report that no one is leaving Rosebud Camp. Mad respect for Chase Iron Eyes. He's a true leader. Every time I am around him I feel safe and like I can look up to him as a leader. The first camp established was in April. I filmed the horses going in. There were good hopes for the future.

Much props to New Zealand. And Australia. I'm pretty much all over the world. People are tuned in.

We are needing donations for our next project. This is going to be different. The world's first Drone2bwild pipeline tour. Hitting all these pipelines all over the U.S. Documenting how to fight these pipelines. What's going on. The people, the prayers. I'm Standing Rock Nation. I want to start going out and reaching out to other fights.

He gives more updates in another live feed. He's in body armor and a ball cap. Hundreds of people jump on the live feed right away. His videos are getting thousands and thousands of views right away.

Doing pretty good this evening. Always good to send positive vibes. Frost bite at the tip of my fingers, but it's all good. So you guys want to know it all.

I'm testing out Kevlar vests. Have to find one that fits well. Taking care of myself pretty good. Am I going back to camp? Camp right now is cold. I'm going to present something different. But before I leave for anywhere, I will go back to camp. I will fly the drone there - I will fly it low, like I do best.

People on the feed ask him what they need at camp.

Wood, hearts, drones.

You guys love that stuff, up in your face close. *(He laughs.)* Who watched AJ+ drone video? All I wanted to express was my creative ability. To show everyone what a drone can do. I just took a drone and inspired people. I noticed that I haven't flown a drone in two weeks and a lot of people are concerned. As soon as I see anything negative, I block every one of them. Any kind of drone warmer? I don't know - it's hard to keep it warm out there.

The veterans are still here. Not all of them, but here and there. Still standing. It's going to filter out all the people who were just here to be here. The casino is less crowded.

I'm not leaving. I'm right here. I smile in the face of evil and I speak proudly in the face of all the corrupt. Fear will not take me down. Fear will not let me get scared. It's you guys who empower me and the power of my brothers who stand here and protect me.

It may be really hard to stand and defeat a corporation with so much money, but as long as what you speak about and your words are heard throughout the world, that's more power than any corporation with as much money as they ever will have. It's about that. It's about the message. And that will continue to go on and on throughout the future.

He stops to talk to someone in the room.

Are you hungry, my friend? Order some food. That's what we do. When someone is hungry, we feed them.

The Phantom 4 is 1200 dollars – some are down to 800. As soon as I get a Phantom 4, I am going to fly it over to where at least they don't know where I'm coming from.

Someone asks about the snowmobile attack.

We are doing this the legal way. We are taking them to court.

The FAA didn't lift the no fly zone. There's a petition, I encourage everyone to sign. I still fly the skies. It's all Indigenous lands, Indigenous air. Mother Earth didn't actually put anything there to get sold.

A new Anonymous video came out tonight. I have to give Anonymous some credit. In the past I was doubting them a lot. But they have come to a new light. I have much respect and honor for Anonymous. They do what they gotta do and for that I respect them. Anonymous is standing with water protectors in Florida. Awesome. Anonymous does watch my feeds. It's the power of my followers. I am always careful.

December 11th

Overcoming the greatest odds

"If he walks with his mind and heart attentive to Wakan Tanka and His Powers, as he has been instructed, he will certainly travel upon the red path which leads to goodness and holiness. But he must cry for a vision a second time, and this time the bad spirits may tempt him; but if he is really a chosen one, he will stand firmly and will conquer all distracting thoughts and will become purified from all that is not good. Then he may receive some great vision that will bring strength to the nation." ~ Black Elk

He live feeds this morning.

Updates and news for the day!

I caught up with my sleep. I'm over all dealing with all that bull, that's history. I have some new stuff coming up. Big surprise.

Right now they are not drilling. They want to drill, but they are not drilling.

It blew out of proportion. For future reference, when something like that happens, let's not put it out there publicly. Putting it out there like that does upgrade the level of being wanted. So much love throughout the whole world. Even down the darkest roads. There's still love in Bismarck. Love does breed peace.

He talks about the water cannons on November 20th.

Subzero temps. IEDs - were protestors using them? Infiltrators are highly possible. They have been poking at us, hoping we will do something. But we are smarter than that. There's always going to be infiltrators coming into camp. The most powerful weapon in the universe is the heart.

Dave versus Chase. Where do I stand? Even though a lot of people are holding Dave with the confusion with the money - and we have Chase, excellent human being. I am with both of them. I stand with both of them. They are both my brothers. I'm not going to choose sides. I support both of them.

Even though a brother goes down in what he does, you have to bring him back up. And Chase is right there to help us up. Much respect to Chase. And to Dave too. I bet being a tribal chairman is really hard. It would be less stress if the whole tribal building worked as one unit. We'd have one strong Nation. We're working on it. We're all just human.

Law enforcement likes to watch our feeds. The night we were being chased, they were watching. Shouldn't they have been stopping the guys who were chasing us at 100 miles an hour?

We're going to overpower Morton County with lawsuits. Not all Morton County law enforcement are bad. They are not all racists. There are some good people who are going to do the right thing. If you know something, don't be scared. You have a whole world of people who are willing to back you and support you.

People laid my past out on the table, get over it. You can't live in the past. It's not about the past, it's about the future.

He asks for hearts.

They need a new book. A new edition. An Indigenous edition. Water is life. Indigenous people are the first protectors of this land. We are real, we feel it. We are alive.

The human race does matter. All these big oil corporations, think about what you are doing. You are destroying the planet. Where are we going to go? Mars? Only the rich will go. The rest of us will still be here praying and singing and healing the mother.

The guy they did catch, that is him. You can see his goatee. The other guy, the quiet guy. The red button nose guy. I think you guys know who it is. Facial recognition technology. Why would he commit a crime like that? Still could be tied into law enforcement. They use them like puppets. I hope he loses everything he has because it's the consequences.

He's probably not a bad guy. It all ties in to the bigger picture. There's a lot more stuff out there. Bismarck has honest cops. They are trying to do what they can. MSNBC called me this morning. That's how bad they need to solve this. If this goes unsolved, that's going to be bad for Bismarck.

I shouldn't have to walk around in a bullet proof vest all the time. I wear it for protection. Bismarck police department are not the corrupt ones. Morton County, everybody has their doubts.

I know it's hate we are fighting against, I know you really want to do physical harm, but you cannot. We fight that with the power of standing. We can stop all the hate. Do this out of the goodness of your heart in a good way. Not out of hate or jealousy. We lead by example. We lead by example. No matter how many times they might harass us on Highway 6, we lead by example. And from there, things will change.

To tell you the truth, we will never get rid of hate. We are human beings. We need hate to show us true love. We need racism to show us who they are and where they came from.

December 12th

Morning updates and news

Remember how we were missing drones, we were supposed to be getting drones in? Everybody is missing drone footage. I've been taking time off drones to shed new light on other things.

He shows a message: $10,000 worth of drones cops intercepted in the mail might be the ones people sent to you.

If they are going to stop everybody with a thousand dollar fine from coming to camp, they will stop the drones. Messing with the mail is a federal crime.

People are complaining about GoFundMe accounts. It may seem that Drone2bwild has 13,000, but it doesn't. To solve all things, I'm just going to get rid of that GoFundMe. I never wanted to have one. The GoFundMe started drawing attention. Only way to keep them quiet is to take it down.

There's going to be new camps soon. It's all about money. People like to complain too much about money, they forget why they are here. I don't need the money.

I have confirmed that the drill is not drilling. I even said it was, but it is not. There's still hope. Hope is something that if you believe long enough, it will be right.

A lot of people are angry about how the vets were treated when they came. It's these fundings. Money hasn't been released yet.

He shows a photo of the man who harassed him at the mall.

He was contacting me after all this was going down. Said he was sorry for his actions. This is the big surprise. We are going to be changing the way people, our communities, look upon one another and the way we interact. If you have been following me and you have seen the love in my heart, this is what we're gonna do. Ready people? His name is Chris. Let me just recite what Chris is saying:

He's sorry. He says, "It's not okay with me what happened to you. I know I could have handled myself better. I would never wish that on you. I would never put you in a situation like that."

So me and Chris started chatting. It's about making changes, taking risks. Before we start calling things out, give this a chance. We talked. We actually got to know each other. We talked for an hour. Trust me, this is some serious stuff. I'm changing the hearts by working together with other communities. We have that same vision of a happy safe future. We are trying to dial down the image of water protectors being violent. We need to stop that.

If you truly believe in me and trust me, trust me on this one. I have seen Chris and he has a heart and a great mind. We are both out there. His past is out there, my past is out there. But I am looking toward the future, so is Chris. Everyone stops looking toward the future when you bring out the past. Trust me on this one. This is our mission statement.

It's time to combine efforts and band together publicly. Chris said that.

We are going to get together in an undisclosed location. He's going to be alone. I will have one water protector to watch over. We will both be live feeding. We are going to sit down and talk to each other like human beings. Chris really is a good guy. I pointed him in a direction. Words can guide the hearts of many to show there are greater things to connect with than anger. We are not perfect, but together we can promote peace and deescalate the attacks.

We need to stop with the verbal threats. It will not heal your soul. Know that by not doing anything, you are doing the right thing.

He surprised me. It took a while for us to trust each other. I assured him that nothing will happen to him.

In another live feed:

Just some quick feedback. I want to share some of my followers' messages.

138

His followers call him wise. They say that he's grown so much. They are proud of him. He continues to read the messages.

You spoke like an elder. I got a lot of knowledge from you. You are on the right track. It's all about the children, they are the future.

He reads another follower's comments. She's giving him advice.

More spiritual essence, challenge yourself. Challenge yourself to go higher. Spiritualism.

He reads another message. It's hateful.

You gotta give them time to change. It won't happen now, or in the next few days, but it will happen in a lifetime. People will change for the better. Whatever people think about Chris, I've been talking to him for a couple of days. I can comfortably call him and we speak good words. I am not putting myself into the hate, they are just words. I look forward to the live feed with Chris. We are going to be 100% open and honest. We just want to create a better community for Bismarck and Standing Rock so everybody can walk around with no problems. Together we can all just get along.

He shares a story about an eleven year old boy who needs help buying Christmas. And a story from Izzy Edward, whose children were taken from her. People look to Dean to help them and Izzy contacted him to share her story. Many Indigenous children have been taken from their Indigenous birth parents and given to Caucasian/European adoptive parents. It is just another way the government tries to assimilate Indigenous people and wipe out the Indigenous culture.

He live feeds about Izzy and her children:

Bringing home our children. They are the future of this planet. Protectors of seven more generations.

Welcome to this late night live feed. I want to put this article out there. If you could reach out and help her get her children back. Children are the future. They are the future of the next seven generations and generations after that. We really got to bring more knowledge to light here. Indigenous children get lost in the system. But we need to start protecting them. Children are sacred. Children are powerful. Children are precious. So help her out. Thank you for accepting this good message in a good way.

December 13th

Drone2bwild returns to camp!! Getting ready for the pipeline tour 2017.

I just got confirmation that they may have started to drill today.

In a live feed from a hotel room he shares:

BREAKING NEWS: Pipeline spills 176,000 gallons into creek 150 miles from Dakota Access CAMP!!

Two and a half hours from Cannonball. If someone knows the exact location, put it in the links. That would be helpful. *(He shows the article.)*

The ground they cross here has always been sacred ground. That's what we've been fighting this whole time.

He reads the article: Despite victory, which it wasn't - just for that day, many water protectors are wary of the future. The leak was contained, so they say, within hours of its discovery. The woman who said that to the news said it to CNBC. Anybody with CNBC connections, if they can look into that.

There's more important things than trolls these days. Trolls just aren't important.

He goes back to reading.

It's not clear why electronic monitoring equipment didn't detect the leak. Now isn't that what they said - this pipeline was supposed to be so darn top of the line, it was supposed to be a secured line, right? All the time those guys are promoting this pipeline like it's going to be the safest thing in the whole world. Please. Something failed, just like all pipelines. Some button somebody didn't push or maybe it got clogged. Who knows.

The investigation is ongoing. Last week the Army Corps of Engineers denied the segment DAPL needs to complete the final stretch of the 3.8 billion dollar pipeline. And I just got confirmation that they may have started drilling today. They may have. I'm not going to put the map out here publicly, but if you guys want the proof, we'll leave that for later on. But yes, they are drilling guys. Supposedly. I'll find out for sure this evening, or within the hour.

Actually this would be a good Drone2bwild comeback. If someone could mark where that spill is. If it's out there, we gotta see it. There's no coverage of it. Now it's time to get the drone out there and go cover that spill. I'm gonna need the exact location with a map set out to drive there and a vehicle. I bet it's all forted up too, like the pipeline here.

About 60 workers were there Monday and are averaging about 100 yards daily in their cleanup efforts. Some of the oil remains trapped under the ice. About 37,000 gallons of oil has been recovered.

There it is guys. This all states that the pipeline they're putting under the river is not going to be safe at all. Guaranteed to leak. But they still want to put it in. Corporate oil and their greed of money. I bet they literally wipe their butts with that money.

Here's some updates about this guy over here. The president elect, Donald Trump, has voiced support for the Dakota Access pipeline.

Yes guys, the banks. We all need to start taking our money out of the banks. Someone once asked me, you don't have a bank account? I said, nope. That's how corruption starts.

Oh not to mention, this whole thing, it's not mentioned once on mainstream news. Fox news, CNN, MSNBC. Nobody. So all major news networks are not covering this spill. So that means the Drone2bwild better go up there and get the world's exclusive then.

Maybe we can get me and Chris to go up to that busted pipeline and we'll go cover it. The internet has been acting weird lately.

The feed is suddenly cut off.

He live feeds again later.

More updates on the pipeline spill near Belfield, North Dakota.

He shows pictures of the pipeline leak. He shares the oil company's apology online. We deeply regret.... It was bubbling up out of the ground. Discovered by a farmer.

North Dakota wants more law enforcement. So they can keep violating protectors' rights. Due to blizzard conditions, the pipeline broke. But they are supposed to be top of the line, unbreakable. Obama is reviewing election season hacking. New day and age.

He shows Morton County's page. He calls it the terrorists' page.

Some guy is saying law enforcement are getting donations from everywhere. People are paying for their meals. Sheriff Kirchmeier talks about the support of the people. He says that every county has sent officers so things stay safe. He talks about all of the sacrifices of the police.

You need to see the truth, bro. We could put up all kinds of stuff about sacrificing. They thank someone from Standing Rock Sioux Tribe for bringing coffee and treats. You should have brought me some first. I would have gave them the leftovers.

He reads the comments. A lot of people thank him for everything he is doing.

I want to live in safety. Despite the DAPL cloud that is poisoning the minds of people. I'm trying to cleanse everyone's minds so they can feel that freedom again. Knowledge is free. Nature is free. We are going to fly the drone today. Let's just hope that they don't have top secret drone weapons.

When you write hateful messages, it can scar and hurt people. I want them to understand it and learn it.

I have posts and someone's deleting them. They deleted a post about these children... water, children, earth - these are all things we are fighting for.

Live in 5 minutes. Shiyé & Chris closing old doors and bridging together new ideas of a safe and welcoming environment for all of North Dakota and its wonderful citizens and great warriors alike.

He and Chris are sitting on the floor. Chris is the man who harassed him at the mall in Bismarck. They both say hello and introduce themselves. Chris lives in Mandan and is part of a couple of community groups there.

Chris: We figured it was about time to sit down and have a discussion.

Dean: This is a special live feed. As for me, all of my followers, we are here to present everybody, the communities of Bismarck, Mandan and Standing Rock, we can all come together and we want to make statements to promote that. This guy here, when we first met it was all over social media and we were on different sides. We had a confrontation or an introduction where one of us took out his aggression.

Chris: The way that day went down was just a bad deal. I had seen some things that really frustrated me. And I got caught up in the trap of emotion and reacted in anger instead of going up and introducing myself and starting a conversation. And I think a lot of that is going on all over the place. So for Dean and I to get together and start talking on the phone and saying, this is crazy. There's no reason we have to hate each other. We don't have to be best friends either. But a mutual respect is what we really need. We're getting to know each other pretty well. And my opinion has really changed from what it was. I was just going off live feeds. I didn't give him a chance as a person. It's funny what happens when you actually do that.

Dean: You want to show the truth. In order to do that, all things gotta be open. There were things put out on social media that pretty much provided our whole past and our history. Each side trying to play each other. Trying to attack us. Personally, attacking our past isn't going to cause anything, it's not going to fix anything. It's not even going to damage anything. But it is going to put our families at risk and the people we love. And we don't want that. It's not about our past, it's about us looking to the future and doing that common good. Just take that first step forward. You don't have to like each other. You don't have to know each other. But just taking that first step and going through that first door and closing those old doors, and crossing that bridge where it is two communities. We both, on both sides can experience and enjoy a lot more things in life. But we can do it together.

Chris: We're at a point now where it's not even about water or the pipeline. We just need to deescalate what's going on - on both sides. Protectors aren't going anywhere. They're going to keep on voicing their opinions and they have every right to. We just need to be able to do two things. Allow them to do that and feel safe in our communities. And I think if we had more conversations like this and give each other a chance, I think there would be a lot more comfort involved. A lot of the fear would go away. I'm sincerely asking Bismarck, Mandan and Standing Rock protectors to just back off the threats, from the spreading of personal information. Dean and I were both victims of the doxing about our kids, our families. Nobody needs that. So we've talked a lot in the last couple of days and we're going to do our best to try to get the people we know and that we've met through all of this to just take a step down the ladder of escalation. Because it's not going to help anything. Whether it's threats or actual physical violence or just making people feel uncomfortable. A lot of it's just fear. We get scared of something and fear overtakes and hate turns into violence. I'm not scared of Dean anymore. We got to know each other and I'm down here at the casino. I was sitting there gambling by myself earlier. I felt safe the whole time. I've met a bunch of good people today. They've been nothing but respectful. Two weeks ago, the way things were presented, I never would have expected this to go so well. And that's my bad for having that stereotype and that fear of somebody who had a different opinion from me or looked different than me.

Dean: First of all, I want to apologize from the bottom of my heart to all the people in Bismarck and Mandan. I'm sorry if I came across to you a little jerky or a little offensive. I never meant any harm. I never meant any terror. I'm a humble guy. I do what's right in my heart. I say what's right in my heart. I either speak the truth or I show the truth and that's all I can offer. And not only for our kids' safety, but for your kids' safety. In each community. Stop the hate. Appreciate. And respect will start going on both sides. And even if you still have a little hate in your heart, it's okay. I feel you guys. It's okay. We're all human. But eventually you're going to feel that change, you're going to feel that shift. And when you do that, you'll feel a lot better in life and you'll learn to love things. And change will happen. It starts with each one of you guys. It starts right here in your heart.

Chris: And with that said, I would like to sincerely apologize as well. For the way I acted toward Dean that day in the mall. I didn't give him a chance. I jumped at the opportunity to try to prove a point and it proved nothing. It proved some things about me that I wasn't proud about. That's not a side of me that I like. It's not a side of me that I ever care to use, but I showed it. So for that, I'm sorry Dean, for not giving you the chance face to face like we are right now. Just sitting down and talking about it. I think the saddest thing that has come out of this is that it's become such a racial divide and racial war when that's not the issue. I'm not going to get into the politics about the pipeline and water, but it's not about race. That's one thing I know for sure. It's not Indigenous versus white. It's people having different opinions. It's not a race, religion or where certain people are from. I don't want my children brought up in an atmosphere of racism. That's one of the great reasons that we are sitting down talking and getting to know each other. We've been talking a lot about people's reactions in our groups, as far as us getting together. A lot of people in the BisMan United group were questioning my intentions and my motives. We're not here to try to change each other's opinions about the pipeline at all. Our only goal is to deescalate this down a little bit. So nobody ends up getting hurt. That's the biggest thing. Even if we go back to where we were a couple of weeks ago, the last two weeks it's really escalated fast. And it's scary because the next steps are not good ones if it keeps going in this direction. And none of us need that. We don't need to take any mothers away from their children, any fathers away, anybody's children away. Anybody getting hurt or killed. That's the way this escalation is going. That scares the heck out of me.

Dean: I love clean water. I think everybody loves clean water. But we will not always have clean water. But while we do have clean water, I enjoy it. And we're just going to have to deal with the evil in the world and with the good in the world. We all just have to make good decisions and make them from the goodness of your heart.

Chris: I see points from both sides. Pipeline and water. A lot of people on both sides have valid points. I won't get in the middle of it. We need to create an atmosphere of safety for everyone. On both sides. There's no positive to putting people's personal information out there. There's no positive to making a threat. It's not going to solve anything. The first time we met face to face it wasn't a good situation at all. But we spent the last hours having conversation. We just want to deescalate it, just down to where we can tolerate each other. You don't have to express that hate and dislike. And if all of us can do that, this will go a lot more smoothly. We're not looking to change anyone's politics. If everyone's on edge, it's just going to take one little pin drop for things to blow up. It's explosive right now. Let's put the matches down.

Dean: I want to apologize once again. Even to people on my side. We're sitting here at the casino and I miss this casino full of people who want entertainment. And I do miss driving down 1806, it makes getting here so much faster. If we work together maybe we can express from both sides of the blockage that love and compassion that we have, let's work together to push aside those blocks. And welcome each other into a new breath of renewal. This whole incident is happening around us. It's cause and affected us in a lot of different ways. Deep down mentally, spiritually, physically, it's affected us in all kinds of different ways. But we are all learning from this. Even from hate and fear. It empowers me. It makes me a greater person. It allows me to see the world as it really is. It has empowered me to do a lot more things. It changed my life a lot.

Chris: Block John. We don't need that negativity.

Dean: This is where we are a little different. Someone leaves a little hate on my comments, I just leave it, because people need to see that stuff. If they see it, they will learn from it eventually.

Chris: But that's a friend of mine.

Dean: Maybe in time you can talk to him again.

Chris: We aren't enemies. All of this is new to us and we're learning. We don't need to make enemies. We don't have enemies here. I was in Iraq. We had enemies there. This is just a difference of opinions.

Dean: If you have a little anger, a little hate, learn how to let it go. I just miss Bismarck, Mandan and Standing Rock the way it used to be. We all share resources. Don't let DAPL divide us. We'll build unity. Do not let greed consume your soul. Greed is very powerful. I've seen it in my own community.

Chris: Greed is very powerful. The anger is running high. People are tired of dealing with a situation they are not comfortable with. Seeing new people around. All I ask is to take a step back before you throw out a racial comment or something that could have been perceived as a threat. If my kids were with me that day in the mall, it never would have happened. So next time you're thinking about it, ask yourself what your kids would think. They see what we do and they will grow up and copy it.

Dean: I want to give a shout out. Because there are good people in the world. There are also good law enforcement in Mandan and Bismarck. And as much heat as they are taking right now, I want to thank all law enforcement. There are good officers who are upholding the law.

Chris: I give a lot of props and respect to Dean right now because he brought that up.

Dean: When you see me, don't be afraid. Come up and shake my hand. I'm human just like you.

Chris: I want to say to Standing Rock, I've gotten hundreds of messages of support for doing this. There's no reason we can't get over it. Dean and I are both live feeding. I think there's two sides of this and there's groups of both everywhere.

They read over the comments.

Dean: Basically we are fighting the same thing. We all have our differences. We all have our bad days and our good days. We don't have to like each other. Children, water, earth, productive.

Chris: I know this person. It says, can you please tell Dean that they are going to inspect the bridge and if there's no damage, it will be opened.

Dean: Wow. See, it's already coming together. Two different people come together and express to all the people out there. The law enforcement of Morton County, I'm asking you guys, for the family of your own generations. Do what's right in your heart. I want you guys to have your law enforcement jobs. Can we all just get along? Just do what's right. I do believe it's the police escalation that's inciting all the fear. Just speak with a good voice and it will be okay. Do not let corruption set in. Show the love, express it, feel it.

Chris: I will say that's one area where we don't agree. It is standard to wear that gear and to hold a line. I'm not going to point fingers, but I will ask that both sides stop it. I know a lot of the local law enforcement and most have good intentions. I hope we can have some more of these conversations.

Dean: I've learned to let him express it without trying to block him.

Chris: We could point fingers back and forth all day. We need to move forward in a positive way. We're not trying to all get along. Just to take it one step down.

Dean: I apologize to everyone again. Including the law enforcement that I flew my drone around. I'm sorry if you were scared or offended. I was just documenting history. It was a movement coming together. The whole world is looking at Standing Rock and Bismarck right now. That opens up opportunities for us to show the world that we can get along. Just learn to live together.

Chris: Hopefully we can get a lot of feedback and get together again with more people. Just keep having conversations. I don't want to see anything bad happen to Dean. He doesn't want to see anything bad happen to me either. Or anyone.

Dean: I love drones. It was fun. It was the greatest feeling ever. The feeling of pure freedom. I got a message from a ten year old kid who had put together a video with Legos. I've inspired people in Bismarck and everywhere. My vision, my side of the story, it changed me for the better.

Chris: I think we all know that the problems going on with both sides have to do with corporate money. Does Chris plan to go to camp? I would love to. Especially after this feed. Is it really safe for me? Things that happened, things I did.

Dean: It is safe. You have my word. If any of you want to have the experience of going to camp, come on down. It's just like everyday people. Drumming, singing, cutting wood. Chris really is a good guy.

Chris: I've learned to have respect for Dean too. It's paid off for us. Hopefully that can help spread a positive message.

They show a graphic someone already made. It says, Respect - with Dean and Chris' pictures.

Chris: I just have a big mouth.

Dean: It's okay, sometimes I'm a little jerky. Chris has to go to camp. People are commenting.

Chris: I will. With us both learning every day how to go forward with this.

Dean: We'll do a live feed from camp.

Chris: Okay, I'm down. Thank you for listening.

Drone2bwild (Shiyé Bidzííl) returns to Oceti Sakowin Camp

It is a live feed from camp.

It is very dark and looks very cold out. You can see DAPL's lights behind him. A woman asks him some questions - where's Candy? What about this cough? He doesn't know.

He says to Chris: You made it to camp! You are with me right now.

He shows the moon. It is big and bright. They walk over to people. The feed goes in and out. Chris does not stay very long because it is so cold outside.

It's cold out here guys. I'm gonna walk around in the dark now. Dang it's cold. It's too cold out here. It's cold, it's cold. Whoa, I'm gonna slip.

The screen goes dark. He goes inside of a tent and finds a light. You can see his breath. He reads comments. He shows his drone.

Yes, I know it's winter. Christmas is coming, we got a snowman on the hill. You guys want to know where the money is? I got something juicy coming about where all the money went. And all the other stuff too. It's still here. Time to get this fire.

He gets lots of great feedback from his meeting with Chris from his followers and from media groups.

"Chris and Dean have chosen to work together after they did some reflecting and apologized for their past actions. They're ready to unite for a better future not only for themselves but for their loved ones and their communities. We truly hope some good can come out of their interactions and wish them the best of luck!" ~ We Are The Media

It is reported that North Dakota is not getting any financial help on the federal level. Even though they have repeatedly asked for more funding, more law enforcement, more help in general. One article says North Dakota feels completely abandoned by the federal government.

And a recording from a corporate meeting about the Dakota Access pipeline is leaked. It tells about their underhanded methods to get this pipeline in the ground and oil flowing through it.

On December 15th he adds a photo of an emergency management SUV with a huge, sturdy antenna on top of it. He also adds photos of stingray equipment. Plus a couple of graphics that describe how these are used.

I want to address this post. They will deny it every time, but I believe this is what The Forces of DAPL have been using throughout the times when our Indigenous media was at a strong point!!!! Anything at their dispense to cover the truth!!!

He shares an article: How to block Stingray Devices 2016

Water protectors time to fight back and defend our phones?? Against this device!!! Try it!! Keep posted will have links for all phones!!!

He shares a YouTube tutorial: How to set up VPN on Android Devices.

This you need to use if you are in any public Wi-Fi service. Remember water protectors we got to keep up with technology to constantly keep in tune to updates and new software for the future of our cause and doing what's right for Mother Earth.

"Peacemaking doesn't mean passivity. It is the act of interrupting injustice without mirroring injustice, the act of disarming evil without destroying the evildoer, the act of finding a third way that is neither fight nor flight but the careful, arduous pursuit of reconciliation and justice. It is about a revolution of love that is big enough to set both the oppressed and the oppressor free." ~ Shane Claiborne

What keeps me going every day I breathe and live my life of fighting environmental injustice. Not against LAW ENFORCEMENT. NOT AGAINST A COMMUNITY. NOT AGAINST A STATE. But against positions in many levels of control within humanity!!! We citizens of the Dakota lands seek culture, a way of life, and the acceptance to be who we all are no matter what differences we may have or opinions we may say!!! We are all one. And that's what America truly should be. FREE!! #StandingRock #Mandan #Bismarck

He shares an article: Uranium Mining at the Grand Canyon? #HaulNo!

This has to stop! This is one of the greatest landmarks in the entire world and they want to mine out of it. How dare they! Time to step up water protectors and create canyon protectors!!!!!!!

Drone2bwild pipeline tour 2017!!! Exposure is coming!

He shares an article: Sabal Trail pipeline seizes Florida properties

With the rise of Standing Rock we have gathered the strength and prayer to send this knowledge throughout the world and to attack every black snake that has ever been laid on all of Mother's sacred grounds.

He shares a YouTube video: We are legion - the story of the hacktivists

Although I am not Legion, nor a hacker, I am just a listener with knowledge that I accepted by the energies of our actions. Defeats and oppression have bred a new generation of water protectors out of this fight with the Dakota Access pipeline. This can bring great change with stronger hearts to battle a new system of control between environmental us and the destroyers known as oil monsters!!!!

December 16th

He live feeds from the hotel. He talks about a troll who does a lot of videos and posts about the water protectors. He is in good spirits. Angelo Wolf is there with him.

He continues to talk about technological weapons that may be in use against the water protectors and the digital warriors too.

An article comes out in German about his work. They think he should get a Pulitzer Prize.

There is another troll who has been making rude and horrible comments about him – especially on his GoFundMe page. This troll plays dirty – trying to stop the drone movement at the funding level.

This guy's been popping up in everyone's FUNDING ACCOUNTS. The bottom left pic is how he gets around and hides. Once you accept his friend invitation, he invites five friends beware!!!!!

Perhaps this is A CLUE TO THAT MISSING VETERANS GOFUNDME ACCOUNT?? Hmmm. I do have my suspicions, but I will let my followers take a pick at this one.?????????????????

Digital warriors find the troll's information online and share it.

December 17th

In a live feed, he shares music by Nataanii Means. He captions the feed:

Just be honest in your heart. Why?

The people want to know.

Something just doesn't add up?

He shows an article.

Kenny Frost exposes stockpiled supplies in a warehouse. There is a photo of a mountain of boxes piled up in a warehouse. Kenny believes that Dave Archambault is involved in hiding these donations. Now Dave Archambault has told water protectors to leave camp. Will he keep all of these donations?

Shiyé Bidzííl gives an example of how DAPL helicopter tactics are used against Environmental Drone Activists!!!

It is a short video of drone footage.

There's the helicopter. The helicopter tries to fly close to the drone and says we are trying to crash into them. That's bull. We are out of the air space of that helicopter which is flying too low for FAA regulations.

Talk CELLPHONE spies, disconnection and defense, and other technologically advanced warfare tactics with Shiyé Bidzííl and guest Josh Long, tech entrepreneur.

He shares more information on technological spying and weaponry. An article about how drone data can be intercepted by hackers. And a live feed with Josh Long who gives extensive information about technology and how to stay safe.

December 18th

Angelo Wolf tags him in a live feed. Angelo is at camp on Media Hill. He plays a video. It is the Governor of North Dakota with a message about Dakota Access pipeline.

The governor says that the Obama administration has stalled this project and that has put North Dakota citizens and law enforcement in harm's way. He says that he supports the pipeline and talks about how great the pipeline is and how safe it is. He calls on the White House to issue the final easement.

Angelo: Get to North Dakota. This fight isn't over.

It's time to step up water protectors. Support the revolution so that we can overcome this dark shadow of corruption and greed!! Oh trust me you can be the most honest man in the tribe, but if you look at the darkness of the oil industry and the power of the money that they will throw at you, you know in that second your heart is already consumed with the black death of your human soul!! For all my people this has been the hardest temptation to ever overcome. The only way to stop this is to be true to yourself. To not look to yourself, but look to the future of the next generation and beyond that next generation that will ever be untouchable by this system of control. Support the revolution and like the page and stay in tune. For tomorrow is a brand-new day. Shiyé Bidzííl

OK WATER PROTECTORS TODAY'S PROJECT IS TO CAPTURE AND RECORD YOUR PHONES ACTING STRANGE OR ANY WEIRD ANOMALIES AND PLEASE SEND TO ME ON MESSENGER SO WE CAN PRESENT A FEW ON THE NEXT LIVE FEED AT 1PM CST. WE WILL DISCUSS MORE INTO SIGNAL JAMMING AND MEDIA BLACKOUT AT OCETI SAKOWIN FRONT LINES, PLUS DRONE DEFENSE.

Josh Long & Shiyé Bidziil

Talking about weird things going on with technology. Phones, computers, Facebook, drones...satellite signals. Moving information. Send me questions or stories about problems you've had. I've never experienced anything so weird than what's happened.

Water protectors check out this app and see what it's made of!

He shares an article: Google maps has been tracking your every move and there's a website to prove it –
Anonymous

Shiyé Bidzííl late night talks:

From an outsider who has never been at Oceti Sakowin Camp here at Standing Rock. And more on Stingrays and other high tech intelligence on DAPL & the case of RED FAWN!

Dean: This is one of those surprising late night talks. We're gonna get straight into this stuff. We have a random caller and they go by the name of Morgan.

Morgan talks about cell signals and how they can be blocked. Dean shows a graphic of how a stingray works.

Morgan: They can operate your camera or mic in any device. These are often used by police and military. They are looking at your info without a warrant this way. Technology changes day by day. Say something to your lawmakers - the more people who do, the more impact we all have. Maybe your device is acting up, doing things it didn't use to do. If you are in the physical area of Oceti, it's probably acting up. It's probably been compromised. Don't put your software updates off. Be sure you have a firewall, be sure you are secured. This is about our constitutional rights.

Dean: Snowden has brought this up. It's up to us to continue to update. Some people open their eyes, but then they go back to sleep. But this is an awakening.

Morgan: If your phone is acting up more than usual, look at your data. Look at your settings. Look at data usage. If that does not look kosher to you, do something about it.

Dean: You haven't been to camp yet, correct?

Morgan: Correct.

Dean: You did have friends who came, correct?

Morgan: Correct.

Dean: You believe your friend's phones were compromised, right?

Morgan: Yes. I am sure that my friend's phone and other devices have been compromised. Phone companies have allegiances with government and corporations. Save everything to uncompromisable areas. Save everything. Never take your privacy for granted. Always believe you are being watched and act accordingly.

Dean: Know your device is not completely secured. Always go in thinking they are listening. Never let it go out of your mind and you will always be safe. It's common sense.

Morgan: You can't trust anybody. You have to know everybody you are talking to. We are up against big corporate dollars here. These corporations do not care. They will hire anyone and do anything to satisfy their stock holders. What you say and what you do is being watched and they will use it against you. You have to be in the letter of the law all the time, and that's the only way to protect yourself. Being on the defensive means being aware all the time. What you say and what you do can be used against you in a court of law.

Dean: Red Fawn's court hearing is tomorrow morning. What's your take on that?

Morgan: It's obvious that what the police say happened, didn't happen. It's a real blow to us as water protectors and people who just care about people.

Dean shows pictures of Red Fawn on his computer. He scrolls his laptop while Morgan is talking. Morgan encourages everyone to donate to help them get justice.

Dean: If everyone has to donate one dollar, it makes a difference. Just one dollar.

They watch the clip of Red Fawn being arrested.

Dean: I hate to see people, not only our people, but any people, get oppressed and pushed back like that. My thoughts on them not allowing our water protectors to use video evidence, is that's not right. I'll make sure everyone uses their own evidence to protect themselves. If they don't let people use their own rights, then what are we doing in this country?

It's everybody in this society. People are the power. They like to keep us under control. But pretty soon we are all going to wake up and then they can't stop us. All the time the money seeps in even to the most honest and loyal people on the planet. But we can all overcome that power. People just have to have strong hearts. Take care of yourselves. You can look at a billion dollars and just walk away. That's the greatest power you have. If they shoot you in the back, you won. Because they can't take your power away.

Money don't mean nothing. You could just delete it all, there's true power like that. One day they are going to find out. I spoke truth and that's what they don't like. They did suppress this feed. Not nearly as many viewers as usual.

In a live feed from a hotel room, Dean and Josh Long talk.

Water protectors' cell phones & other data signal phenomena. The TRUTH from Standing Rock. Oceti Sakowin Camp information. With Shiyé Bidzííl & Josh Long

Dean and Josh cover a lot of topics. The chemicals that were possibly sprayed over camp, signals being cut off. Posts deleted off of Facebook. They talk about Red Fawn and what happened to her the day of Treaty Camp raid. He shows the video of Red Fawn's arrest in slow motion and they talk about it. They also talk about stingrays and other technological weapons that the government can use. The video cuts off.

Another live feed comes up soon.

Shiyé Bidzííl & Josh Long got shut down and of course we all know why!!

We have fan followers and they are called TROLLS!!!!!

Dean: Hey guys we're back on. Number counter is coming back quick.

They talk about trolls. There is dead air time while Dean looks up information.

Josh: Mainstream media is reporting that it's all over with, so it's up to us to get the news out there. Let's talk about hackers - databases - malware. These are tools everybody has access to. They target people's phones, even if they aren't out there in person.

Some people have court tomorrow. The prosecutor said they aren't going to allow video evidence. A lot of these tactics aren't being totally utilized probably because of the holidays. This would be the most opportune moment for police to shut down live feeds in camp.

Dean: Maybe we should try to rally against Facebook now. Only 10% of people are seeing the videos. Censored. I encourage everyone to send messages to Mark Zuckerberg. Tell him to stop censoring us.

He loses Josh's connection. He calls Josh back. It takes a while to get him back on.

Dean: Can't be afraid of them. We've been up for two and a half hours. Wow.

Josh: We should do a Monday morning live feed when they are too busy to mess with us.

Dean: I have a ton of questions here. 8am central time. Everybody set your alarms. If you want to know all the juicy details of everything you want to know about. You saw them cut me off. You saw them mess with the messenger call. Someone knocks at the door. He says, "Uh oh..that's them right there...No, I'm kidding." *(He laughs and ends the video.)*

December 19th

Today is the Water Protectors' trial.

Will Justice be served for the Indigenous Water protectors???

This live feed has several problems with signals and goes in and out. He still manages to feed for more than 3 hours.

He shows Angie Spencer at courthouse in a live feed.

Angie: Last time I was here was when I was in jail here. I was held in a dog cage right in this very building. We're here watching the first jury members chosen. My trial will be mid-February. We're here to heal this wound and have compassion for our perpetrators, for our abusers.

Angie walks around and talks about the trials. She talks about forgiveness.

Dean shows messages of people who are having trouble viewing live feeds - screens going out. He talks to Tangerine Bolen about how water protectors could go after the oil companies legally. They discuss the first amendment issues at hand.

Then he shows a live feed of Joye Braun who is outside of the courthouse. She's being interviewed by Johnny Dangers. Joye reports that a group of potential jurors were released. The trial was pushed back to late January. There will be other trials this week.

Shiyé Bidzííl talks dams and flooding. We are just too much Native!

His videos still get tens of thousands of views. Even the very late night feeds.

Dean is in a hotel room. He plays music from A Tribe Called Red.

If we have haters on here, let them hate. It's all they can do. We're going to do a little flood 101 education. *(He shows a map.)* Here's the flood plain. Here's camp. Sacred Stone's safe, right here. *(He points it out.)* They are right next to the flood plain. Now when that dam releases all that water out there... We'll look at dams and see if we should still be standing there or if we should be moving by now. Because if we are going to be smart Natives, we need to start focusing our energy. We have to focus on more than just destroying the pipeline. We're gonna get to that, but we have to all work together right now guys. A lot of people are getting too confused. You're forgetting what we're doing here. *(He shows a video of a dam breaking.)* Look at all that power there. You guys get the idea.

The Army Corps of Engineers are going to raise the water. They are trying to raise it so they don't drill. But in reality they are hitting two birds with one stone. Stopping the camp, making water protectors move out, and stopping the pipeline.

What do you think? Of course they are going to flood us out. It's common sense, we're in a flood plain. We need to move. If you are building houses on the ground, you need to think about taking it up. We need to move it up to higher ground. We all need to work together. Nothing is difficult. When we work together, we can get things done. Another lesson we're going to go through is unity.

Floating houses. Somebody's thinking outside the box. I like that one. If you're going to be here in the long run, we'll have to start improvising. That camp is not going to be there forever. It's going to flood. It's going to happen. They're trying so hard to get us out of that valley. I'm showing you the reality of what's going to happen. This water generates power. Do you really think they are not going to raise it? Good luck if you are going to stand right where your tipi is at. I'm going to be up on the hill. I'm just giving you guys a reality check. The highway doesn't get washed out. Probably media hill will be the beachfront when the snow melts, plus the flood.

He continues to show dams breaking.

Look at all that water. It will eventually fill up the whole river. The funny thing about this truth is they're not shutting this live feed off. They want me to show you this.

Get a houseboat or move up on the ridge. There's a thing we cannot stop, that's evolution. Adapting to the land, adapting to the world. But can we be one with the world and still progress? How can we really evolve back to earth? We only use 10% of our minds, so we should all come together and start thinking outside the box. We need to sign off the psych ops, we need to snap up and realize there's a whole big world. Corruption will eventually work its way out.

There are 1,200 to 1,500 people at camp - rough estimate.

You just can't stop the power of water. *(He shows more dams.)* Get all that hate and anger out of your minds. We're talking about water. We're trying to come together and think. Keep asking questions. But we're not talking about drones, we're talking about water. That's why this isn't cutting out. Just like everything else in the world, they're suppressing it, they're controlling it...the water.

We all have common sense, now we gotta use it. Let's just forget all that happened to us in the last four or five months and just watch the water flow. That's a lot of water. That's a lot of hearts. They're not cutting the feeds. We love water. Here comes all the water. *(He has beautiful music in the background. It makes the video more dramatic.)* Beautiful truth with a beat. Never just sat back and watched water flow, huh guys? Don't panic. Just drink a gallon of water and start moving your camp up on the hill.

He shows a picture of camp.

This is all going to flood. I've seen all of this flood. It's possible. I'm just telling everyone, just be smart. Start making plans now. Don't worry about the camp. If we all come together again and enjoy ourselves, DAPL will wonder what's gotten into the campers. We're rejoicing. The frontlines are everywhere. Not just at camp anymore. Sure gonna miss camp though. Moving on up.

We will still have Turtle Island, but we give the spirits respect. We don't conquer the hill, we pray for the hill. It's time to just move camp. It's time to all start going back together. That pipeline may go through. But there's something that came out of this. And we all see it and feel it. No matter how much the military or the government throws at us, we're still right here living and breathing. Don't let those psych ops get to your mind. I know they did us wrong. I know they shot at us, sprayed water on us in the freezing cold. We just got to stick together. No more letting that money get between us.

Money doesn't bring happiness. There's one thing I'm always going to remember and that's the camp. Remember we can't hold onto everything forever. We gotta learn how to let go of things. It'll make us stronger. All that history, all that hate, all that we came from. We just gotta let it go now. I got everybody riled up. That's how you make a thousand million hearts. This is how you tell the truth without getting cut off. It's everybody's truth.

He shows a picture of the ocean.

That's a lot of water. But it's getting polluted. Toxins are getting dumped in there. We bring awareness and our voice. And we don't have to be at the pipeline or at camp. We can be anywhere in the world. Yes, space is also getting polluted. There's so much junk. If we don't start taking care of it, we're not going to have a future for anybody. This is how you positively report inspirational news that just jumps out of the box, off the page, off Facebook. Because we're literally just watching a YouTube video.

He shows a photo of earth from space.

If we just step back and see the world in the bigger picture. The world's so big and yet we're fighting over treaty lands. Look at how the earth consumes you with so much color. Inspires you to do anything. The mother is crying out loud and she's weeping and telling us, stop. Before it's too late. We have all kinds of environments on this earth. Deserts, wetlands, jungles.

Standing Rock created awareness for the world. It changed everything. It changed all of us. It opened up our water protector eyes. There are more things that need to be protected. Mostly water though. Water is life. There wouldn't be life without water. We're one speck of dust in this whole universe and we have water.

So that's a little journey...just wanted to get your minds out of chaos, out of hate; what's making your minds fight each other. We could go back to the old ways, but it was the power of the internet that made this movement. But all we need is ourselves. We are the living, breathing stories.

Standing Rock opened the world's eyes. It's only been less than a year and look at what we've done so far. We've changed a lot of things. We gotta show the world what we're standing up for. It's gonna get worse. Standing Rock was nothing. It's gonna get worse, but after that you'll feel it. Stopping oil and mining corporations.

He shows another picture of camp.

We're part of history. We shaped that history. Because we're water protectors and it's going to take more than getting shot in the back with rubber bullets, getting sprayed with water, more than money, more than greed to take us all down. The major media come over here wanting to write a story and I tell them to put their cameras down and go cut some wood and tell a story. We want to hear your stories.

Back to the flood. All the atrocities that happened here, if this flood does come through, it's a cleansing. It's going to consume all that hate and take it down. And then the land will be clean again. There's the big ugly snake that was foretold that it was going to come. It's going to go across the river. Whether you like it or not, it's going to go across. We know because we're still standing here with our injuries. It's too important to them. Everybody's so caught up in the system, you forget sometimes that you need to let go of everything and just listen.

Someday we'll all walk these lands again. That fortress is going to go away. If it doesn't, we'll just have to organize an army of drones and monitor it ourselves. Each one of these hills is a prayer spot. These valleys, that's where our ancestors walked to connect. Now we have pipelines coming through. That's how much ignorance our government and people who want to control the world have. It's not about money, you can't take it with you when you go. If it does spill, I believe we can create a worldwide clean up. We gotta start thinking out of the box. If we cannot prevent that black snake from crossing the river, then we need to present ours - a system to collect the oil. Maybe we could save 18 million people's drinking water. We have to think of something better.

Look at this, before we ourselves tarnished that land - it was green.

He shows a picture of the land before it was camp. Then he shows a picture of the United States.

All the power on the east coast. All the dreamers on the west coast. All the hard workers in the middle. Pipelines, gas lines, electrical wire filtered throughout the land. Another hundred years, we're going to be so polluted. The oil companies need to look from up here. They don't do that because their minds are stuck in the right here and they only worry about themselves. They don't worry about future generations. There are a lot of great minds out there, but this is what they have pushed us to. We're so powerful that we gotta go around the world and start policing everybody else. We gotta take the weapons down first and start getting into their minds. Not psych ops, but happy things. It's a new world, a new generation.

If there's too much violence and hate in your mind, it will take you down. We gotta be there for each other guys. No time to start calling each other names. What would Sitting Bull do? He tried to do it but people wouldn't listen and they shot him. Let's take that history as a lesson. He would be sitting right where the fire is at. He would call upon all of them and warn everybody not to fall into that white man way. Don't be falling into that money way. We don't lead, we guide. We can all be leaders. We can't expect someone to know all the right answers.

We were never in the box, we were in the circle, the circle of life. In the old ways, we think outside the circle. But in the old ways if you are outside of the circle they called you backwards - but sometimes you need to be out of the circle.

Standing Rock is the beginning of a worldwide movement. Protecting the water everywhere. Respective power that we will have. Pipelines will never be built again. We got a lot of things to clean up now. We got Sabal pipeline. Feel welcome to post links to all pipelines, mining, everything. Those links are going to be our guide. I think Drone2bwild is going to go to Sabal. Could go to the Grand Canyon. For the good of the earth.

We did a good job. We went to hell and back and we're still here. Dust it off your shoulders, suck it up. We'll take them out in court and we'll go on to the next pipeline. That's what we do now. I forgive you guys if you dipped into corruption. You're only human, you can change. Standing Rock will change us all. Don't think too hard. Dream of water.

December 20th

It's because of the Drones

I AM A TARGET!

His feed goes in and out. It stalls and then comes back.

I'm being targeted because I tell the truth. It all started with the drones. The drones exposed a lot of things they didn't want people to see. The drones went to the front lines. Now those front lines are cyber space. They are trying to keep it hidden, but it's all over social media.

Money and power. Money and power. It's all America cares about. They don't care about the people. First they threaten you. They threaten to shoot you. They want to put in fear. But you gotta be strong. They make up videos mimicking you. They are paid. They are going to extreme measures.

A lot of people in the last few weeks have sent me messages about how my feeds are interrupted. I tell the truth and that's what scares them. Why aren't other feeds interrupted?

I know for a fact that they are censoring everything on Facebook. It's keywords. When said, feeds interrupt. A lot of people who haven't even been here are being affected. Suddenly their devices start messing up.

There's corruption on all levels. There's corruption and even framing. Oil industry will go way beyond the limits of civil rights, treaty rights. They don't give a crap.

If you don't feel anger, if you don't feel pissed off at all, then you aren't human at all. I know you guys care about me. I know you worry about me. But I am going to do something here that's going to change everything and open the world's eyes.

He shows an interview he did.

Dean: I've been documenting what's been happening on a whole different level. I have been shooting this from a cinematography level. I have been here since before it all started. I was the first drone pilot here.

The power of the drone gives me the whole awareness. I hone my skills in this technology. Through this, I am free. They may have built walls and trenches, but that does not stop me from exposing the truth. I can fly wherever I want to see. It's just video and it speaks for itself. It's truth. You can't manipulate it. I have so much respect for these drones. I call it High Hawk. I talk about drones in the spiritual sense. When they try to infiltrate us, we speak spiritual language, they won't understand us.

We bless these drones before we start. We give them power like the thunderbirds from our creation stories. I am here to protect the water and the land. My dream was to bring all these drones out and document truth. They spent billions of dollars building walls and hiring people to come stop us, but they underestimated DJI drones. It just takes one little drone. When you shoot one down, five more are resurrected. The power that the drone gives to the people. They feel safe because they are protected by the drone.

It was the drones that started all this infiltration. We are going to take the drones and fly again. We got some new drones. I am inspired to fly again.

In another live feed he shows Cindy from 88.1 FM FARGO/MOOREHEAD talking about Facebook live feeds being hacked and trolled. It is over an hour long feed. It gets stuck often and goes in and out.

Cindy talks about how to protect your devices online. She talks about the airplanes that fly over camp. She talks about stingray equipment. She talks to a caller about technological weaponry. Her live feed is also DAPLed a lot.

December 21st

Welcome to tonight's show. This is social engineering pros and cons and the mystery behind it all!!

His battery goes dead quick and he plugs in for more power. The audience builds quickly. Josh Long and Meko Haze are his guests and they talk about technology and what is causing all the devices to mess up. Not just in Standing Rock, but everywhere. Josh can't get online much at all – something is messing with his connection.

Dean: Sometimes you don't even have to be at camp and you have these problems.

He reads a comment: Christopher Chase: No, it's because you keep doing meth and are so paranoid. Maybe if you would quit doxing people and actually got some sleep you might not be so paranoid. How would you like it if people started posting crap about your kids or family members?

They talk about trolls. They talk about Dakota Access and how much money they are making. Both guests have trouble staying on the line. He ends the feed with some music and drone footage.

Has Facebook secretly been censored by Trump and his upcoming administration??? Or does the government have a new secret kind of weapon that distorts, scrambles and listens to everybody's computer, cell phone and landline phone without their knowledge?

He shares an article from Digital Trends: Facebook's secretive censorship guidelines leaked in new report

Another Public lesson apology between two worlds of people from this great NORTH DAKOTA STATE. He's a Bike Rider named Zach from Bismarck, North Dakota and Shiyé Bidzííl, a Drone Pilot, Water Protector from Standing Rock Nation. Together by RESPECTING personal differences & views WE CAN SHOW THE WORLD we can make a DIFFERENCE!!!! RIDE ON. A'HO

Dean: A special apology video. Between two people who grew up in different backgrounds, who see things through different perspectives. We want to settle these things. We all make mistakes and we all want to get together and make a public apology for how I went about things and for how he displayed certain things. I'd like to welcome Zach to the show.

Zach: So basically I made the video and it was funny. I wasn't trying to hurt anyone's feelings. I saw a live video and it looked fake. So I was just joking around and said, let's make a video. I didn't mean no harm, no foul on people. I didn't think about how many people would see it in the first place. Then it blew up out of proportion. Then, all of a sudden I was getting called out. It blows my mind that someone would get so upset over a video. It's just a dumb video. Let me be perfectly honest, I'm not pro DAPL or against DAPL. I don't care. I just want to clear the air because with my address being flashed out there, I don't want anybody doing anything stupid. That's the bottom line.

Dean: So what are we going to do then? We're trying to settle our differences here. I want to publicly apologize for the actions that me and my little team did. Sometimes we do things we don't want to do and it's out of our anger and emotion. I can see your point of view, it's funny. Hey, water protectors are funny. I guess we entertain people. From our side to your side, we're a community that wants to grow together, whether we have differences or not. You like riding bikes, we like protecting water. It's all good in the end.

Zach: It's really dangerous when you start putting people's addresses out there. That's really threatening. You don't know who all is following you. It gets out of control.

Dean: You took it down right?

Zach: Yes.

Dean: We took down your address too.

Zach: A video like that, I can see where you got mad, but when you put yourself out there for this many people, someone's bound to snag on it.

Dean: That's the thing we've been learning. How the power of social media works. There's pros and cons of it and this is basically a con of it. It can hurt you or it can make you feel better. Seriously, it did a lot of damage though. So to settle all of this, I'll go first and you can go second. Zach, I'm sorry for my actions this morning. I did it out of anger. I hope we can start a new friendship here.

Zach: I'm sorry if I hurt anyone's feelings with that video. I really am. But I was just trying to be funny.

Dean: I'm glad we went this way and now everybody can settle down.

Zach: I want everyone to know that my club does not have a stance on this pipeline. With them being brought into this, oh wow. It really got blown out of proportion. People in your live feed were saying to throw ball bearings at them going down the highway.

Dean: Hold on. All my followers. This is what we are trying to show. People are human, you have to give them that opportunity to let them change. People can change. We can inspire people.

Zach: For some reason people think I'm a racist.

Dean: Differences. I have trolls that troll my feed and reveal my background. I just don't pay any attention.

Zach: If my address wasn't posted yesterday, I wouldn't have done anything. I have Comanche blood in me. From my dad. I'm a mutt though. Whatever I'm racist against, I'm probably part of.

Dean: There it is. We've apologized and we're good to go.

Zach: This will give my family peace of mind. We're good here.

Zach hangs up.

Dean: How long have you been following me? Some have followed since the beginning, some for months. You follow me because I make random videos and play music. But most of all you follow for the drone footage. I'm going to go back to droning.

If you follow me so much, I would appreciate it if you take it easy on the people. Just because he has an image or a different attitude, doesn't mean you have to treat him different. When I was in Bismarck things were said to me that I'll probably never tell. It was meant to hurt me and I just took it in. You just gotta walk, just keep walking. Don't look back, don't look sideways. Continue on your journey and your path. A lot of people in this world say a lot of messed up stuff. When we were all at the front lines, there was a lot of cussing coming from our end and their end. I told them, don't say that stuff, it's going to come back to you. And sure enough, it did. It came back in the videos.

If we want to be Indigenous, we gotta hold ourselves strong. We want to be proud of what we're here for. We want to be proud of protecting the water. We can't be that image on the frontlines, then come back and start talking crap about someone else. I make mistakes too. I'm not perfect. I do let the ego get to me a little bit. I do let the anger get to me a little bit. But that's what makes us human. And we need that so we can boost our energy full of more love, more solidarity; more wisdom.

You gotta dwell in each and every one of your feelings. You gotta get hurt. You gotta get called a savage. You gotta get called everything else in the book. If you don't get called that stuff, then it makes you weak. You don't know how to handle society as you grow older. And then all of a sudden some people can't handle it. It breaks their soul. But that's what makes you stronger. You gotta get hit from all sides.

A lot of my water protectors are like, how come you didn't get out there and kick those guys' butts? Why? It's just going to make us look bad. I'm sorry I went up there by myself. I just wanted to be accepted for who I was. But I wanted to show the world. In a way it was a good thing. The whole world is looking at Bismarck now. The whole world is looking at Mandan. The whole world is looking at Standing Rock. That's what I provided.

We could take it this negative way and start beating each other on either side. No. I brought the world to these communities here so we can work together. So the world can see what we can do as Bismarck, Mandan and Standing Rock. Not fight each other. Not hate each other. Stuff happens. Believe me. Not everybody here is going to be a bad person. Not everybody here is good. That's just the way the world goes. The world isn't perfect. Nobody's perfect. If the world was perfect, then what's the point of living? I like to protect the water. He likes to ride bikes. That's his freedom and I'm fighting for that freedom. It doesn't matter. I could talk all night.

The truth. It's the lies, the deceit. Come on guys. You're better than that. You're Indigenous. So before you yell at somebody or use a racial term, we're fighting racism. 500 years, man. Let it go. We have to let it go. They got to let it go. And if they don't, in time, they will learn. Because we're just people. All we want to do is live a happy life. Yeah, some of us want to change the world, but it takes people who like to work together on different sides and different perspectives from different angles. Different opinions. But they still gotta work together. That's why we gotta stand together. All of us. Don't let DAPL corrupt us all.

Now I think I've shown that there are good people in Bismarck. There's bad people in Bismarck too. There's good people in Standing Rock. But, oh believe me, there's bad people in Standing Rock too. We gotta show the reality on both ends. That's the only way we're ever gonna see the big picture. I hope I teach you guys all a lesson. I try to have and I do have respect for everything. I know that there's some warriors still locked up for life. But in a way, think of it as them showing us. Let them be our guidance. Let them be our door. Balance. There's always going to be evil in the world. There's always going to be corruption. There's always going to be greed. There's going to be happiness too. There's going to be joy. There's going to be tears. But we need the evil so we can feel it in our hearts and that's what's going to drive us to put our foot forward and do things that we would never do in our lives before. But that's how you guys make change. That's how you make solidarity.

I had to go on that side to understand where he was coming from. I know all of you guys won't agree with what they say, but it's my choice. You guys can either look at me for an example or you can look away. But you're all tuned in here for a reason. And that reason is to learn. To respect. To enjoy life.

With that said, I feel like we can finally just cool down on Facebook. But it ain't gonna stop me from exposing the government. Exposing secrets. Secrets as Americans we actually need to see and hear. Not secrets and exposing families on Facebook or anything like that. No. Let's just take this for a lesson learned. It's reality. We are living in a sick world. We are living in an evil world. But we're living in it right now. And when we survive, at the end of this, it will make us stronger. It'll make our kids stronger. They're going to get stronger and pass it down from generation to generation to generation. And their kids up there, they'll pass it down from generation to generation to generation. It's all about family.

And in a few more days it's going to be about family. It's the holidays. It's the time of coming together. Enjoying the moments. Enjoying your kids. No matter what you did in your past, I'm pretty sure we all got punished. I'm pretty sure we all learned from it. And we adapted and it made a different person. We grew. We grew like trees. So Zach, you have a Merry Christmas, bro. Tell all your kids, Merry Christmas. And your mom and your dad too.

I hope this was a very special holiday greeting and a very Merry Christmas lesson. And I hope what everybody witnessed tonight brings everybody a lot closer.

Everybody is settling down. The warriors are still at camp. Go to Bismarck. Go Christmas shopping. Don't be scared. Take that fear, that DAPL fear that they put in your mind and get it out of there. We can do that because we're Indigenous. But you don't have to be Indigenous. We're all human. We have that power to control our destiny, our bodies, and our actions.

Have a happy holiday. Much love. Take care. Peace out.

December 22nd

He notes that he is feeling determined.

Now that Shiyé Bidzííl has shown you all his truths from our world, he will continue on his journey to speak, share, and to express his deep affection for our mother. Seeking all contributors to help aid this adventure he will take you all on. Out of chaos comes control, wanted but wild. DRoNE2BWILD.

Looking for the meaning of life. The forces of evil that control our lives. This is the schematics of the system. Acknowledge now and protect our generations. Share and unlock the secrets of Pandora.

He shares a post: The top secret network of government and its contractors

"You call me paranoid.

I call you uninformed." ~ Unknown

December 23rd

In a morning live feed with Josh Long he goes over the veterans' stand on December 4th. They talk about links and being careful not to click on unknown links.

He shows flight patterns for airplanes all across the United States. It shows that no planes are coming into Bismarck. It's the only place in America where there are no planes.

He shows a video of the governor. He is calling the National Guard and emergency management systems to come to Standing Rock.

He shows a photo of a woman. He says that he messaged her, but she never messaged back. He wants to know what she has actually seen. He says that someone says they saw crop dusting.

They talk about a local airplane that went down. They wonder if it could have been caused by signal interference.

Dean's computer is acting up. He shouts out a message to Morton County: Have a holly jolly Christmas. Think about your resolutions. What are we going to do next year? Fight another pipeline.

Drone2bwild takes it to another level @Standing Rock, ND

It is a live feed about the drone being shot. He plays music in the background. He shows the drone after it was shot.

Dean: There were ten shots that hit. These five were ready to shoot. GPS was damaged. As you can see NO HELICOPTER was HARMED during this confrontation with DAPL military police and Drone2bwild. Everything took place at very low altitude.

According to Loretta Lakalay, an aviation attorney who teaches Drone Law at Vaughn College of Aeronautics and Technology, the statute also prohibits interfering with anyone "engaged in the authorized operation of such aircraft" and carries a penalty of up to 20 years in prison. Since drones are considered aircraft, threatening a drone or a drone operator, according to Ms. Lakalay, would also be a federal crime subject to five years in prison under this same statute.

Mike Fasig posts a photo of himself and Dean, sitting on the floor at Prairie Knights Casino and Resort. They are looking at a laptop computer.

Mike says, "Dean and I going over footage, nothing special pic."

December 24th

I wonder what the world would say about all the cracks and breaks that the Energy Transfer Partners knew about. Did they responsibly follow up with their company's safety & guidelines procedures and environmental laws of the common citizens?

NO, because of their addiction to greed and power and a deadline.

"They just covered it up neglectfully knowing the situation of major catastrophe around these areas," says a previous Dakota Access pipeline worker whose name I will not mention for the protection and safety of the worker.

Take for instance the crack, rupture, break in the pipe line that occurred 150 miles away from camp. They will silence you. They will send you death threats. They will manipulate your community and the law enforcement around you to oppress your freedom of thought, speech and actions. I have proof of all of these locations. Proof and evidence of Facebook censorship of this topic. They are now preparing a bill that will soon hold protectors accountable for so called terrorism actions.

They call us terrorists but yet they are applying use of the most violent acts of injustice against a peaceful people who just want nothing but to protect what is right and the rights of the land and waters. Energy Transfer Partners and all of the oil industries are the only Terrorists

He shares an article: BREAKING: Oil company openly states they will defy Army Corps Order in Standing Rock. Energy Transfer Partners says the Army Corps' decision not to grant a permit to drill under the Missouri River does NOT change plans for Dakota Access.

Same old situations but TRUST me, new LEADERSHIP will RISE out of this new world order!

He shares a photo of Birmingham, Alabama in the 1950s when law enforcement used water hoses on African Americans during peaceful demonstrations.

December 25th

Angelo and Gabi live feed from a hotel room. Dean joins them on the phone.

Dean: We are putting together a tour called Drone2bwild pipeline tour. Getting a lot of resources together to get every pipeline in America. Merry Christmas everybody out there. I'm with my children. I don't feel lost any more. I'm ready to go after the holidays.

"I'm just a human being trying to make it in a world that is very rapidly losing it's understanding of being human."
~ John Trudell

Shiyé Bidzííl and Josh Long wish everybody out there a merry wonderful Christmas. We will be discussing new world order, DAPL, and the 45 secret government organizations within the United States of America.

In a live feed, he shows pictures on the screen of his laptop. They talk about camp security.

Dean: The computer went down on battery. There are people who have negative things to say on this feed. But they are still here. I don't know why. The best thing you can do with money is to burn it and keep warm.

He continues to show photos.

The only reason major media was out there was because the vets were coming. They got scared. This day is the first day when they used the psychological warfare, when this guy right here pointed his weapon at children. While a plane is spraying. And all of this together is psych ops. Everyday continued with shooting rubber bullets. Shooting at the groin. Shooting behind their backs. Shooting them in their faces. You see your brothers and sisters beat down.

They all have something against us. One Morton County cop says he watches all of our live feeds. You gotta start thinking into what their minds are thinking. They are hiring thugs and brain washing people. These cops think they are slick, but they are not. We're getting bad interruptions.

The live feed cuts out.

Part 2 Shiyé and Josh Long talk truth and the future of our society

Dean: Back again. When we start talking the truth, they cut us off. Still here. Played a Frank Wahn song. He's from Rosebud. A lot of artists came through and sang songs for us.

Josh talks about using your voice, your rights. They talk about making a better system for North Dakota. They talk about lawyers from other states coming in to help water protectors.

Dean: There are lawyers out there who want to come help, but they will not let them.

They talk about defund DAPL and the divestment movement. He shows pictures, graphics, memes from his laptop.

He calls Didi Banerji. She's in Toronto.

Didi: People can be so ignorant. I go out to Christmas dinner and people don't want to hear it. I show people pictures and they don't want to see it. I got to go to Washington, D.C. Everyone was there. They gave me two minutes to speak. I was in the worst spot ever after a rap band.

Didi talks about chemicals possibly being sprayed and how she's still coughing.

December 27th

Johnny Dangers posts:

Breaking News: Police Arrest and Violate the Religious Freedoms of 4 Peaceful Water Protectors Praying by the Mni Wiconi on a Peaceful Prayer Walk! Share Everywhere!

How better to understand the truth

He shares an article: How Dakota Access will lead the way in exporting America's crude oil to foreign countries

Shiyé Bidzíil knows truth and nothing but the truth!!!

"Truth, the only thing that people don't believe." ~ Unknown

Karma is gonna get you!!!!

Look it up on YouTube guys. Sometimes it's easier to look for yourself and see what we all can dig up.

He shares a video. They call Standing Rock a staged protest. They say they are paid protestors. They talk about the veterans showing up. They say events are staged and not real. They say Standing Rock uses chaotic situations as backdrops for their stories. They say 400 people were pinned on a bridge. Then, at the end of the video, it is Dean's voice. As if he participated in this video. But he clearly did not.

OK everybody out there, the truth is going to bed. So sleep tight, don't let those lies bite!! No more corrupted dreams. Wake up in the morning for more truth.

December 28th

Up in your face!!!!

It is a live feed showing law enforcement on top of Turtle Island. Water protectors are on the bottom. He is sharing this video from someone else.

On top of the hill there's about 20 cops. On the other hill there's about 30. So anybody tells you it's over, it's not. It looks like Drone2bwild needs to go back in the air. The blizzard is over. On top of the hill there they are standing on our sacred sites, so we're gonna have to come back.

Now I do have two drones ready. I'm ready to get back up there and do what's right. As long as we keep doing these actions Drone2bwild will be in the sky. The rivers are frozen so we can walk across now. Let's play a game of who comes closer into each other's territory. Literally, it's all our territory. Let's just start walking across the river. What else do we got?

Remember, they have insurance. So if anything gets out of hand, they're gonna get all that money back. Remember you guys, be careful. As long as you go up there in solidarity and prayer, and that's all we do is pray, we will be okay. So do some more of these actions here so we can get them all documented. Let's get them going guys, they're probably bored.

"People should not be unfamiliar with strategy, those who understand it will survive. Those who do not understand it will perish." ~Sun Tzu's The Art of War

He does a couple of live feeds about surveillance, hacking, IMSI receptors and other government tactics to use and stop technology.

Walk away investors. Walk away. Do what's right from your heart. Make the right choice to just not give your funds to the wrong hands of corporate greed. Happy holidays, much love.   Shiyé Bidzíil

He shares an article: Investors delay two billion purchase of Dakota Access pipeline stake

December 29th

Wow!! A load off my desktop!! At least they came out honest in the end.

He shares Waste Win Young's post. It is the minutes from a Standing Rock Tribal Council meeting.

Just FYI...the Standing Rock Sioux Tribe has passed a resolution allowing them to use the NoDAPL funds to pay off the tribe's debts...instead of using them for camp.

"THEREFORE BE IT RESOLVED, THE STANDING ROCK SIOUX TRIBAL COUNCIL HEREBY AUTHORIZES REALLOCATION OF UP TO $3.2 MILLION FROM THE NO DAPL ACCOUNT, ON AN AS NEEDED BASIS AND SUBJECT TO TRIBAL COUNCIL APPROVAL, TO FUND VITAL TRIBAL GOVERNMENT."

These are funds that people from all over the world donated for the resistance against Dakota Access pipeline. They were not donated for the tribal council's general use.

And still, the comedy continues.

I laughed my freaking ass off.

"I heard that Myron Dewey, Prolific The Rapper and Shiyé Bidzííl did a drone threeway that got too explicit to post on facebook. #DAPLrumors" ~ Dallas Goldtooth

December 30th

This is a live feed with him, Kevin Gilbert and Josh Long.

Let's get to know Kevin Gilbert a little more everyone!!?? Be nice and polite.

Dean: Welcome Kevin. Where did you come from and what's your stance on protecting the water in Standing Rock? Where do you see the future for water protectors?

Kevin tells that he came from England in 2006. He stayed mostly in the Midwest. He says that he comes from a background of addiction. He was first made aware of Standing Rock in August when a friend was arrested there. He says that it was really hard to live stream there.

Dean: You can live feed anywhere in the camp now.

Kevin: I was blessed to be able to get signal on November 20th when the actions on the bridge happened. That footage was picked up by Jill Stein and Bernie Sanders.

Dean: They were cutting your signal out several times, right?

Kevin: Yes. You could hear my voice most of the time, but the picture was really bad.

They talk about how technology was shut down at Standing Rock. All kinds of things happening to their devices and their followers' devices.

Dean: So what's your thought of money and the control of it?

Kevin: Specifically around the pipeline?

Dean: The money that surrounds all of us every day throughout funding, throughout government, throughout the pipeline.

Kevin: I'm going to sound a little hypocritical because I'm using technology and stuff that needs money, but all you truly need in life is you need food to eat, water to drink and you need shelter. We've been led to believe that we need all the other things by advertising on tv.

Kevin talks about building your own shelter and growing your own food. He goes on about how government is scared of people not using money and going green.

Dean: I believe before great change, there's great chaos. I believe what happened at Standing Rock is the beginning of great change. I believe that pipeline will go through and it will leak. But what we learned here as family is that Standing Rock is everywhere. Everywhere you dream it. Everywhere you believe it. We can fight more than just pipelines. We can fight humanity for the better good.

Kevin talks about what he's doing next. Dean asks about him shaving his beard and everybody laughs. It is a nice exchange between the three of them. Kevin wants to network.

Dean: You are going to have to come back to Standing Rock.

Kevin: People in Bismarck don't really like me. I've had death threats.

Dean: Me too. You have to come out of that. You are a different person, stronger in the end. And the fear just blows away with the wind. Don't be afraid.

Kevin: I don't think so.

Dean: Just wanted to get to know a little about Kevin Gilbert. See who he is. A lot of people have a lot of different things to say about Kevin. But before we say, we need to get to know him. We learn how to be a good judge of character. To let the other person speak and see what they're about. And that's what we did tonight and it's all about coming together whether we're Indigenous or other colors. It doesn't matter. We're all here for the same thing and that's to protect the water. And now it's gone beyond protecting the water. It's about what's right in this world.

December 30th

Shiyé Bidzíil, Josh Long, Cindy Gomez-Schempp talk about the camps and water protectors' legal issues and where to go from here, and the future of Standing Rock!!! Tune in followers!!

"Just be honest with me or stay away from me. It's not that difficult." ~ Unknown

Looks like karma has already found its way!!

He shares an article: Utah Attorney General says he'll sue Obama over national monument: Protect Bears Ears

December 31st

Shiyé Bidzíil / Drone2bwild Photography & Video has reportedly been detained. He is safe. Please send prayers for Dean.

Chapter Eight

January 4, 2017

Shiyé Bidzííl says to all my followers I am ok!!!! Thanks for all your love and support!!

January 5th

The coolest lady I've ever met I'm glad we are friends!!!!!

He shares a screenshot of actress, Frances Fisher.

In a live feed late that evening:

Steven Jeffrey Chrisjohn and Shiyé Bidzííl talk Camp and the future of Camp life in the new year of 2017.

Dean: Welcome everybody. I'm okay. I'm doing good. I'm healthy. My spirits are good.

He plays some music... smiles... There is a Standing Rock flag behind him. Steven asks if he can hear him.

Dean: Yes, I can hear you good. Good late night talk with everybody. I'm doing good. I'm healthy. Looking good. I will not reveal where I'm at for the safety of myself. People always try to call everybody when you're doing a live feed. But I'm okay, as you can see. We have Steven Jeffrey Chrisjohn.

Steven talks about experiencing PTSD. (Post Traumatic Stress Disorder)

Dean: Yes, I have experienced PTSD. It's not pretty. It's a scary feeling. It doesn't affect me 24/7. You want to be honest with yourself. It comes to me in really weird ways like the time when I was traumatized from just turning the world's eyes on Bismarck. When I got threatened at the Ramada Inn. For a good week, I closed myself in. The only way I felt safe was being connected on Facebook. And I was hell bent on finding out who those people were. It opened a lot of doors to things I didn't want to know about.

People will start resorting to drugs and drinking. A lot of people talk about me sometimes. And it's true I have resorted to taking drugs. It's not a pretty sight. It's a way of dealing with the situation and stress that DAPL has put on all the water protectors. But in the end it makes us stronger because before there's happiness and strength, you gotta feel the devil, you gotta feel death, you gotta feel fear. And in the end it builds your character, it builds strength. I've dealt with it.

A lot of people want to talk crap about me. Oh he's a meth user, oh he's a drug user. The new one is oh, he's a drunk. If I was a drug user and a drunk, then why are so many people in tune with my page and why do so many people believe in me? But that's what the PTSD does to a lot of folks, a lot of water protectors and I've seen it in a Diné brother of mine. I won't say his name. But people who are connected will know who I'm talking about.

For real talk, it messes with your mind. And this all goes back to psych ops and what they are doing to the water protectors as far as illusion. It's the water cannons, it's the tear gas, it's all the stuff they've done to us. And after 500 years of genocide and oppression and the world is witnessing what happens. It goes down through the generations.

What happened through this whole movement is that it created a new kind of human. It created water protectors. It created a new breed of water protectors. And this new breed is living through 500 years of oppression, alcoholism; it's living through drug abuse, domestic violence. It's living through all this stuff from just being human beings. And we live with all of that and we come, we're fighting the system, we're fighting to protect the water. We're fighting for herbal rights. We're fighting for a lot of things. In the end it does build our spirit. But in the end it can also crush our spirit.

So we gotta be very careful about how we carry this knowledge and how we carry our spirits. We need bad things. To accomplish the good things, we need to experience the bad things. We always need evil in our lives. We need hate to experience the good and the love. So there's never going to be an end to bad stuff. There's always going to be bad stuff. But we learn from our mistakes.

Steven agrees with him. Dean shows a graphic about PTSD. He reads over it.

PTSD shows up in your everyday actions and in your thoughts and your dreams. Am I nervous? I've never been nervous since I got so talkative on Facebook live. Am I abandoned? At times I was. I make myself abandoned at times. Am I guilty? I used to be guilty of a lot of things, but I let it all out. Am I helpless? Sometimes I make myself feel helpless. But is it natural. I believe it's your mind that makes you think like that. Nightmares? When I was in jail I had nightmares all the time. It had to do with snakes, it had to do with spiders and it had to do with fog, dark fog. And flashbacks, yes. Every time we talk about certain situations, I have flashbacks.

And fearful, this is one thing. Define fearful. I don't experience fear. Because I have a lot of people, people who support me through my live feeds and people who I know in physical form who really do ... Oh thank you Frances Fisher... oh by the way guys, this makes me feel happy. She sent me something in the mail today. She sent me her little book of all the pictures she took while she was at camp.

He shows a beautiful photo book.

It brought a lot of things back to me. There's my drone. There's Turtle Island.

He shows pictures of water protectors. Photos of actors, Mark Ruffalo. Shailene Woodley. Jane Fonda. The youth council.

What we've done here on Standing Rock, we've turned eyes here. In that valley we will all remember what we started and what we did. But Standing Rock is everywhere now. Standing Rock is in everyone's hearts. We don't have to be at the camp.

That's what I keep telling everybody. Everybody keeps saying, Dean, you need to go back to camp. I've taken in a lot of things and learned a lot of things at camp. We can go wherever we want now. Because we are water protectors we have the knowledge and the strength in our souls. We have that unity and that family and our family is worldwide. We have support wherever we go. We have support around the world, in every state.

We can go to every pipeline and we can show them and speak the knowledge and speak about the skills and we can speak about the hardships that we've been through at Standing Rock. We can take it to other places. We can take what we've done here and we can take it to every environmental cause. And we can go beyond environmental causes. We can go and protect the children. We can go and protect the elderly. We can go and protect the sick. We can go and take care of corruption. That's the power and knowledge and strength we've gained as water protectors and just as people who have been through 500 years of oppression. Alcohol, violence, drugs, addictions, greed, corruption; everything.

And we can make it better. We can enlighten a lot of people and a lot of souls and we can show people that there is change. We can show it, we can feel it. It's all about the love. And for me it started with the drone. That first purchase of that drone opened a doorway, a window for me to dwell in this other world of everything I never thought I'd be doing to this day. I don't know if I'll ever hold a 9 to 5 job. A lot of people say, you gotta get a job, you gotta do what's right for your family. I am doing what's right for my family. The world is my family. My children are my family. And I'm going to do what's right and that's speak about what's right.

I'm going to keep protecting the earth, keep talking about children's rights, elderly rights and Indigenous rights. I'm gonna do what's right. And I can call it my job. I love it. I love what I do. I don't want to go back to a 9 to 5 job. I'm sorry. Whoever's out there who works a 9 to 5 job, I'm not going to say anything against it. You all work hard for what you have and what you've done. But for me, I live life to the fullest. I live doing what I want to do and how I want to be. For me, holding a 9 to 5 job is being a slave to a system that wants you to feel comfortable so you don't have to cause the government or the system any problems. Pay a lot of money to learn a lot of education when education and knowledge should be free. But if you do it the right way you can get knowledge and education for free. There's ways to snake around and go above and below the system. You just gotta be smart about it and you gotta think outside the box. Or in our case, the circle. You gotta think outside the circle.

But in reality the government calls us extreme domestic terrorists. We're beautiful people who like to protect what we love. It's what we do.

Steven talks about money and greed.

Dean: You brought up money and we got two angry faces. It's funny when you bring up money something triggers in the brain. Excitement, hope. All kinds of vibes come out of it when money is spoke. As much as we're fighting a system that is based on the almighty dollar, Steven does speak the truth. Yes, money does talk. But, we can use money to the advantage, but we have to use it in a good way. We can't just get greedy and get corrupted.

We're gonna talk about money. People keep saying stay away from it... but we're going to talk about it. Money is colonialization. Money, money, money, money, money. Money is everything. It takes money to buy drones. It takes money to support a movement. It takes money to pay your bills. It takes money to put gas in your car, to burn that fuel that came from Mother Earth. It takes money to get people from point A to point B. In a way it shouldn't take money. Because before money, we still progressed. We still did all that. But times are changing. And if we are going to get ahead of things, sadly we are gonna have to deal with the money.

We all need funding. A lot of people are posting GoFundMe pages for Standing Rock. To be honest, I don't trust those GoFundMe's for Standing Rock. Not one bit. Here's what I have to say about that. Fund where your heart goes. If your heart is set on certain individuals, fund those individuals. If your heart is set on supporting the camp as a whole, then support the camp. We're all different people. We're not telling you who to fund and who not to fund. You can even fund a prayer sent on messenger. That helps a lot.

Speaking of funding, we're going to get into it. Standing Rock Sioux Tribe. By the way, this flag here *(he points behind himself)* is from Dustin Thompson. This flag was flying on the day they raided Treaty Camp. As much crap is coming out of Standing Rock politics, I'm still going to support Standing Rock because that's where I come from and that's what I'm about.

My take on the whole situation is that money talks, bull walks. In the end it's truth. I don't need money to speak truth. I'll just speak it right now.

You know what's been said. Why put that all out there. People want to be heard. People don't want to be screwed over. People just want to know the truth. And if they took the donations, the 3.2 million dollars, donations from the camp, if they took all that and liquefied it to get them out of debt, I can understand that from a business standpoint. The tribe cannot go broke. The tribe needs money. Because the tribe used all the resources. I saw that. I agree with that.

The casino was getting dried out. I wanted the casino to go back to the way it was. The bar was getting shut down, entertainment was lost. There was no gambling. The casino went as far as to open the pavilion for all the water protectors that were coming. But if we were going to invite the world to Standing Rock, we should have been prepared. What if we invite 20,000+ water protectors? Where are we going to put them? They never thought that far ahead because they were already focused on the money they were going to get.

We needed all the water protectors. We were all here. And we were so focused on the pipeline, the pipeline, Morton County. We're standing in solidarity. It's because we underestimated that there are a lot of good people in this world. But there's a lot of bad people in this world too that we opened the door to. Hackers. Yes, I said it. They don't even have to come here. They can log on from any part of the world and start infiltrating GoFundMe accounts, emails. They looked at Standing Rock and that was an opportunity. Hackers and all bad people take advantage of the movement.

And even our own tribal people. Yes, I said it. Here's how I look at it. If I was a leader, you could look at this almighty wall and you look 1,000 feet right and left and you look up 1,000 feet. You think, I cannot get over this wall, this corruption. But you stand there. If money comes off the wall, you don't pick it up. If there's a ladder you climb it, if there's a rope, grab it. You can't just come to the first 100 dollar bill and grab it and say, oh it's getting easier and easier guys.

As a leader you should not succumb to corruption and greed. You're trying to say that you're trying to save the tribal programs. Yeah, I can agree with that if you're gonna take the money, put it out to the tribal system. Put it out to where it belongs. Put it in programs that help the veterans, that are going to help the children. That are going to help support the camp. And to help build a whole environmental system. Don't be stuck. Think outside the box. Don't grab that whole box of cards, funding cards. Don't grab those and run off with them and say, I just wanted to keep them safe. Just don't take that money and do that. You should have been honest from the start. You should have been honest. You should have told the people. It's not about yourselves or your little family or your dream or whatever you need to get in life. It's called sacrifice. It's called doing what's right. And it's called letting the people know because it's the people's right to know.

It's our reservation, it's our Standing Rock, it's our home. We don't do this. We don't take the money. Just because the whole wall was hard to fight. Just because DAPL had so much money and power and resistance. You can't just give into the first 100 dollar bill they give you. No. You keep standing there and you say no. I'm not going to do this. I'm not going to take your money. I don't care if you give me five million or five billion. Don't take the money. That's a true leader. A true leader that's going to do right for his people and not put them to shame.

And don't say we're going to shut down camp because we want a road open. You're gonna let that system that did so much bad to your people, spray them with mace, shoot them with rubber bullets, disrespected your tribal lands and your treaty lands. You gonna let them boss you around? You gonna let them say if you shut down camp, we'll open up that way for you. No, you don't let them tell you what to do. You are the bigger person. You tell them what you want to do because you're the leader, right?

I'm just saying, it's money. If you're going to receive it, do what's right for the people. Create jobs. Create better jobs. Create better jobs than the casino, because the casino is called a revolving door. Trust me, I've been through it. Create opportunity. Beautiful opportunities for the children so they can be inspired every day. So they can go out and be inspired and want to be something. Not go outside and feel depressed because their neighbors are drinking.

You need better programs. Especially for Indigenous veterans. They protected our country that they've been oppressed by for 500 years. But yet they go to war and do what's right for the country. And the code talkers. Respect them. Especially the Diné code talkers. We created the code that was never broken. I think it was the accent. They couldn't understand Navajo. I love my Indigenous culture. I'm proud to be Navajo, Diné. And I'm proud to be from Standing Rock, Hunkpapa, Lakota.

I am not ashamed of anything. Because why be ashamed of it? I suffer from PTSD. I'm a drug abuser when it really gets to my mind. Yeah. But I don't let it control me. My heart, my mind. I control my own destiny. This world is my own making.

You follow me, you listen to me, you don't gotta listen to me, it's your life. But I love all of you guys from the bottom of my heart. And all the haters out there, I love you from the bottom of my heart because if it wasn't for you haters out there, you're just boosting me more and more.

I'm glad I'm back. I feel better than ever. I'm not going to stop what I'm doing. I'm going to keep doing what's right and I'm going to point out the wrongs. I'll even point out my own wrongs. No one's perfect. I'm not going to hate or put down my own people who are doing wrong to us. I'm going to pray for them. And I know in my heart that I'll make the good choice in the end.

And if they're going to take the money, do the right thing, that's all I ask. Because the whole world's looking at Standing Rock right now. We need to make Standing Rock better. Much love to LaDonna Tamakawastewin Allard and much respect to Chase Iron Eyes. They have strong hearts and I believe a lot in them. They need our support. For the people who are doing wrong in the tribe, I still support you too. I might be a little smart mouthed or a jerk, but I love you guys. You're still my brothers and sisters and elders and great leaders.

So when I cruise around the rez or you see me around, don't be scared to come shake my hand. Especially those at the KLND radio station. I haven't once heard in five months. I miss you guys. I still have love for you guys. Don't hold a grudge. Don't be silent no more.

Oh, as much mail as I never received, I want you to come out Ernesto and say what you did wrong. Then I'll forgive you bro. Here's what I actually got in the mail. Inspire battery warmers. The batteries need to be warmed. Thanks to DroneGear, my sponsor that supported me with a drone. A new battery for the Inspire Pro 1.

Now I'll have more battery life. And we can fly a lot better. This is like Christmas. I never got my check from Vice Canada and that was a lot of money, I was going to use that for presents for my kids, but I never got it.

I want to answer someone's question. Debbie Brown. Yeah I'll get a job and get my kids Christmas presents. They actually got drones, because that's all I had. And I inspire them to love drones. They love it when I fly the drones. And that's what I gave them for Christmas.

I don't know when I will fly again. But trust me, I'll fly again. I'm not going to say when. But you'll see when I'm back in the air. I actually want to do some extreme stuff. Oh and one more drone. We'll get this one up in the air too. Unfortunately all my Phantoms got shot down. They all went for the cause.

January 5th

He shares a live feed from the tribal council. They are talking about flooding at camp and how people need to move.

We can spread it around the world. We don't need to be at camp. But we all know all of this. Let's get to the real truth.

He puts out another live feed.

Dave and Avrol, you guys were the leadership. Now you're saying whoever the leadership is? They are just poking at who's left at camp. Yeah, of course we know a flood is coming. I've warned the people. They will move. But we know all of this. We know the safety. But how are we going to get the truth out about the funding? That's what I want to know about. The supplies.

He shows someone's live feed of the council meeting.

Should we talk about what's really going on? Who's stealing from us? The camp will still be there, it will be on top of the hill. It is in our hearts. Standing Rock is with us no matter where we go. They obviously want to sustain Standing Rock. Financially and spiritually. But I don't hold nothing against these guys.

Move now. The time is now. The road will be open. Make everybody happy. Remember, we got drones, we can fly them over. We could take advantage of the frozen river and do actions. But we need to stop back stabbing each other, stealing from each other. We need to come together. In spring time we will have many more people coming. We can continue this fight until the black snake is gone. Because if we stop this fight, there's going to be a scar forever.

For example, the Black Hills. Now there's four presidents who pretty much disgrace the sacred Black Hills. It's going to live on throughout history. We don't want that.

Infiltrators might have gotten to the council. But think outside the box all my peoples of the world.

A council member on the live feed says, "We'll be there for you guys. We have resources."

Yeah, 3.2 million dollars from donated funds. All I want to know is about the 3.2 million dollars you took in the dark.

Push the hearts guys. More hearts.

I want to hear the real truth. I've heard all this stuff already. I'm going to set up for some live feeds later. There are some issues as far as organizing and certain individuals in the camp. They are reviewing everything I already know.

Today I awoke with a new level of higher understanding of life and death. A darkened world beyond our creation stories. A nation of illusions has brought out colonialism to most extreme progressions. Evolution of extractions of Mother Earth. Spiritual beings we now define as WATER PROTECTORS. Sacred traditions filter through laws and systems of the American dynasty of this manifest destiny. A new evil has surfaced within us that stems from our deepest coincidence of our fragile minds. Hate and Love again in an everlasting battle of beauty and cruelty of man and its environments of Mother.

Dean Dedman Jr. 2017

He shares a music video: A Tribe Called Red - Burn Your Village To The Ground (Neon Natives Remix Video)

January 6th

He notes that he is feeling motivated.

What Shiyé Bidzííl has done is beyond just operating any drone, but to push the technology to its limits and fully expose OIL Operations Nationwide. He has opened new doors to opportunity and advancement on how we can document and survey endangered Indigenous lands and to protect our human civil rights and future generations to come. Now he has been called out around the nation and world to travel and speak to many communities, cities, tribes, fundraisers and schools of many levels of learning to promote and share his story about, "How one drone changed his life forever." What he brought to Standing Rock and The Oceti Sakowin Camp is a new sense of FREEDOM and strength. He shared with the world his vision of free speech and acts of change that inspired a new generation of drone pilots. So I encourage everyone to SHARE AND PROVIDE this NEW TRAVEL PAYPAL ACCOUNT so he can spread the knowledge even further. Thank you for your support and donations.

Groups of water protectors all over the United States are still protesting at banks and doing their best to get people to divest from all the financial institutions that support DAPL and fossil fuels.

This is what you call a picture update. As you can see I'm in perfect, healthy condition and perfectly safe in an undisclosed location. Be safe out there everybody and stay tuned for the next most wonderful live feed yet!! You're just gonna have to follow me and stay updated and aware of all things that are going wrong on Standing Rock!!!

January 10th

I miss my babies so much. They are my world. They are my future. They love and miss their dad so much I hear them in my dreams. Dad loves you so much!!!! You are my strength and future and why I fight every day to keep this world safe just for you.

Water Protectors Invade Snoop Dogg's live feed!!!!!!!

He shares screenshots of Snoop's live feed with the comments. He typed DRoNE2BWILD over and over and over. Other water protectors are also in the live feed typing support messages for Standing Rock and No DAPL.

January 11th

It's official. DRoNE2BWILD has entered The NEW YORK DRONE FILM FESTIVAL. The prize is world recognition and respect. The Power of Standing Rock and illegal activities premier on the big screen. The world is watching.

He shares Alex Kavanagh's post: I've brought in the New Year and submitted my first ever entry into a film festival, The New York City Drone Film Festival. My entry is called: DRoNE2BWILD. On my first day at Oceti Sakowin Camp at Standing Rock, North Dakota, I interviewed Shiyé Bidzííl AKA Dean Dedman Jr. on how he's been using drones and what this technology means to him and the movement by water protectors. How Dean describes a drone is like you've never heard before, the drone is symbolic to him like the bald eagle and the thunderbirds. Dean calls his drone High Hawk. I personally donated my most expensive drone to the cause, as I felt not worthy of owning it and wanted to give them the tools needed to keep up their great work.

Everywhere we go we all have water and community issues same as here in Redwood City, California.

He live feeds from the Drone2bwild page. It is drone footage of above Docktown, California. He says that it feels good to fly again.

Drone2bwild presents: Docktown, California. The Bay Area. The city wants these houseboats, a 50 year old community, gone. The city wants to bring them down so they can build these huge condo apartments which personally I, Shiyé Bidzííl, would say have very bad architectural designs for this type of project and location due to the earthquake zone area. So obviously it's another issue of divide and conquer within Redwood City, California.

In a live feed:

Shiyé Bidzííl welcomes everyone to Docktown!! A floating boat community that's on the brink of being destroyed by REDWOOD CITY. A water community under attack. Spreading Standing Rock Solidarity. Special Guest: Lee Callister

I know you missed the live feeds. I took a break. I'm doing a new travel thing. I'm going out and spreading Standing Rock solidarity. They are still up there in Standing Rock fighting. I am not there, but Standing Rock is right here with me.

What I've been doing for the past year. It's an intense fight. They are still fighting. But I was dealing with some bad negativity. Everyone knows it. Everyone sees it on Facebook. It's because people are úp there telling stories, telling lies so people will leave and they can shut the camps down. It's all about that psych ops, that psychological warfare. They're turning our own people against each other. They're making believe people sold out. All kinds of tactics. It's crazy.

Well, I'm here and I wanna get to it. I'm actually in Redwood City in the Bay Area. It was a pretty intense flight. I arrived here last night. Had to circle the bay twice. It was crazy, my stomach was getting all crazy.

I'm going to kick it for a minute. Get to see California. Going around and spreading that awareness. Standing Rock is everywhere. In every state, in every country. Of course I'm from there. Standing Rock is my homeland. I know everybody's saying that when everybody leaves, I still gotta be there, but I actually left in a good way. A lot of people were worried about me. Where's Dean, we need drone pilots here at camp, but there are drone pilots at camp. I am aware that Chase Iron Eyes has a drone. There were a lot of drone pilots there.

But for some reason everyone kept texting me, telling me to get to camp. Every time I was itching to get to camp, I had a lot of people saying, stay away from camp. Don't come back there with the drone. It's either because they don't want me there, or they are protecting me. All of the strange occurrences going on at camp, it's better being safe than sorry. You always gotta stay one step ahead of everybody.

A lot of people were wondering where I was. I just was hiding out. Not really hiding out, but being safe about things. I knew camp was negative so I stepped out of camp. But what we can keep doing is we can keep sharing the awareness and solidarity. Because right now we can't go across that line anymore, they have insurance. They are going to get their money back if anything happens to that pipeline. It's cold and it's time for survival. People go into survival mode and start doing things they don't normally do and they start thinking in ways they don't normally think. In the end if you are a strong warrior, you'll come out of it all.

He introduces Lee. Dean says that he takes care of Docktown.

It's like a floating town. He's been following Standing Rock, big supporter.

Lee: A lot of people in Redwood City support you....you are our hope. We've been looking to you as a role model because you've done such a good job at standing up. We have about 180 people living in floating homes. Now they want to get rid of us. Pressure from developers. They say we are harming the environment. None of it is true. Lawyer filed a lawsuit...terms are is that we have to leave.

Dean goes outside and looks around. He shows some houseboats.

Dean: They have been here over 50 years. The city wants to get rid of all these boats. They want to build big condos. Remember earlier I was talking about houseboats. This story is out with the old and in with the new. Also a story about how they want to control all of the water.

I know a lot of you were worried about me. I'm perfectly fine now. My spirits are high, I feel a lot better. Throughout the time of December when I disappeared, a lot of people are saying a lot of things. They can say a lot of things. I do what I gotta do and I say what I gotta say. If you don't like what I say, why are you still following me?

Those of you who do still follow me I'd like to say once again, thanks for staying there with me. I get a lot of messages every day. Even when I don't live feed. It's been pretty crazy on this journey.

In a later live feed:

Shiyé Bidzííl gets a closer look inside a boat house at DockTown,

It's dark out. I'm walking on this big plank here and it's a dock. And it leads to all these boat houses. It's pretty neat. You can just have a boat and pull it up here and live here. It's a pretty cool idea. Remember I was talking about boat houses? This is a boat house. These are nice boat houses. They have three story boat houses, they have regular boats. We are walking - going inside... careful.

Someone tells him to stay to the middle when he is inside.

Dean: Oh it's a moving house.

They go inside. A dog makes noise.

Owner: It's a bit of a wreck. I have to clean this up... it's just all my stuff.

Dean: Right now I'm rocking the boat. Kinda feels like I've had something to drink. But it's a house floating on the water. A boat house, I think I could get used to this. It's a good idea, but it's pretty crazy. I'm pretty sure you'd puke, Didi. But at least it's not snowing here. You get used to it after a while. The big difference is it feels like you had a six pack. There's a full moon out. A king tide comes in. The water rises. It floods. We came earlier today and it was flooded. They are building these huge condos. It's a very bad design. A waste of foundation, less living space. They are an eyesore. Chris Turley's looking in on the live feed. What's up Chris? Beautiful moon out. Marshall. Steven. Tomorrow I will be in.... so many towns, I forgot where I was.

Drone2bwild rap beat: Song Coming Soon. Shiyé Bidzííl & Justo St Clare cruising the Bay Area. Spirits High!!

Dean is riding in a car. They are listening to music. He shows a NoDAPL art build page. They are in traffic. He puts on Indigenous flute music. He shows photos of Standing Rock. Canoes, camp, actions, flag row.

Later he shares Angelo Wolf's live video. Angelo has managed to get Didi Banerji, Ed Higgins, himself and Dean in the same live feed.

They make plans. Everyone talks about what they are doing. Dean plans to go to Santa Cruz with Justo. Nobody is sleeping well. They are all surprised that they are on a four way live feed. Everybody misses everybody.

He is tagged in a post by Joye Braun:

"The Oceti Sakowin Horn is taking down its fire today and coals are going back with the bands. The fire, relit after all these years after the battle of Greasy Grass, is beyond historic. There has been much learning that has happened since this summer. The bands reunited as was prophesied by Crazy Horse and Black Elk and others. The fire is not out, it is traveling back to be amongst the people."

Camp Updates: The fire is once again put out. So finally the last few must pack up camp and move to the new Oceti Sakowin Camp which is right across from The Cannonball Store on the other side of highway.

But we will never forget what we brought before all the corruption started. Stay strong last few warriors.

January 12th

He puts out a live feed from the Greenpeace Warehouse in Oakland, California.

He walks around a warehouse. There are Water is Life patches hanging up to dry. These same large patches have been seen in water protector videos and in live feeds from the actions at Standing Rock.

Dean: It's a warehouse where individuals are all about what we do.

He Introduces Mary. She is screen printing. She is creating the patches for water protectors.

Mary: These are the same images you saw us producing at Standing Rock. We only give them away to water protectors. Especially those on the frontline. We make buttons, graphics...we deploy art. Flags and banners. Then the media can capture it on film and send out the message. It is also art therapy. Anyone can do this.

Dean: I'm looking and searching and seeing how big the DAPL awareness goes. Standing Rock is the epicenter and the source. I've taken that source and I can go with it. You're seeing where my journey is leading me to. There's a lot of good people doing good things for the earth. Doesn't matter who you are, you can do things like this. Come together, accept each other. This is a pretty big warehouse - outside of the building are a lot of graffiti tags. I'm an artist. This makes me want to spray paint something.

It's not really made by Indigenous, we have to stop thinking that mentality. This is about everybody. We divide and conquer ourselves every day. We have to stop this.

Free Red Fawn shirt....Free, free, free...everybody wants to be free. You gotta get yourself out of that control. Don't think like that. A year ago I didn't know I was going to be out here, I didn't know. I thought I'd still be at Standing Rock working a grocery store job and thinking, is my life going to be like this every day? Then again, that's about the future. We don't know what comes. We don't know where we are going. But does that stop you from doing what you really want to do? No, you just do it.

A lot of you people on here, could be trolls too, are saying come back to camp. Come help us. I showed you guys, I opened the door, there's even two windows you guys could look inside and it's pretty simple. Get a drone and start being your own drone pilot and continue on what I did. I'll be back, just when the time's right. Right now I'm enjoying myself. Public speaking. I think it brings more change.

Change is happening every day of our lives. We don't accept it yet because we don't have patience and that's another thing. We need to have patience. It's hard. You want something and you want it right now, but you're not going to get it, because you don't deserve it yet. To deserve it you gotta learn it, respect it. But I'll be back. I'm just going to go out here and tell the stories. If you guys want to know who should be telling the stories, probably shouldn't be me, but I'm doing it. I gotta do it. Who better to tell the stories but someone from Standing Rock, the drone pilot. I don't know if I was destined to do this, but it feels good. It feels good. It fills my heart with happiness. I'm glad I got out of Dakota, I needed to. Not necessarily stepping back, I'm stepping forward, but in a much bigger picture.

A man named Michael approaches him. They know each other and greet each other with a hug.

Dean: Frontlines. Let's talk about frontlines. I was on the frontlines twice. Two of the most unforgettable days. One at Treaty Camp raid. It wasn't nice. You got people out there on the frontlines every day, getting arrested. Everybody did their part. Everybody's still doing their part. Winter really did come. Most respect to the warriors still there. You really did test your mind, your strength. You either learned something or you didn't learn something.

He introduces David. He was at Standing Rock. He is an artist.

David: Creating a vision, an art narrative, that's storytelling and that's our way of expressing how we feel....through colors, letters, posters. Even sound and lights. Working all together. I think it gives it a more powerful feeling.

You look at these oil corporations; they have multi-million dollar public relations campaigns. This art project in this warehouse kind of duplicates that for the movement. They use their media, their arts, to keep things the way they are, or make things worse. They use advertising, commercials, public relations. We have to fight back on that level.

Dean: That's how I created a visual medium for the drones. Using the drone's vision. And attacking and documenting what we're fighting against.

David: You making drone videos puts you on the frontlines of the information war.

Dean: I'm past the frontlines. I'll go all over the place, go all the way over to where they're sitting at. That's the whole freedom that the drones gave me as a visionary artist. I never felt imprisoned, I never felt oppressed anymore. It's a good feeling. And I can see that you guys carry that, when you organize things and get them together. All of these people helping out to support the planet.

He looks around the warehouse and shows everyone the amazing art that is being created there.

Dean: You guys want to help but you can't leave home? You already do. By pushing the share button and the heart buttons. I'll get you an address, a page for them. Promote that. Keep it going, just keep it going. Good messages. And keep all those good thoughts on the comments. Even if you want people to hear what bad you have to say, then say it. Or don't say it at all.

If you want to continue following me, you're doing a good thing. Much respect to all of you guys. I do respect all of you guys. You guys take care of me a lot. You're riding along with me in this journey that I'm taking. To show you that there's a whole other world of possibilities. And check this out.

He goes outside of the warehouse and shows the beautiful graffiti on the side of the building.

They used to tell me that graffiti isn't art. But graffiti is art. Anything creative that you do, the way you speak, move, the way you act, the way you feel, the decisions you make in your life, your past, your history - you put it all together and it creates beautiful things like this.

It's not about calling someone out. Calling out the wrong. If you don't want to do that drama, just start surrounding yourself with people who don't do drama. If you're in something really deep and can't get out of it - just step away. But that's about life for me. I'm over here in California, I don't got much. I'm not doing this for personal gain.

Like I always say, Standing Rock is right here *(he pats his heart)*, it's never left. And what better way to have Standing Rock go all over the place and tell everybody what's going on, what's really going on at camp and the future of everything.

But the only way to be real is that you gotta be truthful. And if you messed up in your actions, just be honest. Just admit it. Let that crap go and it will all go away and we'll all start getting along a lot better. There's all kinds of other pipelines out there, you know.

Yeah, it would be nice for Dean to come back and film what's going on with the drones, but to be honest guys, that pipeline is going to go across. No matter how much we document it. We've documented it so much, we have so much evidence. I have so much evidence. Evidence I haven't shown anybody yet.

We'll put these people where they belong, they'll get prosecuted, they'll get jail time. They'll get what they deserve, but there's other pipelines around where I could actually help. I can't just stay stuck in one idea. There's a lot of ideas out there. We got Texas, we got Florida, we got Mount Rushmore too. I really want to drone Mount Rushmore and talk about how that shouldn't be a national park. That's a desecration park. It never should have been like that.

We're media story tellers and we tell the stories and that's what lives on through all of us. That's how much power we all have. We don't have to show statues like the ancient world did. They did it to show their power through all the generations. When they left the physical world, they put them up to remind everybody of who they were. No, that's not Indigenous people. Indigenous people didn't have to do that. We tell stories. They try to turn the stories into myths, but they're not myths, they are truths. I want to drone everything wrong with this America. And it's going to be awesome. So I hope you guys stay tuned.

The freedom act of flight 101. Drone2bwild presents: The Greenpeace Warehouse

He shares drone footage of the warehouse.

The drone footage starts outside with an overview of the whole area. The Bay Area. He flies over a train, over the highway. The building is covered in bright, interesting, beautiful graffiti. He flies right up to himself and a couple of guys in front of the building. Then he goes back out. Then into the warehouse. He flies over people making posters. Then he flies the drone back out, looking at the graffiti. He gives really nice views of the city, the highway. He flies back into the warehouse, then outside and lands. He puts up his fist as the drone touches the ground.

They say don't forget where we came from!!

I never forget because Standing Rock is always my home and will always be in my heart. If you all don't understand that then you must still be caught in the system of divide and conquer.

Remember DRoNE2BWILD started it all with a simple drone. The camp's first drone pilot who never got charged by law enforcement. Why? Because I battle this dark force with knowledge and power to do what's right in this world, when most of us blindly walk around what's truly happening around us and our planet. A door has been opened now and the first step of this movement is over. It's the second coming that will end in strength and courage. So please you who read this, don't forget to know yourself before you SPEAK! Listen!!!

He thanks many people for donations and shares his funding link.

January 13th

Spent the day at the Pulgas Water Temple in prayer for my family at Standing Rock. Preparing for the event tomorrow in Santa Cruz. I hope to see many of you there. Prayers up.

January 14th

They talk about trolls. Everything you need to know and everything you don't want to know!!!!!!

He shares Conscious Media Alliance's video about hacking.

I am not feeding a monster, but just bringing awareness to these situations like this.

It's unfortunate that our military programs the soldiers but doesn't deprogram them before they get released back into society. Most of the people sending us DEATH THREATS are soldiers who think they're still at war and they want the Sovereign Nations out. #WhereIsTheFBI??

If any of my followers are being harassed by any of these people please screenshot all of it and send it to the drone page. We're collecting quite the dossier.

He shares a profile and messages from a troll named Joshua. Joshua is in a military uniform in his profile picture.

Joshua says he knows about all the crimes that all of the water protectors are committing. He says that the "protesters" are engaging in one of the most massive harassment, intimidation and extortion campaigns. He says Sophia made the explosives that almost took off her own arm the night of the Backwater Bridge attack.

Joshua: Lmao we have more than enough drinking water in the world kiddo. I can run clean drinking water out of my faucets for centuries and it's free at my apartment.

When the rivers get polluted like the Mississippi will, they will tap into your private well. They've already done it in Iowa. How's your water gonna last when you're sharing it with 33 other states? You actually think your private well is private? They're going to turn it into eminent domain just like they did in Iowa to the farmers!

Although the U.S. Government is in control, and maybe in conspiracy to also hold water protectors accountable for crimes they never committed, read and act on your own risk!!!

Maybe if everyone who's being threatened (followers & water protectors) reports it here to the FBI they will be pressured and actually start doing their jobs.

Also please report these military accounts to the nearest military base. They want to know if any of the troops are committing online crimes and want to shut down false accounts. Stay safe out there my followers and protectors of the water.

#DeathThreats #Military

He shares the Internet Crime Complaint Center's link.

Wells Fargo is going EXTINCT!!! #DefundDAPL

He shares a link: Wells Fargo is closing over 400 bank branches

Are we all really going to look the other way as he violates our national security on twitter, is drowning in conflict of interests, and is in violation of nepotism laws? If he wants to be president, divestment is a small price to pay and it is also the law. And why is he still an executive producer on Celebrity Apprentice? Does he want to be a reality TV star or the Commander in Chief?

He shares a couple of Trump's crazy tweets.

Shiyé Bidzííl & Justo St Clare on the way to Santa Cruz. Together we can all make a difference no matter where we all come from! Respect for all of the Bay Area.

He shares music: One Tribe featuring Justo St Clare & Sober Junkie

Drone2bwild shares a graphic of a missing Indigenous woman. She is 18 years old. Another issue for Indigenous people, especially women, is kidnapping and murder. It happens far too often on and near the reservations.

It is also another toxic side effect of oil drilling. Man camps are set up for the workers. Women are often kidnapped, raped, tortured and killed by these temporary workers. Especially Indigenous women.

He puts up several posts about missing Indigenous women over time and always asks everyone to share these posts in an effort to bring these missing Indigenous women home.

January 15th

Santa Cruz Drone2bwild runs with the wolves!!!

Marshall Lee, Angelo Wolf, Salina Manson, Gabriela BK, Iam Drezus, Justo St Clare, Sioux Z Dezbah and other water protectors are there.

Dean: I'm just gonna do a live feed real fast. Sitting here by the fire. Nice and warm. That's the Oceti Sakowin fire right there. *(He laughs.)*

I went to the Running with the Wolves event and I spoke. It was an amazing night. People took it how they took it. I gained a lot of knowledge about how people come together and stand against pipelines and other issues. But I did address a lot of things about camp. Some people didn't like it. Some people had to accept it. Some people listened. It's good to listen.

It's a good feeling though. Everyone had their say. This is one of many gatherings that the water protectors are going to do. Going around and spreading the truth. Spreading our experiences that happened to us at camp. And our roles, what we did. We hold that with us. We don't let it dissipate. We stand strong every day. Fighting these kinds of battles and situations in your own home, like my reservation, Standing Rock, it'll change you. If you're strong, if you're smart about it, you can get through situations like that, when your home is invaded by corporate greed and big money. Spirituality and prayer tends to get attacked by all of that.

Remember, it's about balancing your energy, the good and the bad. If we all do that as individuals we can all get along and understand each other on a higher level. And work together in many ways. And understand each other's differences. Accept them. Work with them. Always make the right choice. And do it in a good way.

He reads some comments: Stay strong...all the hearts are cool...the troll situation, don't mind them, it's a scare tactic. I'm documenting them and putting them away because you never know what kind of court case might come up and you need the evidence.

A lot of people look out for me. I have been getting threats while I've been in the Bay Area. I'm aware of it, but I don't buy it. If they want to come get me or scare me or put fear in me, it's not going to work. You guys are gonna have to just step it up to a new level cause I'm not buying it. If you want to do something to me, you would have already done it at this time. My connections are strong, my spirit is strong. I'm powerful within my heart. And there's nothing you can do to take it away. You can come with your guns, with your tactics of fear. I've been through all of that stuff through the month of December. Everybody on the live feeds saw it. And you get used to it. It doesn't affect me anymore.

You guys can keep believing in me. I'll keep providing the truth and the motivation to do what's right and move forward. And don't let all the bull you hear go to your head. At the same time, when I do take a break and don't get on live feed all the time, don't worry guys. If there's something that's going to happen to me, you'll know about it, guaranteed. You don't gotta get all freaked out. Relax. You don't want all that stuff to get to your head too and they start infiltrating your followers. Because you guys provide me with unbelievable information at times.

He reads comments.

I don't think I'm a leader. I don't put myself out there that way. I'm just a good listener. There's lots of leaders. I just label it as having common sense.

I'm enjoying the Bay Area. Lots of great people. I've been here five days. A bunch of good, caring people and I feel like I'm at home. Home is where you make it. I support the message that you don't have to be at Standing Rock all the time. The ones who hold that strength and power and love and go to spread the message, that's power as well. We're all doing our part. I like to touch their hearts and make them aware.

People gotta experience from all levels. You don't have to have guns anymore. It's all mind manipulations. They will infiltrate our actions, our daily thoughts and dreams. They make us turn against each other. Some people say we shouldn't talk about it, but we should. We need to look into it. People exaggerated. When there's great change in the world, there's going to be lots of bad things happening as well. If we're all aware of all these bad things, we need to start putting a stop to it. There are things that people do that can take them to hell and back, I've been there. I've been through a lot of things. Every person I've met I acknowledge and learn something from them.

Standing Rock is coming back. I believe that. That's my home. Standing Rock will never go away. You always hold it in your heart. That's how we keep the strength. Hold that prayer in your heart. You can still feel that power and embracement. People are just not thinking right. Be more aware of your situation and surroundings. We need to defend ourselves from the psychological battles.

Indigenous people are more aware of the battles. We've been oppressed for 500 years. They have laws to protect those who do things that are wrong and you can get away with in America. Now it's that the country that it was born for, those constitutional rights? No. It took something that the Indigenous had and it took a lot of things in life that make you happy and joyful. They stressed our spirits out.

Now that's the system that we are fighting for. It's beyond the pipeline. But the pipeline is the door to open to see all these things in life. Agreed? Understand? Don't ever let those psychological attacks get to you. If they start getting to you, sometimes people do things that make them uncomfortable. I dwell on those things sometimes, but just think about it. Turn off all your electronics. If you think you are really being watched, turn your phone off and put it in the microwave and close the door. Learn how to defend yourself from surveillance, cyber-attacks and threats.

It's been a wonderful time here. Tomorrow I'm probably going to go speak on the radio. We don't know what's gonna happen when Trump gets in. In life you always gotta give someone a chance. But if things don't start looking right and we feel like the president and the government doesn't start making decisions that do not benefit the earth, we will all step up. And we will do things that will change a lot of the ways that we produce. We're going to stop everything that might be sucked out of the earth and we're going to stop all the coal mining. We're going to stop all the radiation and we're going to stop all the issues for the planet. And it all started with Standing Rock.

Standing Rock was the key to a lot of issues and it opened everybody's eyes. But we still have work to be done. Because while I was at the water temple yesterday, we talked to some people who didn't know what was going on. They had never heard of Standing Rock. That shows me that this message still needs to be spread out more. So that people can be more aware and attuned. And if we keep sharing these messages, share them with your friends. Tell people, these are our stories.

Remember I was telling you, we've always been media because we were the original story tellers. We tell our stories far and wide. As unbelievable as they seem to be for today's listener. But it's more than listening. When you start to understand listening, you go into another realm of understanding and that's where the stories are told and felt. We have these stories now in cyberspace, it's called Facebook live. They'll probably disappear off Facebook, they'll probably disappear off the net, but this going on right now, you guys listening to me talk, you heard it, now it's stored in your brains. Now you pass it on that knowledge too. It's the only thing they can't take away from us. It's that strength in the power of connection. Listening with all of your senses is the connection of being human. They can't cut that away from us. They can't suppress it.

From here on, lawyers who can take any cases, contact me and review any footage I have to help protect the water protectors' rights. As you guys know, Morton County and North Dakota will charge them with anything, it don't matter. You walk across the road and they will charge you. There's so much drone footage that I've never shown anybody yet. Not on Facebook. You guys just saw all the exciting stuff.

There were so many things that happened, things I really haven't told anybody yet. I believe that's why they won't allow the drone footage in court. The drone footage gave everything away. You can tell that they committed so many illegal things. But we'll fight them. If they don't wanna prove their case in a court of law, then we'll just go ahead and put it out all over and we'll let the people of the world decide who was right and who was wrong in this situation. And when we got so many people aware, then that law can just go right out the window, cause that law ain't working. You can't just create laws to defend criminals. But that seems how it is.

You've got laws to defend criminals and then when the good people go out of their way to defend something for the greater good of mankind, they create a law against that. It's stupid. They postpone, that's how the system works. They will slow down the process, they will speed up. They will plant something on you.

They manipulate, they are the controllers. They love to control everybody on this planet. And that's what they do. Even if you take it all the way to the Supreme Court. They don't call it supreme for nothing. Cause the supreme law of the land. Is it really the supreme law of the land? No. Just because they establish that system, we gotta agree with it? No. It doesn't matter what kind of system.

The only system we should abide by and we should respect is the law of the land. The natural law of the land. We just got to believe it. Come on guys, we can't be that connected to this system. People can wake up. People need to wake up. It's just that easy. *(He snaps his fingers.)* Snap yourself out of it. Don't be scared. You think we're crazy? We're not crazy. It's just expressing ourselves. In ways, people are looking at us like, I don't know man, is this guy really telling the truth or not? And then they start going off from there. Start emailing other water protectors, start creating drama. But there's good drama too. It creates suspense.

Iam Drezus comes over. Marshall Lee comes over. They talk about Drezus' new song. Marshall talks about how he was at camp until Christmas...now working on merchandise.

He walks outside...everybody is out there. He talks to people. Sioux Z. Dezbah. She tells him she is heading to Washington D.C. and that she will be speaking at the women's march and other places. She talks about Occupy Washington D.C. and how they want to get as many Natives there as possible.

He talks to E'sha Hoferer. E'sha talks about protecting the pine nut trees next. He talks about how they are cutting down pine nut trees. It is a part of his culture and his tribe's survival to collect pine nuts.

Dean: The fight continues on. The fight is everywhere.

He walks around some more. He talks to Izzy Hernandez. He shouts out Cheyenne River Sioux Tribe.

Dean: I might think about staying here. It's a real good atmosphere.

The next live feed comes soon after the last. He is still at the house where all of the water protectors gave talks and are interacting.

He shows his Superman tattoo on his neck. He introduces Chaske Nebow. He was the tattoo artist that did this work.

Dean: Me and this guy, we met about a year ago. We came from the same community and ended up finding each other at camp. He was part of security, standing in solidarity. The other tattoo is the last design of the water protectors from Ernesto. After that he switched up designs. It didn't hurt. The superman took about twenty-five minutes. I believe the other side was about ten minutes. I always said I'm going to get a tattoo, and then I said, I'm going to get it on my neck. That's just one of the things I fulfilled in life. Myron's here. William's here.

Myron: You're addicted to live. This guy's addicted to live.

Dean: How did Oakland trip go?

Myron: Lotta love, lotta solidarity. Coming and going and going back to Standing Rock to support the water protectors.

Dean: We will win. We are survivors. We are Indigenous people. You people out there who shared all of our feeds and love. You are making the change.

Salina Manson interviews Shiyé Bidzííl Standing Rock Water Protector/ DRoNE2BWILD pilot REAL TALK REAL ISSUES.

Dean: I am Standing Rock Nation. Hunkpapa, Lakota. And I am Diné, The People, Navajo nation. Born for the Bitterwater clan on my father's side. I'm full Indigenous but from two cultures and that makes my blood strong.

I was always there. I lived there. It's my home. In the beginning when this got big I filmed this with my drone and found new ways to document.

The front lines were where all the flags were when they first broke ground. I was the only drone. I got my hands on a drone and I documented the first arrests. And a lot of illegal activities they were doing. And it got big, and then the dogs happened.

Salina: Did you know how powerful the drone was?

Dean: I was still exploring it. I thought, what a better way to fly a drone over a fence and document up close. I didn't feel a sense of being told where to stand. The drone let me go beyond their laws.

Salina: When did you catch juicy footage?

Dean: Every day, every second I documented the desecration and violation. It's never been done before. It's never going to be copied. So every time I was flying, it was exclusive.

Two days before they raided Treaty Camp. That's when they first shot the drone. I was flying close and you can see them shoot it with rubber bullets. I never got arrested. Because in a way I believe I had the right to document. They are always going to look for that loophole to prosecute and arrest. But they never did.

Get a drone and learn how to fly it and feel it and connect with it and what it can offer human beings. I have been inspiring a lot of people, especially children. I'm doing a lot of great things in my life. It empowered me to get involved more and understand more. There are a lot of people who look up to me for news and information.

Salina: Would you give anyone a warning about drone flying?

Dean: When you want to put yourself out there and put yourself beyond the limitations, you are going to get yourself in situations that you won't know the outcome of. Don't be afraid. Don't fall into the fear. Just do it. Balance out the fear. Balance out your skills, your vision. Do it every day in a good way.

Salina: Anything you want Bismarck to know to help them understand?

Dean: If they're against us, they're against us, but we gotta understand our differences to get along to make the best of it. Anyone targeting me...I'm glad I'm making you do something productive. At least I'm inspiring you to open your eyes. This guy is telling the truth. I do get death threats, so I must be talking about sensitive things. People think it's crazy, but it's not. This world is filled with beautiful things, but also chaotic things.

He appears on Angelo Wolf's live feed later. Everyone is eating. Angelo walks around. Cempoalli Twenny is there, Prolific is there. Angelo talks to Dean for a minute. Dean looks exhausted and says he's all live feeded out.

On Facebook, actress Frances Fisher shares a YouTube video: Standing Rock 12/02/16 Meet the drone operators of #NoDAPL

She posts: This is why I love Myron Dewey & Shiyé Bidzííl ~ Breaking the rules but not breaking the law. Witnessing. Direct #Drone Action. #EyesOfTheSky

Since April of 2016 I started utilizing a drone to document awareness on Standing Rock about the oil corporations and the Dakota Access pipeline that is now being built half a mile north of my reservation. And that will be crossing the Missouri River. They have already illegally desecrated and disrupted the sacred burial grounds of my ancestors. Since this construction started in August, I have been documenting heavy evidence of them illegally violating our Indigenous rights, treaty lands, and violence toward our water protectors who have been peacefully praying and standing in solidarity for the last six months. It's been all over Facebook, yet major media has not reported on these issues. Since I now hold strong evidence through my drone footage I have been harassed and I am now a target.

Since my footage shows the truth, people around the world have asked me to share my knowledge of drone technology and how I have used them to fight environmental injustice on Indigenous lands and beyond.

In order for me to go to these other reservations and pipelines in Texas, Florida, and many other states and countries to gift them with my knowledge I need the following:

Phantom Drone due to the fact that DAPL security has put up Stingray devices which caused all my drones to malfunction and made them inoperable. Others were illegally shot out of the sky by Morton County.

Zoom lens for the drone

Night Vision for the drone

Faraday cage - I want to try one to see if it blocks the Stingray technology

Airfare to get to and from the different reservations/pipelines

Travel expenses - hotels, rental cars, etc. as needed

My goal is to get to these places and teach a day long drone class for a minimal fee. I'm going to be very transparent about all money and receipts will be posted online.

January 16th

He shares Johnny Dangers' live feed. Law enforcement attacks a peaceful prayer walk. Law enforcement shoot and spray water protectors.

The people of Standing Rock won't agree, but I am gonna have to side with Gary John Montana on this!!!! Guess this is what happens when you're not being transparent when it comes to all TRIBAL!!!

He shares a post:

According to sources there are approximately 287 Standing Rock donation sites listed and thousands more not listed on the master GoFundMe listing. Not only that $11.2 million that was collected, but the 80,000 packages that were halted by Chairman Archambault and redirected to warehouses somewhere on Standing Rock. The warehouse owner allegedly wants storage money or has threatened to auction the boxes off. The membership should request a federal investigation!!

It has been confirmed. This is the reality and second coming of this world wide movement!! Time to step up and protect what we believe in!!! Time for DRoNE2BWILD to return home!!!

He shares Wes Howard's post:

I was checking up on a helicopter that was spotted landing on or near the Missouri. Instead I found what appears to be a surface to air missile located on the DAPL work site near the Missouri River.

DRoNE2BWILD TRUE STORY

I was flying the drone backwards, revealing the area when all of a sudden the Inspire Pro 1 Drone hit a California Tree. SMH

The Drone had to camp out in the tree for two days until the people of Docktown community and Pineda Tree Service came to the rescue and saved the day!!!!

Late night live feed. Ask me questions. My followers follow me for the raw truth. Before we start wanting to stand in solidarity and unity, we gotta be right with ourselves first. No, I am not going to Washington D.C. Are you crazy? They'll pick me up right away. They'll detain me. In situations like this, we gotta laugh.

Everyone at camp is moving across from the Cannonball store - on the west side. The camp's all moving there. There's some people that are still building, but you guys gotta let that part go. That camp is gone. It's time to let that camp go. You can't hold on forever. We'll have the memories. The camp should be right here. *(He points to his heart.)*

There's all kinds of things that do break down the human soul and this movement is one big training ground, experience, experiment, psychological propaganda. It's teaching us to be real humans. It started with the pipeline, but it went beyond the pipeline.

How are we gonna stop this pipeline? We change ourselves as human beings. We come and stand against big oil corporations. They have all the money in the world. You have all the power in the world when you have all the money. You have the power to end anything you want or get anything you want.

We're not going to fall to corruption. It affects everyone, even the most wise of all the elders. Their mentality is growing up with the spirits. They aren't used to this kind of information right away. They don't want to listen. The elders told me, you always gotta listen. The greatest power is how you carry yourself. You don't need a gun, force, army; you just need yourself and how you carry yourself. And when we're all standing together, we'll have all the power. Not forceful power, but beautiful power.

In each one of us, one person can stand up and change the country. It's happened in history. One person, any gender, religion, race, can stand up to all that corruption and greed and oil corporations. Stand up for all the things that aren't supposed to have a price. People have been through more than me. They've been through Wounded Knee. But a lot of people who stand up are met with the same death threats that I get every day.

Someone spun the lug nuts off a truck that was supposed to pick me up in Bismarck. They could have been killed. Those two were protecting me and I feel I put them in danger. But they knew the danger they were getting themselves into.

I feel like I've lost another great person. We've never met, but we've talked a lot. And the situation that happened on Cindy's show. It's about both sides trying to show the truth. Of course Morton County is going to lie. But we turn against each other. There are bad people on our side too.

They are turning us against each other and working to bring down water protectors and stop a movement. They are being paid off or threatened. There are things beyond what you see and it's playing out right now. Morton County and Standing Rock are working together. They will deny it. If you don't like what I'm saying, turn this off. Block me. Send me a hateful message. I can understand better. But if you hate this and you still watch it, maybe you're curious about what I know.

And for individuals who hold positions in politics, you talk and walk politics, you gotta choose one side. Either be a warrior like Crazy Horse or be a politician and do what you're told. You can't be a politician and a warrior at the same time. Crazy Horse went on his own to do his thing, whether the people believed in him or not. He didn't get mad because they didn't believe him. He found his own way and his own vision and that's why today he goes down as one of the greatest warriors of all time.

You gotta find your own power in yourself. You can be strong as much as you believe in yourself. But you can't get down to criticizing. You have to respect each other's differences. Whether right or wrong, you gotta let them speak. If you have the right answer, share it out. Don't hold that in. You're selfish if you keep it to yourself. Why be greedy. Spread that knowledge.

You set little goals for yourself. First you change yourself, then you can change the world. Once you know your limits, you pass it on. As a community you start to grow...then you start change the country...then we change the world. Then we go beyond the world. We start explaining those unsolved mysteries we always wanted to know.

The pipeline is not just about the pipeline. It's about world, human, animal, genocide, hate, racism, everything in this world that we can change. It happened on Standing Rock for a reason. It was foretold by the elders that there was going to be a black snack. That's the pipeline.

We do need negative forces. It's the ingredient for changing the world. If there were no negative forces we wouldn't have anything to change. When you make a decision, it's not just for yourself. Will your children benefit from it, your people? You take that all into context. You can't be selfish because you hold a position of trust. All the great chiefs were great because they were wise and knowledgeable...maybe they just had common sense, or maybe they prayed a lot. I'm not always right. Sometimes I can be wrong. It's up to you guys to find out.

Yes, I am going to go back to Standing Rock. I am being targeted and threatened every day. A lot of people who help me also get threatened and they get paranoid and soon they block me and I'll probably never hear from them again. I'm not out here in California to seek fame, I was invited to tell my story. But I feel like Standing Rock needs me again. I see military positioning themselves. I see the evil and fear, it's within camp. But I feel strong enough to walk back into camp.

If you need help, I will help you. I understand you. Whether you are into bad medicine or spiritual, I will always understand you. I never turn anyone away. I'm not going to judge you. I will be there to listen. I can give you what I know because I've been there. I've been to all those hurtful and angry and selfish feelings, that paranoid world. All that evil I put down inside me. It wasn't because I was addicted or weak. You have to be willing to put your mind through a lot of stress. You have to be willing to feel the realms of chaos to feel the honor and bravery. You can transform it into peacefulness. You can close your eyes and feel the energy.

People are too caught up in possessions and manipulations and ego. Respect yourself and others. People are freezing, trying to stay warm, trying to stay in solidarity. People of the camp, it's time to move out. We don't have to be in exactly that location for us to stand in solidarity with this movement. I'm praying for you guys. I understand you don't want to leave. You got to put snow on that fire and put it out. It's in your hearts. It's going to flood.

Military guy says it's not going to. Who are you going to listen to? I pray for you. But you made the decision to stay there. Whatever it is, I won't hold nothing against you guys, but don't say I didn't tell you so. Start moving up to the new camp. I'll be back soon. I was going to continue on to other places, but that's something else I want to talk about. Other water protectors are going on - people are saying that all the previous water protectors are going on. We're just spreading awareness all over. People forget, because we're not at camp, don't judge us. I left because I needed to. I was smart about it. I didn't stick around camp to feel the freezing cold. It's called common sense people. You want to test Mother Earth, she is powerful. She creates the most destructive storms on the planet. She will fight back, all the oil corporations, fracking. It's causing earthquakes. That's Mother Earth shaking her head. That's when the volcanos, hurricanes, floods...the more we destroy the earth, the more Mother Earth is going to respond in anger.

Right now she's sad. She sees the protectors fighting against each other instead of protecting her. She's sad because the oil corporations are destroying her body. Water is life and this planet is the only planet with this much beautiful water, and we want to destroy it.

The government must know that there's planets out there with plenty of water, because they don't care about this one. We'll be here living on a planet and it will be dead. We will be down here suffering from all the destructive forces of mother. Once she knows we've neglected her, she'll die...there will be long periods of destruction. All those rich people will be gone.

Use your money in a good way. Money is the root of all evil, but throw it into something good. We can never get away from money. We live, we die, we kill for money. That's what it does to humans. We get so weak over paper. We could just burn it. Here we are fighting.

We all have less than 100 years to live. If you have a skill to use, use it in a good way. All you hackers, don't be scared. God gave you skills and talents, use them for a good reason. All you lawyers, protect the good people. I know I'm not the only target. Every water protector out there. Truth speakers are targeted, absolutely 110%. But why is everyone so afraid to speak the truth. We have to be like the warriors before us. Run all the way up to the military truck and slap them. That's what I did with the drone. I created something new. A new style.

The new president - he's not going to make a year. He's going to go down as the worst example of a human being. It's going to fail. We always need the bad and the good. But there's so much bad, we need more good. We need to balance it out. If we're going to police the world, lead by example. Learn how to show peace and unity. Respect their differences. Learn to trade and be honest.

You gotta feel. We can all know what to do. The real message is the real deep down inner thoughts and heart and actions. Fear of propaganda and it's been started since this country was born. That's why we have police and secret military known as Blackwater. Why is everyone afraid to say that name? Everyone gets a little jumpy. Don't be scared. The AIM. Indigenous are proud of it. Non Indigenous - are getting a little jumpy. It's not about physical force, it's about educating yourself and understanding your mind. We only use 10% of our brains and look at how much power we have. Don't underestimate yourself. Don't think you can't achieve something great. If you set your mind to it, you can do it. Sticking to the tasks, accomplishing your goals. If you fall down, pick yourself up. Mind over matter.

January 17th

Hey Shiyé, I can only imagine what you are going through, the challenges and difficulties. You are a really good person. You are an activist but you are also a thinker, a real deep thinker. I've listened to a lot of your speeches and conversations and you have such a pure mind. You aren't caught up in petty things but have the biggest and greatest goal in your sights to keep you from being distracted. You seem to have come very far in mastering yourself. You are a realist... Stay curious, stay pure, you are one of the most pure men I have ever heard speak. You know who you are, you have a strong intuition and great wisdom. Your judgement, your courage, your character, your virtue - this is what is what is so great about you. This is why so many follow you and love you.
Sincerely: Nick Ruderman

Shiyé Bidzííl would like to Thank Alex Kavanagh from DroneGear. The DJI Inspire 1 is truly inspiring people and the world around us!!

He shares a short video of the drone flying over.

West Cliff, Santa Cruz, California

#SantaCruz #SantaCruzSurfers #WestCliffSantaCruzBeach

It is beginning to get dark outside. This is drone footage from the beach. He flies above the ocean's waves. He flies down to the beach where people and dogs are walking. He flies along the shoreline. Then up to a lighthouse. He flies way over the ocean, far away from the shore. The drone goes over lots of surfers. He gets a couple of surfers as they hop up on their boards and ride the waves. He gets amazing shots of the surfers and the water.

In the next live feed, it is getting even darker out. He flies over the surfers. He sends the drone out to an island in the ocean. It is a huge rock that comes out of the water. There are lots of birds on it and a seal too. He flies the drone close enough to see the seal really well. The seal looks like it is looking at the drone and talking to it. He flies back over the surfers.

Future generations to come. We will always be remembered through our children's stories. The year Standing Rock changed my way of life forever. The greatest sacrifice that led me through hell and high heaven came from the precious love of family. Shiyé Bidzííl

Johnny Dangers is the nicest cool dude I met!! He has been there since the beginning as well, capturing live feeds and the truth just like all the others. Remember they will manipulate the truth on anyone!!! Those allegations against him are pure trickery to make us look at each other and find our false demons. That's how DAPL is attacking us media, supporters, drone pilots, and water protectors!!! Open your eyes world. Can you see it????!!!!!!!

He shares a graphic: Misinformation Effect (cognitive psychology)

Shiyé Bidzííl talks psychological tactics known as Face Plant!!!

He shares Withstands With Wolves live video.

Angelo says there are rumors going around Facebook and they are not true. He says that everyone who's been at camp since the beginning are all good people.

Dean gets on the live feed.

Dean: I just want to talk about Johnny Dangers. The battle has moved into psychological. DAPL, they can't fight us. We're strong. Physically we stand up in solidarity. We pray on the frontlines. They know how ever many times they use force and do whatever they do, we're still going to be standing there for what's right.

So what next are they going to do? Doxing people. They have hackers. They have money. They find information on everybody. Who has the most flights, who's a tribal leader. They will go into all of your background and they'll look through your history, your previous life, and they'll use all that stuff against you. And they'll put it out and they'll try to plant you.

That tactic is called a face plant. They're putting out ridiculous information. They're trying to disguise themselves in profiles like they are someone who's at camp. You guys really got to think about this. This ain't no mumbo jumbo. They're getting into our minds and they're turning us against each other. They make us think twice about water protectors, like, are they really here for us?

Johnny Dangers, he's been there. He's still there. I met the guy. And I'm proud of what he does. And they see that, so they are trying to attack him. That's how they infiltrate us. Through our minds. And we gotta think. They're going to break down that family. They're going to break down that solidarity. They're going to break down our prayers. They're going to break down the human spirit because they are getting to our heads and it will make us turn on each other. That's real talk. That's how they battle us now.

It's not about guns, it's not about warfare, it's not about force, it's not about intimidation. Yeah, all that stuff is in effect. But the real weapon is our minds and that's how they fight us. Believe it or you don't have to believe it. It's up to you. You guys have to make that decision.

As far as support for the camp, it's still there. Of course it's going to move, it's on a flood plain. But it's like I tell everybody, Standing Rock is in our hearts. It's in my heart. We can go anywhere we want to and Standing Rock is always going to be with us. We're out here in California, of course we're enjoying the views, the people, the atmosphere, but at the same time we're spreading the message. And we're bringing awareness because there's a lot of people here in California who support what's going on at Standing Rock and they want to know, they want to hear, they want to experience our feelings and our thoughts because we were there, huh Angelo....

The more we talk about it in a negative way, the more we fall into the trap. It's a spiritual battle and a battle within ourselves. So we really got to find ourselves and what we can do, what we can strive for - and when you understand yourself, you can stand up for anything you want in the world. It really does only take one person to stand up and you can change the world. It has happened. We have seen it in history. Every one of us has that power. We just have to feel it and experience it and believe it.

I am sorry that my own tribe is telling everyone to leave camp by January 29th. With all the lies and half-truths filtering Facebook, camp, and the council, we must find a way to continue this fight no matter wherever we are on this planet, and it starts with you, as an individual.

January 18th

After I give my speech at UC Berkeley I'm coming back for a special purpose!!! Fly the DJI INSPIRE PRO 1 and document all the illegal actions!!!!!! By the way I'm calling DRONE NATION to return again!!!!!

Johnny Dangers' LIVE FEED clearly shows that DAPL is highly active and National Guard gearing up for what?? The Drones are coming back!!!

Anyone in the Bay Area willing to DONATE any and all drones, or even be willing to drive up and fly your drones at Standing Rock to document all what has been playing out these past few days?? Please Message me if so!

UC Berkeley Tour! We will be speaking!

He live feeds as he walks down a hall. Angelo is there. He walks around a common area. He looks around. He says that it has been raining all day. He finds water protector posters framed on the wall. Shaun Begay's work. He shows the signature.... also black lives matter and other issues posters around.

What a very nice gift!!!

ISHI In Two Worlds

A biography of the last wild Indian in North America by Theodora Kroeber

A man gifts him a copy of this book at Berkeley.

Wassup!!! UC Berkeley

He starts a live feed. He is outside walking around. People are gathered inside watching a video. He looks in through the glass.

Good evening everyone. Just out here on this rainy evening. Rain is good because rain is water and water is life. Myron's here. Everyone's having a good time. Spreading awareness. Doing good in the world. *(The feed cuts off.)*

The next live feed is of a panel of water protectors. They are there to share their stories about Standing Rock. Including E'sha Hoferer, Angelo Wolf, Gabi BK, Salina Manson and others.

Dean introduces himself when it is his turn to talk.

Dean: How many people have been at camp? How was your experience? Different? You'll never get anything like that in the city. Or wherever you're from. The thing about Standing Rock is that it's my home. I grew up there. There and in the Navajo Nation. I grew up chopping wood, taking care of grandma and grandpa. All the good stuff we do in life. Things that we need to enjoy. Things that's we've lost. The little things in life.

This pipeline is about more than a pipeline. Standing Rock was changed. It's still changing. It's changing the world. The way the world looks at environmental issues, at Indigenous issues. It changes a lot within ourselves. More understanding of ourselves. If we want to stand up in solidary and unity, we need to figure out ourselves first before we change the world. Change yourself, then you spread the knowledge to every other individual in the world out there. Then together we start understanding ourselves better as a movement and as a whole. As a community, as a state, as a country. And from there, the world.

It takes patience. You have to be a good listener. I always say that you always have to give yourself that opportunity to listen to people. Even if they're wrong. Listen to what they have to say, whether it's positive or negative. Always accept that people come from different backgrounds and they have different ways of acting and talking. No one's never right and no one's never wrong. We're all water protectors here and we're not perfect.

People look at us because of what we do on social media and what we did to Facebook. We made Facebook interesting again. You probably should clap for us. *(There is laughter and applause.)* Standing Rock was trending last July on Facebook and all of a sudden, it's not trending anymore. When it's trending, everybody's talking about it, round the nation, round the world. But all of a sudden, people are still talking about it but they wonder why it's not trending anymore. It's all part of media censorship. They are censoring us, every one of us in this country. This country is coming to a point where we're going to have to pay money just to breathe fresh air soon. They're already attacking our water. We're paying for water.

All these little freedoms that we first had when we first started on Mother Earth thousands of years ago. The Indigenous people were one and we were connected and we were equal. We treated everything equal. The animals, the plants, the air, the water, the earth...even space and beyond in our spirituality. But we all forgot about that. We forgot about those little ideas, those concepts. We started evolving ourselves within a system of colonialism. It's in everything. It's what we do every day, it's our jobs, it's us being students, it's so much. But we can be aware of it and start changing it.

But understanding yourself is at the core. Looking into your mind, looking into your heart. Your heart can be your strongest weapon. Then again, it can be your weakness. This movement has done a lot of things for all those involved, whether it was looking at Facebook, or actually going there to fly drones or to be on the frontlines. It's affected us in a lot of ways. As far as me, when this first started out back in April, let's say last February, I bought a drone. I knew about them for some time, but I knew they were expensive. So I decided to just buy a Phantom. Little did I know, a year from then, I'd be sitting here in front of all of you guys talking about what this drone did for me. I just wanted to fly a drone.

My friend, Dustin Thompson, he's a Standing Rock member too, said, Bring your drone, you're going to film something. It's going to be really cool. You'll like it. Joking he said, I'm going to make you famous. I was like, what do you mean? He said, just bring your drone. You're going to cover a run. For what? It's an awareness run for that pipeline that's about to come through and destroy our water. So he fed me the links and I read up on it. And I thought, Wow. It's an honor to serve. So I took the drone. It was my vision. And I went.

January 19th

#WATERISLIFE

West Cliff Santa Cruz California

Trying to see if there's any surfers out today. The tide is high today.

He flies over the light house and up and down the coast.

In the next live feed, he shows drone footage from above some surfers. There is not much going on. No big waves. A surfer is just floating. The surfer gets hit by a couple of waves then the feed cuts off. He does several short live feeds with drone footage flying all over the area.

The power of water

He live feeds with his phone from a very rocky beach. He walks down the beach. White waves hit big rocks below him. There is a walking path with some benches. There are people sitting. There are seagulls flying around. The waves smash against the rocks on the shore line and the foam goes high up in the air. He walks over to the edge of the rocks and looks down. He walks down closer to the water. The waves are white capped, powerful and beautiful. The foamy white water hits the dark rocks again and again. He turns the camera around. It is very windy.

Wow guys, here we are. The ocean. This is what we're here for. That's what I'm here for. To understand the water and pray for the water. Everybody else is going to say, it's just waves crashing into rocks. But if you listen, you can understand the water. It's a pretty amazing sight guys.

He shows more of the white foamy water around the rocks. He walks out even farther.

Alright guys watch this.

He walks up into the edge of the rocks. He screams and laughs at the same time as the water comes up and hits the shore and sprays him. He gets soaked. He looks amazed at the water.

That's what you gotta do. *(He is laughing hard.)* That was fun! Here we go. Here it comes! One more time! Here comes a big one. I'm going to get all wet again. Aww, come on. Here it comes! *(It is only a small wave. He gets a little closer.)* Here it comes!

More water sprays up on the rock where he's standing. He looks like a kid playing. He gets hit with water again and laughs hard.

It's cold! One more time. Alright guys, that was fun. One more time. Water is life and now I'm all wet. *(He laughs.)* That was actually fun. Having fun with water. Things like that you gotta enjoy in life. You can't just sit on the bridge. You gotta go down and let it touch you. That was fun. I think I got the highest one.

People in the comments tell him how dangerous that is to do.

In the next live feed, he flies the drone.

He flies over a rocky beach and a lighthouse. He flies over the water and shows the waves coming in. It is a gray day. He flies around the big rock out in the water. There are waves swirling gracefully around it. He goes way out above the water. You can hear sea gulls. He flies above surfers. At first there is not a big enough wave for the surfers. Finally one surfer pops up, but wipes out.

That was nice. I kinda got close, but I'm still trying to master the waves. You have to get timing going. This is how you train yourself to be a good pilot. You just do it. Water is pretty powerful. We have four surfers on this wave. Let's see which one can do it. There you go! A surfer is up. That's how you do that. This is cooler than anything. That's how you document surfers. That was awesome dude. Do it again, one more time! Here he comes.

Here comes a huge one. If you know any surfers who want to be droned, I can do it. Here they come. Be cool to go to Hawaii and get the hundred foot wave. Never been done before. I want to get one more in. That was fun. Next time we'll get a little more closer.

I forgot that I soaked myself in water, so I'm freezing. Here we go. Come on, come on. *(A wave goes by.)* Nope. Battery level is low. I'm just looking for one more. He's got it. *(He flies the drone right above a surfer riding a big wave.)* I got it. Now I gotta get it back over here before I lose battery. That's drone footage 101 on how to film surfers. Better than zoom cameras from the beach. And here we are, right here, filming it.

All this chaos that's going down is telling me and I feel that I am cutting my trip short and getting ready to return ASAP!!!! With a whole lotta drones!!!!

He shares Mike Fasig's live video. He is at the Backwater Bridge near camp. There are many people standing there. Some are singing. Some have shields. There is a lot of snow everywhere. Mike is walking around. Video goes black. You can hear him say, "Everybody keep moving! Keep moving!" You can hear people running.

The picture comes back on. There's smoke and he reports that one person was hit hard in the face. Law enforcement came to take down a tipi.

Law enforcement is now on the water protectors' side of the bridge. Mike yells at people to get behind his truck. He says they are shooting at the water protectors. He finally has an opportunity to move his truck and he has to drive backwards. He tells the people in his car that they are safe now.

Next, Dean shares Mitra Singh's live video.

It's late at night. Law enforcement is on the water protector/camp side of the bridge. She says that they took a lot of their shields earlier. She says that they could just walk right on into our camps. She says that they have to pray for them because they don't know what they are doing. They are lost.

She walks up to the frontlines. People are singing. She falls and someone picks her up. Someone yells for a medic. Someone has been hit. Water protectors are standing on the barricades, in the barricades. Singing. Some dancing. Someone yells, "You are cowards, shooting unarmed people!"

She says that our guys are telling us to move back. Everyone starts to move back - quickly. The law enforcement officers run toward the water protectors. Tear gas is thrown by the law enforcement into the running crowd. She finally gets off the bridge. You can still hear the singing. Then you can hear shots. People yell for a medic. They say that this is an elder. A medic vehicle comes in. The video cuts off.

In a live feed Dean and Angelo put a call out for help.

Calling all to action. Help us get home ASAP!!

Dean: We need to get home ASAP. No bull. What we've been seeing on the live feeds, what we've been feeling...it's a feeling of ... we need to get back home and we need to get there fast. This is a call out for everybody who is tuned in, everybody who can get us home. We're talking plane ticket. That's the fastest way to do it.

Angelo: If you're unable to get a plane ticket, a rental car. All this stuff is hitting really close. We need to get back.

Dean: It is bad. I need to go home. I need to go home and fly the drones. I only got one drone, but I need more drones. Myron Dewey's coming back, I heard. But we need to get home.

Angelo: I got two drones waiting on me when I get back up there. We've been here fundraising, but it's not enough to get us all back. We need to be back.

Dean: I know you all have been leaving me messages saying you gotta come home, and you're right. I do gotta come home. I can feel that I am needed back there. Angelo is needed back there. We see it. We see what's going on. And we need to get back up there. This is a call out to everybody that can help us get back to camp ASAP. And everybody who has any drones that they can donate for that eye in the sky, I guarantee you that they are going to get shot down and they are going to get taken out. But the more drones we have, the better equipped we are for the eyes in the sky. Share this. Spread this message out. Please pray for the water protectors on the front line and all of us here. Get us home. We need you and you need us. Please pray tonight. We'll put the info in the live feed comments. We need to get home. Terrible things are happening. It's best that I go home and fly that drone the way I do.

January 20th

He shares Dallas Goldtooth's video of a march in Washington, D.C.

2000 gather in the streets of D.C. Only to be joined by another 1000 more marching on this day when this so called president is being sworn into office.

He shares a link from the Bismarck Tribune: Cannonball asks protesters to leave the district

January 21st

Things at camp have become very chaotic. My soul is pulled there so I must return with the drones as soon as possible. All help in making that happen is appreciated. Even if you know someone who is driving out as long as they have room for 2 more could work.

January 22nd

He shares Angelo Wolf's live video of the Women's March in San Francisco, California

Dean is there with Angelo. People are holding signs. It is very wet out. There is a huge crowd marching. When they yell it echoes all the way down the street. All ages are there. There are little kids marching with umbrellas. Someone starts singing.

People need to realize it's not about the physical atmosphere but more of the spiritual sense when we all came together! We came together for a special reason and that reason is brought forth by the millions of people we have captured around the world who felt, believed and witnessed a revolutionary change within ourselves and our future through solidarity & unity! Which we all hold and carry with us every day forward now. Speak and spread awareness of our sacrifices and experiences as today's individual from Standing Rock, my home. Now we must all spread the very definition of change to the world!!

He shares a post:

Standing Rock Tribal Council approves evacuation order for all camps.

From the river of Cannonball to the Pacific Ocean!! Water is Life!! #MniWiconi

He shares a video. It is of slow motion ocean waves. It is a gray day. The waves are very white and foamy.

January 23rd

He shares Sioux Z Dezbah's live feed from Pilgrim Pipeline Splitrock Prayer Camp.

Shiyé Bidzííl has seen a lot of water protectors coughing but hasn't felt the cough himself!! I believe it's something more than this!! Something that was in that water!!!!

He shares a link: Growing concerns that ROZOL poisoning could be the cause of "camp cough" at Standing Rock camps.

Sebastopol, CA

This is a Drone2bwild live feed. It is dark and he is outside. A woman walks up to him and says that she just found out that it was him in the video when the buffalo ran.

Dean: Yes that was me.

Woman: One of the people who made that buffalo inspiration saw that video. And you're in it, but you're right here! *(She hugs him.)*

Dean: Just giving an update. We are here out in the middle of nowhere in California which has been pretty cool so far. Since I've been in California I got away from all the paranoia, all the rumors, all the lies. Got away from a lot of things in North Dakota.

I was brought out here and at first I thought it was to take me away from a lot of things, but actually I found out a lot of things while I was here. It gave me a new sense of direction to go and do what I am doing now. But I am going to go back to Standing Rock.

A lot of people have been messaging me that they need drones to fly over. But my sources at camp say there are drones flying over right now, but they only come out at night. And they say that there's red and green lights on them. So obviously that's a DJI drone. So somebody at camp has a drone and they're not telling everybody what's going on. Or DAPL could have a drone and be spying on whoever's left at camp.

I am going to go back and meet up with quite a few districts in my community that still stand up for the good of water. Not everybody on Standing Rock is against and not everybody is trying to make people be afraid that they have to get out of the camps. I'll say that again. Not everybody agrees with what the Standing Rock council has said. There are quite a few communities I noticed down south on the South Dakota side, there's quite a few people who still stand for the water. There are good councilmen who haven't wanted to be a part of what they are doing.

I want to give props to LaDonna, I wanna give props to Chase Iron Eyes, one of the few people that's going out of the way and sacrificing and utilizing all their skills and knowledge to still bring awareness and to still keep this fight up front.

I also want to talk about the recent findings of the poisonings and the DAPL cough. I personally think that it's more than the poisoning. I was never affected by the DAPL cough. But I have been in contact and shook hands with a lot of people who were coughing, but I haven't gotten the DAPL cough. So you could say it's not contagious by hand. I think it's something else. I think it was something in the water that was sprayed. From the airplane. It has to do with water because everyone who was hit with the water cannons are pretty much coughing. But we'll figure that out.

Everybody keeps telling me not to go home to Standing Rock. They say they are going to put me in jail until June. That's what the tribe says. They say I'll be jeopardizing everything everybody's done for me. But if you were actually with me 100% support, you would believe in the good things that I will do. I'm not going back there to be a pest to DAPL. I'm not going there out of vengeance.

Angelo comes out. They say that they are both going home on Thursday. Back to Standing Rock

A panel of water protectors speak to a group in several live feeds over the evening. In the first live video people are coming into a meeting hall. It is very loud. Dean looks around.

Angelo is live feeding too. They watch each other's live feeds. He and Angelo mess with each other playfully. They tell each other's followers to come to their live feed.

Dean: I'm in California, at a place that kinda resembles a bingo hall.

The meeting starts with a prayer song from one of the water protectors.

Dean: How many people went to camp? (*Several people put hands up.*) How many people supported, watched live feeds? (*Many people put hands up.*) How many are just learning about this now? (*Just a couple hands go up.*) That's great.

My name is Dean. I'm Shiyé on Facebook. Standing Rock is my home. It's where I'm from. My mother is from there, Hunkpapa from South Dakota, Standing Rock, the south side. And my father is Diné, Navajo. I was born for the Bitterwater Clan. My father is from Arizona.

I joined the fight because that is my home. That's everything. We protect our home, no matter what costs or sacrifices we have to put down. As far as what we have been accomplishing, we've been putting the word out and spreading awareness. I feel it's an honor to be here among you wonderful people who are all for the cause and support Mother Earth. Standing Rock has changed my life forever. What I'm doing here is a good thing, for my own children and for your children and for their children. For the next seven generations again. Thank you for welcoming me and I'm glad to be here from Standing Rock.

Other water protectors on the panel speak. Then they pull down a large screen to watch a video. It is Oceti Sakowin Camp in the snow. The video shows flag row and tipis. After the video the panel speaks again.

Dean: A day in the life of a protector? I got up every day and flew the drone over the camp, over the pipeline to bring awareness to what's going on in my home. To show all the people in the world who don't know what's going on. There's still people unaware of what's going on at Standing Rock, that's pretty crazy. Even within 100 miles of my homeland, people didn't know. Just a few media outlets were putting anything out.

Waking up every day is harsh, but it's beautiful. When the camp was at the high point in September, October, that's what camp was like. Whoever was there experienced the whole aura of it, the lifestyle. To me, it's actually the only place where you can experience true freedom. And you could be yourself. You could be anybody you wanted to be. You feel that sense of beauty, of creativity...anything.

There's always going to be negativity everywhere and right now the camp is dwelling in negativity. That's because the people who got out, like us guys here, we did not leave camp. We left to spread awareness. Like I tell everybody, just because camp might be closing, camp won't be gone. Camp is going to be with us everywhere we go. And it's in you guys.

Standing Rock is worldwide now. In every country. It changed my homeland forever. It changed the way people are looked at in Standing Rock. Standing Rock was the door and the window that everybody needed to look through and go through to see our world, our planet, our Mother Earth is under attack. And these corporations, this government, this system are draining those resources to make their almighty dollar and they don't give a crap about us Indigenous people. They think we are lower than them. They are gonna pass bills, they are gonna make laws to desecrate and destroy our sacred lands. This is true and it's happening right now and it's been happening for the longest time.

They put censors on it because they control the media. They control the media because they control the system. To suppress the people who believe in their rights and believe in true freedom and where they come from and their creation stories. They want to destroy our spirits like that. They lock up people who speak the truth. They lock them up for no reason and they'll be political prisoners for the rest of their lives. It's a crazy story, but it's not a story. It's the truth.

People have to open their eyes and look at the world and the way it's evolving. They're doing it to every one of us right now. Every one of you people who view things on Facebook, I'm sure your phones have been acting weird. Your computers' hard drives are malfunctioning. Things go strange and it's not really normal. The world is censoring us.

Trump's in control. A lot of people hate Trump because of the racist qualities he's brought out in a lot of individuals. Even though we hate him, or we dislike him, or we don't agree with him, we have to give him a chance. And we have to accept that this world is evolving whether we like it or not. Whether you think it's good or you disagree with it, we're going to have to accept it and work around it.

We can overcome things in life, these difficulties, if we always think in a prevailing way. Don't let anybody bring you down. Some people say it's impossible, it's impossible to change, but that's not true. It's possible to change for anybody. Whether you've done so bad in your life, you could actually do good and change the world for the better. And to do that we gotta change ourselves as individuals. And when we accomplish that, we work together and that creates a movement. A good movement. A different kind of movement. A movement that is unity whether it's in cyberspace or actual physical reality.

Like in communities. Like coming together in this building here. And bringing support and awareness that these environmental issues are impacting our daily lives and our sacred sites and our ancestors which we are created from, and born for, and going there to pray for.

For me personally, I'm not only standing up for the water in Standing Rock. I want to bring awareness to all Indigenous and environmental issues worldwide because it took Indigenous people to stand in solidarity - to open everybody's eyes. And it's going to take a lot more. And now, for me, it's beyond Indigenous people. It's all people. People who have that goodness in their heart to actually stand up and bring awareness to all these issues I am fighting for.

Angelo talks about winterizing camp. Dean reads the comments. They are eating pizza in front of a good sized group of people. Someone stands up and thanks them for what they're doing and for being there. They say that they appreciate all the live feeds to keep them in the loop. Angelo talks about when the Army Corps said the easement would not be granted on December 5th. He talks about the roller coaster of emotions. Then the chairman said to go home. Two or three days later - then the fire, they decided they would ceremonially put it out. Then Oceti Oyate came up and was a new camp. It wasn't clear. Is the fire still going?

Angelo: The fire is a symbol of the fight we have. It was intense. It was cold. It's dangerous.

Dean: The fire is not put out. It's in every one of us that's been supporting camp. You carry it wherever you go. We take these things we do, it's a flame here. We take it with us. And as far as anybody going to camp, if you go you have to be self-sufficient. Think of this as a test. A test of your will. Have enough food. Have enough water. It's up to you to see how much you can endure. Think smart. Have common sense. You can survive anything that comes, any elements.

The meeting ends with applause and whistles.

He walks through the crowd. He goes outside and smells the air. He takes a deep breath.

January 24th

Inspiring the youth is the most important message

It is a live feed with an adorable little girl.

Dean: You like water protectors, huh?

Girl: Yeah.

Dean: What do you like about the water protectors?

Girl: They tell you about how to keep the oil out of the water.

Dean: You don't have to put oil in the water?

Girl: Yeah. I don't like oil.

Dean: Are you inspired by all the messages? You're going to grow up to be a water protector too, huh?

Girl: Yeah. And then I'll come back here to say my own words.

Dean: Oh, I like that. That's very empowering. What would you like to say to the world out there about water protectors?

Girl: I dunno.

Dean: Destroying the water is sad, huh?

Girl: I know. I just don't know the words.

Her mom says, "What do you say? Water is life."

Girl: Water is life. That's what I want to say to the people.

Dean: I like this little girl. This is what we do. We inspire kids from all over. This little girl has been a blessing to me and to all the water protectors and to the world out there. This is what we fight for. Right?

Girl: Yep.

Dean: High five! Awesome. I like that.

"I prefer dangerous freedom over peaceful slavery." ~ From a Latin phrase

Let's evaluate this post pic!!

He shares a graphic with information:

Bismarck, ND - Breakdown of costs from Aug 10 thru Jan 20 by the North Dakota Highway Patrol in response to the Dakota Access pipeline protest and related illegal activity.

Personnel 1,956,533

Travel/lodging 431,928

Equipment/supplies 330,824   Total 2,719,285

Total with regular time and mileage 4,433,329

Number of state troopers logging emergency declaration time 155

Hours of regular time 41,039.75

Hours of overtime 39,113.75

Hours of on-call time 59,289.50

Miles driven on regular time 349,139

Miles driven on overtime 412,983

He shares a post from Texas.

ATTN ALL: Kelcy Warren meeting in less than 48 hours now++ SHARE IT UP PEOPLE! ++Invite Media because they invited "Light Security" ++ Bring Drums and Signs and Water and Land Protectors++ This Thursday 1/26/17 is the day we will see you in Austin! Austin, TX 9 A.M

Texas Water Protectors say NO! to Kelcy Warren

He shares a photo of Trump signing papers.

OK I know what I said about giving this guy chances!!!! Well if you're going to be making these decisions within the next couple days as president then we're all screwed!!! Time to step up and tell this guy why it's all bad to continue taking from the earth!! This guy looks like he doesn't even know what's going on!!

Trump's censoring EPA updates but it's ok for him to tweet away stupid rants?!!!

He shared a link: Trump bans Environmental Protection Agency employees from giving social media updates.

Diné means "The People" Not "The White House"

I pray that my Diné Nation makes the right decisions this coming year and not buy into the corruption and greed!! Remember protect Mother Earth at all cost!!!!

He shares a link: Navajo to work in White House

"Stop it.

Stop losing hope.

Tighten up, refocus and keep fighting. It's time to come back together because even though it feels like the whole world is against us, remember the whole world is watching. We have the lead on this so let's keep showing the world we still stand. Never give up the fight for the generations to come.

We are the resistance.

We are change." ~ John BraveBull

He shares a video. He is riding in a car over the Golden Gate Bridge.

"Thank you Gabriela BK, Angelo Wolf, Shiyé Bidzííl, Steven Harrison Jr. For coming to events up north in California. I am truly grateful for the past two weeks. Wishing you all safe travels. Know you have a community of people standing with you as you go back to Standing Rock. I hope you carry us with you. When it's hard, remember Sacred Center and every person who hugged you that day and gave you love. Remember all the people and the children who look up to you." ~ Valerie Treloggen

It's in our DNA!

He shared Fusion's video: The broken promises that built Standing Rock

We're again on the front lines.

#BREAKING: President Trump just signed an executive action to advance the Dakota Access and Keystone pipelines. Once again, Native Americans must fight to protect what is theirs. #NoDAPL

This video explains how the construction of the Lake Oahe dam took out a beautiful ecosystem to provide electricity for much of the north central part of the United States. The dam was completed in 1962 and President John F. Kennedy visited South Dakota to celebrate the completion.

The Oahe Dam flooded the Standing Rock and Cheyenne River reservations. It displaced hundreds of Indigenous families and destroyed 160,000 acres of their most sacred land. The dam destroyed the wetlands and the food source. The government began food commodity programs to compensate.

The 1851 Fort Laramie Treaty that reserved millions of acres of land for the Oceti Sakowin Nation has been broken since it was signed. White settlers never stopped moving in on the land. Things only got worse when gold was discovered in the Black Hills. Congress took even more land a decade later from the Nation.

Each of these events completely disrupted the Nation's culture, spirituality and way of life. The Great Oceti Sakowin Nation has been encroached upon since Europeans first arrived.

I've learned something at Standing Rock.

When we prepare our way with prayer, a transformation of consciousness takes place. Subtle at first... but then, the senses gradually become heightened, the fears melt away, and life's endless possibilities begin to open up.

Come prayerful warriors.

Tunkashila awaniyanki ktelo.

(Creator will watch over you)

He shares a moving video about what camp means by John Gonzalez.

January 25th

Prolific The Rapper has done it again!! Powerful, chaotic, beautiful storytelling.

He shares a great remix of Prolific's music video.

Must watch this: Welcome to BLACKWATER. A look into private security education.

He shares a YouTube video: Inside Blackwater: Iraq's most controversial private military contractor

He shares a couple of live feeds. He is riding in a car. There is music in the background. It is a gray, cloudy day and there is a lot of snow everywhere. He is back in Standing Rock.

Shiyé Bidzííl says: The Withstand with Wolves page will be back up shortly and Angelo and Gabby are ok as well. Keep prayers and strength coming.

January 26th

DRONE FOOTAGE WILL BE NEEDED EVERYWHERE!

He shares a link: Iowa pipeline leak brings attention back to Keystone & Dakota Access

Education in action is a beautiful thing!!

He shares a link from Greenpeace USA.

Update from the climbers who hung the "RESIST" banner above the White House today. Please show them some love in the comments! #ResistOften

Looks like they are targeting water protectors. It's called snatch and grab!!

He shares Steven Jeffrey Chrisjohn's live feed.

Steven: Disturbing news from frontlines warrior. *(Steven introduces Fixico Akicita. They are at the front gate of Oceti Sakowin Camp.)*

Fixico: Night before last we went on a prayer patrol, me and two other people. Twelve snowmobiles and ATVs came down in a u formation and surrounded the vehicle. Boarded the vehicle like pirates. They banged in windows. We tried to get back to camp, but we got stuck. They yanked us out. They were choking me, pulled us out by our hair. The snatch and grabs are getting bad. I felt like I was in a hostage movie. Some of them weren't even wearing badges. They arrested me. They didn't read me my rights. They took me to Bismarck.

CAMP IS FRONTLINES!

Fracking Free Ireland!!!

Standing Rock Awareness!!!

Share it up!!!

He shares an article: Irish government rules out fracking in the Republic of Ireland

I support this guy John!!

He shares John Bolenbaugh WhistleBlower's video.

Information for your own good knowledge!

He shares a release: Public Health Warning: It is about possible rozol (dangerous rat poison) exposure.

You're all wasting energy talking about negativity!!!

Come to camp and pick up trash is as simple as it gets! Let's get that camp cleaned up!!! Thank you all for listening. #CleanCamp

Time to wake up!!!

He shares: VICE Canada: RISE premieres January 27th

The first episode is Standing Rock.

More truth for all of your knowledge!!!

He shares an article from Forbes.com:

Solar Employs More people in U.S. Electricity Generation than oil, coal and gas combined.

January 27th

Pop some popcorn and enjoy this 90 minute wonderful movie about water. Inspiring education everywhere!!! Listen to the sound and let Mother heal you.

#Education #SaveThePlanet #StandingRock #WaterProtectors

Slowly but surely they are covering up and getting away with all the evil they've done!!

He shares a link from theDickinsonPress.com:

North Dakota House passes eliminating reporting of small oil spills.

Dave wants to have a meeting with trump!! Talk business? Or protect our tribe and what it stands for?

He shares an article: Chairman Dave Archambault of the Standing Rock Sioux Tribe has asked President Donald Trump for a meeting.

BIA has stepped up with additional police assistance from North Dakota!!!! Wow!! It looks like they want everyone out of the flooded areas!!!

He shares a link from KFYRTV.com: Additional BIA (Bureau of Indian Affairs) officers to be dispatched to North Dakota to assist with DAPL protests. This will bring the total number of BIA officers at the site to forty.

This just happened on Wednesday and TRUMP pushes for more pipelines!!!????

He shares a link: Iowa pipeline leaks 140,000 gallons of diesel following Trump's push for pipelines.

On January 24th of 2017 a major oil leak happened in Canada!!! Meanwhile Trump signs to bring up KXL and DAPL!!! SMH

He shares a link: Canada oil pipeline spills 200,000 liters on aboriginal land

I'm not an NDN. I'm an ACTIVE NDN!

Will the Morton County/ Fargo police get felony charges for shooting at the drone while the drone was documenting history?

He shares a screenshot of law enforcement officers shooting at the drone.

Stand up!!! That's all we gotta do!!

He shares a YouTube music video: Stand Up / Stand N Rock Official video

The video has many water protectors and celebrities in it.

Have you heard about the #NationalStrike February 17th? Nobody works, travels or buys anything. Shut the country down. Disrupt. #Resist

January 29th

The battle begins: Looks like there might be delays!!!!

He shares a link: As Trump reboots the pipeline expansion, an unexpected delay emerges. The projects will need to be approved through the Federal Energy Regulatory Commission, but a resignation will leave that five person panel with just two people.

I awoke in a blessed way!! Well TIME 4 LIVE FEEDS ALL DAY!! Time to crack this NUTSHELL open and get those long remaining questions finally answered!!!

Let's spread the boycott message worldwide!!!! We don't need any TRUMP PRODUCTS HERE!!!

He shares a link: Here is the list of 32 retailers that carry Trump's products. Join the movement aimed at boycotting them.

Shiyé Bidzííl would like to take this time to post and express my deep thoughts and prayers for both my tribal affiliations. May they be blessed and honored!! Despite what the world thinks of these two tribes I will still stand and fight to protect my people!! To educate our children through experience and culture!!

He puts out a late night live feed with a follower named Nick. Nick is on the phone.

Dean: The greater understanding of the humans and why they all congregate together. I want to understand you. What you think about the rise of Standing Rock. You have been in Vermont. Do you have any Indigenous blood in you?

Nick: No, I'm Irish.

They talk about community - Civilizations fail because they get too big and lose their values.

Dean: Before you see the light, you have to experience the darkness. It's a good thing Trump is the president, because everybody's waking up. What we do is one little step process into the future and our kids' kids will see what we started. We can't change it like we change our clothes. But to create and make change in a world that is so huge, where do we start from? But it's not impossible because you can see earth from space and you're on this little speck.

The most important tool we have is the power to listen. To people, to earth, to the air, to the trees, to the animals. You can pick up a lot of sounds that can guide you. A lot of people have forgotten this. Maybe this is why our ears are going to get smaller - the things we don't use that much, in evolution, grow smaller.

It's the bad talk, the gossip that gets me. But that's all a part of this psych ops. It's what has brought down this whole movement. People turning on each other. It's all the misinformation.

Do you know what I have to deal with? They don't phase me anymore. All these stupid trolls. Like Jared saying, don't send Dean money, he's been arrested, he's been doing illegal drugs. They feed into that. It's my past. It doesn't even bother me.

What really brought me out of the state of fear, that all came out of me on December 5th at the Ramada. A lot of water protectors wondered what I was doing. If there wasn't going to be a million people tuned into what was going on at Standing Rock yet, I'll create an issue. Not create, but what I tried to do was to create another window to open up the world's eyes. What better way to open it up but to show the world Bismarck still has hate crimes and still has that racist image. And terrorizing.

What happened to me that day was shown all over the world. But what I did there caused a lot of people to be angry at me. Especially the BisMan people. Saying I was going up there being disrespectful. The tactics I used were a little jerky, but I never meant any harm. I've been going to that mall half my life. We all go there to shop, to do business. We say hi to the people, that's how I live my life, I'm a humble person.

The camp was a beautiful thing in November. You should have come. September, October, November - that was the golden age of camp. I still feel it. I still carry it in my heart every day. I'm Navajo too and they have water problems too. I think it's a bad idea to take anything out of the earth because this planet is a living, breathing spirit. Think of it like another human. Think of it as a living creature. How would the oil corporations like it if we had them strapped down and started putting needles in them and started testing them and start sucking out their blood. I don't think they would like it. That's the connection that they've lost. We've got to start teaching those people how to connect again. It doesn't matter if you are Indigenous, black, brown, white, green.

I went to California for a couple of weeks. It was beautiful thing. I felt free in that state. Even without a drone. It's a pretty expensive state to live there. That was my training ground for Standing Rock again. I really like to be comfortable when I fly the drone. You can't really be scared. My drone got stuck and spent two days in a tree. It was $150 to get it out. They climbed up the tree. A lot of people took care of me. The flight was six hours. Four hour delay. I was looking out the window as we circled twice. I felt like the drone. There were brutal winds.

If you're gonna be a consumer, consume knowledge. Consume education. You don't have to pay for that. That's just a part of the system to put all the knowledge in one building and make people pay for it. When really, you could just learn all that knowledge for free. Literally you could just go on the internet now and teach yourself anything you want to know. When you put truth out there like that, it's going to disrupt the system in time. In time though. We're not going to change this planet in one day, but in time we'll change it. It takes patience, it's probably not going to happen in our lifetime. But think about how this country progressed from when Columbus came over here to the way it is now. We gotta get out of this fossil fuel age.

I haven't had a car in three years. This is my futuristic ideals, but I think we need to get away from cars and trucks and anything transported by fossil fuels. And we need to go wind. We have such amazing thinkers in the world, why aren't they thinking out of the box. Edison and Tesla - people are afraid of what they don't know, so they gave the people Edison.

I'm learning too. I'm not always right. When you're wrong, you gotta learn to accept that you're wrong. And keep moving forward. A lot of people are under so much stress. Especially on the frontlines, there's a lot going on - you're not really straight. You're not really thinking right. You're feeling fear, they start controlling you. All those agitators that have been smacking crap.

The most powerful thing you can do to someone who is against you is to look them in the eye and walk away. Even on the frontlines you can just stand there and pray. You don't walk away, but you just stand there. No matter how awful it is, just stand there. Let yourself be consumed by all that tear gas and see how much you can handle.

Sometimes I have so much knowledge that it's overwhelming. Sometimes I don't even understand what comes in my mind. But I don't question it, I just feel it. Sometimes it comes to me in dreams, but sometimes in words. Before you change the world, before you stand up for water, you're going to have to learn to understand yourself. Really look into ourselves to see who we are. We can then bring it to other people in the community, then it can spread out to the tribe, to the state, to the country.

I was willing to take that pain to show the world what was going on, but they never shot me. They never shot me. They never charged me. They never really got to me. But that day at Treaty Camp, I think it was just because I had a Washington D.C. sweater on, probably bad for their publicity. I joke about that.

I don't pray every day, every other day. But I always pray in my dreams. A lot of people say you gotta pray every day to make it work, but that's not entirely true. You could pray once and make it work. You take all of your thoughts and feelings and put it into the prayer. That's how you connect. You connect to Creator or Tunkasila or some people call him God, Wakan Tanka. I hold my spirituality and my foundations good. Like in Diné country, Navajo, I lived there until I was 12 and I grew up really in a traditional way.

We knew how to be self-sufficient. We had to haul our own water, pump our own water. We had to go up to camp in the woods to cut our own wood to burn for the winter. We herded our own sheep. We sheered our own sheep. We cooked our own sheep to eat. We had our own horses, we grazed our own horses. We had chickens that laid eggs. We were self-sufficient. It wasn't a big camp. All the Navajos were spread out in remote areas. But we learned how to live off the land. We learned what plants to use. It's really still like that to this day. It is getting bad with all the drugs there and it is taking over the younger generations because they don't know what to do. That's where the government locked up all those people. Now those people are in a little world. They oppressed them so much that they don't have any hope for the future. But that's not true.

I respect all my elders. I have gained a lot of knowledge and wisdom, but sometimes elders can be wrong too. They can succumb to greed even. These medicine men, they sell the ceremonies, and will he actually do it right? A lot of medicine men are taking advantage of their connections. Spiritual laws, they are misusing them. They are buying out the medicine men. I want to talk to the medicine man, but I don't want to give him money. I might give him a drone and tell him a story. I want to do a whole body ceremony to cleanse myself. But I don't want to cleanse out all of the negativity. I kind of like to have that in me all the time because in a way those evil feelings, or those chaotic feelings, all that bad stuff, it can save us one day.

Use the anger. Use the fear. Use the sadness. But don't ever give into all of it though. But we do need it in our daily lives. To find ourselves. To strive to be the perfect human being, but we're never going to be perfect. It's perfect when it's not perfect. It's like art. Putting blobs of colors everywhere. People wonder what it is. But I've been around art and artists my whole life.

Be careful of desire too, sometimes it leads us into a whole can of worms. Love is the strongest feeling that we can hold in our hearts. It can empower us to do things that we didn't think we could. To protect the people of the world. But then again, that love can also be your greatest weakness. It won't even be in your own heart, that weakness could be in your kids or someone you love and the enemy goes for it.

Love what's beautiful. I almost forgot the little things in life. I was so consumed in Facebook and the drones. I almost got disconnected from all of the little, tiny things in life that matter. What's happened to me, I'm going to have the greatest story to tell my grandchildren. I talk to my children like I talk to you. I think it's more natural for girls to understand earlier. Women are more powerful than anyone on the planet. They go through a lot more stuff than we do. It's the man's ego that wants it to fear and last forever, even when he's dead.

I feel so enraged right now because of what they are doing with the Crazy Horse monument. They want to put it on the sacred Black Hills. He fought for those hills. Look what has come to his story, it's all wrong. All we need is his story. We don't need a statue to remind us. We don't do that kind of thing. We tell stories and they get passed down. Every culture had a beginning.

You can't just say you're going to control the whole world. Aliens do exist...maybe they want to build something to go to another planet. We're the most advanced living beings in the universe, but we are the most stupid too. Most naive.

That's the mentality that people are putting on this pipeline - Trump is going to push it through - after the vets left after the bridge, all they have in their minds is that pipeline's already in the ground and they screwed you guys all and it's over. I don't even pay any attention to them, but I listen to them. It's knowledge when you listen to people who don't understand.

I really look at everyone's comments. There's quite a few comments that I can talk about next time. Trolls will figure out that I won't even pay any attention to them anymore. All those trolls, they don't mean nothing to me. They don't phase me. They can try to make my emotions run, but I don't care. They're just hackers. That's what they want to do in life. They can say all the things about my past.

Supposedly I'm the biggest meth dealer at camp. I'm the biggest pot dealer at the camp. I am a disgrace to camp. I just smiled. He doesn't even know me. In a way he was doing something that made him happy. But I never showed any aggression or anger. I don't allow it to affect me. It's just people talking. They're just lawyers. In tribal court, I'm going to represent myself and fight the marijuana charge. In a way I broke the tribal marijuana law, plain and simple. But people change. We need more understanding. Certain things that can be better. And make revenue. Grow something that can make revenue. I drink, but I'm not an alcoholic, my father was though. We got to weed ourselves out of that system. It takes time. You gotta indulge in a little bit of that colonialism, that fire water.

Sometimes I have all the love and all these good words that I can pass on, but at the same time, I'm still hurt inside and feel sad and lonely inside. I think it's part of the PTSD. Mine is not out there, not dramatic. It gets triggered by helicopters and videos of what happened.

It's all up to us. We all know what we have and what we're supposed to do with it. We just have to stand. No matter how dark the battle looks, don't be afraid to step into the light. This is the face of change. Good has to look into the face of evil and evil has to look into the face of good. Evil needs to understand why goodness needs to prevail. We need evil in the world so the good can prevail.

Out of chaos comes control. The chaos is slowly happening. People don't agree. This world is in uprising. It's going to get worse before it's going to get good. But it's going to be worth it. It's going to be worth every sacrifice we ever gave in our whole lives. It's going to be worth all the hate, fear, destruction. Because after that, we'll all be at peace again and the whole world is going to renew.

Our knowledge is so caught up on just this tiny little planet. If we understood, we would already be on other stars. We had all those connections in ancient civilizations. We're so caught up in life. We don't need a colonized system any more. I'm not going to allow this government to suppress anybody, any idea, any culture. I'll be right there to help protect.

We're going to put money on water and sell it. We don't put money on our resources. Not on water, air, but we do. We are consumers. Before you say it's too late, it will be over. It will start over again.

I hold a lot more meaning to myself and what I do and my community. I can say that with honor. No matter what my tribe at Standing Rock is going through, if they stole something - I still support them. But I need to educate my own tribe that if you are going to have money, you're going to have to use it in a good way.

Alright guys I'm going to go sleep in solidarity and I'm going to dream in unity. Next major live feed will be of camp tomorrow morning. I've been taking care of my babies. I spent the weekend with them. I will wait until they go to school and then I will go.

It's the first time since the beginning of December. I went a few times, but to fully be at camp again. People are saying, Dean, don't go to camp. Don't come back to camp. I appreciate everyone's thoughts and concerns, but I am going to make that decision. And you know my decision making, it can lead me to the world watching.

I selected the very best drone footage and I gave a couple of them to the New York Drone Film Festival. There's so much I haven't shown. We made a video. It's entered. I believe the prize is world recognition. I want to use it to help spread Standing Rock still. Talking on live feed is one thing, but to go out there and actually appear in a community where people really support, we're making them believe anything is possible just by showing up. They have been feeding off your knowledge, your strength. They see you. They feel you. It gives them a sense of hope and direction.

Everyone says I'm a hero, but I want people to start picking up everything I'm talking about. They want Drone2bwild to leave camp, so there aren't any drones...but Chase Iron Eyes had a drone. He didn't use it to the limit, but he used it. He kept up on camp life. He did the right thing. Drone2bwild came back. I came back because these are my people, this is my community. This is my life.

There were only two Standing Rock tribal members that went to California. First time for both of us. Experiencing a new way of life. Beyond Standing Rock in a land of oceans, spreading the wisdom. I brought back a more focused plan and more knowledge. My brain does not stop. That's what drives me. I love my life. I'll sit, I'll cry. I will never deny. I will always just tell the truth, whether it's bad or good.

Sometimes people say I do too many live feeds. Maybe I do. I just live feed images with some music. Anything I put out there, people love it. I put good music with it, good vibes. I might just take the drone up and go right over to the pipeline. I'm not trying to stalk these DAPL security, but just to check on them, make sure they are still alive.

I have a funding page going up. A lot of people don't want to talk about funding. Money involved, the negative just comes out of nowhere. We were in a wealthy county and they asked us what we needed and I told them, drones and GoPros. With fifty drones we can document and attack a whole pipeline in a couple of days.

January 30th

Shiyé Bidzíil is back at camp with one of many residents Steven Jeffrey Chrisjohn

He walks around camp. There is a lot of wind and plenty of snow everywhere. It is a bright, sunny day. Roads have been cleared in camp.

I'm at camp right now, feel a different vibe. Still feels great. Feels awesome. Still feel freedom in this place. It's kinda eerie right now. If you're used to when everybody was at camp, it still feels like that, but it's more empty. A lot of abandoned yurts, tipis, tents. Seems like there's people in there, but there's nobody in there. And that's the eerie part. But once in a while somebody pops out of one.

He shows trash dumpsters. There are many sitting in a row.

California was fun. It was great. We met other water protectors. It was a vacation and a learning experience. There's a lot of people who this means a lot to. Just being here, in Cannonball – with DAPL security right up there.

He shows around camp. He is walking around. The wind is strong and it is hard to hear. He sees a Burger King poster hanging on an abandoned tent and stops. A young woman doesn't know who he is. She asks where he's from. He walks through water, slush, snow.

He talks about donations with another young woman. She is trying to sort out the good stuff so it can go to different camps. Some of it still has the tags on it. A young man doesn't know who he is. He says he is concerned about Dean's live feed. The young man says that live feeding inside of camp is not allowed. Dean talks to him about it and moves on.

He talks to a man from Pueblo Camp. He shows Dean around his camp - including the stove and how it works. He talks with another man in this structure. Dean talks about Standing Rock spreading out and how beautiful it is. They talk about being free and how scary it can be without money.

In a way, this camp is everywhere now. It's spread out all over the world. People came through here. They donated what we needed.

Abandoned tents

Emptiness

Chilling resistance

Echoing shadows

STAND RISE PRAY

The day I first met this guy he was humble and had a good heart with a lot of truth in it!!!! He is known as The Oil Corporation's Whistle Blower that cost Embridge BILLIONS. His name is John Bolenbaugh. A man with NO FEAR and COURAGE of a lion!!!! *He shares dapllies.com*

PROOF THEY ARE MEETING TONIGHT!! @pkc. They didn't want any Facebook Live Feeds coming out of this secret meeting!!!! Let's hope they still support the camp and the resistance against DAPL!! Despite the Standing Rock Tribe telling the camps to leave all areas. They don't have that right to say such a thing!! The people who have that right to stay or go are the WATER PROTECTORS themselves!!! Money isn't everything!! Money can't buy you happiness!!! I, Shiyé Bidzííl, am in full support of every warrior still out there at camp!!! Stand in Solidarity together and forever brothers & sisters!!!!

After the meeting, he shares a couple of videos and posts about what happened. Many different governmental offices will be sending people to camp to help with the cleanup efforts. The concerns are about protecting the water, so that none of the camping gear or trash gets washed away in it in the expected flooding. They also talked about keeping the campers safe and avoiding an armed conflict. Water protectors will also help in the cleanup and those who want to stay will move to higher ground.

Calling all veterans of this great nation to Standing Rock once again to stand and fight!! But most of all protect the water protectors from the Domestic terrorism such as our own government!!!

As the day turns to darkness!!

I took a walk throughout Oceti and what I felt was the spirit of Standing Rock!!! Our home.

#ShiyéBidzíílPictures

January 31st

It's official!!

He shares an article from Cramer.House.Gov: Approved - Dakota Access pipeline Receives Federal Easement

He shares KFYR-TV's post:

Senator John Hoeven issued a statement with Vice President Pence and Acting Secretary of the Army Robert Speer:

Today, the Acting Secretary of the Army, Robert Speer, informed us that he has directed the Army Corps of Engineers to proceed with the easement needed to complete the Dakota Access pipeline.

Let's see if this is debunkable???

He shares a live feed from camp. It is cold. You can see his breath as he talks.

Talking about info that passed thru everybody - I try my best to put what needs to be seen and heard and said, but you take it how you want to take it. The info I put out there doesn't say if it's the whole truth. So help yourself out. Don't always rely on everyone else for the truth. You have to do your part and look into it for yourself. It's up to you if you believe it or not.

If you all heard, they approved the work. Very sad. But you shouldn't be sad. You should be happy. Be good. Don't let information and news like that break your soul down. You gotta keep on going forward.

We all have to work together. Start doing your own investigation. Start learning the way of protecting and documenting. We can all be our own personal reporters. Take all the posts I put out there, you take it upon yourself to believe if it's true. The truth is out there, it's right in front of us. We just gotta open our eyes and put down our guards and step into uncomfortable positions.

We are doing fine and are safe here at camp.

"I need us to stand NOW! This is the final hour." ~ LaDonna Tamakawastewin Allard

Standing Rock is Shiyé Bidzííl

He shares a video. It is slow motion steps into very deep snow.

Every step we take is always a challenge but that's our first step when breaking the ice here at Oceti Sakowin Camp!!!

Shiyé Bidziil talks about stepping forward and taking the risks!!!

He is in Steven Jeffrey Chrisjohn's live feed. They are near the river. They are walking around in very deep snow. They walk to the frozen water. It is windy and very cold. There are dogs out on the ice.

Dean: Here's a neat idea. On this side of the river is the reservation. On the other side is farming and a whole different kind of living. We could use snowmobiles to outreach to each other. We could cross the river, it's frozen. We have to start thinking outside the box. Make a bridge, a connection and start reaching out to each other.

He walks out on the frozen water.

Dean: This is the risk we all take. This is life. Sometimes we are going to step in dangerous situations. Life is full of dangerous situations that we put ourselves into. You gotta have no fear and just keep stepping forward. Until you start hearing cracking. *(He laughs.)* Don't be afraid to step out of your comfort zone. This isn't my comfort zone, but it's beautiful. It's cold, it's stinging, it's a frozen river here. But here we are, enjoying it. It's what we came here to protect. It's moving, it's life.

Steven does a little dance on the ice.

Steven: We're on the way to shower, but this is too beautiful not to stop.

This can be looked into: There are half a dozen BIA patrol trucks in the parking lot of Prairie Knights, also patty wagons.

BIA MOBILE HEADQUARTERS parked in RV parking at Prairie Knights Casino and Resort. Don't let that stop you from casino entertainment!! Stop in!! Enjoy yourself!!

Backwater Bridge and the lights still burn!! With Shiyé Bidzíil & Steven Jeffrey Chrisjohn

He still gets thousands and thousands of views on his live feeds. Even more since he is back at camp. They are sitting in a car near the Backwater Bridge.

Dean: They need to open this bridge.

Steven: We are policing ourselves, nobody can come up here - so they will open up the road. But they have station points where they are watching on lookouts. We can't pass these yellow signs. These are treaty lands. They said our actions were a liability, but we fixed that. Camp is getting cleaned up fast. We have front loaders, bull dozers working very fast. Where did this money come from, I don't know. Are the feds coming?

Dean: Some say they are already here. There are an extreme amount of BIA cops. They are pulling lots of people over.

Dean shows the concrete barriers on the bridge close up. And the stadium lights.

Dean: This is treaty land. We have the right to be free here. This is our own world. That's a lot of hearts guys.

We are observing, just like they are observing. There's a camera there with the lights.

They get out of the car. The wind is blowing hard, can't hear much. They get back in the car.

Dean: Shout out to DAPL, watching this live feed. Don't be scared, we're just people here trying to fight for our future. Nothing wrong with that.

Chapter 9

February 1, 2017

Update on Treaty Land Territory

This live feed is very late night/early morning. The camera is looking at lights on top of a hill. DAPL lights. Spotlights. There is snow everywhere. He shows more DAPL lights and then more DAPL lights.

Kind of windy up here, but I just wanted to do a live feed. We all heard they got the easement through. Even with this high wind, I can hear machinery working. They're moving around up there. They already started drilling, they're working.

We Need You Now!

He shares a link: Final easement for DAPL appears imminent

It's official: Calling out all veterans to Standing Rock!!

He shares another link: US Veterans to return to Standing Rock after DAPL decision to continue

If you are coming back to Standing Rock please remind yourself to be self-sufficient and ready for winter as we are still in the freezing season here in North Dakota. Also when you make that journey do not settle in at the BIG overflow camp known as Oceti Sakowin. They are in the process of cleaning it up and in the process of transitioning it back to its original state. We are asking everyone to go to Sacred Stone Camp to gather and camp. Bringing all camps together as one.

He shares Joye Braun's live feed:

Anyone who fails to vacate when cops tells them to - flood, blizzard, other natural disaster. You will be charged $5,000. March 1, 2017

Shiyé Bidzííl says listen to Dallas Goldtooth on his view and take on the easement decision!!!!!!

He shares a live feed from the day before. Department of Army recommends Corps to grant final easement for DAPL.

Dallas says it's not necessarily true that the final easement has been granted. It has been recommended, but not granted. He believes it could be politicians trying to get water protectors worked up so they will do crazy actions and escalate things for themselves.

Backwater Bridge gearing up.

In his next live feed he is walking down the road. It is a bright, sunny day and his shadow stretches out on the ground in front of him. You can hear a drone flying nearby. He is walking toward the bridge. It is so cold that when he tries to zoom in on the bridge, the picture is very shaky because his hand is so cold.

On the bridge are vehicles and big flood lights. There's a thick blanket of snow everywhere. The road has been cleared, but there is still snow and ice remaining on the pavement.

There is a small airplane flying over. The sky is clear blue. He turns and shows six vehicles sitting on top of a hill. He looks around. He looks back at the bridge. Now some law enforcement officers are standing outside of their vehicles, but nothing is going on. A helicopter flies low. There are a few people walking around on the road. They are looking down the road at the bridge.

Water protectors walk across the bridge. There are a few people ahead of him. They walk toward the law enforcement officers. There is a man with a big camera with the water protectors. The officers start walking over toward them. There are five or six officers. They talk to the water protectors.

It is very windy and it is difficult to hear them. Dean points out that Chase Iron Eyes is there. He is talking to the officers. More law enforcement officers walk up. They are still talking.

Officer: This doesn't help your cause. There was some good communication going on, but you guys ruined it today. You ruined a lot of things. So when you go out there as a leader and get these people spun up, you won't get away with that. Who was on Facebook? It's going to fall on you. My advice to you is to call them. If you end up there on the hill, you are subject to arrest. We gave them a warning, but they keep going. We don't want any damage.

Chase: This affects our lives.

Officer: What this is about today is that you are trespassing on private land. Let them know they got to start leaving. It's private property.

It's hard to hear Chase. He talks about passive resistance...illegal things our government does. No face mask, but you're wearing face mask. You are the power. Trump is going to be asking you to do some illegal things and you need to look inside of yourself.

Officer: You just need to go home.

Chase: You need to go home too.

The two groups walk away from each other. He talks about how cold it is. His hands are frozen. They walk for a while.

Dean: That was a meeting. It's really, really freezing and cold. Behind me, looks like the new camp that's being put up on top of the hill is going to get raided. But the main camp is okay. Oceti is okay. People are still cleaning up. The camp on top of the hill will be raided. They are standing in prayer. The cops said we just all have to get off the top of the hill. Can't break laws, can't go on private property. Again the U.S. government tends to screw us over.

More people are gathering in the road all the way to the bridge. He passes them as he walks back toward camp.

Dean: Everybody's going to get arrested on top of the hill. Whatever happens when they raid on top of the hill, if anything bad should happen, if anybody gets hurt, they said they are going to pin it on Chase. They are going to blame him.

But he said that we are just standing in prayer and we are. Basically the government's enforcing their laws, making up laws, making up laws to protect those laws and more laws to protect those laws and basically screwing us over.

He shows the helicopter flying overhead. People are walking back from the bridge. He runs up the road. There are militarized vehicles behind him.

Officer on a loudspeaker: Everyone on the roadway needs to get off the roadway. All vehicles left will be towed and moved now.

Dean shows a water protector standing in the middle of the road in the way of the militarized vehicles coming up the road. Dean continues to move back.

Officer: If you remain on the roadway, you will be arrested.

The militarized vehicles come toward the water protector.

Officer: Go into the main camp. Get off the roadway.

The water protector is still standing there. There's a long line of law enforcement vehicles coming. Another water protector walks up in the roadway in front of the vehicles and puts his hands up. Several other water protectors join them. The officer just keeps telling them to vacate the road over the loud speaker. Then the LRADs go off briefly.

LRADs are sound weapons. They are also called Sound Cannons. They were also used when they raided Treaty Camp and on several other occasions. They produce painful tones. Headaches, permanent hearing loss, loss of balance and movement are some of the horrible things LRADS can do to people.

I'm back. Had to charge up the phone. The government is at Oceti's door right now.

He walks over to a large group of people standing in the road. There is some singing and drumming. There is a line of law enforcement officers. Water protectors line up and face them. There are a lot of officers.

Water protectors yell at them. They call them terrorists. The law enforcement officers are fully geared up from head to toe. Water protectors try to talk to them about the water. About keeping the water safe. The officers just stand there.

A woman starts crying and screaming about how they could have been responsible for her not being able to have any children. She says that she was hit with a rubber bullet in another action. Some of the things the water protectors say are deep digs, but it is truth. The woman keeps wailing. Someone holds her.

People start singing and drumming again. An officer says that on top of the hill is private land. He says, "This is way above us. We can't do anything except hold the line. We are just following orders." He points to Oceti camp and says that is Corps land. They are allowed to be there.

Dean gets good shots of all their gear up close. He shows that there are tipis and people standing on the hill. He gets a close up of an officer's eyes. The feed cuts off.

Morton County is under government control!!!

In the next live feed, Dean is moving around. There are a lot of people on the road. Law enforcement officers stand blocking the road up to the hill. The officers have full body shields up in front of them. A water protector walks by with no shirt on. There's a militarized vehicle behind them. There are more officers behind them. He walks up and down the line. The water protector without a shirt on walks by again. Across the street from the hill is Oceti Camp.

Dean: Steven is still on top of the hill. His battery is going. Pray for Steven. He's probably going to be arrested.

People start singing and drumming. He walks around the crowd. A militarized vehicle is running in the background. Water protectors try to talk to the officers. "You'll have to kill us," somebody says. Water protectors talk to them about the importance of clean water. Someone says, "I'm from Michigan and our water is poisoned." There is an Indigenous grandma there right up on the officers telling them shame on them. The guy with no shirt walks by again. He says, "My prayers keep me warm." Someone says, "I don't know who's idea this is, but it was a bad idea. Camp's going to be gone, what's the point."

Dean: Camp's cleaning up right now. Heavy equipment is here to help. People don't want to leave. I'm not going anywhere.

Everyone yells loudly. Water protectors hold up their hands. They hold up their fists. He zooms in on top of the hill. There are tipis still standing. There are many people standing.

The raid continues!!!!

I'm sitting in a vehicle so I'm pretty warm now. The new camp is getting raided right now. They've opened up a trailer and are going through it. I don't know if Chase has been arrested. Steven's page, he's live streaming on the top of the hill. The yellow helicopter is flying. The wind is bad. That's the government these days, making up laws as they go. Awww, Steven's live feed went down?

He zooms up on top of the hill. People are still standing around the tipis.

Steven's feed is down. Hopefully somebody up there has some juice to plug in and get the live feed going again. I can't deploy the drone right now because it's malfunctioned. The controller won't connect.

He gets out of the car. Someone has a drone flying. It is above the hill by the tipis. The feed cuts off and comes back. Someone is holding an upside down flag in the road. Someone starts singing and drumming. A water protector asks if he has any wires for a Phantom 4. He thinks he does. The feed picture goes gray when he sits the phone down. You can hear people yelling in the background. It goes on for several minutes. He comes back and says, "Sorry guys. Go to the drone page. I'm going to take the drone up."

Drone2bwild is back!!

Drone footage by Shiyé of the actions reclaiming land today!

He flies the drone over camp. Over water protectors who are gathered at the bottom of the hill. Everything is covered in snow. People whoop and yell.

As he flies up the hill there are law enforcement officers and their vehicles. He goes up higher. There is a truck or two. Then on top of the hill there is a group of water protectors standing. A fire has been started and some smoke is going up. There are tipis in a circle. Some are not completely up. The helicopter constantly flies around.

We got it close and personal with the camp that's going to be raided. We're going to stand strong.

He flies the drone over the militarized vehicles parked to the side on top of the hill. There are people walking down the hill. One person is walking up. He flies back up to the tipis and the water protectors standing around them.

He flies over water protectors being led in handcuffs by law enforcement. They are put in red vans. He gives everyone a look at Oceti Camp, right across the road from the hill. The battery signals low. Water protectors are still gathered at the bottom of the hill.

They took Chase in that white van. They took off fast. Chase got arrested. We're doing this for documentation purposes. To document all the illegal land taking. (*Dean shivers in the cold.*) We gotta push these to the limit. Share it out. Share it around the world.

Chase Iron Eyes has been arrested!!!! And the police have been taking down tipis at the new camp!! Because it's on private land.

He shows law enforcement going up the hill and on the hill. Water protectors are still standing on the road at the bottom of the hill.

Update: The camp got raided. As far as people cutting off live feeds, it's cold so maybe the batteries got drained fast. They took down all the tipis. They seized a white trailer. They have not raided Oceti yet. They just went on top of the hill.

They're going to leave and expect us to go back up there. I wonder if there's going to be a base up there. That's their excuse to come a little closer to camp. They said it's private land, but they are staying up there. These red vans are what the water protectors are in. There should be quite a few people in there. They are taking them up to Morton County.

Red vans drive down the hill. Water protectors yell and whoop as the vans go by. They cheer for the arrested water protectors in support.

Chase got arrested. Pass it on. Steven most likely got arrested too. Last I checked he was on the top of the hill. He had the choice to come down, but he decided to stay up there.

A group of water protectors in the back of a truck go by. He says that it looks like they got the camping gear in there. A tow truck goes up the hill. Another red van comes down. People are standing with signs. They cheer again. There is a beautiful sign that says: Protect the Sacred.

Say prayers for them. At the drill pad right now, they are drilling. Go to Myron's page, you can see the updates. Drills are in position.

I can't tell how many vans, probably six or seven vans. They are going to tow away a water protector's vehicle. Someone said they blocked the road to camp from the Pit Stop. Hmmm....should drive up that way and take a look.

BIA has blocked road access to main camp by Cannonball Pit Stop.

He is in a car in the next live feed.

I drove up here to check if they really did block the road and they did. Check this out.

He shows law enforcement vehicles with lights flashing in the middle of the road. He decides to go closer. He drives down the road. It looks like law enforcement officers are pulling a car out of a side road. There are a few people walking around. Cars are parked all around.

First of all, people are saying it was a bad idea for Chase...the point is this is our treaty lands they are taking over. We got to do anything. I don't care if we build a hundred camps. The point is that this is wrong. We got police forces, government forces, infiltrator forces, people coming at us from all over the place. People say that camp was pointless. That's beside the point. We'll build another camp, we'll build a hundred more camps. The point is that's treaty land, that's treaty land, that's treaty land. *(He pans the camera all around, showing all the land all around him.)* That's treaty land, that's treaty land. All of this around us is treaty land.

So whether we built one tiny little camp that we knew they were going to raid, you're missing the whole message. We're telling the world that this is wrong. We'll put up another camp and another camp. We'll put up camps all over these hills. What Chase did there, he did for the world. You don't see anybody else trying to come up with plans to try to defend and protect our sacred lands. We go into these things thinking we're making the right decisions. Even if it's not the right decision you go from it and learn from there.

Everyone says how are we ever going to prevail, how are we going to win? Stand in prayer, stay in prayer. Yes. Stand for what's right. Yes. Laugh if you need to. The point is we can't make judgements about the decisions that were made, if they were wrong. If you are on that level, you are missing the whole point. You gotta look more deeper into it.

These cops, all this force, that's what it takes for the government to push individuals, water protectors. Now who is powerful? I think the water protectors. And the people who are doing this for the greater power of the earth, don't you agree?

We don't have weapons, we don't have armored tanks. All we got is our hearts, our strength, our courage. We can take all of those and use them to help us stand. That's what Chase was doing. He was showing everybody the way. Now you can be mad at Chase, you can criticize Chase, but all those water protectors on that hill made a sacrifice. A sacrifice for change, a sacrifice for the children, a sacrifice for the future, a sacrifice for the ancestors that made the journey.

This is what we're doing. We're taking our lands back. We're occupying to show the government that we're not going to let you dig into the earth and take all the resources out of the land. We're going to do what's right. We're going to stand here and fight. That doesn't mean physically fight, that means mentally, spiritually. Build our wisdom. Regain our courage. Leaders. All the followers can be leaders. All the people of camp can be leaders. We just gotta find it in ourselves.

So mad respect for Chase. Follow in his footsteps. Look at what he's doing. He's showing us the road to our freedom. Right now what's happening is history. Good things happen. Bad things happen. Chaotic things happen. Things happen that you don't want to see, don't want to feel, don't want to experience. But you need to feel it and see it.

Look at all those cops right there just to stop unarmed water protectors. *(There is an extremely long line of law enforcement vehicles.)* Our prayers are strong, obviously. It takes a whole lot of them to come down and try to stop our power. Throughout the blizzard, throughout all the storms, all of these water protectors are still standing here strong. And personally to me, felon is just a word. It's just a label. It's just something to label us with.

What the water protectors did today were not felonies. What they did was sacred. They were standing in prayer, putting up tipis. Showing the life. I want all of you watching this live feed to take a deep breath. When all of this goes through your brain this evening, say a prayer. Say a prayer for Chase and Steven and all of the water protectors that were on this hill. Say a prayer for everything, for everyone you've ever known in your life. Say a prayer for all the children, the future generations. Say a prayer for the elders. Say a prayer for yourself and your family. And say a prayer for Morton County police officers. Say a prayer for the government because they are digging their own grave.

He looks around with the camera. It is windy and cold. There are flags flying. He steps out of the car and walks down the road. A large group of water protectors are still gathered. There are militarized vehicles there too. Officers stand beside the vehicles. An officer gets stuck in the snow in a small vehicle. Other officers finally push the vehicle out.

He walks past an officer who has a gun strapped on his side. He walks right up to the officers. There are water protectors taking pictures of the vehicles. Officers step up on the side of the militarized vehicles and then down. Then back up again. A water protector says, "Let them go!" Several minutes pass here with officers standing on the sides of vehicles. A water protector yells, "Return to the north side of the bridge!" Everyone laughs. The militarized vehicles finally start to turn around and move away. There is drumming and singing in the background.

Dean: Those cops are taking that trailer. Don't know if they are doing it illegally, stealing it.

Some officers get off a vehicle and walk down to a truck and trailer. The truck and trailer pull out onto the road and leave. Dean shows the license plates. He shows an upside down flag patch with AIM on it. (AIM stands for American Indian Movement. Look it up if you do not know about it.)

There are people standing in the road. All the officers get back on the vehicles and leave. He comes across Fixico.

Fixico: No rubber bullets, no tear gas. There were arrests made. And we're all freezing. They are going with their tails between their legs.

Dean: My ears are cold, my hands are cold, even though I have gloves on. There you go guys. Our lives, our history. I'm going to go get something to eat. You guys take care.

Pray for Steven Jeffrey Chrisjohn for today he has been arrested for documenting and protecting our waters!!!! Please support him!!

He shares Steven's live video from earlier at Last Child Camp.

Shiyé Bidzííl Photography 2017

"Last Child Camp"

February 2nd

He notes that he is feeling concerned.

It has my attention that Vanessa Castle was also detained for inciting a riot.

Vanessa was arrested for simply live feeding on Facebook from outside of the jail. Law enforcement say she was "inciting a riot." Obviously law enforcement wanted to make an example out of her. Water protectors were arrested for ridiculous things all the time.

He shares all of the phone numbers for law enforcement and asks everyone to call and ask that the water protectors be released.

Phone call to Shiyé Bidzííl aka Drone2bwild, from Chase Iron Eyes & Steven Jeffrey Chrisjohn who are incarcerated from yesterday's raid of Last Child Camp. They are both being held in Morton County Jail but they seem to be in good spirits. They send the protectors words of encouragement.

This is a live feed.

Dean: Update from camp. I'm here at camp and it's cold. There's a lot of mobilizing to get camp cleaned up. Bulldozers scraping up stuff that's spilled out of tents. Over donated food, excess camping gear. But I got a special live feed for you today. It's from Steven Chrisjohn and Chase, coming from the jail.

Steven: We're okay here. It's not about us, it's about the people. It's about sending our voice out. This is a movement.

Chase: 77 people were arrested. Criminal trespass and inciting a riot. They are holding us, not giving us a day in court. 72 hours, they may be able to hold us. We are committed to the peaceful stand we are taking at Standing Rock.

Dean: That was a recorded message from Chase and Steven. By tomorrow they will get out, if not they will be held all weekend. They encourage everyone to call the jails. Half of the people arrested got farmed out to other jails. Get on the phone lines. Blow them up and pressure them to let them out tomorrow. They haven't been charged with anything yet. I'll post the recording. Share that out.

When I finally get the drones, we'll get some drone shots of up on the hill. Where they told us it was private land, now they're just sitting up there watching us. Check this out. A row of vehicles on top of the hill. Stay strong. Keep your prayers going.

February 3rd

He shares Bismarck Tribune's link: Oil spill hits the Missouri River south of Williston

Live at the corrupt courthouse of Mandan with Chase Iron Eyes and Vanessa Castle.

He live feeds from the courthouse. Jordan from The Young Turks is there reporting.

Chase talks about Last Child Camp. He tells how some water protectors who are ancestors of Crazy Horse said to go west. They had dreams. So they did that. They went up on the hill. Last Child's Camp was in Crazy Horse's memory. People were just engaged in a prayer circle.

Jordan asks Chase what the future of the camp is going to be. Chase says, moving to higher ground, cleaning up...still committed, still strong. Over 700 people have been arrested.

Dean: I kinda have to go incognito any time I'm up here in Mandan cause I possibly might be the most wanted drone pilot in America. I'm going to go back to camp, start putting up the drones. Start surveilling everybody, BIA, watch their tactics, watch over camp, watch for infiltrators, and pretty much go to the top of the hill and survey DAPL.

It was just an excuse that they took everybody off the hill so they can get that much closer to us. Without using binoculars anymore. To tell you the truth, we're at war. It's an intellectual war on sovereignty. We're fighting for our rights as humans and Indigenous people. We are beautiful people. We come from many, many stories. We come from earth, we come from the stars.

See Trump thinks he's high and mighty. He thinks he's the king, he thinks he knows it all. But in reality, he doesn't. He's lost. He's a lost soul. It's going to take the Indigenous people to bring that all back. And we're here and Chase is showing us the way.

A lot of people say that him putting the camp up on the hill, knowing what the consequences are... now when we do actions, it's not pointless, it's powerful. It was empowering and these water protectors set up this camp knowing it could be raided but they still stepped forward into the light and they still accomplished Crazy Horse's stories about going to higher ground, getting away from the flood.

Camp is going to be different. Camps are fading out into multiple little camps. But the most important thing now is camp is inside all of us. Camp is in our minds, in our dreams and camp is what we make it. Pray for Standing Rock. Even though they are against us, we still gotta pray for Standing Rock, for they will find a way.

City of Seattle is divesting $3 million from Wells Fargo!!!!!

February 4th

Standing Rock wants the water protectors out of main Oceti Sakowin camp by the 22nd of February. Confirmed by Chase Iron Eyes.

Things are getting ugly water protectors, and we all know that North Dakota court is saying that those who live stream are camp leaders, and charging them with inciting riots. WHAT? Also BIA invaded Sacred Stone Camp and assaulted and arrested water protectors on security detail, and entered a home with documents stating that he did not own the home and telling him he was evicted. What is Standing Rock Tribal Council trying to do? Please stay safe my people!!

He live feeds in the dark. He holds a lantern up for light. He is wearing a face mask.

Good evening people who have been inspired by this great movement. I am one of the few reporting media coming from camp. It seems like since I've been back there's nothing that's ever going to stop what we're going to do. Nothing they can put in our path can stop us. We're either going to go around it, jump over it or work together to pick it up, get it out of our path and continue forward.

Now, here's my really deep down thoughts of camp life. It's not Standing Rock doing this to the water protectors. Here's where we're going to correct this place. The people here are Standing Rock. I am Standing Rock. And I am standing in solidarity right in this camp.

It's tribal council, and on behalf of David Archambault, the chairman, that are making those kind of rules. Why has Dave Archambault allowed his legacy, his position, to a position where they are just oppressing his own people? Putting up road blocks at the Cannonball Pit Stop. Keeping other water protectors from going to camp now. To me, it's wrong. They say it's for the safety, but for the last six months we've been getting shot at, we've been getting terrorized, getting smoked out, getting infiltrated through our computers, and through our minds. Now they want to bring up safety.

When this all started up, Dave was in camp. It was powerful. All the people coming together from all walks of life. Standing Rock brought everybody together. And we'll say this again and again, Dave Archambault said all the good words, all the good wisdom. I believed in him. I believed in everything he was about. He was the guy that when everything was confused and chaotic around us, I felt better when he was around. I felt protected. I felt safe. But now do I feel safe when Dave's around? I wouldn't know because Dave's never around anymore. He's off to other places. He's taking a different journey. I want all the followers to understand, don't hate him. Don't disrespect him. He is only human. He is taking his journey to a whole different level on his own. I want to wish him the best of luck. We all make mistakes. I know Dave will learn a lot from all these upcoming actions they will be doing for all the water protectors to not be in the camps anymore. BIA is under government control. Now Dave wants to work with BIA and Morton County. Personally, I would be working with the water protectors.

The feed cuts out then comes back.

I'm back again guys. I'm used to that. All you gotta do is pause it, wait for it, boom. Comes back on. At camp, wait a couple of days and they're going to start coming back in. Earlier today it was reported that BIA went into Sacred Stone camp and they arrested a couple of water protectors who were on security detail. Now Sacred Stone, that camp, they've got it down. They've got all the valuable resources. They have all the stuff to survive. That was the first camp. And that's going to be the last camp standing.

There's rumors going around. They say the land owner called it in. That is nothing but bull. Don't believe everything you hear. It's not LaDonna. Not in a million years would she do that to her people. She's done so much for everybody here. She's done so much to bring awareness. Women in general have stepped up and shown all of us men how to do it. I've been watching cause I've been the eye in the sky. Who's always on the front lines? The women. Yeah, there may have been a couple of men calling the shots all these months, but who do you always see on the frontlines? All the women warriors.

Women are more powerful than men, I always say. Because they are. They have no fear because they are here to protect the water. And the water is life to everything in this world. It's the most sacred element, the most precious element. To me, it's life. Water. Water is life. Water is everything. And if the Standing Rock tribal council and the tribal chairman don't understand about water, then let them not understand. Don't step in and try to correct them. Let them talk. Let them feel special. Cause we don't need that kind of power. We have a different kind of power. It's a power that a lot of people are missing. A lot of people are misunderstanding. And the few people here in Oceti, they feel it, they see it and they know it.

So is everybody going to be out of here in time for the raid? I don't think so. There's going to be water protectors still standing their ground because that is what this whole movement is about. It's not about safety for us. It's not about getting out of the flood zone. Anybody can survive a flood. The flood was in all creation stories. Even the Bible. And what prevailed out of that flood? New life. That's what's going to happen here. New life. All from water.

All through the Missouri River they built dams because they wanted to control the water. This is all the little steps of controlling Mother Earth, controlling Mother, controlling the water, controlling the air, controlling the weather. We're only human beings. We shouldn't play God, or Tunkasila or the Great Spirit. We're supposed to be here, connected to the roots, connected to the earth. Now we are going to stand here. It doesn't matter how many little hills we take and set up camps, if it does get raided, we still do it. Because that is the message.

We're going to show Standing Rock and the world how to really stand. How to put your foot down. How to keep moving forward. We're past the light. We're stepping into the darkness. Again. That's why I hold this lantern. Because it's darkness. Do we know what we're getting ourselves into? Maybe. Maybe we don't. But that doesn't stop us. It's about sacrifice. You gotta sacrifice everything to stand. You gotta sacrifice people you love. You gotta sacrifice possessions you had. You gotta sacrifice your freedom. You gotta sacrifice your life. You gotta sacrifice your body. Right now, we're sacrificing everything. And we're here.

Right now this camp is getting cleaned up. A lot of people are saying that stuff is going to stay there and pollute the water. It's going to go against everything all the water protectors have been fighting for. Now all those people, they speak too soon. Just because you think you know the outcome, doesn't mean you actually know what's going to happen. This goes all the way up to the elders here. You never underestimate the power of Mother. For she has the last final word on who is to prevail on this planet, or not. She's been surviving for billions of years, eons. And throughout those billions of years, that's where our creation stories evolved from.

All this stuff I talk about, you can take it into your own meaning, how you want to think about it. It ain't up to me. I'm just talking. You're the person who makes the choices in your life. It's up to you. It's up to you to stand. It's up to you to decide if you want to back down. People are getting arrested. Is that going to stop them from standing in solidarity on another treaty land? They're going to keep standing. Getting felonies, getting arrested.

It's a system we shouldn't be controlled by. The system we're fighting needs to die. It needs to disappear. If we can't make it disappear, we need to contain it. Put it in a sacred bowl and pray for it and tuck it away, hide it somewhere where no one will ever see, hear or know the knowledge about the corrupt power and system. The true system is all around us.

And people don't judge them, teach them. Make them understand. And if they feel bad about it or disagree with you, don't correct them again. Just allow them to say what they got to say and in time they will understand. In time they will learn to forgive themselves. I hope they do. Everybody can be forgiven. Even all the police. Even all the DAPL workers.

We gotta pray for those DAPL workers. They have no idea what they are getting themselves in to. They dug up a lot of sacred sites and a lot of our ancestors who were buried here through all the generations. What's going to happen now is all those remains that they disrupted, the spirits are all flying around us. Because we are all one interconnected. Some of life, we don't see it. It's in front of our eyes. It's the spiritual.

As long as our two feet are connected to this earth, that's more powerful than any political tactic. That's more powerful than any non-lethal weapons, or even actual firearms. That's more powerful than the United States government. There's where our true power is. It's our two feet that the Creator provided, connected to the earth. That's more energy than any star in the universe. Never underestimate the power of energy you have within your mind and your soul and your heart and your body. Because we have so much energy within our spirits, it could explode into a whole new universe. We don't think like that because our minds aren't trained to understand it on a deeper level.

We're gonna rewrite history and we're going to write new laws. These new laws are the natural laws of Mother. Now we don't need to enforce it. Because she enforces the law. If she feels like she's upset with a community, she has that right to start an earthquake and cause chaos and destruction. We have no control of that. But we try to control it ourselves. We make weapons of fear to destroy things. Because we want to be that prevailing human at the end of civilization.

We want to drain and suck up all of the earth's resources just because we want to reach to that farthest star over there. You don't even need to drain resources to do that. All you need to do is close your eyes and connect yourself with earth, with Mother. And feel that connection with water, the trees and the wind and that will take you to the farthest places in this universe. We don't even need to physically be there. Spiritually, mentally we're already there. That's more powerful, a more spiritually grand feeling than draining Mother Earth's resources just to get to that star. We are already there. Why? Because we came from the stars. We are star people. A lot of people have forgotten the star people. That's where we came from. We came from the stars. We're travelers. We came to this planet.

There's always good and there's always evil. But it's the good that will prevail after the chaos. It's a continuous cycle. But we are going to win. We are going to show the world this is standing in true solidarity. We don't have weapons here. And right now, I'm fearless. That's where we need to be in our state of mind. We need to be fearless. But in order to get to that level, you got to go through fear down to your deepest inner emotions. You gotta put yourself out there and feel the fear and feel that presence of death, destruction.

Now I knew all of the decisions I was going to make in this movement. I knew all of the possible outcomes, but did that stop me? A lot of water protectors said I'm pretty crazy for doing what I had to do. But somebody had to do it. Someone had to show the world. But it only takes one person and that's what I tried to show. Now with the drones, we all know drones now. A lot of Indigenous people know about drones now. Now my advice to any drone pilots out there in this camp, Drone2bwild says, if you're going to fly a drone, and it's our drones, the camp's drones, the movement's drones, please get a hold of security and let them know you are taking a drone up. I don't know who else is flying drones out here, but that mostly like is DAPL's drones. They say they don't use drones. But think about it, be smart. If there's a bunch of DJI drones flying around, and you're the enemy, wouldn't you want to get your own and fly it into camp? That would be the perfect cover. People don't think that far ahead.

This is more strategic, more planning, more moves than any chess game ever created. This is a new kind of chess game. Everyone says that DAPL has the upper hand in this movement. No they do not. They're already in fear. They're up there with real weapons, we know. And non-lethal weapons and they've got all these little gadgets to protect themselves. And here we are with our voices, our hearts and our minds and our vision and our prayers. And our feathers and our traditions and our stories. We arm ourselves with all that knowledge and we can stand and walk. And that's more powerful. We can already see that the United States government is in fear because that's why they have weapons and tanks and try to do psychological warfare. They try to incite fear by bringing in tanks and parking them there for a few hours or a few days. That makes the people see them and they start freaking out and saying, that's where we gotta stop guys. But just because we see a big ole tank coming on that hill doesn't mean we gotta start shooting things. There's where we gotta start controlling the fear. Observe it. Study it. Because we are going to go all the way to the end.

This is my home. I'm standing, fighting for all of the people at camp. And I'm also standing in solidarity with all the other camps around the Nation. In Canada too. I'm standing here in solidarity for the future of all generations of children. And not to forget, I'm also standing here for all the environmental issues going on. South America, Brazil, we got issues going on in the forests. We got a lot of issues going on all around the world, more than just this pipeline. We got trees getting cut down. We got the mining. Who said that once, they are mining our spirits. Someone once said, you're digging into this earth, you're mining, you're mining our spirits too. And you're releasing all these chemicals. All the toxic chemicals that are not supposed to be in this kind of atmosphere. It's supposed to be staying in the ground. In the earth. Because that's where it's supposed to be. Not exposed and exploited for fuel. To make a machine move.

Now we need to start being more creative with alternative energies. Here at camp we have the old school wood stove. We got a structure made of wood and canvas. We make it here and we survive here. A lot of people say, but you stayed in a hotel for three months. It's because I needed to. Because I was smart about it. A lot of people, and I give them that much more respect, they stayed here and they dealt with all the elements and all the fear and all the cold. Sacrificing their well-being to stay here. And every second that they were standing on this ground, this movement got more powerful. It grows.

Think of it like this, we are all leaves. We are all leaves and we are all connected down to every branch, down to the trunk of this great tree of life. Now there's going to be a few leaves that are going to fall. Get plucked from the twig and fall down to earth and lay on the ground. You can say, metaphorically speaking, that's like the council, or Dave Archambault. But that leaf still has life in it. Even after falling to the ground. It degrades, it turns, it gets connected back into the earth. And from there it sprouts new life again. With a dab of water.

And this is why we're here. To protect the water. Because in the future all of our good water is going to be gone. We won't be able to find pure water. Because all the water is medicine. We need water to sustain life. When I was in the womb of my mother, I was in water. That's why to this day I give my mother a lot of respect. I believe we should give all the mothers a lot of respect. And the grandmothers a lot of respect. Because that's who I see out here, it's grandmothers and women who are standing and fighting. They are showing the way.

We are all leaders. When we come together with our bits and pieces, we got a leader. That's how leadership should be taught because we need to change history. We can't follow a leader because when the leader goes out of camp, that's where that disconnect is, we're disconnected. That's why we all have to train ourselves to be leaders. Not to be a bigger leader or a better leader, but all equal leaders. So when one leader heads out of camp, we don't have to worry about it, because we're all leaders here at camp.

Now this goes for LaDonna. She is very busy. She holds those great leadership qualities. She's beyond a leader. She's the whole ideal of women and tradition. But once she leaves camp, BIA comes in and they start bossing everyone around, making up their own rules, making up their own warrants. Targeting certain people.

Sacred Stone is a camp that's prepared to survive and live there for many years if they want to. Now with that camp being on point and more organized, of course they are going to infiltrate it. They are going to try to regulate it. They are probably checking if the camp is up to date on safety hazards, they are probably checking to see if certain things are being done. And that's how they're going to try to control that. I encourage everyone at Sacred Stone to be respectful of others. Don't be going places you don't belong. This is why we're all here now. Because they took over land where they don't belong. But we don't take land. We share the land. We understand the land. And always be mindful of trash. Even if it's one little piece of trash. Pick it up. Throw it away. Take that time out of your busy life. Take that time to preserve Mother. Three seconds.

Now I'm going to give you the instructions of this new law. We pray. This new law is around us. We don't need a building to hold all of this knowledge because these laws and understanding and knowledge are all around us. It's inside of us. We listen and we follow the rules of Mother and she will guide us in ways we will never understand. These are just the trials and the challenges of the physical world. This is only one part of life, the greater part of life is after death. That's why when warriors long ago went into enemy camp, they knew that they might possibly die or get injured, that didn't stop them. What encouraged them was that they were doing it for the people. Doing it for a reason. Doing it for hope. Doing it for the children. Doing it for the future.

This is what we are doing right here. Live it, love it and respect it. The wind will guide us. It might take us and change our direction. We see a stream of water and we might follow down that path. Or we might see a flock of birds changing their direction. See that's the power of earth. The power of Mother. We can't control her. She controls everything on this planet. But she can guide us in ways we really need to understand. That's why I'm fighting and I'm standing and I'm staying right here. And this is why I continue to tell it like it is.

Camp is going good. There's a few remaining water protectors here and we're going to stay. IEN, Indigenous Environmental Network, a big shout out to them and respect. They are going other places and reporting. We're all one big organization of water protectors addressing environmental issues all around. But they're not here at camp anymore. I am. TYT politics, Jordan, is. We got Johnny Dangers. We got Steven. And of course we got all the media that's at the casino.

But I'm surviving. And as far as this funding, I don't even have funding right now. Some say that I have funding, but I've been having problems with that funding for a while now. A message to all those trolls out there, it doesn't matter how bad or how much negativity you write about me, I don't see it like that anymore. So you're wasting your time because I'm beyond all of that. But thank you for allowing me to feel what you guys feel toward water protectors so I can understand it more so I can teach the world how to understand that kind of tactics. It doesn't work on me anymore.

We human beings are so quick to judge. We're so quick to act when there's danger. And we're so quick not to act when there's danger. But everything happens for a reason. The other day, those actions on the hill, Drone2bwild came back. I'm kind of limited right now with the drones. My problem right now, for some reason, when I came back to camp I couldn't connect the controller to the drone. Now is that stopping me from what I'm doing for the future of our people? No. I don't let stuff like that bother me. Because I still have my voice. I still have my livestream. I'm still here.

We changed the way we look at media these days. We are our own media. Indigenous media. We were doing media long before MSNBC, way before FOX. They just took the best parts of media and stuck it in their big building and all of a sudden they felt this power. Now they try to control and manipulate it. When you have a great power like that, you cannot misuse it. You gotta show it to the world and keep it free. You gotta keep everything free. Knowledge, learning, education, wisdom, water, air, the trees. All the sacred sites in this country, leave them alone.

But what they are saying about us, that this camp here is going to be flooded, it might flood, it might not flood. But how are we gonna allow Standing Rock, Dave Archambault, Morton County, North Dakota, anybody else who is against water protectors, how are we going to allow them to say whether or not Mother Earth is going to flood this camp? We cannot speak for Mother, for what she's going to do, because we don't know, we don't understand it. They might have a little control with the dam, but that's just a little bit of control. It's up to Mother Earth to decide if she's going to flood this camp or not. I respect it. Whatever her decision is. It was meant to be.

No matter how much greed and corruption is all around us, please be strong and don't take any deals from the devil. Do what's right. And if you do want to play the wild card and you do want to accept DAPL's money, turn that money into prosperous ideas for the people. Turn that oil money into good if you want to play it like that. We need to present more programs, we need more within our community. If I was Dave, I'd get out of that office for a minute and I'd go interact with the community. I'd go interact with the children. I'd take time off from that political position, that position of power and control and I'd allow myself to always nurture my human spirit.

Dave Archambault, go down to Little Eagle. Go down to Bullhead. There's Standing Rock communities that have been forgotten for a long time. Way before this pipeline was ever brought up. So don't ever play that card of saying to involve ourselves back into our community because on the South Dakota side, they will agree with me that before this pipeline was ever here there was that issue of community. It's like South Dakota was left out of everything. North Dakota got everything. Are we learning from our mistakes now tribal council and chairman? Or are you just taking for yourself?

I know every one of you guys on the council and I know you too Dave. No matter what I say here, it doesn't mean I hate you guys or I look differently at you guys. I'm not criticizing you. I'm just telling you, do it for the greater goodness of our community and our people. And you can still support the water protectors here and still do what's right for the Standing Rock Sioux Tribe. We're human beings. Anything is possible. Now don't get yourself in the mindset of the U.S. government. Yeah, we do have to work with this government or they can take our sovereignty away. It's just a word. Sovereignty is just a word. They can take that away, but we'll still feel it. It's inside of us and they can never take that away.

There may not be a sacred fire here anymore, but the elders should have known, even I know, that the sacred fire is not out. The sacred fire is burning within my heart. And it should be burning within all of the water protectors' hearts. So did the sacred fire ever really go out? Physically, yeah. But spiritually, mentally, that fire still burns within all of us and we gotta understand that and we gotta take that and just warm ourselves up with it. And when you have that fire inside of you, you can do anything. You can speak your mind and you can dream a lot of things and you can be a lot of things.

Now am I going to see the change that we started here? I might not ever see the change but am I about that? No. I am about doing it for the long term but I don't see it like that. I just gotta do it. Sometimes you just gotta know that you are doing it for the right goodness.

I was watching a couple of live feeds today and one live feed stuck out there. I'm not going to say any names, but I'll talk about the idea of it. Now this live feeder was kind of agreeing with Dave, but it's just interpretation. It's just reporting from the outside. These people are not even here. So how can they really, truthfully understand what's going on here if they're not here. That's why I came back.

When I was in California I knew what was happening, but deep inside I couldn't connect. I had to be here. I connected with Standing Rock, it's everywhere, but I needed to be here. A lot of people were saying Standing Rock, that's the heart. Go back. You know who you are. But are you here? No. But I respect you and you go on and tell them about that journey. This is Standing Rock, this is my home. I will come back here and I will still speak and I will still fly the drone. And I will speak for all the people here. Does that make me a leader? No. That just makes me a person who is very informative and very outspoken. I could talk all night, but I'm going to allow my spirit to sleep tonight.

You guys all have a good evening and pray. Pray for your family, pray for all the water protectors here and pray for Dave Archambault and pray for Standing Rock. And pray for all the other pipeline resistance camps out there. They need us too. Standing Rock connected us all. It connected me to you. But before I was connected to you, the drone connected me to a lot of things I never knew would happen in my life. And all it took was me stepping out of my comfort zone and to keep stepping. That's how you create change. No matter how much psychological warfare or roadblocks, you keep doing it. And that there is the strongest you will ever be. I tell everybody just sit there and pray. If you pray so hard those non-lethal rubber bullets will fly all around you. Can you believe it? I do.

"So the gravity of what is going on finally hit me. 5 years in prison... that's what I am facing. Obviously I won't probably do the maximum sentence because I have no criminal history but it still scares me. Not because I am scared of prison, but because it will hurt my family." ~ Vanessa Castle (Arrested for doing an informative live feed.)

February 5th

It's past 3am here at Oceti Camp and there are two snowmobiles blazing all around the open frozen mni wiconi like it's the X Games!!! Screaming and trying to war whoop!!

It is a very dark night. You can hear him walking on snow. You can see all of the bright DAPL lights.

As we were sitting in the yurt, I heard snowmobilers racing around. Brought back memories of when they were chasing us. I'm climbing this hill, but they are probably watching me with night vision. But it's not like I'm trying to hide myself. I'd rather step into the light for the people. I wouldn't be surprised if they weren't nearby on snowmobiles. This hill is pretty steep. There they are right there. I feel like I'm on top of the world here! Woohoo.

There's camp. *(He shows that it is mostly dark.)* That little dot there, that's north gate. Don't be surprised if Tiger Swan jumps out of these bushes here and tries to tackle and take me down. There's the bridge barricade and beyond that is the other blockade to the bridge. Obviously they're just cruising around up there like it's the X games. It's 3 o'clock in the morning and we're going to shine the light. This light is going to represent the solidarity and the unity of what we're doing here. We're going to shine the light. Bou-yah. Let there be light!

He turns on a very bright, handheld light.

I'm going to hold this high for all the DAPL security and all Morton County to see. To show them that we can stand in the dark too. This is what I'm talking about guys. You need to get out of your comfort zone and you need to get on the highest hill and you need to report the truth in the dark. Sometimes you gotta go to the darkest places and turn on the light and speak the truth. But at the same time, you don't say nothing. Silence. And it's good.

Obviously I don't have any gloves on right now. There's no really cold breeze. Here's what we are going to do. We're going to shine this light. We're going to hold it above our head. *(He holds the bright light up.)* And signify to DAPL that we're not afraid of them. This is our treaty land and we're the original protectors. Yeah, this might seem ridiculous, holding this light up, but so what. It's about empowerment.

Look, those guys there, they are watching. They are running around on snowmobiles and trying to war whoop. Why not go on top of a hill and just shine the light on them. Shine the light on the people there. There's a switch. Only if it were that easy to change the world with the flick of a switch.

Yes, I know they are known to just come out of nowhere. They hide in the shadows. They sneak through the tree lines. They act like they're ninjas. But when you are fully aware and understand what's going on, you don't need to see them, you sense them; you know they are around. And right now I feel freedom. As Morton County surrounds us, they are with BIA, so literally surrounds us.

There it is guys, I got a response. They turned on their lights then they turned them off. Looks like he's getting out, probably looking through his binoculars at the crazy water protector standing on the hill. This hill is beautiful. You can see everything. There again, this hill is significant to history. A lot of people came to the highest points, especially being in this valley here, when you hold yourself at a higher atmosphere, a higher perspective. And we all know about higher perspectives. In a way we are a little closer to the stars. Now the snowmobilers aren't around anymore.

The feed cuts off.

He starts another live feed soon. He is still outside in the dark.

Here's how you make them move around when they start getting bored. You take a light and you shine the light on DAPL, right? But when you shine a light on them they scatter like cockroaches and they start moving around. And it's funny because it's just one person up here. It's just me. Oh, I forgot! I'm empowering all of Standing Rock. That's why they're moving around.

Right now, since I've been up on the hill, there's a lot of movement up there. *(He moves his very bright light around.)* I'll point the light right up there. You can see that's Turtle Island, where all the actions took place across the water. And over here, you've got two spotlights kinda shining up straight into the sky. It's funny. I kinda want to stay out here and just keep live feeding. Push them, you know. Make them move.

They're probably almost ready to fall asleep until I turned the light on them. Woke them up. And then those guys over here, they're parked on top of the hill where Last Child's Camp was taken down. There's nothing we can say, do or think about what happened that day, cause it already happened. So we all just got to let it adjust, settle and digest and move forward.

Okay, action. Here come the snowmobilers now. I'd like to see if they make it up the steep hill. Live feed them as they fall backwards, you know. And then I would say, I told you so. It wasn't me, it was the power of the spirits. But see, it just takes one person up here with a light and they all start getting active. I bet right now there's probably a team moving in on me right now. But this is a good view. I can see everything around me. Steepest part of the hill here. You can see all the way over to... Oops, there goes a truck. They probably think this light means something, so they're all moving to their stations. I'm right here guys! I'm always right here.

Guys, don't worry about me. This is what I'm trying to get to you all out there. Don't be scared. Sometimes you gotta step into the realm of danger and be alright with it. I'm showing you guys every time. I hope you're adjusting and I hope you're understanding. And I hope that maybe you can put yourself in the danger zone and see how you deal with it. Because why not. This is our land. This is Mother Earth.

And if I want to go on top of this hill at 3:30 in the morning and shine the light on all this corruption, I have the right to do that. Because last time I checked, this world was meant for true freedom. And when you have true freedom, I should be able to walk down in that valley where the river used to be. Now should I? Or do you think I'm pushing it? Do you think I should run all the way up that hill there and count coup on the DAPL trucks? But the point of this is just to get them moving around. They were probably falling asleep. And I wanted to see where all the snowmobilers are at. They're probably on top of the hill. I should run all the way up to the bridge. Tiger Swan is probably hiding under the bridge already though.

I have a feeling, if I stay here another five, ten minutes, they're probably going to come out of nowhere. But that's what I want to happen. We need some action here. We got spiritual action. But we need some action. See what kind of toys they are playing with. See what kind of stuff they got. From the looks of it, it looks like they're slacking. I should have taken the drone out. I could have just been sitting in the yurt, flying the drone.

I wish I could stay, but this extreme cold really drains the batteries. That's the thing about cell phones and drones. Let's answer some questions before the battery goes out. Yes guys, we know we all put ourselves in danger zones, but know that we know that we are putting ourselves in danger zones. You gotta understand, you gotta just let it be like that. Although I do appreciate all you guys' concerns. I appreciate everything you all have done. By sharing the live feeds and listening to us. Because we all have a voice. And when you use your voice for the right cause, that's the most powerful weapon. More than anything DAPL can throw at us. As you can see they're already in fear. That's why they're loaded up with guns. Are they that scared of prayer? That's how much distance they put themselves from being connected to the earth.

I want to do a shout out to Steven Chrisjohn. He's been through a lot in the last couple of days. I'd like to give a shout out to Chase Iron Eyes. Because he's showing us the way. I want to give a shout out to LaDonna. Whatever they say about her, it's always going to be not true.

I was watching the live feeds earlier. BIA, how can you do that? How can you exert that much force on a woman? And whip her and beat her with your baton? Now I seen you guys, you're really huge. Is that really necessary? Now what if you were doing that to your own mother?! BIA cop. You might be watching this. What if you're whipping with your baton on your own mother or your own grandmother? Would you still be doing it with that much strength? Would you do it that hard? Now you think about that.

He pulls down his mask.

Yeah, you've always known who I am. We've always had run ins. Remember? Yeah, I saw that live feed. They're taking some plays out of Morton County's playbook. So as you can see, we're surrounded. We're surrounded by BIA, DAPL, Morton County.

What Chase did, it wasn't Chase, it was Crazy Horse, and the power of water protectors coming together and moving and making decisions as one. Not singling out any one individual. Because we are all leaders, every single one of us. Young to old. What Chase did up there on the hill, a lot of people say it was wrong to do. But we need to do more of those. All of these hills around here, we have that right to do it. And we'll do it again. We'll keep spending Morton County's money. We'll keep making them do work until they hate this job. But what he did up there, he was making a difference. And if you guys don't understand that, you guys are forgetting. This is treaty land. If you are Indigenous, you'll hold strong to that. This is all Indigenous land. It's treaty land. We have that right. But in the end, no one should have that right because this is Mother Earth. And in the end she makes the decision of who goes and who stays.

I feel like walking up to those guys up there. They probably know that I'm tempted to do that. And they're probably coming up with plans. Something's coming up. I hear a truck really cruising. Right there where that light's at, there's a little red dot right there. That vehicle pulled up right there, so they are watching me. I was informed that they are watching us with high powered infra-red binoculars. So I'm going to wave this light. They probably know Morse code. I should do some Morse code and say something that's gonna make them mad. DAPL's boring. They're not fun anymore. Remember when we used to step out just onto the highway and they'd pop out of nowhere. They would come out of the woodwork.

Now they're probably getting tired of their jobs. I probably better let them be. See they are getting bored, they turned around and went back up the hill now. They probably are tuned in. It's probably one of these trolls on this feed here messing with us. I would if I was them.

He looks side to side abruptly.

Let's be safe about this one guys and let's head back to camp. Maybe tomorrow or the next night, we'll mess around with those guys on top of the hill there. If they want to shoot a rubber bullet at us, what better than to do it on live feed. We're not inciting a riot. I'm inciting someone to shoot me with a rubber bullet I guess. Keep prayers up.

Calm Down. My people, Shiyé is ok!! Just a late night suspense live feed for you all!

Dave Archambault was seen driving his truck along with others in Oceti Camp today!!! Hmmmm...

Have you changed your mind about the movement Dave? I feel that you have seen the light!!!! Follow your heart Dave. Support the people who think highly of you. It is not too late to come back from the darkness!!! I still and will always believe in you on whatever journey you continue on.

Reality update: Check on Oceti Camp life and the future of Standing Rock and all the water protectors.

He puts out a live feed that day.

We are here on Facebook Hill. This is what's left of camp. They cleared out major portions of this camp that were abandoned. 45% estimate of infiltrators walking amongst everybody here. The tensions are high. Everybody's on high alert. We got a charter bus there. A lot of foundation structures. A lot of buildings built on the flood plain.

There's a lot of abandoned structures here and tipis. No one's an angel. I've witnessed Standing Rock people come and just take tents and tipis. No one is going to use them, but maybe they were. I just found this out last night, even a horse was stolen from camp. There is theft going on in this camp. If you're taking stuff and you go back to Standing Rock to your backyard and selfishly take it for your own, you guys out there who probably watch my feeds, think about what you are doing. How dare you take those back to your homes. You do that you're just as bad as those people way up on the hills. They are taking everything without asking. Think about that people of Standing Rock and of this movement. Think about it when you're at home benefiting from this camp. When you took a generator or tipi poles. *The feed cuts off for a minute.*

We're back on now. I want to believe that Dave is stepping out of the darkness and he's looking at the camp for direction. I believe he wants to see the light again. He's a good man. Whatever Dave decides to do, it's going to be a path just especially made for him. He's going to experience a lot of new things. Listen Dave, if you want to lead a Nation, don't forget about the water protectors or this camp. Use them to refocus and make the tribe a lot better. Even if you take money, use it for the good of the people. Help the veterans. Help the youth. There's a lot of issues here on Standing Rock. You made a clear point to put out the fire. And to close everybody's eyes to what's going on.

Come back to camp and give a good speech. The more you hide and don't acknowledge the truth, the more it will get worse for you. If you are doing everything good for the tribe and being an honest leader to help Standing Rock prosper, then tell the world your true feelings and inner thoughts. Tell the people that you cry and you're sad. You have all the control. Only you control you, Dave.

Morton County is at the door step of Oceti. They're just right up there. They don't even need a scope no more. They are watching us. That's the reality of camp. Will there be a raid? We don't know. The only people who know are the people who want to raid us.

We're just getting too strong and powerful. We are all here for a reason. And for all the people who have lost the understanding of that reason, let them go. Soon they will come back. I did.

I've done a lot of things, I did it all for my people and the world and all my water protectors, and the water and the earth and the sky. I do it for my children and I do it for your children.

These tipis, these yurts, all these possessions, don't hold on to them. In the end, they can strip everything from us. What matters is our mind, our heart and our feet. We can keep standing, keep moving. I'm calling everybody, come back to Standing Rock. Don't believe all these stories. All these stories of passion...hate. Come back for your river. Come back for every gulp you take. Every splash. Every rain drop. Come back people. Let's show the world that Standing Rock is stronger than ever.

Also calling back all the other Indigenous media. We're in this together, remember? That's why I came home. A lot of people think it's crazy, I ain't gonna let that stop me. I'm going to keep supporting Chase, LaDonna and all the water protectors. They are here doing what's right. What are you doing? Yes, you're sharing the knowledge.

If you're still confused, go outside and put your hand on the ground and sense it. If you're still lost, grab it; all that dirt. If you're still lost, go to the river or the ocean and dive on in.

The camp is not going to get raided, but if it does, we're going to stand and pray and stand and pray. We record it, we broadcast it. We broadcast solidarity, sovereignty. I'm decolonized. Nothing holds me down. Just gravity. Take all those ideas, take your time. But be prepared to make your journey back up here. Be prepared to endure difficulties. You're going to feel the cold, the fear, all these different emotions you never felt before. But you'll survive. I did. Doesn't matter what they throw at you, terrorists, trolls, a confused tribal chairman, corrupt police and one guy that sits on top that thinks he knows what he's doing but he don't. The president of the United States isn't the man for the job. He's supposed to lead the people. But it's the people who lead. We're going to make him do time...for inciting.

February 7th

He appears on Steven Jeffrey Chrisjohn's live feed with Ernesto. They are at camp. Clean up is going on around them.

Dean: You guys want to know the cure for PTSD? There is no cure. You just live it and you control your own destiny. You don't let that PTSD filter or make your mind go crazy or evil. Because we are already beautiful and evil and crazy. That's why they fear us and that's why they oppress us. They know the power that we're capable of. Our knowledge is more powerful. It's universal. It started through Indigenous roots though.

They are clowning around...laughing...joking.

Live with Shiyé and Steven

They are at camp. There is lots of snow. Lots and lots of snow. It is cloudy out. Big snow piles are all around them.

Dean: Good afternoon everybody. Just wanted to show everybody camp. Early this morning, a group of Morton County law enforcement came down this road and stationed themselves up there. And they're still sitting on top of the hill. There's a lot of people still here. We got EPA over here cleaning up. Using the scrapers. We're doing it the right way. Take all the politics and back stabbing out. Don't turn your backs. If we turn our backs we're all walking in different directions.

Steven is talking on his own live feed. "No one can go on the bridge yet. Only Morton County," he says.

Dean: Steven is upset because his tipi is gone.

Steven: This guy has taught me valuable lessons about detachment. I was going to try to use it to get a kitchen... Johnny says there's money, but hasn't produced any of it. Yeah, you Johnny, I heard what you did.

Dean: That's what money and a little bit of power and control does to people. All these material things, they are just materialistic things.

The signal cuts off. It comes back when they are in the car.

Dean: They cut our signal off. You guys are all waiting for us.

Steven: It's negative sixteen out. Johnny hasn't produced nothing... Jay actually lives in the kitchen....we don't need much. It's disheartening that someone would take the tipi.

Dean: But it's just possessions and it's just money. If you don't understand, just stay away from it. Don't let it control your life. Don't let it be your future. This is our future right here, just us, going around telling how it is. People are still at camp. People are still standing strong. People are cleaning up. People are confused.

Steven: How many Standing Rock people were cleaning up this morning?

Dean: Standing Rock's EPA is doing a good job here. Most of the guys that are cleaning up come from the same community as I do, the same neighborhoods. In the beginning, all those boys that are cleaning up, they were here putting up tents, being involved, changing the world. Standing Rock members are here. They have always been here. I'm going to show you guys the hill.

He shows all the law enforcement on the hill.

Dean: They're probably watching themselves on the live feed. They are literally trespassing right now. They've been trespassing this whole time. Steven's not talking about Johnny Dangers, he's a good guy.

#7gwarriorskitchen With Brandyy-Lee Maxie: Songs and good food

It is a live video from the kitchen tent. There is drumming and singing.

Dean: What's going on here?

Brandyy: What's going on here is that this is our last supper in this location. This is the main mess tent. We are taking our tents down and are going to relocate to higher ground. Today we had some bad news, but we're trying to keep spirits high here. We're still in prayer. We're still here. Jay Pino is our main chef here. He's 23, a professional chef.

Later that evening, he live feeds from the dome a couple of times. Water protectors are gathered and Nataanii Means is putting on an amazing show. Everyone is having a great time. There is singing, laughing. The dome glows in the feed.

Later he live feeds as he walks around camp and out to the road. It is dark out. It is windy and cold.

I had this whole idea of walking on the road. And guess who comes out of nowhere? Digital Smoke Signals. He's up the road. Driving a truck. I'm walking.

To the left of me sits DAPL security. Tune into Myron to see some nice beautiful scenery of this treaty land that's been overtaken. I'm pretty sure we can see because these DAPL lights light up the whole sky. They are misunderstanding. They are using the light in the wrong direction. We are the light.

The live feed cuts off.

Counting Coup on DAPL security

He is still walking around on the next live feed.

Welcome back guys. Sorry to scare you all like that, but we are the media. Behind me you hear a drone. It's Digital Smoke Signals. We're going to show how much they are blocking the roads.

The feed cuts off again.

He brings up another live feed soon.

It's either the cold or they have devices that are blocking the live feeds. We are counting coup. Don't worry I'm not going to do anything sporadic or surprising. I just want to shed some light and give an update on camp. The lights are so bright. We don't need light anymore. I'm pretty sure they're watching the live feeds from across the bridge. All the trolls. When you're walking down the road of courage and you have a drone flying above you, you can do anything you want.

Someone asked me, how do you deal with all the ugliness and the hurtful things that are put upon us, our own people, the water protectors, even from our own people. How do we still do it? How do we stand strong and keep walking forward? It's cause we got to keep walking forward.

We got until the 22nd and camp's going to be gone. But camp is never gone. Camp will always be with us. They aren't cutting this live feed off. That's good.

The drone's in the sky. They are being watched right now. There are three vehicles up there. A lot happened on that bridge. A lot of hate, hurt, pain. A lot of freedom was taken away. A lot of spirits rising. But don't give up on water protectors. We are a story and it's beautiful and this is a message to all the people who feel lost and hurt and chaos and violence...just keep moving forward.

I hear snowmobiles. Probably coming across from the drill pad. They can get around quick on snowmobiles. They leave their marks. We see their trails. How do you deal with all the hate they throw at you? I just take it all in. I absorbed it all in. I looked at it from a bigger perspective. It goes beyond me. It goes beyond everything we are here for. You guys get the point. We empower ourselves for our future generations.

I could stand right here in the front and not be afraid. I can go walking right toward the DAPL security. Are they pointing a weapon at me? Maybe. Are they watching me with thermal? Maybe. It feels good to be right here people. It feels beautiful. I feel free. I feel the coldness, but you use that to step out of the darkness and into the light. Here comes another vehicle coming down. I'm always aware that these guys can come out of nowhere. There's probably an infiltrator sitting on top of that hill.

On the 22nd of this month. That's the final countdown. If I'm wrong, does it matter? They are just going to push us away with their weapons, but we're just going to pray. Ain't no one on Standing Rock, anyone, who's going to say that camp is going to get flooded. How do you know that? They are using the flood against us to incite fear. Who stays, who goes, who has the final say so? Mother Earth. Not Morton County, not DAPL.

There's the drone. Check out the drone. *The drone comes up right over him. It has little green lights.* It all started with the drones. It allows us to see everything from a grander perspective. *It comes right up to him then goes away.*

We're going to start a fire and get something to eat and have a good laugh. We are in good spirits. I stand here to tell everybody, we just keep moving forward. A giant could be standing in front of me and we just keep stepping forward. Everybody says it's stupid, go away, the pipeline's gonna get laid. Yeah, we know that already.

Early today BIA was all over Cannonball. A show of force. Like forty BIA cops and also feds, border patrol and the ATF. All these agencies out here. Infiltrating us. They are all staying at Prairie Knights. But it's all good. We're literally housing environmental terrorists.

Don't forget guys. Don't forget all what happened here. A lot of things happened here on this bridge. Those memories will be petrified in my soul. It brought out a lot in me. My whole life I had this purpose and this purpose is right here. All the things I put myself through. And my tribe says go home water protectors. But they forgot, I am home. Where do I go?

The more I talk, the more vehicles that come out. Don't ever let anybody put you down to their level. No matter how much they come at you. Whether it's an enemy or your own family.

He walks around quiet for a minute.

What's the purpose of this live feed? It's called counting coup on DAPL intelligence. In a way it feels like they are moving in. They are moving around. I can hear them. I hope everybody is sharing this live feed. This is from the Backwater Bridge. A lot of bad things happened on that bridge. It will probably be taken down and I won't be surprised if they slap Morton County's names all over it in remembrance. They have to inscribe everything to keep it going. But things fade. This physical world is soon going to be gone. All this life is a testing ground.

Like Myron Dewey said, when you really want to get deep into it, all of these lands out here are powerful. And DAPL knows it. That's why they come at us so hard. To protect their illegal actions. They are stripping our treaty lands and desecrating our sacred sites. With Trump there hasn't been one drop of anything good coming out of that guy. This world is changing.

I want to thank every one of you who have been a part of this movement. This is about the true inner connection to the frozen water and the stars. We're all connected all the way to our hearts and to our lands. I am proud of you all. We all made a difference here. We grew. As Indigenous roots we just went into the ground deeper.

All you warriors who were on the frontline and were hurt, I understand. I get you. I was there. Understand yourselves and start looking at it from a bigger perspective. To understand the hate and pain from others, we have to understand it in ourselves. So we can grow as intelligent people, roots people; people of universal understanding.

There is life within this camp. We gotta give it back. But never ever forget. Use it to empower a tribe, a Nation. Sometimes we don't want to talk about it, but we can't censor ourselves. We can't learn if we censor ourselves.

It's so cold out here that the cold just seeps into the layers that are supposed to keep you warm. The wind doesn't help. These are the elements of North Dakota. We get two or three months of hard, strong winter. Be prepared. Don't be afraid of the camp. It's still here.

Pray for us. Occupying these tents. They are clearing out abandoned tents. Bulldozers are here to clean it up. All the media that's saying we're destroying this camp, that's not true. All the things that come out from the outside world, they aren't even here. We're freezing, but we're holding strong. Camp is going strong. Despite all the stories. We're holding prayers, we're laughing, we're singing, we're enjoying. Flag row is still here.

There's so many rumors. The real life is inside these structures. It's not dying. We're walking above frozen water all over this camp. It's a little slippery at times. People fall, but they just get back up. No matter what they do to us, solidarity and the people are still here.

This camp is beautiful in darkness. The major media reports things from the outside. They miss all the true stories on the inside. It's not about the outside of anything, or the looks. It's about your inner self, your heart, your blood; your values.

February 8th

Dean appears on Steven Jeffery Chrisjohn's live feed in the morning. Steven says, "Dean has the DAPL cough and we're going to go take care of him."

He shows up again in another of Steven's live feeds.

I want to thank everyone today, it's a beautiful day. It's a wonderful day. It's an appreciative day. It's a day in history. I saw all these world class actions *(he sounds like he has a cold)* posted all over. But today I woke up and I didn't feel any actions. I felt peace. It's a good feeling. Then I felt disconnection. Then I felt confusion. Then I felt all the illusions.

But we are at the camp, at Oceti, I feel we are slowly being faded away. We are getting disconnected. They've got huge antennas right on top of the hill where the Last Child Camp was raided. Since this morning we cannot get any signal whatsoever. So that means it's just getting a little darker, until the 22nd. They want us out of that camp. They're going to get us out of camp. They're making it harder on us. I'm pretty sure we'll all get arrested. But that's just how it goes. That's the white man for you. Taking control and manipulating everybody against each other.

Money starts making everybody think different. Money makes some people go crazy. People are lost. They come back here, but they don't know what they're doing. So if you don't see any more Facebook live feeds from me, don't be scared. (Steven is laughing at him for being dramatic. Clearly he does not feel good.) Don't be afraid. I'm still around. I'll always be around you guys. If you've been listening to me for the last six months, you would understand why there's no more Facebook live feeds from me. (Steven continues to laugh.) Time to take a break and disconnect from the internet.

But that doesn't mean I'm going to be off Facebook forever. When the time comes, I'll pop back on. But I need to take care of some business and that's myself. I will still be inside of camp, I'll just be underground. They're trying to make us disappear, so I will disappear myself. Thank you guys for taking the time out of your day to watch this happen to my home. I want to thank everyone who has done everything in their power to do what they did, because it needed to be done. All the things you shipped, you donated, you prayed, you a'ho-ed. All the prayers that went up. And even for the prayers that went down. It doesn't matter, we're all one.

Just smile in the face of corruption and forgive them. Life's going to go on. We're going to pass and go on to the greater world. All these things we've learned in this life are lessons. Don't ever take anything for granted. Whatever you have in your life right now, enjoy it. And bless yourself. Because you are a beautiful person. You are a wonderful person. Don't let anyone think less of you because we are all one.

We just showed that huge oil corporation that we can stand up and we can say we don't want this and we can change the way. We don't have to see it in our lifetime because deep down truly we can understand patience and in the future, this fight will continue. Our children's children's children will finally get to accept what we've been fighting for as we open the door for Standing Rock. And they will finally get to enjoy that world peace with connection to the earth, stars and the moon and the sun. And even if it's just for one second, that was worth fighting for. So this is my last live feed because I gotta get business done. I will always be around. I'll never go away. Thank you guys.

Mni Wiconi

Water Is Life

Sacrifice is why I stand with my remaining brother & sister water protectors here at Oceti!!!!!

Where are you????????

Sacrifice. I am ready!!

We keep the FIRE burning here at Oceti

Native expression

He puts out another live feed from the dome that evening. There is singing and drumming. A large group of people has gathered.

Music is the medicine for our soul. As we water protectors take in the awful news, we stand. We express our existence with sound.

Looks like the government along with FBI and NSA are targeting water protectors!!! Time to go into back into the shadows!!

February 11th

We need to heal our minds and our bodies.

If the words are good, I will be right beside you. If the words are bad, I'll be in front of you. Ready to give my water & people my greatest sacrifice!

I am in a place where the earth touches the sky. The bluebirds sing, where the water flows. You will find me there in the ripples of life. Shiyé Bidzííl

Once again hackers have infiltrated my Facebook account and had their way with it!

I guess you can literally say they raped my truth!!!

February 13th

BTW I don't have the DAPL cough!!

He live feeds from the Backwater Bridge.

Hey guys, it's me. We're at Backwater Bridge. They took down the barricade on the other side of the bridge and now they are putting up what they are calling a temporary road block. They are only going to allow medical ambulances and law enforcement through.

He walks up to a law enforcement officer and asks what is going on. The officer says, "Watch the news at 5."

Dean: You don't watch anything else? What's your favorite sports team? You guys got anything to say?

Officer: It's nice out.

Dean: How long have you been here? Have you been camping out or going back and forth?

Officer: Whenever I can get back, I get back.

Dean: You guys are from Mandan too, huh? Bismarck?

Officer: We're from across the river.

Dean: So only ambulances and law enforcement can get across?

Officer: It's my guess that this is the start of opening up the bridge.

Dean: Has it been checked since all the actions, the bridge?

Officer: There's a semi on it, so I'm guessing it's been checked.

The feed cuts off.

February 16th

The buffalo nation has returned!!!

They graze as they walk towards the military base Morton County and DAPL have put up since the last disappearance of the Tatanka Nation.

Unlike Dave Archambault this leader knows his journey of protecting his people and sacred lands and waters!!!!

Last weekend Cherry Creek Pow wow honored us water protectors. It brought new hope for us and a tear to our eyes. Knowing that Cheyenne River Nation has never gave up on us and that they are in it until the end. Much respect to them and my people.

Sacred Stone Camp got served an eviction notice by BIA.

Shiyé Bidzííl gives his thoughts about Standing Rock and the future of Drone2bwild.

I don't understand, you're not even here but you act like you know what is right for us! Out of respect, I respect your words, but until you are here on the ground, when you see and you experience what we're going through and what we're fighting for, then maybe I will maybe listen and take your words into light but this is my home!!

Yes, stop all the posts about raids!! Funny because all the posts are from people who are not even here at camp!!!! Hahaha!

Sticks and stones may break me but DAPL trolls and comments may never hurt me!

February 17th

Would you guys believe me if I told you I dressed up as one of them and secretly reported from the other side???? Hehehehehe

"Native Americans' sacred grounds being desecrated, #WaterProtectors being labeled trespassers on treaty land, and peaceful prayers labeled as riots are the tactics of state-sponsored terrorism (North Dakota's #MortonCountySheriffsDepartment) and are aimed at ignoring constitutional, civil, and human rights guaranteed by this very nation in love with its laws." ~ Shamus Beyale

February 18th

How can you let this happen to your own people Dave Archambault???? When will you stand up to your wrongs and look us water protectors in the eyes??? And tell us you're sorry for selling out your people!

Shiyé Bidzííl says if you're in the Oak Flat area today be sure to tell Dave Archambault to get back home and do what's right for his people!! Thank you.

No fear. Stand your ground it's your sacred ground!! My people!!

To all media water protectors, have your portable chargers ready, have your batteries on full charge. Live stream from multiple phones. No matter what happens make sure record is always on.

Don't worry my people, Shiyé Bidzííl will still be here after everything goes down! Peace & Prayer for all of my people.

Let's Sage down all those BIA officers!!!!!!

BIA Checkpoints

He live feeds from inside of a car. An officer asks if they have any building materials in the car. They say no. The officer asks if they mind if they look.

Hi guys, just made it through the BIA checkpoint. There's the rest of what's left of Oceti Camp. I'll just go live until I can't go live anymore. Apparently they've been shutting off my live feeds. (*The live feed cuts off.*)

February 19th

He live feeds from camp. He is showing the law enforcement on top of the hill right across from the main entrance of Oceti. He zooms in to see the law enforcement better. Then he looks around camp.

Hunkpapa hill deck overlook!! Good morning neighbors!!!

People are working. Flags are flying. He looks all around camp. There is singing over the loud speaker. People are walking around. You can hear equipment of some sort - maybe a generator. People are walking around taking photos.

We are making history here. We've been making history since the beginning. We are the people who make history. Story telling. That's how we keep our generations alive. Story telling echoes throughout eons. To them, they call them myths. But they are so old. Our stories are still alive.

He talks to a man from California. The man is a film maker. Dean talks about making a film. Someone takes his camera and turns it on him.

Today is a good day. Today is a nice and sunny day. We got our neighbors on the top of the hill. They can't greet us, they are hiding behind barriers, but it's okay. They're scared. But it's okay, we won't hurt them. We're here in prayer. We're here in peace.

I've been documenting all the camps. Everyone's complaining about how bad this place is, don't believe it. All the stuff they say on the major news is totally wrong. They're using it as a tool. All of this stuff is meant to suppress us and keep eyes shut on this place.

And all the talks about biological warfare, it may have happened, but until there's legitimate proof, what really happened here with chemical weapons, it's just a story. But it never hurts to be cautious. You can still come here. Oceti is always going to be here no matter what. They're trying to get into Sacred Stone, the courts here in tribal law are trying to manipulate their own laws.

They're trying to get LaDonna with her acreage and land because all her people don't have ties to it. So now all the people have to buy into a little section. But you do the math, the land is only so much, so there's going to be a limited amount of people if they go that route. But like I said, they're manipulating tribal laws. They're being influenced by big brother, the government. That's what we're fighting here every day. It's infiltrating our government system and our tribal chairman.

Where you at Dave? I heard you were in Oak Flat. I hope you had something good to say to the people there. Remember now, we believed in you. When your wife was telling the story about how bad she was hurt and how she was sad, I felt her pain. I felt all of that. Now to go ahead and do this to our people, especially your children, you think about what your decisions are doing in the next couple of days. Because it's going to have a big major impact. When this camp gets raided, you take that all on your shoulders Dave. You think about your decisions. I still love all of you guys on the council and I still love you too Dave. But you really got to step up and address this here, what you're putting your people through.

I say this here in sobriety and I say it with all my heart. I love all you guys out there. But we need to come to a final solution where we can all get along in peace. Now I see divesting is working. The banks are losing money. They put out a letter saying something needs to be resolved between the Indigenous and big oil. They don't want to lose money, they actually stated that. It's in the best interest that they reroute this pipeline.

Even if they do that, the destruction has already been laid. There's burial grounds that will never be the same. The spirits have been dislocated. They are probably roaming around this camp right now. They've probably infiltrated the spirits of those people on top of the hill that don't know no better. But we need to fix that. Spiritually, physically and mentally.

We gotta take care of each other. It's not about this pipeline right here. We already won. There's no oil flowing through that. But we gotta take care of each other here and that's what we're doing. That's what I'm doing. Encouraging and uplifting people's spirits. That's a good thing to do. That's another way of helping the community.

Shiyé Bidzííl, Thomas Touches Lightning Bettles & Eddie Simpson: Our next journey to establish the first Indigenous Roots Camp located in Iowa. So come and be a part of the teachings & understandings of being a part of this life and who stand in Solidarity and prayer for Mother Earth and her water. #WaterIsLife

He shares a schedule for the conference in Iowa.

The BIA checkpoint! This dark Sunday night!

There are law enforcement vehicles on the road with all their lights on. He is quiet while he just watches. The law enforcement stops cars then lets them go.

This is Shiyé reporting and they are letting people through. It's a good thing. Be safe. Prayers up.

In his next live video it is dark out. It is quiet. It looks cold. He is walking around outside at camp. He shows the Truth/Fear sign. There are fires burning in camp. You can hear a guy on a microphone telling someone happy birthday.

He looks at the DAPL lights. Right on the hill across from camp. He looks at some beautiful water protector signs.

Wow! 200 plus people watching a live feed, walking in the dark. You all must want to know the truth. I am walking down the highway. This is what is known as the public zone. DAPL don't own it. Army Corps don't own it. The reservation don't own it. It's a road where you can meet and greet and be in prayer. Whatever you want to bring to this highway.

It's a nice, nice, nice evening. Pretty dark. No stars in the sky. No moon in the sky.

He is cut off for a few moments.

Back on again guys. Seems like every time you want to get in a good conversation, they cut you off. There's certain areas where live feeds bounce on and off. Right now I'm along the fence area. Way over there you can see BIA has held up traffic. They're not letting anybody through. It's all because water protectors were establishing a woman's ceremony in a tipi on the road here. We told them to be patient and let the ceremony go on through. So they sent over their tribal communicator. And they negotiated.

We just told them, just let them do the ceremony. Now the tipi is taken away. To me they're just being big babies because they're being stubborn. Now they're acting like this whole road is on lockdown. But it's not. I can see clearly here that you can go on through. They let emergency personnel come on through. But they're trying to say it is because of the tipi. If I was someone in charge there, I would continue to let medical personnel go on through.

Now BIA, maybe we should walk up there. It's not too far. But then again, you don't want to do that. We'll stay safe right here. There's fires lit. There are people still here. They are letting sleeping bags come through. But as far as any building foundations, they are not allowing them to come down to Oceti camp or

Rosebud camp. This bridge is pretty good to go through. They should just stop crying around and open it. Let emergency personnel go through.

The live feed cuts off again.

All truth. Nothing but the truth, so help me creator!!!

Through the power of prayer we can get through anything. Good morning!!

He shares Earthjustice's post: DISGRACEFUL: With a signature, Donald Trump just eviscerated the Stream Protection Rule, which was intended to protect waterways and drinking water sources from toxic mining pollutants such as lead and arsenic.

"It is shameful that one of the first bills President Trump signs into law is an attack on clean water protections for communities facing the harmful health and environmental impacts of coal mining operations like mountaintop removal mining." ~ Jenifer Collins, Earthjustice Legislative Representative.

He shares an article about the return of bison to Canada.

After more than a century, bison return to Canada's oldest national park, Banff National Park. Local Indigenous communities also have strong cultural and spiritual ties to the bison and have welcomed their reintroduction.

Camp in progress

Good afternoon everybody. We are walking across the river. But that fear, if we fall in, we keep walking across the river because that's what we gotta do. Quick update: Oceti is getting cleaned up. *(The video cuts off and comes back.)*

I don't know if I'm live. We got helicopters coming out of nowhere now. Oh we got hearts! We got cars parked at north gate all morning for a prayer walk. Oh! There's everybody popped up out of nowhere! I'm back on! We love you guys. I don't care if you're a troll, I don't care if you're DAPL. Of course we care if you're water protectors. We love all of you.

I'd like to give a shout out to all my haters and all those trolls. If it wasn't for you guys throwing us all that negativity, it wouldn't have allowed me to be where I'm at right now. I've influenced a lot of people and that's good. We're all learning from each other.

Oh we got a truck stuck again. The truck has a big trailer on it. There are cars driving all through the mud. Never underestimate the power of Mother Nature. Those guys are having fun. Spreading the seeds.

An SUV runs across the mud. The truck is still stuck.

Daily operations of camp life while we got the countdown going. Back to reporting. Veterans are here. They are in camp. They look like normal, everyday people - elders. But they are here to stand. Some of them want to reintroduce themselves but they don't need it. The veterans know what's up. They're here for here.

Reports say that they're going to go right through the BIA checkpoint. So what I got to say about that is BIA, you better step aside and let the veterans keep going and secure our own barricade. But everybody's prepared, everybody's still moving out though. Expect the unexpected in a couple of days. Right now there's a helicopter flying over. That same ole yellow helicopter. Probably some Bismarck people too scared to ever come to camp, so they just fly over. I wouldn't be surprised if FBI was in it.

Eddie Simpson: A full blooded Indian? *(They laugh.)* Fry bread Indian? FBI. Flat broke Indian. *(They laugh again.)*

Dean: Oh that's just Dave...in a way he misses camp too but he doesn't want to be seen, so he takes the infamous helicopter.

Just a week ago this was all snow, stuff, debris and things that were abandoned. Just last week a bunch of people came back for their stuff. We all heard the stories about people taking things, but hopefully they took it and they use it in a good way. All the stories you've been hearing, the good and the bad, don't let that get you out of focus of why we're here. We're here to protect Mother Earth, stop pipelines, stop uranium mining, to stop taking the resources of Mother Earth. Stop all that consumerism. Start understanding our individualities. Start understanding ourselves.

We're battling a superior government now. The government is going to do what the government is going to do. Bottom line. So what do we got to do? We gotta do what we gotta do. That's utilizing our culture, our tradition, our skills and last but not least, our prayers, to continue battling what we started here. It's not over, they can take this land back, but in the end, they're going to have to leave. Because we always gotta hope for the best.

Don't ever think negative about the outcomes of the next coming days. Always hold yourself in prayer and stay humble and mindful and always be understanding. Whatever happens, these water protectors here have been standing since day one. Give them that respect. Even though you see some negativity. Give them that respect. Because they're here doing what most of you guys want to do too. They're here fighting the fight, doing what's right, for all of you. Not just Indigenous people, but all of the people of the world.

The feed cuts off and comes back on. He is talking to a man who has a big RV. The man says that they are working on moving, but not sure they want to. He says the pipeline is still there. "Bismarck didn't want the pipeline, how can they say this is right?"

They are disconnected from the ground, from the land. That's why they can do this. Some people call it environmental racism. It's about unity worldwide. Doesn't matter what race or anything. Indigenous roots started it. Beautiful connections with things from the earth. That's how we do it. Good people back there. We're all equal. We should continue on in prayer. Have a good afternoon.

The dome crew

Hi guys. I just got off a live feed and now I'm back on another live feed. I'm sure you guys can recognize this structure behind me. It's the dome - just the metal, bones of it. That is what we know as the dome. This is where a lot of meetings were held, a lot of questions were answered. A lot of good stories were told. A lot of good knowledge was shared and music.

He asks someone: Who brought this dome here?

Man: This is Red Lightening. We've been at camp doing clean up.

Dean: So where is this dome going to?

Man: To L.A. We gotta do some repairs before we take it out to Burning Man.

Dean: Burning Man?

Man: Yeah, so we're a multi-nation and we meet up every year at Burning Man.

Dean: Have you learned anything at Standing Rock?

Man: The importance of peace and prayer. We're trying to bring out some of this sacred tradition to Burning Man. We're bringing out a bunch of elders to Burning Man.

Dean: Well there's the dome crew. They're passionate people who do a lot of good for a lot of causes. It don't matter where you come from, it doesn't matter the color of your skin. We're all working together. We all gotta understand each other. We're all human beings. We can all work together and we can all relate to one another. Put our differences aside and our opinions. If we do what's right before we think about ourselves we can build a better future for America. For the world. Be that inspiration for everybody out there.

Muddy muddy muddy

In a short live feed, he is walking through lots of mud. There is a lot of standing water all over camp. It is not flooded, but it is certainly soaked. There are tire tracks everywhere.

Love that wild salmon!!!

He shares a picture of Native caught, smoked Wild Salmon from the Columbia River. A lot of Indigenous Nations donated food, wood, money and help.

In the next live feed, he shows people wading through muddy water. They are still taking the dome down. It is sunny out. The skies are very blue. There is ankle high water in places. There is still a little snow.

See guys, we've been working. So just document for all those people who are talking a lot of crap about us not putting the camera down and doing our job to clean up. I've been busy helping out, taking down major structures and organizing and going through the resources we have left here at camp and utilizing that for the future. To keep using what is here, to keep fighting what we're fighting against. And that's oil.

Whatever resources we have left here we are going to gather them and sort them and see what we can utilize and transport to Iowa. We're going to Iowa. What else do you want to know for today? Everybody hits me up for all the information. What's true, what's false. Now you guys are going to tell me you got nothing. No questions for me?

Yes, we're going to keep up the fight. Keep up the battle. Yes, it is far, far from over. Another thing about the negative talk, people are going to talk negative talk. You just let them talk. We got our own things to worry about. Trolls don't affect me no more. What's the next step? Well you tell me, what's the next step? I know what my next step is, but I'm not going to share it with everybody. I shouldn't have to.

Everybody should know what the next step is. That's to defund all the oil corporations and to stand up for what's right for this planet. Trump's a big player. He's not a big player to me. A lot of people out there saying how come a water protector isn't reaching out to Trump. I'd like to reach out to Trump. I'd like to have a one on one talk with him. Yeah, he may talk business, but I gotta talk spiritual business with him. Put our cards on the table, since he likes putting cards on the table. You mess with water protectors here at Oceti Sakowin Camp, you're gonna mess with all water protectors. It may seem that we're invisible to you because you haven't gotten one phone call or complaint from here, but this whole world was yelling, screaming, war whooping and shouting mni wiconi here while you were trying to barely get elected into office.

So Trump, you wanna talk to a water protector? I'm right here. I can understand that you're the president of the United States, but you're talking to a water protector. You recognize that. You look at this face here. This face is all the reasons that's coming for you. I hope someone on this live feed knows a person who knows a person at the White House, perhaps a buddy of a secret service or Trump himself. Make sure he gets this live feed. I don't care how long it takes or how difficult it is, make sure this message gets to Trump. Because this is the guy we're going to have to take down. Not in a negative way, in a spiritual way.

He might make all these decisions to destroy the EPA. Well we're going to destroy the existence of colonization. We're going to destroy the existence of republicans. We're going to destroy the existence of this so called government. We're going to construct a new aura of knowledge and prayer. Next, after that, comes understanding. That's what that camp is about in Iowa. And it started with Indigenous roots and it's going to go beyond Indigenous roots. It's going to beyond a lot of issues because it encompasses every issue in the world. It's the people of the world, united as one. No matter what color you are, no matter where you come from, no matter if you're rich, no matter if you're poor. You stand in solidarity, you stand in unity, you stand for the Indigenous roots that we are all connected to, it doesn't matter what color you are, again.

So I encourage every one of you followers out there to spread this message out loud and clear. Make sure this gets to Trump. You messed with the wrong water protectors. We know our voice is loud and our voice is huge and our voice is out there. We're coming for you Trump. Recognize that. Respect that. You're gonna get so scared, you're not going to know what to do. Because you don't understand the power of prayer and spirituality. It's something you need to get reconnected with.

February 21st

A huge streak of lightning has just struck across the sky!!!! Right above Morton County and DAPL!!!

I believe the thunder beings are watching!!

A storm is coming for the ages!!

U-Haul situation clear!! Next mission get it out of the mud!!! Hahahaha!! FR

He is live feeding as he walks up to the police.

Dean: Is there any reason why we aren't allowed to go and get our stuff out of here?

Police: You can go.

Dean: Oh okay. I thought you guys weren't letting anything through. So you're allowing empty U-Hauls to come through? Cool.

Eddie Simpson: But no loitering? No. Move along. What about those white guys? Let's get hopping, this is good news.

He is at camp in the next live feed. People are still cleaning up. It is daytime, but the sky looks dark and a little weird. There is still camping gear in camp. He shows the Standing Rock flag. There are many people moving around. People all over camp are yelling. Whooping. There are tipis still up. He shows the DAPL lights up on hill right across from camp. People are working.

There is lightning all across the sky. People are walking around, taking photos. There is more lightning. Everyone yells. He is walking around.

It's going to be one big storm. All of our prayers are being answered. What's the importance of a storm? Of lightning? Mother Earth is cleansing. It's a beautiful thing. *(He takes off his mask.)* It's a beautiful thing when you can take off your mask and smell the fresh air. And the wind. The importance of why we come together and why we give our respect to the earth.

I was helping dig a post hole and put up a wall. This wall is being built out of unity and prosperity and love for the good of why we're all here. Right now I'm going up to the north gate. There's lightning after lightning. The thunder beings are talking. Huge lightning bolts just streaked across the sky. The biggest one I've ever seen in my life. I believe it's a message. Mother Earth is going to protect us, no matter what. She's showing us that she's here with us to guide us. She's telling everyone to show no fear. Always be the true meaning of who you want to be.

Tomorrow they are going to raid from 11 to 2. There's people here. They are standing. People in the community still believe, people in council still believe, they just don't want to say it or show it. Because they've been blinded by the money, but it's okay though. They can still look. You're just a normal person, you're just a human being. We all make mistakes.

Wherever you're at Dave Archambault, you need to be here for it. Be on top of the hill and see what your people stand for, what you took for granted. Watch them. Watch all of the people you let down and all the water protectors that were there for you. No more funny business people. This is really serious. It was serious from the start. So wherever you're at, I know you're not here, I respect you.

For all you National Guard who are friends and people on the other side, perhaps soldiers, I respect you too. You're just being told what to do. Following orders, it's okay. But it's starting to rain now, it's a beautiful thing.

Pray for us and be there for us. That's all I ask of you guys. Thank you.

My last prayer to Standing Rock to a new beginning.

Thank you for tuning in for another live feed people. (*He's walking around camp. It is evening time.*) I'm up here walking by the north gate. In the face of law enforcement, I wonder how tonight's gonna go. With this beautiful, beautiful thunderstorm we've all been praying for, it's coming. It's a sign. A sign of good things to come. Because when it rains, it's giving life to the earth, feeding the plants. And people who are sharing the earth can refresh themselves, take a bath, drink water, plant their gardens. So it's a good thing. Rain that is coming down right now, it's a blessing. It's a blessing to all my people out there. And even to our enemies too. Show no hate in your heart. Show a lot of love and we'll accomplish great things together. This isn't the end of Standing Rock. It's the beginning of Oceti Sakowin. We all came here for a purpose. All of you that came and went, I want to thank all of you guys from the bottom of my heart. But people are moving out.

The veterans are here. I got to talk to a veteran. He's going to be here until the end. And his message is to tell the American government and the military, there's another way of doing things. This is not the way. I give him all of my respect. He's here for a good thing. The military is even stepping up and coming to Standing Rock because they see what's going on here with the water protectors and the military and they know it's not right. We don't have to have a weapon or superior force. People can be free. Free to do what they want to do. As long as they do it in a good way.

But here's the camp. (*He turns the camera around.*) Here's a U-Haul. We are packing and getting ready to go to Iowa. Tomorrow is coming. They are going to come with their force and their National Guard and their military. Just to suppress people in prayer. And once again I want to thank all you people who followed me through a journey. A journey of self-realization. People change and people go through a lot of things. If people are willing to put themselves out there and show the evil and the good.

I hope and I truly do want every person who followed me out there to take a piece of what I've talked about, take a piece of my mind and save it, use it. Use it for the good. Use it to protect. All we want is clean water. And a better way of life. Is that too much to ask? But I'm going to Iowa guys. You guys take care and be safe out there. I love all of you guys. You're all my people. No matter who you are. No matter what I've done, I still love all of you guys. So thank you.

"The wakinyan have always been with us but our minds (ego) have not let them do what we asked. When the Inyan Wakanyakagapi Oti was in its infancy they showed themselves to us that were in camp. Prayers were offered and what we experienced was incredible. Believing is Seeing." ~ Virgil TakenAlive

The biggest water ceremony is about to begin!!

Tomorrow we will incite prayers for the world to see!

February 22nd

Oceti: Fire burning. Singing. Drumming.

Through songs we sing we are teaching the world.

He is live feeding from camp in the late night/early morning. He is beside a nice, small fire. There is singing and drumming. It is dark out. A man says, "Welcome to Oceti's first pow wow."

Standing Rock 2-22-17 Where were you?

There is a guy telling a joke. They are having a good time. People are talking and laughing.

Dean: We had some prayer songs going on earlier. We're just going to celebrate.

He walks away. The ground is very wet in places. There is some snow. You can hear drumming and singing in the distance. He shows the DAPL lights. You can see silhouettes of tipis and huge fires. There is smoke rising from the fires. There is drumming and singing in the background.

A man is talking about how much the water protectors missed out on in their lives being at camp...birthdays, births of children, weddings....

He walks around on the road. A car goes by. A truck goes by. You can faintly hear a drone. Someone asks him if it is his and he says no. He walks past parked cars. He zooms in on DAPL on the hill. There are militarized vehicles and huge lights.

How's it going out there everybody? What's going on? That's what's going on and it's been going on for six months. Oil companies such as DAPL are tearing up sacred lands. If anybody is just tuning in to what is going on at Standing Rock, I stand right here in the middle of the road, behind me is DAPL. This is where their blockade is now. Right at the front door of Oceti Sakowin Camp. Everybody here is going through a lot of things.

I walked down through camp to get the feel of the situation and everybody's feeling happy, joyous. But some of them are feeling sad and angry. That's okay though. Camp is alive. There's many bonfires going. Keeping warm throughout this cold night. It's still going on. Camp is still here. I believe the whole camp is staying up tonight. Nobody's sleeping. We stopped sleeping days ago.

I guess in a way everyone's anxious. Everyone's just waiting for that outcome. To see how bad Morton County and DAPL are going to come take care of us. Are they happy that change will happen right away? I don't know. We'll find out. Two o'clock.

I don't know what to say. We stood our ground. We prayed. We sang. We prayed. We gave honor. We gave knowledge. We gave strength to everybody here and to everybody out there. So is this the final message? Morton County, once again, coming into treaty territory and staking it as their claim. Are we going to allow that to happen? No. We're not going to allow that to happen. Because we're Indigenous people and we know what's right for the earth. We're smart people. We got people in the court systems now, we got people in the law systems; we got people here on the frontlines. Everybody is where everybody is supposed to be right now at this point. We all contributed a lot to Standing Rock and this movement. Right now, ain't no money in the world gonna save what's going to happen today. But through our live feeds we will tell the story, so everyone be prepared.

There are drums playing softly in the background.

Right now it seems like a Morton County patrol or BIA kinda pulled up. They are parking about 100 feet in front of me. He got out and they are talking in front of the vehicle. In front of a big van looking thing. We'll just stay here and watch them. Oh they're laughing, they must be telling a joke. Too bad we don't have Facebook night vision live. Yes, they can visually see me. Maybe they are ready to raid now?

The truck moves past him. Then another big truck goes past him.

Oh it's the media. Eyewitness News 5 truck. Maybe we could get an interview with these guys.

He walks up to the truck and tries to talk to someone. The truck is loud and you cannot hear what is being said.

Eyewitness News 5

In the next live feed, he is standing by the Channel 5 news truck.

They aren't doing interviews until 6 am. They're in there planning what they are going to do. They are busy, really busy planning out where they are going to be tomorrow. They said law enforcement told them they couldn't be on this road tomorrow. They're not like us Indigenous media. I told them the best place to be was right here. Indigenous media reports where we want to, when we want to because it's our treaty lands. So they're following their little rules and laws. They're abiding by the law enforcement so they're not going to be able to stand here and report the news.

Another live feed comes soon.

Alright everybody. We're sitting here in front of the sacred fire. There's a lot of sacred fires going on tonight in camp that started with one sacred fire. And we are sitting here with Touches Lightening and... that's one thing about sitting next to a fire... have you ever noticed how the smoke just comes all on you and you move and then all of a sudden the smoke comes on you again? That's the fire talking to you guys.

He shows the DAPL lights right across the road.

That's how close they are to invading our spirits and our treaty lands. I'll be live feeding all night. Stay tuned. This is Shiyé. I'm going to sit here and enjoy this nice wonderful warm fire.

In the next live feed, he is walking around camp. There is snow. There is a huge fire. He just about slips. He walks through the snow to the big fire. There are people standing around the fire. They are yelling, laughing. Whooping. There are other fires around camp too.

It seems to be that the structures are the new fire. The structures are now the new sacred fire.

He shows another fire and walks toward it. People are still whooping all over the camp. Mni Wiconi!!! He gets closer to the fire and it is apparently a building. He walks around it. People are there standing around, talking. Unci Maka!! He turns the camera around and the embers blow behind him up into the sky. He reads some comments and walks around some more. You can see him when he gets close to the fire. Most of his face is covered.

You can hear snowmobiles in the background. The structure is still burning. Dan Nanamkin starts singing and drumming. Someone else is taking a video. Dean gives him thumbs up. They watch the huge fire. The embers fly high into the air. People are talking, laughing.

He walks by Mike Fasig. Mike says, "It wasn't me. It wasn't me."

Dean: that's the best joke of the night. Did you hear that Cindy? You let loose of information too soon that time. But I forgive you. We all mess up sometimes.

The next live feed is drone footage.

Going to the front gates. Check out the bridge.

It is completely dark except for the DAPL lights. He flies the drone over the lights to a far light. He goes over other lights. Then over camp. He flies over a big, big fire. You can see some tipis. You can see people at the fire.

He buzzes the fire and goes back up, back down and around the huge fire. He flies way back up and comes back toward the fire. The drone swirls down toward the fire. Then back up.

He flies over the road again and to the lights. He flies over a law enforcement vehicle.

I did that to document what's going on, the truth. That's what's protecting me. I say that in a good way. Just testing out Drone2bwild's flight skills. It's been a little while since I flew a drone, but it looks like I've still got it.

Good morning people of the world. Got up at 7:24 in the morning. The Hogan, one of the biggest in camp, nobody started it, it was meant to be burnt down. People stayed up all night. It's snowing here. It doesn't look like the clouds are going to break up. The biggest snowflakes we've ever seen in our lives are falling right now. It's a beautiful thing. Mother Earth is sending us a message. We are here. We are strong.

A lot of people are worried about me, they say, Dean, think smart. Just get in the car and go...but in this case, we're getting a U-Haul. We're going to put it in drive now. Here we go, we're gonna go guys. Oh no, we're stuck in the mud. That's why we can't get out. So anybody with a truck, come and get me out of the mud. So we can pack our U-Haul and get going. Eddie, what do you have to say?

Eddie Simpson: We are stuck. One prayer at a time.

Early in the morning. Time for some wake up coffee. Power to the people. Power of prayer. We need to get our U-Haul out of this mud. You guys are gonna make that happen. Pray for us so we can get our U-Haul out of here. We are gonna fly no matter what. This is a once in a lifetime, historical... *The feed cuts out.*

In the comments someone shares ABC news: Pipeline protesters burn camp

No live feeds at the moment, sorry for the interruption. If you are in the vicinity of Oceti Camp due to the Raid on Treaty Lands this morning, DAPL will target you, prosecute you and lock you up for protecting clean water!!! Welcome to the new corporate America!!!!!!!!!!

Liberation gone wild today. The United States government fears us!!!

In this live feed his face is fully covered with his goggles on. Smoke rises from Oceti Camp. People yell and whoop in the background. He shows that the road is very muddy and wet. It is snowing. He walks up to a vehicle and the people will not talk to him. They are with some kind of news media. The feed cuts off and comes back with him walking again.

Those guys back there are part of the news. They are ashamed to be on live feed. I wonder why. Think they're going to be feeling guilty about all the lies they are going to put out? Let them say it. I'm going to walk all the way up to the front. And I'm going to find somebody to talk to. See what they have to say about these last few hours of eviction. We got water protectors everywhere. Thank you. I respect you.

CNN's here. They are already painting a story. I'm going to go bother some news people. See if they're worthy of being media. Of course we're not going to trust mainstream news.

The feed cuts off for a little while.

We're back on about 300 steps later.

He hugs a woman. She thinks he sounds like Chase. She says that she has covered the camp for the last six months with the Bismarck Tribune and she will never forget the people. She cries. "It's a hard day to say goodbye to this camp."

We need to choose how we exit with dignity. Those who are marching out, praying out. We look after each other. We will do that until the end, we'll do that into the future. A lot of cars parked around here. I'm going to go around and ask. Knock on their window. That guy was looking really mean. Probably an FBI agent.

Beautiful place. This is the beginning, where it all starts. It's hard being kicked out. Smudge. Mainly smudge the BIA, they are gonna need it today. We heard there was going to be a gathering, a march to the bridge... *The feed cuts off again.*

The next live feed starts in a few minutes. He still has on a face mask because it is very cold and snowy out. He also has on huge mirrored goggles.

It's really a challenge to do live feeds here because they are cutting our live feeds short. The only media that is profiting is major media because they have all the connections. They are suppressing our media. We got ACLU people here. We got a couple of organizers who are helping everybody get out safe. The closer I am to what we need to get out, the more the live feed shuts down. We are trying our hardest to get these live feeds out, but they are cutting us off really bad. We walked up to the major media people and the police came at me and I was advised that I shouldn't be there. Which is bull, we all know that. The more I walk toward the Cannonball River, the better the live feeds get.

We got people heading out. We got people with prior felony warrants who are making the choice to stay here and protect the truth or to get out of camp and protect the knowledge and keep it going.

A man asks him if they ever caught the guys at Ramada.

Dean: One of them.

Man: Did they prosecute?

Dean: Yeah.

Man: But it wasn't cops?

Dean: No but the cops played it all out. Little did they know that day that brought all my fear out. Now I'm not afraid. I'm not afraid to use my voice. I brought the eyes of the world to the racism in Bismarck. That's a popular topic, so people tuned in. I put myself out there for that. For the people to see the fear in me and to show that. A lot of warriors said, why didn't you go up there and kick his ass, but that's not the way. There's more power than physical power. When we show that we're not afraid, we can stand up to the fear and to the racism and to the terrorizing. You don't have to be a group of people, you can be one person. I showed that to the world and brought a lot of people a lot closer.

For us, it's a part of ceremony. When you've occupied something for so long. You burn down the structure. Burning all our prayers, all our sleep, all our fights, all our courage, bravery and strength going up in one fire. So that's a part of it. Everything we do here has meaning. People don't understand that. When they don't understand, it creates fear. So they come out with a story. Some people are still unaware of what's going on here.

The government has manipulated the system to make themselves more powerful. But they didn't remember the spirituality. The natural law that runs through the trees and the planet and the snow. The lightning. The Thunder Beings.

I'm standing. I'm still alive. This camp may be burning down, but that's just the beginning of it. In the beginning, when man first saw fire, it was a beautiful thing. It was a world changing moment in evolution. It's a way of life. The flame. The fire. Once we lit it up and it was burning, it's been burning ever since. People don't understand the relationship between themselves and the fire.

Man: *(He reveals that he is a reporter. He asks if Dean minds being a part of his story? Dean agrees.)* Can you tell me again what the symbolism of burning is?

Dean: Burning camp, burning your tipi, burning your building, the place where you called home because the enemy is coming in is because they are coming to take over and we don't want them touching anything. We don't want them coming into our tipi, our home. So what do we do? We burn it. We burn it. For us that's letting it go back to its natural state of being.

Nothing should be left here for them to come and try to make it into something different. We take our stories. That's the thing about it. They think this is the story. The real stories are the people like me. All these live streamers, all these warriors. We're here to protect Unci Maka and that's the mother and her water flows freely through her for all the people to be free to drink, to quench our thirst for what we want to do in this life. Truth, prosperity. All the values we grew up with. Taught by our elders and taught by their elders continuing to the first generation of the world. We have creation stories. All these things are signs. You talk about the Thunder Beings, the eagle. It's here, we just gotta open our eyes and see it.

That's all we need, if we believe. We don't gotta be a part of any group. We just believe in the good and in the bad too. That's what empowers us to do greater in this life, because we see all the evil and all the bad in this world. In a way this is evil invading our treaty lands, treaty laws and our rights as Indigenous people. We are diplomatic people. We are people who are free from the system of the government and the government knows that and they don't want to let that out to the world.

The difference this time is that they created something that makes them fear and that's water protectors. We're here protecting the water, but we're also here protecting what's right in the world.

Man: Is there a difference in you since you came here?

Dean: Yes, my followers have seen me grow. There is a difference. To be honest though, I'm still learning. I'm still evolving. But I have gained more spiritual knowledge. I found my purpose. I wasn't looking, it just happened. It created a whole foundation for my purpose in life to say the right words, to do the right things. To show the bad too. And also, at the same time, we are never perfect. We indulge in bad too, but that's what grows us and makes us more powerful.

Man: Did the pain of all of the many, many years of being invaded before this affect you while you were here?

Dean: I used that to empower myself.

Man: How will you continue?

Dean: To speak out. We all have a voice. We continue to speak and show the truth. Always care for the people. It's not only Indigenous, it's all the people who want to unite. It's Indigenous based. It was Indigenous who stood up and said what we are doing to Mother Earth is wrong. And in the end it's not DAPL or Morton County or the government or the water protectors that have the last say so. It's the power of Unci Maka, Mother Earth. She has that right. She could end it right now if she wanted to. But right now you see in California, the oceans are rising up and there's a lot of flooding going on.

Those are all signs and it's all connected to this place. All of it because we prayed here. We prayed so hard that Mother Earth heard our cries through every valley, every pond, every lake, all the oceans, all the animals of the seas, the skies and the land, they all heard it. You notice all the geese migrations; they're not even supposed to be heading out. But they know.

Man: In the future, is this a sacred site?

Dean: This is more than a sacred site. It's the foundation of good. It's going to live on forever. If Morton County is going to come in here and set up tents, say they are going to clean it up, they are going to stay here. They don't want us to come back and stake claim. There's so much militarized force here that we're literally going to go to war. What are we going to go to war for? They are ready for a war in a small country. But there's so much fear in them. That's why they have to do that. They have to show people that their superior force can control any situation.

Man: So in that way, you already won.

Dean: Of course we did. We won!

Dean thanks the man, the man thanks him. He's from Fargo.

Dean: We need to stop the currency of the world for just one day. Don't spend or make money for one day. It's going to affect the world big time. People are being brainwashed. They can stop and say, I'm not going to do that. I'm not going to provide the system any more. It's just fake power. And it's going to allow them to keep taking over. Keeps everyone in fear. But you can use fear to fight fear. I used all that fear to empower myself and do what's right for my people.

Right now they are drilling over there. But for me, that doesn't affect me. It doesn't make me hurt, it just empowers me more every time they put a new drill into the pipe, that's just empowering my heart to do more, to do what's right and to say what's right and just keep speaking out against these oil corporations. And about how they are mining out all of Mother Earth's natural resources. That is like her body. Like they are digging out her soul.

The feed cuts off again.

Live here at Rosebud Camp!!!

In the next live feed, it is windy and snowy.

This will probably be my last report coming from Rosebud Camp. You can see all these camps here, there is no smoke coming out of the chimneys here. They have all either moved to higher ground or gone to new camps. There's a few standing here. I believe these are buses about to head out. We're about to head out. Right now we got this big, giant U-Haul. They said as long as they know we are getting out of camp, that they can't just stop what we're doing and make us leave our stuff here. So we're getting our stuff. But we need some help out here guys. There's Chase right there.

Chase walks over to him.

Dean: We're all suffering from trauma too.

Chase: We should be honoring all the people who got hurt. They are pushing us back - again. We are being declared trespassers on our own land.

You can hear yelling in the background. People stop and whoop once in a while.

Dean: We are our own leaders in our own lives.

Chase: There's been a spiritual awakening like no one has ever seen here. They can't take it away from the people who have been here. We love everyone who supports. People have given their lives for the last six to eight months.

An airplane flies over low. The sky is gray. Everything is wet. There is an army of law enforcement vehicles right across the way.

Dean: Pray for Steven Jeffrey Chrisjohn. It's his last live feed. He's standing in his yurt and holding his ground. Chase is a warrior of truth. Our last day here at Rosebud Camp. Take care of Steven Jeffrey...his sacrifice to his freedom, message him and let him know that we're praying for him right now.

He stops to talk to a man. He asks if the officers are in camp now. The man tells him they are. Holy Elk is standing until the end and she is live feeding. Dean asks everyone to share with everyone they know.

Eddie Simpson comes over. He thanks the people that got the U-Haul for them.

Eddie: I can't be funny right now. I just wanna get out of here.

Dean: It's been a journey with you guys. I love all you guys, but we gotta get out of here. Because remember guys, you gotta be smart. My voice, my network, I do best out there in the world, so that's my mission, my obligation, my goal. To make sure that every individual in the world understands.

Intimidation, that's just one of many tactics that they use against water protectors. In a physical sense they can harm us in any way possible. Doesn't matter. It's our human spirit they can never penetrate.

Share this up people. It's been a privilege.

I couldn't go live so I documented for later, enjoy guys this is our BIA from Standing Rock! They are now basically North Dakota's new law enforcement puppets!! Pray for 'em!!

In this video there are law enforcement officers standing on the road. Dean's vehicle is waved on through. They pass federal law enforcement vehicles on side roads. They just keep driving. He says that they cannot go to Sacred Stone any more. He shows down the road where you can see more law enforcement cars and flashing lights in the road. The video cuts off.

In the next video that he shares, they are still in the car and are passing the law enforcement. Law enforcement has all their lights on. They are waved through again. They are told that they are good to go into Cannonball. They pass a park ranger.

Indigenous Environmental Network puts out a statement:

Our hearts are not defeated. The closing of the camp is not the end of a movement or fight, it is a new beginning. They cannot extinguish the fire that Standing Rock started. It burns within each of us. We will rise, we will resist, and we will thrive. We are sending loving thoughts to the water protectors along the banks of the Cannonball River, today. May everyone be as safe as can be.

February 23rd

Our brother, Media Water Protector Eric Poemz speaks hard truth on Morton County and DAPL militarized police so powerful that they literally dash toward him and forcibly take him down and at the same time they fractured his hip! Now do you see why they suppress our LIVE FEEDS!? Now you see they control the media. They can arrest the media. Including Indigenous Media. They basically fear the truth.

Oceti is forever in our hearts. It is the fire that burns in our hearts that empowers us with the strength and the courage to fight these monster corporate entities.

SHARE YOUR SUPPORT FOR ALL WATER PROTECTORS! FREE Ed Higgins!

Many water protectors were arrested during the camp eviction by law enforcement and military force. Several are veterans who stayed to protect an Indigenous grandma. She was also arrested. Ed Higgins is arrested with his hands cuffed behind him while his press credentials hang on his chest right in front of him.

Shiyé Bidzííl sees what is supposed to be free people of the world being targeted, shot at, and aggressively being arrested while the North Dakota governor signed in a new bill to double the penalty of the broken laws. Not to mention Donald Trump (Our United States President) giving the order to raid the water protectors' camps of Standing Rock. I want to take this time to express how much strength is gaining within my heart down to my spirit. This is the second coming of the U.S. Government invading our treaty lands. Sacred grounds that hold a lot of meaning and knowledge to my people since the dawn of our first world from the creation stories we all know and share to this day. My tears pour from my Indigenous eyes. I watch as the drones capture the skies. They flow. They fly. As each tear drop falls, my people, my children, our Mother shall regain, receive and rejoice the liberation of water protectors worldwide. This water protector definitely has a story to tell. Through history and to the future.

Shiyé Bidzííl and the rest of the water protectors will be taking this fight all the way to the International Court of justice!!!

Find the truth and it will lead you to your answer.

February 24th

We left Oceti

Come to find out Oceti

Followed US!!!!???????

Our room was flooded. With Eddie Too Swift Simpson & Ducka Zo Yooxot Likipt

Dean: The whole entire room was flooded. We woke up in water. They are at the hotel desk telling the clerk.

He walks outside.

Dean: Pierre, South Dakota. We slummed it last night cause times are hard. The maintenance man doesn't seem to know what he's doing. I have sleep deprivation.

He walks into the hotel office. There is a map on the desk. Eddie is pointing to it.

Eddie: You understand we're coming from Standing Rock? What will happen when that pipeline breaks?

Hotel owner: Would you still be protesting if you weren't being paid to do it?

Eddie: We aren't being paid to do it.

Hotel owner: I have a lot of rental properties around and I've rented to Native Americans who were getting paid to protest.

Eddie: Where can I get hooked up with that? How can I get paid to protest?

They laugh.

Hotel owner: You were all on private land, you left all that trash. 2,500 loads of trash. It's all on private property. I don't want to get into this. You won't be charged for any damages.

The guys walk out of the office laughing and asking: Do you know where I can get paid to protest?

Dean: That guy voted for Trump.

They laugh. Ducka shows that the sole of his shoe is falling off. They laugh again. Paid protesters. They laugh again.

Water Protectors do what we gotta do!!! No doubt. No shout. Do it for the people. Don't chase the???? Follow your heart, don't belittle others. Follow what you preach. Humbleness is doing more than what you already know. Share and educate. Thank you. Peace out!!!!

The TRUTH about DAPL and the U.S. Government militants and goons!!! That's FEAR!!!!

He shares We Are The Media's post: Grandma Regina, a Wounded Knee Survivor, speaks out after arrest

Grandma Regina Brave, a survivor of Wounded Knee II in 1973, was released yesterday after being arrested for her actions standing up for treaty rights as police raided Oceti Sakowin Camp.

February 25th

Good morning Sioux City, Iowa

When a post is out!! Eventually some truth follows!!!!! Let's see if this works.

He puts out a video that only lasts a few seconds. Then it cuts off. There are still thousands of views. People are still very tuned in.

We are still going to SUPPORT JOHN B. The Oil Corporation Whistle Blower!!

In times like this we need to all put our differences aside and opinions. We all have a past. We all have our own addictions. We all have our own battles in life. This stand we take is one for the ages and our future. That's what's important in life. So tonight John and I will be hanging out and talking about Trolls, DAPL, our projects, but most of all our TRUTHS. On LIVE FEED.

People change. Accept that. Respect this man he has done a lot for America.

Every saint has a past. Every sinner has a future.

My Facebook has not been hacked. Perception. DECEPTION!!! Follow. Unfollow. It's not up to me to change people. It's up to themselves to accept their own change.

Propaganda has our truth chained down. So what you do? You jump into that propaganda and unchain your truth to set it free!!!

Water Protectors United

He live feeds from a dinner banquet. It looks like they are in a gymnasium. There is a large group of people sitting at several round tables.

Water protectors are gathering. We are establishing a camp here in Iowa. We are eating. Prolific's here. LaDonna's here.... others... We are uniting right now...eating...sharing stories, prayer, unity. Let's go down and take a look.

Basically we're here to establish a camp for the people who are at Sacred Stone and Oceti. It's to bring them here to keep them out of danger, to keep them safe, keep them in prayer, keep them in unity, to regroup, to re-strategize and basically to keep the fire going. We're doing a naming ceremony tomorrow.

I'm glad and proud to be a part of it. But we are all going through things and people are calling me a troll. *(He laughs.)* I'm not a troll. Don't take those posts to heart. Like I was telling you, there's a lot of propaganda, just don't buy into it.

We are in Williamsburg, Iowa. Come down, be a part of it. If you're at Sacred Stone and you want to be a part of it, come on down. We'll give all of you support.

February 26th

In this live feed they are putting up tipi poles. The sky is bright, beautiful, blue and sunny. It is quiet there. There is just a little wind. The U-Haul is there.

He walks around. There's a little fire in a hole in the ground. Another tipi is going up.

We're here in Iowa trying to set up a tipi. It's peaceful out here. It's nice. You can see all the trees. I believe it's fifteen acres of land. We come here to build a solid camp. To have resources for other camps and just in case of situations like at my home, they are raiding the camps. Still need to get that foundation going, you come here. But you come here in a good way and we're going to do things the right way. We don't have to worry about DAPL or Morton County police anymore. This is all legal land. We can camp here. There's many trees, so with the abundance of wood, there should always be a fire burning.

What's going on with Standing Rock is a lot of propaganda. You guys probably heard about it yesterday. I even dwelled into the propaganda myself. A lot of people are getting mad. Why are you getting mad? It's just propaganda. Whatever I say to you, it's not up to me, it's up to you guys to take it. Whatever you want to take it for, what it is or for what it's not.

Quiet. It's really quiet guys. Grass, see grass. It's not that cold here either. It's a nice sunny day. Gonna be nice all week.

Keep praying. We're all healing. A lot of people are saying, Dean, go get healed. They don't understand, I am healing. I am healing every day. Whether I go through negativity or I go through positivity. It doesn't matter. There's no right or wrong way to heal. Every day I take a step on this planet, every day I take a step forward. That's me breathing. That's me understanding. That's me growing my roots stronger into this planet and into the stars. People don't understand. What we're here for is fighting for the good of the planet. Call this place Water Protector United Prayer Camp. And it's going to be beautiful here. Water supplies life to all Nations and to all races of this earth and to the four leggeds and to the wingeds and to the stars and to the trees. So everybody is welcome. But you come here in a good way.

Bald eagles are here too, so it's already been blessed. But we will be here. We might make a trip to Cali again. Next month I'll go back to Standing Rock and see how that goes. Come back. Depends on what the court's going to do to me. But I will stick up for myself. It's just the tribal court system that needs to be redone, needs to be relooked at. There's just some flaws that need to be out of the system. And that's what we're going to do. We're going to change the system. All the way from the tribal justice to the governmental justice to environmental justice to human rights justice.

And a message to all my haters out there, all my trolls. I want to thank you. You guys are doing an awesome job just giving us more publicity and more good propaganda. If it wasn't for all you trolls out there we wouldn't feel and see all the hate and pain you have in your heart. It's okay though. You can let it go. But I tell you this though, take a break. Get off that keyboard for a minute because by next week you'll have carpel tunnel. (*He laughs.*)

This is the Uhaul we got. So bless the Uhaul nation.

Now the guys are eating and drinking. He shows all the camping gear inside of the U-Haul. Other people are there at camp. There is one camper.

Right here is the sacred fire. Cedric Jr. and a lot of people came out to have the first ceremony for this camp. No, LaDonna is not here putting up this camp. She is going back to Sacred Stone and is going to take care of business...there was somebody in her family that sold... *The feed cuts off.*

Get confirmation from Joye Braun first but if confirmation is a go then the Cheyenne River Sioux Tribe will be allowing water protectors to camp at their pow wow grounds in Eagle Butte, South Dakota.

Going live with John B. The BIG OIL Whistle Blower.

He's going to get everything off his shoulders. We're gonna get everybody motivated and everybody on the right track.

John tells his story on live feed. He discusses an issue he is having with Rod Webber and film that is being used to promote awareness.

Dean: You can back up all your truths, right?

John: Yes. We had to take his thirteen seconds of video out - took two days...he makes a profit off his video.

Dean: He's got 24 hours to throw it all on the table. Once it's on the table, they can't get to us anymore. Encourage everyone to watch John's videos because they are the truth.

When I first met John we were in Myron Dewey's hotel room at Prairie Knights. And Myron, he was just like, who's that guy? I said he's a cool guy. He exposes big oil. Myron went off thinking he was some kind of DAPL informant. I told him to look around at his work and finally Myron got to know John. I can see why he was kicked out of camp because everybody just looked at him and thought he was a DAPL informant. But he wasn't. People judge too quickly.

Live with ROD WEBBER talking about the John B. Propaganda. We always gotta hear both sides of the story right?

There are several live feeds with Rod. They cut off and Dean has to start them again.

Dean: This issue with John, we got to fix that.

Rod: I don't want to talk about that. *He talks about everything he's done. The feed cuts off.*

Sometimes the truth is the hardest thing to say.

Dean: My live feeds have been acting kind of funny. Right after I talked to John.

Rod Webber continues to talk about all the events he filmed at Standing Rock. All of the actions and arrests he filmed.

Dean: People want to know the truth...between you and John. We gotta come together, we cannot separate.

Rod: I don't want to speak about John.

Dean: We can do it in a positive way. This is getting a positive out of a negative. Seems like you haven't been paying attention to the true live feeders. You didn't know Dean was Shiyé.

Rod: I'm busy with the election.

Dean: Our main focus here is unity. Prosperity.

Rod talks about the incident with Dean at the Ramada Inn.

Dean: Rod, I lived through it. You don't have to repeat it.

Rod apologizes for not paying enough attention.

Dean: Let's talk about culture, let's talk about roots.

Rod continues to talk about what he's doing.

Dean: What's your culture, what's your honor, what's your strengths? We gotta understand each other and stick together.

Rod: Absolutely. You're bringing up things you said you wouldn't.

Dean: I'm not portraying you in a negative light. I'm trying to bring the light to you.

Rod: I'm trying to tell you, I've been making art....to shine a light. *He talks about what he's been doing again.*

Dean: When we talk about the future, Rob, we don't really say I all the time. It's about we, unity.

Rod: See now you say I'm not getting your name right, but you're not getting my name right. It's Rod and that's okay.

Dean: Okay Robert. Oh I meant Rod. I just like to call anybody any kind of name. I'm just playing with you. You gotta laugh, you gotta have humor. Don't be so serious. Don't be so uptight. Loosen up. Don't be afraid. Don't have fear. Be the truth.

Out of respect we will no longer talk about John. We will talk about water protectors. And the future. What is it that you can do to help benefit this culture of Indigenous rights.

Rod: Get my documentary out there. Always invite Native Americans to speak for me. *He talks about where he's showing the film.*

Dean: Can I be honest? You're making documentaries, anybody can make those. You know how many came to camp saying they want to make documentaries. That's skill. I want to know what you are dreaming about.

Rod talks about what he's doing again. And the connections he is making.

Dean: You wanna know my fear? You don't give into fear. I don't give into fear, but I jump into fear sometimes. Sometimes I don't want to, but you have to. You have to in order to understand it. Because fear comes in many forms. Fear is everywhere. Fear is all around you and fear is in this live feed. I sense a little fear in you right now. I can feel it. I know it. It's okay though. You just have to let it out. When you let it out on the table, you'll be unstoppable.

Rod: I've made promises to be quiet. To elders, to Standing Rock.

Dean: There's negative attention from elders too.

Rod: That's a problem. A source of shame that I can't bring the truth to light.

Dean: Sometimes truth is light and sometimes truth is darkness.

Rod stutters....respect for elders....will see them tomorrow.....don't like the negativity.

Dean: Don't look at it. Don't let it enter your mind. You can walk across a sea of negativity and come out a better person, you know that?

Rod stutters again.

Dean: We should work together. You should come to Iowa. Let's make a great documentary together. Let's tell a good story and share opportunity....and history.

Rod: I don't want to make documentaries, but I see injustices. *He stutters on about earth, neighbors...*

Dean: We were born innocent. We were born pure. As we grow older that's when it starts getting filtered with hate and all the other ugliness in the world.

We all want to hear the truth. Did you take John's footage from him? Just get it out there and turn it into positive and the whole world will support you even if you did wrong.

Rod: I didn't do wrong. I want to speak with the elders.

Dean: I want to speak with the elders too. Tell them to call me up. The thing about elders is, I respect all elders all over the world, but at times this is a changing world and the elders, they know this. Yes, we're all supposed to have respect. And we're not supposed to say things when there's going to be more problems down the road. But times are changing. And in this day and age we need to set down what we said and what we did wrong and what we gotta do in life and we just gotta put it out there. No one is going to tell you what to do.

Is that elder going to say, hey you, rub my feet and you stay in that room, locked up for ten hours, are you gonna do it? You speak for your own self. Not an elder, not John, not these people on this live feed, not your mom, not your dad. It's you that has control of your own heart and your own decisions. You need to let yourself speak for yourself.

Rod: They're not saying no, this is just me saying....

Dean: Fear can control you sometimes. Have you seen John's video? I think it's a really great video.

Rod: I'm not talking about John.

Dean: I think your videos are good too. I have seen them even though we aren't Facebook friends, even though you wrote me and wanted that video.

Rod: You never got back to me.

Dean: I know because I have a lot of people. But I give you permission to use that video. Use my fear. Show people my fear. So people can have a better idea about what we deal with here in North Dakota.

I was looking for the world's eyes. So what do you do, you call out the trolls and you go down a path. You lead them down the path. You lead them to what time you check in and eventually they pop out. I didn't know what was going to happen, but it happened. And the fear came out and the people saw that because when the people are going to pay attention to something, it's going to be a racial issue. So they paid attention and the whole world saw it. But everybody was tuned into Bismarck.

And after that I got trolled all over from BisMan. But you know what, people change. A couple of BisMan people contacted me, we met on negative terms, but we talked to each other. And now we are on a level of understanding. I know they are on that side and I am on this side, but we still have a communication, we still talk because we respect each other.

I take a chance every day. I do it for the good of you, for my children, for my followers, for the world, for all the water protectors who were abandoned. People who came to Standing Rock to show what's going on. But you gotta stick around bro. You gotta get down there in the mud to help the people. Put down the camera and come help. Put your money back in your pocket and come help. If you really want to help change in the world, help somebody you don't know. Take the time to show someone your love.

You can call me any time you want my friend....we're beyond the universe, we're beyond the stars. Always remember your roots, heritage, way of life, culture. Hold that close to your heart. What you want to do with your life will get more powerful. If you aren't trying to make documentaries.

Rod: I don't try....stuff just happens.

Dean: How's your GoFundMe?

Rod: I'm not trying to do that.

Dean: I cut my GoFundMe off. I don't need money. You can change the world with no money.

They hang up.

Dean: That was really intense just to get a little truth out of that guy. But I respect him. I gotta support them both. We all gotta come together. We gotta stop this propaganda. Propaganda has the truth chained down. We gotta dwell in that propaganda and let it free.

February 27th

Water protectors symposium: LaDonna Tamakawastewin Allard, Grinell, IA

LaDonna is talking about how camp started. She showed her land to Joye and five days later they started a camp. April 1, 2016. The youth started running....she talks about the 4 directions march.

In the comments he writes: All you people just need to shut up and listen to her!!!! Before anything comes out your mouths!

The feed cuts off. He brings a new one up.

LaDonna is still talking. She's talking about bulldozing sacred land. People were being pepper sprayed. Dogs were being used on people. Some other water protectors talk.

When they are finished, he walks up to the balcony.

Dean: I hope you like this live feed. I call it Water Protectors United. The message is still continuing. The actions are still continuing. Despite what happened to Oceti Sakowin. It's not over yet. The battle's still beginning. The battle is within our hearts and our minds and our souls. For our future.

What happened is historical. What happened is water protectors with the intelligence, beauty, the heart and the souls that come together. To come together, to bring that message, to spread awareness and to keep doing what we gotta do, cause we gotta do what we gotta do.

We are establishing, well, I am a part of a big foundation establishing the Iowa camp and it's Little Creek Camp and it's going to be a refuge and a network to bring all water protectors here if camps get raided. And also to build a foundation and a network to reach out to those other camps and to have that connection of resupplying. If they need more water protectors, we'll organize and send out more water protectors to where they need to be. And to also supply that network with unity. That unity of love. That network foundation of intel so we can keep the people updated with real actual facts.

Shiyé is not gone, he's always going to be on live feeds and he's always going to try to spread his truths and all the water protectors' truths. Remember guys, when it comes to propaganda, just let it go. Propaganda is just going to filter through the people who are working the hardest to put the message out. Remember, we all have a past, but it's not about our past, it's about building a foundation for our future.

February 28th

Christine Nobiss talks about the Little Creek Camp located near Williamsburg, IA

He live feeds from a hotel room.

Dean: We are here to talk about the new camp. What we need. What needs to be done.

Christine: We've been getting a lot of questions because we weren't quite ready to go public with the camp yet. Camp is a think tank, action, resistance camp. Also a bridge for what's going on in Standing Rock and everywhere. We hope to provide a place of relaxation. The prayer is already started. We hope to help anyone dealing with PTSD. We intend to put a sweat up soon. We have a lot of work ahead of us. This camp has been there for two days now. We started a Facebook page. We need a few more days to get set up. If you come to this camp, you're getting a job. Expect to do something. We have waivers to sign because you are on private land...can't sue us, no alcohol, drugs, firearms, participate in classes, be kind.

Shiyé Bidzííl last video of Oceti!!!

There are water protectors standing in a circle. He is walking through the crowd. There is singing and drumming. It's wet, muddy and snowy.

Everyone starts to walk. They are walking together. They are walking through the mud. Someone is carrying an upside down flag. The singing and drumming continues. They walk, drum and sing for a while. There is smoke billowing up in the air from the structure fires. Dan Namamkin is playing a small flute. There is a building burning in the distance at camp.

Everyone stops and stands, overlooking camp. They hold their fists up high in the air and sing. It is a large crowd and they are pressed together, looking at camp. There is black smoke over Oceti Sakowin Camp. They are holding signs and banners. They all yell.

He shows people standing around talking with police. He walks up with his phone camera on.

Officer: You need to get that out of our faces. You have been asked to leave. We've been very patient. We are not a part of your conversation.

The officer starts to walk toward him. He walks away.

Dean: Thank you for invading our treaty land though. Karma will come back at you. But I forgive you.

The officer starts to walk toward him again, but turns around and goes back to other officers.

He goes back to the water protectors. They are walking and singing again. Dennis Romero, also known as Chumash, is in the crowd. The video ends.

Sometimes I sit here and ponder and wonder and my mind goes into a million thoughts, questions and answers, darkness and the light. What is it gonna take to change this way of living with culture being desecrated, destroyed, buried with no markings of existence!!!!! Soon this country will be on the brink of revolution!!! Then the people will finally stand up and fight back with knowledge and understanding. You see our knowledge is the answer to our eternal victory for generations to come. The government will soon see they messed with the wrong people!!! Water Protectors United Worldwide.

He shares an article from TheDailyHaze.com. A man was shot and killed by police at the Sabal Trail Pipeline in Florida.

These oil companies aren't creating Jobs!!!!!!!! They are only bringing darkness to the world!! Soon the light will shine!!! Prayers to all Water Protectors!! They need you the most right now!!!!!!!!!!!

I get drunk off Truth and get sobered up with lies!

Chapter 10

March 1, 2017

He is sitting at a fire. He pulls off his hood and smiles.

How's everyone's night going? I'm here at Little Creek Camp. Attending to the sacred fire. Keeping it going, keeping it lit. It was lit three days ago. It's the heart of the camp. That's why we stay here all night. Tonight's my night. So we tend this fire and keep it burning. Feed it truth, you know. It powers the flame to spark higher.

Today was a good day. We had a rain storm. With a tornado warning too. But it's beautiful though. We are blessed with water, out of the sky. Lightning and thunder, yet we're still here. Building this camp. We got one tipi. We got many more structures to put up. Slowly, people are coming by. So far there's about nine people at camp. We're encouraging everyone to come.

This is not like any other resistance camp. It's a camp of prayer. It's a place to find yourself. It's also a place to go when camps are getting raided by the government. It's a place you can call home and you can heal. It's a place you can come to be a part of the future. It's a place where you can come and pray and you can hold ceremony. Despite all that propaganda you hear. I'm sure there's already propaganda starting about this place. There's always going to be propaganda.

It's been beautiful since I've been here in Iowa. This camp is fifteen acres. Our main focus is to make this camp a network camp. A place where resources can be shared. And a place to heal from PTSD. And no, that's not a DAPL cough, it's just an Iowa cough. It's beautiful here. It's a place where you don't see any DAPL lights. You don't hear any helicopters. You don't hear the police in the distance. You don't feel that oppression. All you hear every once in a while in the background is coyotes. It's nice though. It's peaceful.

But I sit here and attend to the fire. Everybody here is sleeping. Getting their rest for tomorrow's build. My main focus right now is to heal myself. On March 10 I will be going to Washington, D.C. I'm going there for the people. Going there for Standing Rock. Standing up for our lands and our rights. I'm going to go there to address a lot of issues, joining all the other water protectors. I'll be heading out on the 7th and I'll be back by the 11th. I don't decide the journey. The journey shows me where I want to go.

I don't know what's going to happen in Washington, D.C., but I know one thing for sure, I'm going to make my voice heard there. There's a lot of things wrong in this country. Yes guys, I follow my heart. My heart ain't perfect though. I speak the truth, whether it's wrong or ugly. I speak the truth.

Here's how you tend to the fire. It's about to go out. So you grab all this stuff here. You feed the fire and soon it will burn again. There it is... fire is burning again. As long as there's light glowing, this fire never goes out. But the smoke gets in your eyes sometimes. Watch it come back to life. Here it comes. Let there be light. See, that's the job of the firekeeper. Make sure this fire never goes out. That fire is the light of the world and through all this darkness, that fire keeps burning and that fire is like the fire in your hearts. The fire is whatever you desire.

Whatever you want in life, you go for it. If you want change, you go for it. The government wants the change in your pocket, but we go for change in the world. It's all about love guys.

Yes. It's cold out here, but we're out here. Yes, we are light bringers, light warriors. You bring love to everyone you touch. Yes, I will be safe. A friend called me from council and she told me that Dave Archambault wants to help the water protectors who are left in camp to find their way home. The way it was told to me was that Dave is feeling really bad about what's been happening this last month. He wanted the water protectors to go home so the earth could heal. But I was thinking, why couldn't he stand up on live feed to the people of Standing Rock, instead of telling people below him to tell the people. I feel he has guilt in his heart. When you have guilt in your heart, it's hard to say what you want to say.

And as far as LaDonna's land. LaDonna has the money to buy that land back that her family messed with. And so, Dave Archambault, if you get this message, LaDonna has the money. Don't do anything corrupt. Let that land be there. That land can be a very educational place. What she established there was knowledge and it can be a very good thing for the people of the world. Dave Archambault, the council, whoever is running things, I want you to understand that removal of Sacred Stone Camp is taking away the knowledge and wisdom of the water protectors. Taking away that knowledge and understanding that the elders brought forth. Taking away the culture. Your culture. You shouldn't do that.

I can see why Oceti was raided. We all prayed and sang our way out. It was never about the cleanup. It took Morton County and the National Guard like two days to clean up. It was never about the cleanup. They just wanted us off the land. Once again, took us off our treaty land. Right now I'm just disappointed. Not in a bad way, in a good way. I'm disappointed because I'm still trying to understand what Dave Archambault and the council did. And I wonder when they will understand that what they did was wrong. You guys were all at the camp. You were at the camp Dave. Your children and your wife were at the camp.

I really do have respect for all of you guys on council. I know every one of you guys. I notice a few of them have blocked me on Facebook. Why? Now you guys come with this truth that you want to help water protectors with gas cards? You want to help water protectors with assistance to get home? I ask you this, if you want to help water protectors with DAPL money you have left, it feels like now you have pity on us, so you're going to help us with DAPL money to get home. I say let us all go to your gas station, Dave, and fill up our tanks. Since it's DAPL money.

Shelter people in your home, council members. A true tribal chairman would be out there with the people in the mud, with all the uncis, with the children. If you truly want to understand where your tribe wants to go, you have to be out there with the people. Not in the office all the time. A real leader would be out on the streets with the drunks. Don't look at people as less or more. We're all equal. Don't look down on them because they're drunks. Go and help them. That doesn't mean buy them booze. It means take them in, care for them; understand them. Listen to them.

That's the number one thing people forget - to listen. When you listen, your knowledge and power and understanding go beyond everything. And you get reconnected with the trees, the stars, the water. That's where it's at. It all starts with listening. That's the number one thing, not just us Indigenous people, not just us water protectors, not just Morton County, not just Trump, he's the hardest one, he never listens, he can't even hear a phone call. That's the one thing we all forget, is to listen to our hearts. We're focused on what we want. And we want it right away.

Patience is another thing. Listening and patience. If we listen and be patient, we can understand the qualities of every little simple thing we have. We could listen to a rock. Listen to the flames of this fire. Listen to the wind. Even listen to the stars. But if you can't listen and you don't have patience, at least listen with your eyes. See what you have in front of you. Because the most beautiful thing is a simple flame that is lit. When the elders tell the stories things crack open and it spurs that knowledge and wisdom out. All those stories and all those elements are what we are missing. That's what we're supposed to hold inside of us. We're so disconnected from this world. We're so caught up in this system. This system of suppressed living, 9 to 5. Bills. It stresses your spirit. Is that the way you want to live your life?

But you know what, sometimes I do feel like giving up. I feel like giving up every day. I feel like getting a job in the oil industry and providing for myself, living a happy life until the day I die. But you know what stops me from that? Our generations to come. It's our generations that bring the light. People are so caught up. They want things to change right away. Well, stop driving cars, stop using gas. You need gas to protest all over. Well, you know what, I don't need a car. I got my two feet right here and I'll use them because that's what Creator gave me. And I'll walk through the darkness and I'll walk through the light.

But difficulties in life, you keep walking. Hardships in life, you keep walking. You meet friends along the way. You guide them. And at the same time, they'll guide you. It's going to take a long time for change. But people in this day and age are so fast paced that they want things to change in an instant. But it's going to take a long time for things to change. But you know, we've started it. It's the doorstep. We will change this world. People like me and people like you guys who have been following this movement since day one. You're all empowering each other. You're empowering many, even me.

I'm not a leader and I'm not a follower. Leader is just a word that people find comfort in. But the truth is leadership qualities are in you. They are in every one of us. It takes leadership in your heart to define who you are. It takes leadership to do what is in your heart. But you can do it because you all have leadership qualities. Looking to someone to be a leader to find comfort in the truth, why look at someone else when you already have it in your heart? That's the real truth guys. We are all leaders.

And I'm only human. I'm never perfect. Sometimes I'm misguided. But I put it all out on the table. When you put everything out on the table, the enemy has nothing against you. My direction in life is to keep doing what I'm doing. To tell the truth, the raw truth. To keep this fire going, don't ever let it burn out. Just like in our hearts. We desire what we think is best for our children and our future. We get what we desire in this world. You hold onto that truth tight. Like the fist we put up in the air. That's the real truth. Don't ever have anything to hide. Forgive yourself. Forgive others. Sometimes it's hard though. But I love all my peoples here. Come to Iowa. Join that truth with me. Grab it with your fist and hold it up high and the fire will keep burning every day. The truth is powerful people. Open your eyes and feel the heat. Come into the fire. The deeper you go, the more love you will feel. The more beauty and that's the essence of life.

Well after all the chaos and propaganda. I would like to give a respectful shout out to Myron Dewey of Digital Smoke Signals. You're a good chapter added to my book of knowledge. Respect

The bank divestment project is going strong. He shares a link: Breaking: Private investor divests 34.8M from firms tied to Dakota Access pipeline

March 2nd

FBI should investigate their own people and the government and Donald Trump himself before they even think about investigating water protectors who are standing up for the goodness of this world.

He shares a link: Senator Al Franken wants an FBI explanation why it's investigating DAPL protestors

March 3rd

Oceti is now gone but we carry the fire where we all go in the world!!!!!

LaDonna Tamakawastewin Allard should be honest with the people!!! Look at the date of this deed!!!!

He shares a document about the land in question.

It is dark out in this live feed. He is walking. He is at Little Creek Camp.

Okay guys. You want to know what's good? Well before I tell you what's good, let me show you what's bad. You see this creek here. This creek is filled with water. Water is life. Right now this water is death. There's dead frogs belly up in it. This water has no flow. This water is death. *The feed cuts off for a few moments.*

I got cut off. I don't know why. The sky is bright with stars. Stars shine bright in the dark. The ground is cold, just so you know. But this creek does not flow. It's full of death. It's full of corruption. Just like my people. The leaders are supposed to lead the people. They gather the masses to fight the pipeline but it's hard to find out that the people who are supposed to be leading are full of corruption.

I'm sorry to hear this and I'm sorry to say this right now, but LaDonna lied. I'm sorry LaDonna. Why did you lie to the people? But the land deed 2015, someone sold pieces of that land and it was your step sisters, like you said. When someone buys this land the people who own it all get a letter. LaDonna knew about this letter. I'm sorry LaDonna. I still respect you. I still look up to you for the woman you are. But lying to the people doesn't make you go forward, it makes you go crazy. LaDonna knew about the land sale. You have this paperwork. I posted it earlier. LaDonna, you knew. Why did you lie to the people? Let's take off the mask. *He takes off his mask. The feed cuts off.*

Shyiye Bidzill speaks truth about Sacred Stone Camp

Soon he comes back live with another feed.

Okay guys. LaDonna got back to me. 31 minutes ago. Apparently she just found out about this deed. Let's hope she makes the right decisions to buy this land and get the camp back up and running. It's crazy how people don't know what's going on. Even LaDonna. Why does it take me to make people wake up? It's three o'clock in the morning and people are waking up. But LaDonna got back to me on that land deed. Let's see if she answers some more questions. We all want to know. In the first place, why did the BIA lie to her? Who's corrupt? The BIA, North Dakota, South Dakota, the council, Standing Rock, LaDonna, Dave? Trust went out the window.

If I had land I would be looking into it. Now all the people are being pushed off that land. People are being told to go home. Why? Because you misinformed yourself? Come on LaDonna. I stuck up for you. I believed in you. I still believe in you. Make this right. Go on live feed and tell the people you did not understand about this land deed. You told me here in Iowa. Just be good to the people. You have a lot of people who look up to you.

Remember, money is nothing. You may have over three million dollars from your GoFundMe account. Buy that land back. Use that money to prosper Sacred Stone. Use that money for good. But overall, the point of this live feed is that corruption can happen to a lot of people. Money makes that happen. Money is so corrupt. Money makes people forget about land deeds. Money makes people go crazy. Money makes people cheat. Money makes people push people off treaty lands. Money makes people do bad things.

So LaDonna, you got back. You thanked me. It's not that hard to find information on the computer. It's easy to find information. All you got to do is google it. So make it right with the people of Sacred Stone. Don't let all those people get pushed off that land in vain. Make this right. Apparently you have 60 to 90 yurts? What are you going to do with all those yurts? You bought snowmobiles at a time when the snow was melting. Are you laundering money? What are you doing with those? Springtime is about to hit. Buy ATVs instead.

Please, please LaDonna. You don't have to lie to the people. A good leader tells the truth. A good leader reports to the people. Not only to the people, but to the people of the world who are watching. Make it right LaDonna for the people. All the people of the world want to know. Did you really worry about the yurts and not the people? We saw the live feed. You couldn't get back in Sacred Stone. Remember LaDonna, it's about your son. About your people buried in the ground. Do it for them.

When you were here in Iowa, something changed. I felt it. Every time we talked you always talked about the important things. And that was prayer. This time you brought up just money. People laugh. Let them laugh. A false narrative, huh? *(He's reading comments.)* Yes, cha-cha-cha-ching. Well, I'm just delivering the story. It's up to you guys to think what you want to think about it. Do you follow this person? That's why I don't lead, I just report. A leader is just a word. It's just a word that people go to find comfort in their truth. Little do they know that they can find comfort in their own truth. Don't go to people to lead because they fall. Or sometimes they get mislead.

You'll find out more tomorrow. In a report. Now the question that everybody wants to know is when did you know about the deed LaDonna? I'm not trying to be an enemy. I respect you. You are my people. But during this whole time, people are losing focus. It's about the pipeline, it's about life. It's about who we are. Don't let money mislead you LaDonna. Don't let money kill the people. Why did you come to Iowa when BIA, Morton County were telling people to get off the land? If I was the leader, I would stay there for the people. I would stay for my people. But that's not my position in this movement. My position is beyond that. But if I were the leader, I would stay there for the people. I would encourage the people. If something were against the people, I'd find out. I'd stand there in front of that gate and I'd tell BIA to go. I would stay and protect the people. But that's not my job. I'm just the messenger.

All those people gathered, just like Dave called all the people of the world to come and stand against the pipeline and then told them to go. But I forgive Dave because he's only showing us the path of corruption. But in time he will heal and in time we will heal. But LaDonna, you're better than that. Tell the truth. Put everything out on the table. Don't leave the people with questions unanswered. Go to your messenger and look at all of the messages you have. You probably have thousands. But try to answer every one. Because what you started was a beautiful thing. What you started was a revolution. Get back to the people. Don't leave them hanging in the dark.

Shiyé Bidzííl says good morning to all my people. Everything I've been through, all the lies all of the deceits, all the ugly truth that we've uncovered together. I sit here watching the sun rise, listening to the birds sing, watching the sky open up. It's beauty. It's magnificent awakening to a brand-new day. I listen to the understanding and knowledge of my ancestors through the beats and melodies. I listen to the beauty of this sound for it is my life and my truth.

He notes that he is feeling funny. He shares a post from someone on Facebook.

"I been thinking Dean is an infiltrator for a while now. He doesn't fly drones anymore, he was able to be on the other side of road blocks, he left before Last Child Camp was raided, like a coward. We know no one wants to be arrested but 76 were voluntarily. He stayed in PKC almost every night but was in camp a couple nights toward the end and was cold, couldn't tend a fire. I think he is either so whacked on meth as his jaw has jacked since the first time I ever found him on live feeds that he is gone to dark side to get his charges dropped... you ever hear him speak about his court dates? He is just so out there now. Praised a pedophile, John the whistle blower. You went to Iowa too, was it to document and leak all this for DAPL?"

Dave Archambault just gave up jurisdiction isn't that just illegal?

I cannot find Chase on Facebook. Where did you go Chase?

He shares Ernesto's live video:

They are inside. Ernesto talks for a long time. Then Dean calls Steven and they all laugh and laugh. Then they call William Hawk and laugh and laugh....

Later...

Dean: I'm healing. It's crazy what propaganda can do to people. It makes people bring up my past again. It makes people do hurtful things when they see a post or something I put out there, but it's okay. I'm glad to be sacrificing my image and my knowledge for you guys to have understanding. Watch it if you want to, don't watch it if you don't. I see you watching and using all your energy in comments when you could turn that around and do something positive and constructive. Don't waste your spirit.

March 4th

I am known as many names in this fight but one thing that's for sure is I know my role and I know my fate. And this is what I make!

I don't care what you all find on Chase Iron Eyes!!!! I still support this human being.

The truth in these days, we lead!!!

Oppressed NO MORE!!

He shares a meme of Indigenous men in suits. Caption: They see us rolling, they hating.

Upgraded my tipi empire!!! Hahahaha

He notes that he is feeling thankful. He shares photos of himself on a bed in a nice hotel room.

Before We De-Colonize ourselves we got to understand Colonization from Within. Please follow Indigenous and American Indian Studies at Haskell Indian Nations University. Creator blessed us with the knowledge now let's put our minds together for the future of this planet!

This is a live video from the hotel room.

Good evening people of Haskill. Educated youth. I'm live streaming on my page too. So the topic today is how do we decolonize ourselves from this system we call America? I believe progress is keeping us all away from connectivity. We have a camp in Iowa, Little Creek Camp, and what we're establishing there is connection. Connection to ourselves. Connection to Mother. It's a camp that's about healing. Healing ourselves from what we've been through at Standing Rock. Because of the pipeline. DAPL. All of the issues that came out of that beautiful place.

There's a lot of beauty, but also a lot of chaos and a lot of negativity that got filtered out. Those camps are no longer there. Last week the Standing Rock tribal council and chairman assisted Morton County to go into camp and raid it, get rid of it. And Dave Archambault, the reason he went that route, he said, was because it was time to heal the land. The land that we overtook to make our mark on this world. And we have made our mark. We made our own watermark.

A lot of people were very sad and disheartened in what social media calls the leaders. Leader is just a word. It's just a word that people go to find comfort in their truth. But we are all leaders. We are all leaders within ourselves. We can look to other people for answers, but we have the answers ourselves.

Before we understand decolonization, it starts with colonization. Like sitting here in this beautiful building that human beings created for protection in this system we have invented. What we're coming to, what we're progressing to is we're making it so easy for us to live every day, getting rid of those struggles we used to have way back, long ago. And we can't forget where we come from. Evolution is always going to progress. We can't walk away from it. We can't run away from it. It's progression. Everything is always going to progress.

But what we know as Indigenous people of this world is that we need to share that knowledge and understanding. That knowledge and understanding of what do we do next. And here's where we start. We start by stepping out. Sometimes we got to step out of the light into darkness. People are being controlled. Not necessarily in a bad way. Not necessarily in a good way. They are learning. They are seeking knowledge. And we all have that knowledge right here. (He touches his chest.) And we need to share it out to the world out there.

I encourage everyone who is going to school to keep going. Don't ever stop your education. Don't ever stop believing in what you want to do in life because of a movement. You can still hold onto those skills and still hold onto your classes and you can still do what's right without changing your everyday life and everyday way of living to change the world. I noticed when Standing Rock happened a lot of people sacrificed a lot of things in their lives. I know a guy who sold his house and came with nothing but his prayers. When I heard that story I realized that a lot of people sacrificed a lot. A lot of students dropped out of school to come stand at Standing Rock. And for that I am grateful, but they didn't have to drop out of school.

But now that this fight is gone from Standing Rock, we are spreading it out like seeds. Like dandelion seeds. All over the world. We're establishing little camps here and there. Fighting the good fight. Building spirit camps. Building resistance camps. And everybody looks to all the live feeders who were there from day one for comfort for their truths. In a way, I can provide that. I have knowledge within myself. Your power, your mind, your knowledge. That's what we hold key to accomplishing anything in this world.

We want to see change in the world, we gotta start right here with ourselves. We gotta support each other. Despite all the propaganda and criticism from people, there's always going to be criticism in the world. There's always going to be people who are negative. But I encourage you to take that negativity and make it into a positive. You can do that by taking that negative in and not allowing it to suppress your spirit. Because this is what this colonized world is doing.

This world that's created for us, by us, for the governmental system, this is meant to suppress our soul, our spirit. We are too worried about bills. Too worried about what you're going to plan for the next day. What school you're going to attend. What job you're going to get. People got to step back every once in a while and view the world from a different perspective. (He turns the camera around to look out the window.) And this is the world we live in. We have the cranes over there just building. It's progress. Nothing we can do or say to stop it. Progress keeps going. It's evolving to be a better society.

But we have to take care of ourselves. We have so much power. People underestimate themselves. We shouldn't do that. We should feel the empowerment of our spirits because the spirit within us is so strong. It allows us to dream. To see another reality for what we want to make it. Sometimes I feel like giving up. I feel like quitting all this knowledge and opportunity to go out in the world and bring a little Oceti and the other camps and bring what we learned. The hardships, the friendships. The chaos. The beauty of the land.

Dave Archambault is right. It's time for that land to heal. For Mother to heal. It's time for the water to rejuvenate. To go back up into the atmosphere and come back down as rain. Cycle of life. Cycle of opportunity. Cycle of natural progress.

I walked around last night and people here support what happened. People still want to know what's happening. People want to understand. They're thirsty for knowledge and that's why all of you attend college. We want to make things better. Don't ever feel like you're going to fail. Sometimes I feel like I'm failing. Sometimes we look at this world and say, how are we going to overcome this? But we cannot allow that to make us feel weak. We are the people.

Standing Rock is a good example of that. We all came together because we felt a calling. I encourage you to spread the good works of Standing Rock. All the positivity needs to be spread out. The negativity is always going to be there. But use that. Sometimes we need a little darkness to see the light. And when you see the light, share it. Share it with the world. With your mom and dad. With the children. Share it with the animals. And share it even if you're out in the middle of nowhere. Like Little Creek Camp.

I encourage everybody to go to that camp. It's a place of healing. And it's a place where you can find yourself. Get out of the big city. Before we can start decolonizing ourselves, we gotta see and understand colonization from within. Places like this are so colonized. We got buildings, we got structures; we got lights. We got artificial light. We came from a flame to just pulling a cord. All of these things are designed to make our lives more comfortable, but we can still accomplish that no matter where we are at. It starts at home. It's the first steps out of whatever you think it is. Whether it's a world of chaos or fear, you just take a step. The earth we walk on, no matter what land it's on, we have the right to step on that land. And protect it. Because the earth needs our protection. The earth needs our love, our unity. And we're going to provide that. And we're going to share that. A'ho.

Shiyé Bidzíil and Ernesto Burbank back together for the people for our mother. A place we call Little Creek Camp.

This live feed is with Dean and Ernesto Burbank.

Dean: I am here in prayer and I am here in healing.

Ernesto: We just made it here. (*He shows the water. There is oil in it.*)

Dean: This is Little Creek. What we're bringing here is healing to mother and we're healing as water protectors. This creek needs healing. It's a little frozen up. This creek is death. This is what it's causing to the grounds of Iowa with fracking and oil leaks. This is proof that Mother Earth is dying slowly.

I'm concerned for all the water protectors out there. Lately there have been a lot of comments of hate. We need to channel that hate and turn it into positivity. We don't need hate. With all we've been through at Standing Rock, we cannot hate, we cannot blame Chase, we cannot blame LaDonna, we cannot blame Dave. We cannot blame ourselves. But at the same time, it starts by understanding ourselves. We have to start healing ourselves, because before we start healing the world and the community, we have to understand ourselves. Then we can help the community and then we can help the state and the state can help the country and the country can help another country and from there we can come together and change the world.

We have this whole entire world and we are desecrating it. Destroying it. Little do they know that this earth is just a little speck of grain, or speck of sand on a big beach of sand. This universe is so big. We tend to neglect that what we have here is so precious. We stand on this ground and the universe is so huge. When you step back and look at our problems, we're this tiny little star in the universe and here we are, destroying what life we have left.

They are inside for the next live feed. Ernesto is tattooing an eternity symbol on Ducka's face.

Dean: We're here with Ernesto, getting marked for life.

He points to his neck. There's a water protector tattoo that Ernesto did some months ago. He says that he is getting this one on his forearm.

My tattoo means mind, power, knowledge!!!!! Thanks Ernesto Burbank!

Ernesto tattoos Dean. It is a triangle design.

Dean: Triangle for knowledge, mind, power. An illusion.

There is loud, Indigenous music in the background. You can also hear the tattoo gun.

Ernesto: It's a tribal design. Rebalance of power and knowledge and the mind. We all hold that in us. At the same time, it's all illusion.

Dean: The pain I feel when I get a tattoo is good. Sometimes it's good to feel the pain. It's an honor to get a tattoo from Ernesto. I got one on my neck back in December. That was the last of that water protector's design. Then after that it changed, but it changed for the better.

The triangle is the most powerful structure. That's why you still see the pyramids standing. Why the tipis are still standing.

He holds up his arm and shows the tattoo.

Dean: Ernesto, one of the finest tattoo artists I will ever let tattoo me. Always does an awesome job. Tattoos do not hurt because I feed off all the pain. You guys have an awesome night.

March 5th

In a morning live feed from the hotel, Dean and Eddie Simpson are standing beside a tall window, looking out.

Dean: Hey everybody. I thought before we leave this colonized city, we leave on a good note. Unity comes in many forms and I think this huge wall painting behind me is beautiful.

It is a large mural of a lot of hands reaching out, painted on the side of a tall building across the street.

That's the world right now. We're reaching out in many directions, but the hands have not yet touched. Some have, but that's the world going on right now. Reaching out for help, for guidance, for truth, for knowledge. This guy is scared of heights, but he's standing here dealing with it. We're about five levels up.

Eddie: I still feel kind of woozy. You motivated me.

Dean: What set you into this fear of heights?

Eddie tells a story about how he was jumping on a bed with his cousins when he was young. One of his cousins fell out of a window and shattered his hip.

Dean: This is what you call overcoming our fears. He's going through a lot and he's learning and he's overcoming. We're all here to teach and learn.

This is the world right now. Some people can touch, some people cannot. Some people are touching the wrong place. But in the end we'll all touch and have unity.

Iowa City, IA

He is outside on the streets with a lot of people. Some have banners. The group he is with has a beautiful Water Is Life banner. It is very windy. There is someone speaking. There are many rainbow flags and banners. The speaker is talking about the struggle.

We just walked downtown. We don't know what's going on but the rainbow warriors are here. We're here in downtown Iowa City. They're speaking the truth. These people are on our side. These people know about change, so let's listen to them. Do you know about Standing Rock? Do you know that it's all true, we got kicked off our treaty land? It's beyond Indigenous roots. We're going to Washington D.C.

He talks to someone then listens to another speaker. He has volunteered to speak. They introduce him. The crowd roars. He raises his hands and smiles.

Has everyone been refreshed with pure water today? No one has been refreshed with water? Defund Wells Fargo. Look into the banks that are funding this. That's what's killing us. I come here as a part of Standing Rock. I am Hunkpapa, Lakota from the South Dakota side of Standing Rock and Diné from Navajo Nation, Chinle, Arizona. Born for the Bitterwater Clan.

I stand in solidarity with my people and you here are my people as well. I come here to deliver a message. And that message is, stand in solidarity and stand for what you believe in. We all have dreams for a better country. And it starts with every individual here. Turn the negative into a positive. Trump is nothing. If it wasn't for Trump we wouldn't have woken up to see what this country is doing. So I'm glad Trump is president. He's showing the world what we can do. I'll see you in Washington D.C. if you are coming.

Yeah, water is life and we need to preserve it for the next seven generations. This battle is not going to be done this year or next year or in the next twenty years. This battle is going to continue beyond our years and we're still going to do it. We're not going to give up. Because of our children. It might not be our children's children. It might be our children's children's children but if we have peace for a second, we've accomplished what we fought for. So believe in it.

Water is life. Water is life. Water is life. A people united will never be defeated. We stand together. We have a voice. The government is not our boss. We have dreams that we pursue.

The crowd roars.

Before we try to change the world, we got to change ourselves and accept who we are. And from there we can work together and we can change this world. So don't believe nothing is hard people. Continue what you're doing. I love you all. For who you are and what you do. We all come from different walks of life. It started from Indigenous roots but beyond that it's all of us in unity. It's beyond all colors and race. We all come together and that makes us stronger in life. We all gotta understand that. I love you all. It doesn't matter if you're the guy on the street or the guy on the top floor, we're all equal. We're all the same. We're all human beings. We all want change. We all want prosperous and peaceful lives. And that's what we're going to build here in this country. But before we see that good in life we're going to experience the chaos and negativity. But we need that, so we can see the light and continue doing what we're doing. I love you all. Water is life.

The crowd cheers as he walks away.

We just happened to be here and brought the banner. These are people that have a voice and have concerns. It all starts with us. Human being is anybody, doesn't matter what you are, what you do, what you've done. This is all unity. People are misunderstood. It's about the children. That little guy that's walking...

A small boy walks over to him and gives him a high five.

That's why we gather. The Dakota Access pipeline blew it all up. People were sleeping and it woke them up. People are gathered for their rights.

It starts with prayer

This live feed is from Little Creek Camp. He is walking with Eddie Simpson.

Dean: Eddie and I are going to Washington D.C. with Janet. She's been active in the movement for a long time. Right now we are walking at camp within the fifteen acres. I just wanted to point some things out.

First, there's always going to be propaganda. People will always be putting stuff out there that points out our wrongs. But people are missing the whole point of this movement. It's not about pointing out our wrongs, they are misleading themselves. It's not about that. What I want to point out is that, Chase Iron Eyes, we need to support that man. We need to pray for that warrior. Everybody needs prayer. But no matter what they put out there about him, no matter what the people think about him, I support him. So does Eddie.

It's about unifying. Money does mislead people and manipulates people's minds. We don't need money. We need buffalo and fish and red willow. A people united will never be defeated. We may have propaganda, but our focus will never change. It starts with this, you take one step forward. Even if you take two steps back, you pray and then you go forward again.

Eddie talks about how difficult it is to be away from his son. But he says he is doing this for his grandchildren who haven't even been born yet.

Dean: Thanks everyone. Every one of us are stars. We are all stars in the universe here. People need to start understanding that and looking deeper into themselves and stop looking at the materialistic things in life. I'm going to end this live feed now because Myron Dewey is live feeding and I encourage everyone to tune into him now. Because Myron Dewey is educational truth. We are all truth. One prayer at a time. Next time Washington D.C. Have a Creator blessed day. I encourage all water protectors who want to redefine who they are and reconnect to their spirits. This camp is for you, people of Oceti. You can gather here and get your energy back. I love you, all of you.

Red Fawn is still in jail from October 27ᵗʰ when Treaty Camp was raided. He shares a post and Red Fawn's new address.

Once AGAIN...my sister was suddenly moved from Bismarck to Rugby, ND. The state of ND insists on moving her abruptly for no apparent reason. We will continue to support her regardless of where she's at.
~ Luta Wi

"The best apology is changed behavior." ~ Unknown

March 6ᵗʰ

"They don't want to see us unite: All they want us to do is keep on fussing and fighting. They don't want to see us live together; all they want us to do is keep on killing one another." ~ Bob Marley

15 days until Shiyé Bidzííl Pre-Trial Date with Tribal Court. Let's see if there's enough evidence to prove that a water protector was selling drugs within Oceti Camp!!!! SMH

Expecting the Storm of the century!!

He is live feeding from Little Creek Camp.

How's it going guys? Good evening. We're about to have the biggest storm of the century. There's probably going to be a lot of tornadoes. There's probably going to be a lot of hail and a lot of wind. It's probably going to test this camp, so stay tuned. I'm ready for this. I'm ready for this twister.

He is smiling. He shows the dark sky and walks around. He finds Eddie Simpson.

Eddie: You about to live stream us going to die? *(They laugh.)*

Dean: Now if we set these right, the tipis should remain standing. Because the way it was built, just like my tattoo, as a symbol of strength. Now these winds should go right over the tipis. It'll still be standing.

I want to bring up a situation, Myron Dewey gave me a call. He was talking about someone hoarding all the camp equipment. My thoughts on that are that a lot of things were done at camp. A lot of people weren't noticing what was happening. They were talking about it but they were called all kinds of names for trying to speak up. But what went on at Oceti behind closed doors, there's nothing we can do to change it. If people want to hold camp supply materials, they are going to hold camp supply materials. Let's hope they use it for the best. Other than that we can all rebuild and start our own camp.

If there's a tornado tonight, I'll live stream it. Water protectors verses tornado.

Grab some popcorn here comes the storm!!! With Eddie Simpson, Christine Nobiss, Thomas Touches Lighting and Shiyé Bidzííl.

We're getting ready for this storm here. There's lightening galore here.

Lightning lights up the sky behind them.

We got our debris goggles on. Ready for whatever flies at us, farm equipment, a horse, a cow. We're going to Facebook live it as it's happening. Hopefully catch a tornado. Drop some tobacco for us. Make sure camp still stays up. During a storm like this, we don't run away. We don't need to run away, we don't hide. We have a house that's offered shelter right there with a basement. Grab a chair, get some popcorn.

He laughs. He is in a very good mood. The others laugh with him.

Pray for Little Creek Camp. We're out here on the road. Eddie is here. This is an educational video. Watch the lightning. Keep watching guys, keep sharing. We're going to stand here until the first lightning hits close by.

They look at a weather map. A very strong storm is close by. Lightning lights up the sky again. It starts to rain hard.

It's coming! It's pouring live! Thunder beings and the rain beings.

In the next live feed, it is still raining. They are in a large garage.

Weather update: Still standing our ground here at Little Creek Camp. We pray, we sing and we eat good food.

Here's my mission for this camp. I'm going to coordinate with some Haskall students and get them to bring a bus of students up here and show them what our mission is for this camp. Our mission is to prepare ourselves. A water protector army. Not an army like you think. An army that keeps themselves fit spiritually and physically. We're talking about putting up a physical course here and sweats. Educate the people about pipelines. Educate the people about hope. Educate people about the environmental desecration that this country is doing. Offer PTSD treatment. And teach classes about psych ops that the government uses. We need to prepare ourselves in every way before we go to other camps. We're building our water protectors in spirit and in strength. Much love to all you people.

March 7th

Shiyé Bidzííl trying to connect with the creator of Facebook

He shares a screenshot of a messenger conversation he has started with Mark Zuckerberg.

Bro this is Shiyé Bidzííl.

Would be cool for you to reach me. I'm one of the few Indigenous people who sticks up for you because I believe in what you do my friend.

He live feeds from a radio station. He walks around the station. They are talking about Little Creek Camp. There is a small panel of water protectors.

I'm the one they call Shiyé. I'm from Standing Rock. I started Drone2bwild. It has been one year since I started it up. I took the drone over the construction site as they were building the pipeline, the first desecration of land and our ancestors there on treaty land. At first the vibe was different. The law enforcement was respectful of what we were doing. Through all of that, it changed. It changed through Morton County and DAPL security. Pretty much by the end of it, law enforcement was evil. But we endured it.

The frontline warriors all suffer from something because of it. But at the same time we all gained. We gained a lot of knowledge about ourselves and where we came from and our Indigenous roots. I do suffer from

PTSD. Whenever I hear a helicopter or even just see law enforcement or airplanes, it just brings me back. As media people we are targeted just for documenting this. It wasn't pretty. But it was a beautiful thing to be a part of history. Protecting our home, protecting our water, protecting our way of life.

There's a lot of people out there in the world who care about what we stand for. It pushes the movement to a whole different level. A lot of people are understanding their own roots. Unity is the key. Education is very important.

Eddie tells a story of how Dean kept putting the flashlight in his eyes, so he waited for him to go to sleep and then tapped his leg and said, "It's DAPL and you're under arrest!" He says that Dean rolled out of bed and put his hands behind his head and without missing a beat said, "I'm a water protector and I am unarmed." The room fills with laughter.

Suffering PTSD in my dreams. That's how bad it filters throughout our minds. This new camp is there to help us heal, to take care of our minds, to heal spiritually and physically. We can all learn from what happened at Oceti and Rosebud and Sacred Stone. We learn from that and we take the good things from that. But we also learn from the bad things. Standing Rock was just the beginning. It was the seed.

My latest read consuming all the knowledge there is in the world. Feels good to hit the books.

He shares a photo of a book: God Is Red by Vine Deloria Jr.

It's always good to be prepared!!

You never know....

This is a short live feed. He has a gas mask on.

Bringing all the equipment we need just in case things get crazy in Washington.

March 8th

I just gotta say, I love my trolls they bring me laughter and entertainment!!!! Little do they know they empower us all!!! Yes even Kevin guys!!

He shares a cartoon meme of himself and Kevin Gilbert. Kevin has a bag draped over his back and a sheep is sticking its head out of the bag. Caption: He was stealing my sheep

We are here at Freedom, Ohio, next stop the capital of this_____. Fill in your truth!!! The Shiyé is back!

"Dear world, if we are having a conversation about equality then all races belong at the center of this conversation." ~ Unknown

Funny how when we address our corruptions we are labeled dividers!

At times we got to admit our wrongs so together we can build strength for the people. That's how we study and understand greed more so we can better understand corruption.

March 9th

Well Shiyé Bidzíil has made his journey to this lost land of Indigenous peoples. District of Columbia! Bringing Oceti and all its essence for our people. We will start praying in solidarity for the politicians and congress people of this country to create change for our generations. Remember education and the youth are everything!!!!!

In a live feed he is walking down a hallway in a hotel.

Good morning everyone out there. Good morning Washington D.C. Good morning Standing Rock, Good morning Iowa Camp. We got in a little after midnight. After watching Myron Dewey's feed about getting pulled over. Pray for him this morning.

We are here to gather and to voice our concerns and to speak the truth and to post the truth. I encourage everyone who's been following this movement to post your truth. We're going to be here to show Washington D.C. the truth of what happened at Standing Rock.

I'm here in this beautiful hotel. Paid for by the people, for the people. The people take care of us because they believe in us. I respect that. I honor that. I never take anything for granted. Sometimes it seems like I'm going off the end, but I'm not. I really do speak my truth and it comes from the heart. That's how I reach the people.

And the thing with Kevin Gilbert, there's more important things to talk about in Washington D.C. And my truths with that, if you look in the comments, it's in there. Maybe when I get back to Iowa Camp I'll post all the truths.

But there's helicopters all over Washington D.C. now. Water protectors are gathering throughout D.C. now and law enforcement knows. So I encourage everyone traveling here to protect and pray. I have hope for our people. Hope for our children. The things I do are for our people.

For the next couple of days you're going to get the humble Dean because this is what we do. We stay humble. We do what's right for humanity. We do what's right for this world. I want to apologize if I offended any elders, offended any people out there searching for their truth. I'm just a human, just like all of us. We're all seeking truth in this world. None of us are perfect. Some of us do wrongs. Some of us mess up. But you got to learn to forgive yourself and move on. We have to learn to admit all our wrongs so we can better understand this corrupt world.

We got to understand greed. We really truly got to understand that method of corruption so we have the knowledge to better understand our people. Even within the Standing Rock Sioux Tribe, there's corruption everywhere. There's corruption in many places, in many forms. Corruption comes to you in dreams, it comes through family and most of all it comes through in paper form. We need to get a better understanding of money. Change the way we use money. Change the way we think about money.

I may not have money in my pocket, but the people take care of me. That's what family does. I want to thank Dave Archambault. He called a lot of people together. Everyone in this whole movement. If it wasn't for all of us coming together, we wouldn't be right here in Washington D.C. I wouldn't be here. It's the first time I've ever been here.

One year ago I bought a drone and that drone opened a lot of things in my life. And showed me a way. Showed me there is a way we can live this life. And it all came from a drone. I'm pretty sure all of you have been watching me, seeing the way I am growing and I am growing. That's what people do. We are all growing. We grow with each other.

But at the same time I have to point out the flaws in my peoples. No one wants to do that. People are afraid to do that. They're afraid to take that message. People are afraid to step out of their comfort zone, their circle and their way of life. But not me. I go beyond things because I have good intentions. I might throw a little negativity in there sometimes, but we need negativity. We need negativity to push ourselves forward. To progress ourselves into better human beings.

I want to pray for you people in Washington and I want to pray for Trump. We're going to pray for all the politicians. Later on today I'm going to speak to some of the congressmen and we're going to lobby. We're going to show and express straight from the Native's heart, why fight, why stand and what I believe in.

I believe in all you people. All you people made it possible. I also want to thank the creator of Facebook. I know we're all having problems with him, but think about it people. He gave us the power to connect with all the people in the world. Through the power of Wi-Fi and a cell phone. So thank you Mark Zuckerberg, I also pray for you. Show you the light, show you the way, show you the true meaning of life. And the true meaning of life is not following the trail of money, the trail of corruption, the trail of deceit. Follow what you really believe in and believe it or not, good things come.

Standing Rock was a movement, we all came together. Standing Rock is my home. I fight for all my people there too. Even if they say negative things about me. We're all human beings. We tend to forget that we have so much power in our hearts and in our minds. So much power that it's equivalent to the universe. This universe is growing every day. Ever since the first creation stories. So think about that my peoples.

An aircraft flies overhead. He stops to look up.

As helicopters fly all over Washington D.C., we set up camp at the Washington monument. In a way we brought Sacred Stone here. We brought Oceti here. We brought Tunkasila here.

Pray for this beautiful day. Tomorrow we'll have more beautiful days. This is Shiyé. Please continue to share out these live feeds. I'm going to be joining my friends, my beautiful friends. We're going to make change in this world.

Solidarity on the wall in D.C.

He shares a short video of artwork on a long wall. It is a painting of a line of people standing beside each other.

That signifies what happened at Standing Rock. We all stood together.

Oceti has come to the Washington D.C. monument. Telling our stories with family and friends reunited!!!

As this live feed begins, he sees and hugs Wiyaka Eagleman and other water protectors who are gathered there.

We're here at the occupy Washington campground. I'll show you guys how it looks.

He shows tipis up at the base of the Washington monument. It is really beautiful to see.

We're here to voice our concerns and bring attention to the movement. All the live feeders are out here. Let's go see if we can find any familiar faces. I see Ernesto Burbank.

There are many people standing around talking. Dan Nanamkin is doing a live feed.

Apparently we're supposed to have some snow tomorrow, but we endured blizzards. It's like the camp all came back together, but in Washington. We're all here in unity, we have not broken apart. Ed Higgins! Apparently we work for the CIA. I feel like Oceti never left. We just came up here.

They laugh. Eddie Simpson is there. Prolific The Rapper is there. He sees other water protectors as he walks around. The Washington monument is behind him. He meets an Indigenous woman. Antonia. She went to Standing Rock and took photos.

Dean: A world united. We brought all the races together for the cause of the world. That's why all our ancestors fought, for us. Now we're doing the same for our children. It's truth. Who is going to step out of the light into the darkness to deal with the corruption? I have quite a few negative feedbacks from my own tribe, but I'm doing it for the better of the future. I have a few trolls. I got two people to agree with preserving life and understanding between. Even enemies can come to understand and respect.

The woman talks about how Indigenous people have always suffered. How the government has tried to kill them all off. How members of her family escaped. She talked about how her mother was so affected by being forced to go to a boarding school as a child that she later became an alcoholic. She left her children and never recovered.

Dean: We, as Indigenous people, are plagued by alcoholism, drug abuse, domestic violence - we're oppressed by all these things, but yet we are still standing here fighting for our generation and for generations to come.

That's what people have to realize, how powerful we are. What keeps us strong is our roots. And you found those roots. No matter how far you had to go.

Occupy D.C. Oceti has taken over Washington D.C

With Dallas Goldtooth, Prolific The Rapper, Ed Higgins

This is a live feed at the camp site. Dallas is speaking. He gives information on what is going on and where the food is. There will be singing, dancing and celebrating. There will be a Round Dance.

I have to say, it's a beautiful time to be here. It really is. For those of you who wish you were here, you are. You're here through the live feeds, remember? That's why we live feed. For you who can't be here. So you can see and experience the things we are going through. So don't ever think you're not here. All you guys are here.

It's the first time I've ever been to D.C. and I like this place. It's full of diversity and culture. I feel like Oceti is here, but I don't feel oppressed to tell you the truth. I feel like we can be ourselves here. And sing what we want to sing and be what we want to be. It's our freedom. We voiced our concerns today. Tomorrow we're going to talk to some more politicians and we're going to state our concerns again and tell them the truth. Tomorrow we'll live feed the march. Remember you are all here. Just watch the live feeds. And share it up.

March 10th

We do wat we gotta do. For the people!!!!!!

Eddie Simpson and Shiyé Bidzííl

They are in a congress person's office making an appointment. The secretary asks what it's about and Eddie says, "Sacred sites being bulldozed and other issues." There's a picture of buffalo hanging on the wall. Eddie asks him if he ever just sits and looks at the picture. Eddie tells him that traditionally his people burn buffalo dung to keep warm.

The truth tellers!! Ernesto Burbank & Shiyé Bidzííl

Occupy Washington March. Native Rising for the World

It is snowing and very windy. The beautiful Water Is Life banner is there.

Beautiful thing that as soon as we got here it started snowing.

People stop by and hug him and chat with him. Someone asks if he got a permit to fly his drone and he says no, but he might anyway. William Hawk stops by and greets him. He finds Myron Dewey and they greet each other. A woman comes up and says she watches Dean all the time.

It's snowing really hard. I think it means our messages are getting through. What we don't understand, as we destroy the environment more and more, the weather is going to get worse and worse.

He shows a very large, very long, black pipe/snake banner that water protectors are marching with. They hold it over their heads.

I'm pretty sure all these trolls are watching. As much as they hate us, they sure do watch us. Trolls spread our message too. We turn it into positivity. We gather to voice our concerns. We gather here to make our mark, to send our message, to show that we love the water, the earth. We're people of all colors and we are united. We don't look at anyone as any less or any more because we are all equal. We all have that right and no one should ever take it away from us.

To all my people on Standing Rock, we're here for you too. To all the people in the country, you are showing your support by spreading this message. We don't lose focus. At times we may veer off the path. But we refocus. People are rising up to protect this earth. As they look out their windows, they need to be on this side. They have no idea.

The crowd roars. They are loud. They are chanting. They shout: Water Is Life!

We're going to start marching in a minute. The people of D.C. have been treating everyone really good. This whole street is filled, one whole block. Bless the trees, bless the pavement, bless the people behind the windows looking out.

Someone with a live feed comes up and asks him to say a few words. A woman stops and hugs him. She says she saw him when he was in San Francisco.

His live feeds go down and he brings them back up. He is walking in the march. This feed is very short. It is snowing.

We're marching down to the Verizon Center. We've got tipi poles. We've got sage.

Some water protectors are drumming. He walks along with the people. There are so many people, so many beautiful signs. There is whooping, yelling, a lot of noise.

Again he brings up another live feed. He is still walking in the march. He shows a law enforcement officer. There is a lot of yelling and whooping. The feed goes down and comes back. People chant: Water is life! Ed Higgins comes up to him and says that he is blocked on all of his own pages. The feed cuts out again.

The next feed is also very short. People are chanting Mni Wiconi! It is wet and gray and windy out. Myron Dewey is right behind him. The crowd is huge. He shows all of the signs, flags and banners that people are carrying.

When the live video comes back, he is walking by the Rolling Resistance bus.

People are now chanting: Water is sacred! Water is life! He shows a Free Red Fawn poster.

Dean: Yes. Free Red Fawn. Ed can't go live on any page.

Ed Higgins: More than likely it's censorship.

Dean: We're here marching. Trying to find the Water Is Life banner, but there's so many people out here. So I'm saying good luck to myself.

The march is moving. We're almost to the White House. I haven't flown any drones because we're in Washington D.C. and they will shoot them down and then we'll be put in prison for 50 years. So we don't out of respect.

Whoops. There's the White House right there.

Ed and Dean walk over to a law enforcement officer in front of the White House.

Dean: That's a big weapon. (*They laugh.*)

Ed asks the officer if he has heard about Standing Rock. The officer does not talk to them. They walk away.

Dean: He has weapons, we have prayers. They are guarding with all the military power in the world. All the security. And we better quit talking about it before they shut this live feed down.

They walk to the Rolling Resistance bus. It is moving slowly. The bus is painted with water protector images and words of support for the water. There are water protectors on top of the bus. Some are drumming. The crowd is chanting: Free Red Fawn!

There are more law enforcement coming up. They got loaded weapons on them, I'm sure. We're going to march right in front of them.

It's not raining anymore but it was good to be blessed by the rain and the snow earlier. Mother Earth hears our cries. We need Indigenous secret service to protect all of our rights, our land. So they can stand there with sage and a feather and protect. As we get closer to the White House, we're getting jammed. I will get as close as I can for you. For all of you who aren't here. You are here through these live feeds and I thank you. Here we go. They are all out front with their weapons.

He walks past banners and people with signs.

Let's talk to this secret service guy.

He asks what kind of lockdown is this? A level three, level four? The officer does not look at him. He does not talk. Dean walks on.

There's more security. Probably DAPL too. They say for us to get off the sidewalk. If you are with the march, please step off the sidewalk.

He is in front of the White House. He meets a woman and her husband. She tells him that she follows him all the time and watches his live feeds. She thanks him.

Dean: I speak truth from humbleness.

The marchers are chanting and playing drums. The crowd is still very large. He points to the White House behind him.

Check out security. Obviously on the phone right now telling Trump that all the Native Nations are on his front lawn.

Anybody with a sign is subject to arrest if they are on the sidewalk. But we can live feed. That security officer right there looks pretty cold. They are all very armed. This day in America. Secret service gotta protect their little house. Indigenous people out here, what should we do? We should give them back their treaty land and they'll go away.

If we can't hold a sign on a public sidewalk, then it's not public any more.

A woman walks up and tells him that she is from Texas. They talk about the pipeline resistance in Texas.

I'll make my way down there. Pray for Texas everybody.

Another woman walks over to him. She is live feeding.

Dean: Prayer in this hand and sage in this hand. We don't need weapons. We have the laws of Mother Earth. All the camps are here in D.C. Standing Rock didn't die, it just blossomed into this here. We are all of color and we're going to take out corruption. They don't know how to run a country. They don't understand. Because they have lost their roots. Their Indigenous roots. We all sprouted from some part of this world. We're all connected to this earth. These politicians need to know that they have roots. It's under our feet. It's the ground. Under this pavement that they put here. This pavement that's been paid for by our tax dollars. So we can step on it and express ourselves and say what we want to say. I never thought I'd have a reason to come to D.C., but I found my reason in Standing Rock. I came here to stand with my people.

We already won. That's why they bring all their weapons to guard their little house.

Another woman walks up and says: Hi, I'm Tangerine Bolen and we're suing the president. *(They laugh.)* It is a lawsuit by women. Tomorrow we're doing a panel discussion. At a Quaker house in D.C.

Dean: Women have led this movement, whether we want it or not. But men are standing right behind you. Respect.

The live feed stops.

Back at Oceti Occupy Camp in Washington, D.C.

He live feeds from the resistance camp. There are people with signs. There are tipis standing. He talks to several people. He talks to a Standing Rock tribal member, a woman named Paula Antoine.

Dean: Why didn't you stop Dave from kicking us out?

Paula: I couldn't!

Dean: We got all the resources in a U-Haul and took them to Iowa Camp.

Paula: My tipi is there. They wouldn't let me in there. Curly stopped me. He said I couldn't go in there because it was his camp now.

Dean: You hear that Curly? You were waving bye when I left the camp.

Another person comes up and hugs him.

Dean: I love this, it's like a reunion. Speak your truths.

Paula: Indigenous rights, we got to keep fighting.

They talk about KXL pipeline and what is happening there. As they talk, Waniya Locke peeks out from around Paula to photo bomb her. They laugh. Then Prolific does the same.

There's round dancing going on. It's cold. Snowy. He talks to Linda BlackElk. People are still photo bombing and laughing. The mood is very light and happy.

The end of camp is not the end of the movement.

Iowa Camp in Washington, D.C.

This live feed is of a large group of people who are listening to Christine Nobiss who is talking on a megaphone about Iowa Camp and what's happening there.

Several people talk. The Washington Memorial is in the background. Raymond Kingfisher gives the megaphone to Dean.

Dean: How's everybody doing today? This is my first time in Washington, but it won't be my last. I'm from Standing Rock and I'm Diné from Navajo Nation. I'm proud to stand with all of you. I love you all. You guys all came together and shared all the live feeds.

These ugly things we go through, we go through together, yet we still stand and go forward for what we believe because we all have a dream. And that dream is to have a better future for our children and the next seven generations. I want to thank you all for coming here. You all did your part. Everyone that's on a live feed and everyone who can't be here is here because of the live feeds. We gotta stand up against all the mining, the pipelines. This is desecration at its finest and we're not going to let that happen. Because all of you guys here are so strong! You know that, right?

The crowd yells. They start chanting: Mni Wiconi. Mni Wiconi.

This ain't the end of anything. It's a reunion. Have a good evening. Come back again tomorrow. As a matter of fact, just occupy these tipis and stay overnight.

We need to focus. Let Dave heal. Leave him alone my people. We must move forward. He is only human. We are all humans. Give him credit because even though there is all of that propaganda on him, he still came to speak his truths!!!!!!

He shares a live video of Dave Archambault speaking in Washington, D.C. that day. Water protectors in the crowd yell bad things at him as he speaks.

Life is a journey. We all go through emotions we express through confusion and hate. But love and unity we find out of those emotions. We need to focus. Let Dave Archambault heal. Leave him alone my people. We must move forward. He is only human. We are all humans.

Calling all water protectors OCCUPY WASHINGTON D.C. TONIGHT!!!

We came. We spoke. We occupied. We conquered!

He shares a video. During the march that day water protectors put up a tipi up right in front of the Trump National Hotel. Water protectors chant: Mni Wiconi!! Black Snake Killas!!

He approaches a hotel security guard.

Dean: What do we do to check in Sir? To check into the hotel.

The security guard does not speak to him.

Dean: Obviously we can't check into this hotel. This hotel is getting shut down today.

He announces that he is in a relationship with Rachael Falcon.

"If you know the enemy and know yourself, you need not fear the result of a hundred battles. If you know yourself but not the enemy, for every victory gained you will also suffer a defeat. If you know neither the enemy nor yourself, you will succumb in every battle." ~Sun Tzu

March 11th

Water protectors are gathered in a hotel room. They are laughing and cutting up. It sounds like they are having fun. Eric Poemocheah is live feeding. Dean gives him a thumbs up. Dean shows his triangle tattoo. The hotel room is noisy. Steven Jeffrey Chrisjohn and Ernesto are there.

Dean: We're in a beautiful building. This is colonialism at its finest. We're in Washington, D.C. Thanks to everyone who congratulated me on my relationship. I love you all. I'm here to take care of you and you take care of me and I'll give back all that love.

The Steven Jeffrey is here. I told you we'd get him here. We got a lot of love here. We're enjoying ourselves. I love Washington D.C. There's diversity of people, culture, history here. We saw senators. We spoke our truths. We made one of the senators cry because of the stories we told him. Others are being a little naive. We don't blame them. They don't understand.

It's all about reconnecting ourselves and understanding ourselves from within before we start changing this world. I know that we see division. A lot of things happened yesterday at the march. But mostly what we saw was unity. People coming together. The chairman, Dave Archambault, was here. He was met with cheers and more cheers, and a little bit of boos. But those boos are positive boos. That's family.

Steven: When family fights, they're going to let you know about it. It's nothing but love.

Dean: So all the people who booed the chairman, bless you. You are only encouraging and blessing this movement to a new level. Besides all the politics and propaganda that was a part of this movement, we all did something that made the world better. Whether it was negative or positive. Whether it was off the road or on the red road. We all contributed a piece of history and humanness to this movement.

So everybody out there, just love. If you want to hate, then hate. It only empowers us more. A shout out to Myron Dewey. Yesterday somebody literally punched him. But that was a punch of unity and love. Some people express love with a punch. Respect to Myron Dewey. When you get punched with love, we're doing things in a good direction. That's rez love. That's Indian love. But we're humans, we all make mistakes. We have disagreements. We are here for Standing Rock and all the peoples of all the nations. So positive boos and punch with love, that's what that was. We decided to stay one more day.

He is still in the hotel room in the next live feed. There are a lot of water protectors there. They give shout outs. Some of them are getting tattoos from Ernesto. The mood is very happy.

He shares a live feed from a march in Olympia, Washington. There are many actions happening all across the United States.

He shares Didi Banerji's live feed. She is at a camp with Chelsea Lyons.

Live from The Stand Camp in Lancaster, PA with water protector Chelsea Lyons.

#NoMorePipelines

March 12th

Arlington, VA

We are live here at the pentagon.

They are holding up the Water Is Life banner and taking pics of it. He points to the pentagon behind him. He puts the phone in his pocket. You can hear him say, "Hi, how are you doing?"

Man: The sign is against the rules.

Dean: We didn't know that.

Man: You're not allowed to have signs around here.

Dean: You need to put more signs up. *(He laughs.)*

Man: I know you guys are just trying to get a picture, but you can go over to the other side.

Steven: We're fine. We'll just go and get a cheeseburger.

Dean: Yeah, thanks guys. You guys take care. Have a good day.

Once he is in the car, he takes his phone out of his pocket.

Dean: Alright guys, we were just told we're not allowed to have the Water Is Life banner here at the pentagon. So we had to delete that picture, but we got it all on live feed.

Everyone in the car laughs.

Dean: Apparently we can take pictures over where the big giant thunderbird flew into the pentagon years ago. Rest their souls. Bless their souls. Courageous people who do what they got to do for this country. But also we got greeted by a member of the pentagon himself. He came out and apparently he must have been watching us. He came all the way out from the building and shook our hands and said he stands in solidarity with what we've been doing, so that was a good thing that came out of this. Did you see him come out?

Ernesto: Yes.

Steven: What do you got to say about this pentagon here?

Ernesto: I did what I had to do here.

Everyone laughs.

Dean: We're going to get out of this pentagon of a place and we're going to Kansas. There's the pentagon in the background. There are good people in Washington. Not everybody is corrupt.

The car stops and they get out to take photos again. He puts his phone under a seat in the car. You can hear someone come over and delete photos on another camera. He picks up the phone.

Dean: Again, we were told by cops *(everyone is laughing again)* to delete the photos we were taking. It's all good. I didn't see a sign. I guess we're not supposed to take pictures. They didn't confiscate our phones. We're from out of town. We didn't know.

March 14th

We are here and we will never fade!!!!!

March 15th

He shares Waniya Locke's post:

"Tuesday, a federal judge refused to stop oil from flowing through the #NoDakotaAccessPipeline, which will likely clear the way for operations to begin next week."

I'm in a 3D movie and next thing I know the loud sounds and bangs started to take effect with my mind like I was back at the front lines of Oceti. The movie was titled: KONG!

March 16th

Thanks to all our people out there who support me and many water protectors out there in the world. We now have a higher level of understanding what this controlled system has brought to a world in chaos. We continue to move forward in many new directions. But let us say we will never forget what happened to us water protectors who endured so much pain, hate, lies, deceits, disrespect to our sacred lands, our community of youth and elders, to a world of people who all opened their eyes.

We cannot have hate in our hearts, but pray for those who fell to the corrupt and those who seek to destroy all that is beautiful. But in the end of this darkness there still was light shed on what was evolving within our people of Oceti Sakowin and the wisdom of a few who held their light of truths, essence of knowledge and the power of prayer. Prayer brought together every people of color and race, brought Mother Earth's beauty of what is truly sacred to this world and beyond to the stars. And that is "water." The liquid foundation of every living thing past and present.

This is only the first footstep into what's true, and that is solidarity to the people for the people. We are all together now as we move united, stepping into our second step and observing all the division amongst the people in positions of tribal/political powers. But we also see unity hang on by a thread by the few people. That's because they held their prayers strong for the future of the children. Sadly a lot have fallen by what I call "fake power" an illusion of power we know as MONEY. But what is left of the few water protectors who roam this world is their truths and live feeds of what occurred over those 7 months of resistance. We will never forget!!!!

Shiyé Bidzííl

If you guide them the FACTS will come.

It's simple people!!! The facts were right in front of our eyes the whole entire time. You see sometimes (facts) truths get blinded by the confusion of people's thoughts and actions!! They get them cloaked in flowers and psych-ops tactics, you can thank the PRODAPL trolls and Kevin Gilbert for that one. Just look at the guy and listen to the way he words things!!! Flowers and Dr. Seuss gimmick poetry??!! No disrespect to the late great Dr. of poetry, but come on people, take your DAPL blinds off and focus on what's important: The water.

Crazy though how I (Shiyé Bidzííl) had to step forward and speak truth for all the peoples before who were already watching and noticing Kevin from the get go! They all got shot down in what they had found out and they all got called "trolls" "instigators" etc. Well now look at what I did!!! Take a real good look!! The truth came back out slowly, piece by piece we will put it back together and the truth will once again reveal that Kevin is a fraud to this movement and many more.

One person can lie and get away with it, but the people together can see all the truths!!! The power of real unity. I love my people. I am always thankful for them because they bring out the truth in many ways which some of us may never understand. But I will never turn my back on them and act on stupid bull some would say "propaganda." I am Shiyé Bidzííl who brings real RAW truth to light even though a few fellow water protectors tell me not to speak about certain things!! YOU ALL KNOW I'M GONNA DO IT ANYWAY! Why I do the things I do? Not because of money!!! I do it for the people!!! Simple as that. Creator bless and have a nice day. Peace.

The people want to know and to address the situation with Chase Iron Eyes and to really get a better understanding on the ongoing process of legal action with the 800 arrested water protectors and what really is going on with the People's Law Project. Now with that stated, we are seeking out some truth in Chase himself!!! As you all should know by now he has deactivated his Facebook account. Now let's just ask him nicely to come out and address this concerning issue.

Shiyé says with all due respect and for the things I do for the people, I am going to stay out of this one with Chase, but will try and personally contact him myself in hopes that he reaches back to me. To let everyone know that since the beginning of this movement I have stood with Chase and his vision of our future and still support him even in these dark times. So because I don't want to blow things up and get the truth let's just say Chase has his way and logic of understanding of things. If any wrongs, I believe he is strong enough to express and bring in his own accountability for his actions. So stay tuned. Chase, get a hold of me. Simple, right?

Always remember it's for the people!

Money can be used for the good but also money can you consume our very values that keep us together. Let's all remember that. It's very important!

March 17th

What is truth if everyone has their own version of it?

Preserving our 7th Generations is a beautiful thing!

March 18th

He notes that he is feeling disappointed.

Wow!!!!!!! Before DAPL came into the picture I was friends with mostly all the people on council and individuals who all work within the tribal building. Now they either blocked me or unfriended me! So much for them having my back. I will be returning back to Standing Rock and I will be having some words with some of these people and get some answers........that's if they even acknowledge me. The question is why??

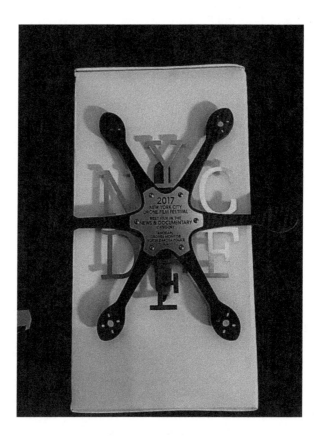

We won! Our piece on drone operators of #NODAPL won the New York City Drone Film Festival News/Documentary category! Myron Dewey accepted on our behalf and gave a powerful speech.

He shares a video of Myron's speech.

He notes that he is feeling blessed.

To me it was more than an award, it was more than the spotlight, it was more than the popularity, it was more than being famous.

I was in this fight for the important things in life and that is for the children who I have inspired to now have a voice. To be heard. And most of all to fly a drone!!!!!!

But I thank you all my people.

March 19th

Wow!!! Pretty cool how a drone changed my life!! Thanks to everyone out there. You are all in my prayers and I love you all!!! DRoNE2BWILD will continue to do what he does best!!! And that's give bad law enforcement haircuts!!! Lol

The Documentary #NoDAPL, winner of the New York Drone film festival, accepted a standing ovation. The founder of New York Drone Film Festival said it was the first ever in the history of the festival.

In honor of all Water Protectors and all those who documented with their drones, not all drones made it out of Standing Rock, many came under siege from the Morton County police department and #NoDAPL security shooting them down.

Thank you to all the water protectors and allies for supporting the protection of clean water for the future generations to come. This is just the beginning.

Many blessings

Digital Smoke Signals

Drone2bwild Photography & Video

Thank you to everyone...followers...us drone pilots. All the children and the youth for being inspired. I'm here in Kansas City. I am good. I have a special lady in my life and she takes care of me. I'm surrounded by beautiful children.

That award that was given out last night meant a lot to me. It's more than that, it's about inspiring the children. I feel good. I feel like all the negativity that was in me for the last months is gone. I live for the cause though. Shout out to Little Creek Camp.

How I fly the drones is that I capture the movement and the action. I like to go in smooth. I like to go in hard. It's what I love to do. I'm going to get back into the drones again. Going to promote Steven with his shirts and Ernesto and his tattoos. We're going to put a Drone2bwild shirt out.

What I meant by I'm going to auction off some stuff, I'm not going to quit droning. I just have a whole lot of props. From all those drones that got shot down. I have like 30 props. Some of them are shot with pellets. And I have some controllers that I would like to sign and auction off to someone who likes them. Doesn't mean that I'm going to give up on the drones. And for those who say just keep them for your children, no. Inspiring the children is what matters to me. Materialistic things, no.

Forget those trolls and what they say. In two days I'll be returning to Standing Rock. Will try to live feed it. We're all moving on. But we're all keeping the awareness going. I'm going to stay focused on what I do best and that's fly drones. I'm also going to work to inspire the kids. To go to school and to stay in school. Of course I'm taking care of myself.

The live feed cuts off.

March 20th

He is looking around a backyard and playing music.

It's a beautiful day here in Kansas. It's beautiful not to wake up and hear Morton County. I'm trying to transition from being at Oceti back to real life. Or maybe Oceti is real life. It's hard sometimes. Sometimes I cry. Sometimes it hurts. Especially now that I see people are driving by the camp where I used to be.

But we all move forward and we all move ahead to a better future. That camp was for the better. So don't ever think it was for nothing. Because look at me. Out of all of that chaos and unity, I came out better. I wasn't perfect. I'm still not perfect. A lot of good came out of camp. Three months I've been clean. You don't need drugs to better your life. You don't need drugs at all. I found something better in life and that's helping the youth and helping the children. I don't need that anymore. My arms are clean. It feels good. It's because of you guys. Good friends like Ernesto and Steven and Angelo and Gabriela. It's good people like them that kept me moving forward. The most people I've ever met in my life was this past year. Good friends like Prolific and William. Good friends like Myron Dewey. It would take all day to name them all.

I'll be heading to Standing Rock tomorrow to deal with my pretrial and to see if they're going to revoke my bond since I violated it. All that weed, it wasn't mine.

I will say hi to my kids. I wish I could bring them with me, but they have school.

March 21st

That's so good to feel that Standing Rock is everywhere!

He shares a video: Okinawa stands with Standing Rock

I am here for the Native American Nations, not for any people of power!!!

Update to the people who really want to know did I really do that?

He is driving in this live feed.

This is a quick update. To confirm that picture of me that's going around of me beheading Kevin Gilbert Braveheart style, I did not do that. I know I talk a lot of crap, I know I post a lot of crap, but that went overboard. It's kind of funny in a way, but I didn't do it.

I did not dishonor any movement, my people or myself. There's been a lot more people who have done a lot more things to dishonor this movement if you really look into it. There's far worse things that councilmen, tribal and other people have done, far more worse than a picture has. So think about it. You don't like the picture then don't look at it. You guys are sharing it. If you don't want it to be out, then don't share it, don't look at it.

I woke up this morning and opened my phone and looked at it and I laughed. I'm sorry, it's funny. But as far as you saying I'm dishonoring the people, do your research before you start pointing fingers at Shiyé. Because Shiyé would have done something far worse than that. I would have added blood and gore and guts. But that's not me. I don't need a picture to tell my truth, I just need my words.

If you are wondering what I'm doing driving, I'm driving back to Standing Rock. Tomorrow is my pretrial. Pretty much I'm speaking up for myself, so we'll see how that goes. I'll try to live feed it. I may have to put it in my pocket. If it goes dark, don't freak out. It don't matter what people say about me. I've already been through the wringer. I'm about speaking up for what's real. How you gonna survive this movement if you're not going to be real.

Yeah, I know I had some problems with Kevin Gilbert. I don't agree with what he has done. But for me, it's not about money. It's about being real and honest to yourself. Not taking advantage of the youth and the movement. Not taking advantage of your own self. Come on people. Kevin Gilbert, you should know that by now. I hope that brings closure to people who were wondering if I did that.

March 22nd

In this live feed, he is still driving. It is gray and cloudy out. He is playing some music.

Navajo morning blessing song. Playing it for everybody going to court today. My court is at 11. I'm on the Standing Rock Sioux reservation. A morning lesson live feed. Minus all the drama. In a good way. There's water protectors being accused of this and that. Let's forget about all of that.

The feed suddenly cuts off. He brings a new one up soon.

Shout out to water protectors due in court today. Especially Eric Poemz. He left a message today. I did the same for him. He said I was one of the main reasons why he came to Standing Rock. Because of people like me. Good to hear that. He believes in me. He inspires me. I inspire him. All relations working together and coming together. We'll always remain as brothers. He stood up there for what's right. He was there. What Morton County did to him will come back to them. Karma does work.

A prayer to all my people on Standing Rock. Some of them don't like me anymore. Maybe I talk too much. Maybe I talk too much truth. There's a reason why we have a great divide. It's weeding out the weak. There has to be a divide so we can tell who's on our side. And who's on their own side. We need a divide so we can unite the true and humble and honest and worthy people who are down for this cause. Not playing with their money. Not at the casinos, smoking those cigarettes and pulling those handles, but then trying to act humble. That's not humble to go to the casino and spend all your money. It's called wasting.

I want to give a shout out to my aunt who just joined this live feed. Sooner or later I'm going to have to come down there and you're going to have to get a medicine man. You're going to have to get together a protection ceremony for me. I need it. The things I'm going to do in the near future, I'm going to need a protection ceremony.

I'm almost home. Almost home to my kids. To my daughter, to my beautiful daughter. She misses me so much. Every day she asks for me. My two sons, my twin boys. Monster Slayer and Born for Water, that's what I call them. There's a Navajo creation story that there was a monster slayer that slayed all the monsters that used to roam the earth long, long ago.

I'm back up here to face the music. To see what this charge is. To see what this prosecutor has to say about me. They don't know me, but they will have words to say about me. But I'll be ready and I'll be live feeding it. Now is this guy truly there for tribal justice or is he just there to collect a paycheck? He's pretty rough on everybody. He even talks down to veterans. He says they use their veteran's status to get out of things. Little does this guy know that these veterans suffer. They don't know. Anybody who goes through this court, they don't know them. They don't know what they are going through.

My whole tribal nation here is hurting. I know because I've been through that tribal court system. They are hurting, they are suffering from alcohol, drugs, addiction. I know that too. Believe me. Suffered addiction myself. But Standing Rock cured me, believe it or not. A lot of people still want to talk bad about my past, but let them. Let them heal themselves by talking down about others. Maybe in a way that heals them. But right now I'm going back into God's country so I'm going to be losing signal soon. Have a blessful day.

Thank you everybody for always taking care of me. I always give you respect and honor. I'm honest to the core. I'll always be honest. What really matters is the actions we put forth. It's about actually doing something.

He live feeds again later.

I tried to go live. I think the FBI agent had some kind of way to freeze it up. Ask me some questions. I know you're itching for some answers. I gotta return for a jury trial. The feds came in and said they could save the day for me. God knows what kind of information they want. The information they talked to me about was who was flying the drones the day of Treaty Camp. I told them I did.

I told them we won the New York film festival and all the drone footage he needs to see is on that video. Which the world has already seen.

Anyone out there who wants to represent me and could do a better job than this lady?

He shows his attorney's business card. He shows his paperwork.

Criminal possession of drugs, intent to sell.... possession of drug paraphernalia. I almost got a warrant for my arrest today. They said 11 o'clock, but it was at 10. Clerk of courts were grouchy. Let's get this taken care of. You guys could all show up. That would be crazy if everyone shows up. This is transparency to the fullest. Email her and tell her how much support Shiyé has.

I didn't sell drugs to this camp. I support this camp through drone footage and the truth. I love all my trolls. They love me so much, they can't get enough of me. The more you guys laugh and throw angry faces at me, the more it boosts this movement. So keep doing it. If it wasn't for you trolls, we probably wouldn't be here. Naw, if it wasn't for my people. We're learning from you. We're going to troll you right back. We got people getting your IP addresses right now. We could blow up your home address, but we won't. You're not worth exposing. I'll pray for you.

I'm okay guys. We're all good people. Even the trolls are good people, they're just lost. What do they do when they are lost? They start trolling. They love to troll us. I feel relieved, but I have to come back. I hope this time I'm going to go in and see all my followers show up in that court room. With all your knowledge of medical marijuana, tribal systems, truth. Come on, I encourage you.

I also talked about the two people who were supposed to be arrested for terrorizing me, but I guess they won't. I told them that I don't trust the Bismarck police. If I take the plea it's sixty days out of ninety and I don't have time to sit in a broken tribal court system jail. With cops that go around the book just to arrest people. I'm not taking a deal. I'm going to be out there fighting the world and doing actions.

Much love to my people. You know the Viceland Rise series? I finally got paid for my drone footage. I'm going to get this cashed. I'm going to go up to Bismarck and buy the latest drone and go over camp and live feed that.

I hate banks. That's where corruption starts. I'm going to cash this and buy a drone. Transparency. It's hard earned money and I'm going to buy the latest Phantom 4 Pro. And batteries and the rest I'm going to spend on my kids and take my mom out to eat. Because I love my mama.

A part of my PTSD, I gotta be holding onto a phone. All those months, you don't know what's going to happen. This keeps me safe. Holding onto a phone. I feel double safe now I have two phones. I hold it close. Ain't nothing wrong with that.

Nothing's going to stop me from educating the people and the youth. Opportunities for the children. I love every one of you guys. I read every one of your messages.

He reads a message from Tony Singing Eagle. It is very nice, thanking him. He reads another nice message. He starts crying.

It keeps me going. It touches my heart in a lot of ways. I love you.

Sacred Stone...or what's left of it!

In this live feed he shows vehicles blocking the road to Sacred Stone Camp.

We're looking at what's left of Sacred Stone. They are guarding the entrance of what was once Sacred Stone. You can see DAPL, the pipelines, off in the distance.

There are BIA vehicles. A port-a-potty. A school bus goes by.

Kids are back to school. That's how we're going to change the world. Keep going to school so we can learn how to fix their mistakes. There are probably a couple of feds in there too. We're going to have to come by and pick up trash since BIA aren't going to. Get some trash bags and clean it up. That'll be a project. Cannonball over there in the distance.

In the next live feed he shows another camp. There are tipis and cars and buildings here.

This is the Cheyenne River camp. The tribe made a resolution to have no camps ever to come back to Standing Rock land. But this little section of camp, they have no jurisdiction over it. So why haven't Cheyenne River returned? Are they scared to be all alone up here and be the only legit camp? Are they planning something? What are they up to?

The flag is still blowing. Looks like these guys live here.

There is one on a bike, one walking. One man comes over to talk to him, but it is hard to hear him for the wind. He tells Dean that there are still people living there.

Well there's the truth about Cheyenne River Camp. Starting off small, but thinking outside the box.

Oceti and Rosebud Camps!!.....what's left of them!!

In this live feed you can see there is still some trash left. The video is a little blurry. It is very windy out. He plays some music. The feed cuts in and out.

Across the river is what's left of Oceti.

The fortress of oiltude!! Yesterday the "NO TRESSPASS" signs were up. Today no sign visible at all. No barricade but still a lot of law enforcement posted at every turn off!!

In this live video, he is driving by Oceti Sakowin Camp.

Dang, straight up all gone. Adios.

He drives over the bridge. He looks back.

Wire fencing all along. Four foot trenches. Razor wire. All that just to protect that oil. Crying shame. Razor wiring goes a long way. The hill that the pipeline went into...more barriers, more cop cars sitting there. Getting paid by oil. More cops.

Feels good to pick up my kids from school!!!

Never give up on what you believe

"Nothing is impossible. The word itself says, I'm possible." ~ Audrey Hepburn

Oceti is still here I can feel it!!! Yup

Fort Yates, ND

The casino is still popping out BIA payroll cars!!!! Lol

He shares a short video of law enforcement vehicles at the casino. Law enforcement presence is heavy still.

March 23rd

Today's wonderful Thursday updates: We have a traffic jam. A herd of deer. LOL

He is in the car and they go over the Backwater Bridge and up the road. Deer cross right in front of them on the road. It is a gray day. They go on. It is quiet. You can only hear the vehicle. There is law enforcement vehicles along the way parked on the side of the road.

March 25th

Today my daughter and I leave our homeland to journey south to seek our way of being and to also help guide our water protectors see and meet up with new friends and family that we have gained along the way.

I drove up here to Standing Rock solo five days ago. I had no idea what this journey was gonna bring me besides my fate in a tribal court system. The most important thing I've learned from camp is that you always need to be there for your people. I found bonds of real, lasting friendship.

I have sought knowledge and understanding. I have gained healing in many directions and from many minds throughout this movement of liberation. I truly accept my purpose in this beautiful life.

I feel deeply about living life to the greatest. I believe in helping one another through hard times and the good times. Keeping each other alive with our purpose of truth and hardship. It's the people you're helping who remind you of the true meaning of love of unity. They remind you of the sense of community. We are water protectors and we are untouchable. I believe it. I feel it. I accept it.

Today I am proud to have Wiyaka Eagleman and Inyan Wakinyan Hehaka on this journey of new meaning.

Our destiny is what we believe in our people and Mother Earth!!! LITTLE CREEK CAMP HERE WE COME!!